Property Rules

Property Rules

Political Economy in Chicago, 1833–1872

ROBIN L. EINHORN

THE UNIVERSITY OF CHICAGO PRESS

Chicago and London

R O B I N L. E I N H O R N is assistant professor of history at the
University of California, Berkeley.

The University of Chicago Press, Chicago 60637
The University of Chicago Press, Ltd., London
© 1991 by The University of Chicago
All rights reserved. Published 1991
Printed in the United States of America

00 99 98 97 96 95 94 93 92 91   5 4 3 2 1

ISBN 0-226-19484-1 (cl.)

Library of Congress Cataloging-in-Publication Data

Einhorn, Robin L. (Robin Leigh), 1960–
    Property rules : political economy in Chicago, 1833–1872 /
Robin L. Einhorn.
        p.   cm.
    Includes bibliographical references and index.
    1. Chicago (Ill.)—Politics and government—To 1950.
2. Chicago (Ill.)—History—To 1875.   3. Chicago (Ill.)—Social
conditions.   4. Chicago (Ill.)—Economic conditions.   I. Title.
JS707.E36   1991
977.3'1102—dc20   91-7781

To David and Edith Einhorn

Contents

Illustrations

Note on Document Citations

THIS STUDY WILL cite and quote extensively from documents in the Chicago City Council Proceedings Files, 1833–71, in the possession of the Illinois State Archives and located at the Illinois Regional Archives Depository at Northeastern Illinois University in Chicago. The collection's filing system was designed by Henry W. Zimmerman, Chicago city clerk in the early 1850s, and relies on the sequential numbering of topically organized folders within each municipal (fiscal) year, though Zimmerman numbered the documents filed before his tenure in a single sequential series. The Illinois State Archives has retained Zimmerman's filing system as well as the original titles for all document folders. Because these titles are usually long and refer to folders rather than particular documents, I will cite documents only by the municipal year and folder number where they can be found. Those wishing to know folder titles or to consult individual documents can trace my citations in Robert E. Bailey, et al., eds., *Chicago City Council Proceedings Files, 1833–1871: An Inventory* (Springfield: Illinois State Archives, 1987). Bailey and his colleagues also have produced an invaluable research tool, the microfiche collection *Chicago City Council Proceedings Files, 1833–1871: An Index*.

Preface

THIS BOOK TELLS A new story of the development of city government in nineteenth-century America. Combining insights suggested
by several important recent (and not so recent) studies with archival
research in a previously unavailable documentary record, this book
builds a narrative that is very different from those most urban historians have recounted. To list my main intellectual debts to the
urban history literature is also to begin to situate this story in the
context of that literature. From the now classic work of Sam Bass Warner, Jr., I learned that an ideology of "privatism"—an outright, una-
pologetic rejection of public-oriented civic responsibility—was crucial
to the development of American city government.[1] From Jon C. Teaford, I learned that the construction of public works, of a physical
infrastructure of streets, bridges, sidewalks, and sewers, was both
the chief business and the chief success, even the "unheralded triumph" of the nineteenth-century American city.[2] From Terrence J.
McDonald, I learned to look directly at municipal finance, to reject
simple identifications between fiscal policies and the presumed "political cultures" of bosses and reformers, and to see the importance of
a "low tax consensus" in shaping city politics in the nineteenth century.[3] From Amy Bridges, finally, I learned that urban political history

---

1. Sam Bass Warner, Jr., *The Private City: Philadelphia in Three Periods of Its Growth*
(Philadelphia: University of Pennsylvania Press, 1968).
2. Jon C. Teaford, *The Unheralded Triumph: City Government in America, 1870–1900*
(Baltimore: Johns Hopkins University Press, 1984); also Teaford, *The Municipal Revolution in America: Origins of Modern Urban Government, 1650–1825* (Chicago: University of
Chicago Press, 1975).
3. Terrence J. McDonald, *The Parameters of Urban Fiscal Policy: Socioeconomic Change*

is national political history, that the nineteenth-century American city was an integral part of the nineteenth-century national political community, truly a "city in the republic."[4]

Yet this story also diverges from those told by Warner, Teaford, McDonald, and Bridges, mainly because of archival materials I was lucky enough to be able to use, the Chicago City Council Proceedings Files. An unbroken record of city documents extending from Chicago's initial incorporation in 1833 to the Great Fire of 1871, this collection was thought to have burned in the Fire for nearly a century, until a state records inventory located it in 1984 in a neglected Chicago warehouse. The Illinois State Archives then rescued the entire collection (some 1,500 cubic feet of material extending to 1940) and launched a program both to preserve it and to make its pre-Fire portions available to scholars for the first time since the 1890s. The core of the research for this study, the Chicago papers revealed a nineteenth-century city government that looked radically different from those urban historians generally have portrayed and one whose history—whose changes over time—seemed powered by social forces and political decisions different from those historians generally have stressed. In fact, this government was more privatized than Warner's Philadelphia, more profoundly influenced by its public works agenda than the cities surveyed by Teaford, more committed to "low taxes" than McDonald's San Francisco, and more closely linked with national-level political debates than Bridges's New York. The Chicago records suggested, in sum, that these historians had not followed their own key insights far enough.

These manuscripts also made it possible to write a new history of Chicago, the second largest city in the United States for a century. Little has been written about Chicago's early history, largely because of what now seems almost a myth of the Great Fire, an assumption that too little evidence survived to reconstruct the history of the city that so quickly reconstructed itself, soon replacing England's (or Engels's) Manchester as the "shock city" of the western world, the international showcase of buccaneering capitalism. Maybe the best way to capture the popular portrait of Chicago's history is by mixing hackneyed metaphors: the phoenix that arose from Chicago's 1871 ashes was an Athena born full-grown, an adolescent giant of a war goddess. It was the *Jungle* of Upton Sinclair and the moral wasteland of *If Christ*

---

and Political Culture in San Francisco, 1860–1906 (Berkeley: University of California Press, 1986).

4. Amy Bridges, *A City in the Republic: Antebellum New York and the Origins of Machine Politics* (Cambridge: Cambridge University Press, 1984).

Came to Chicago. Some Chicagoans intuitively fear their local history
as an inevitable source of embarrassment, believing that research un-
doubtedly would produce yet more revelations of corruption and hor-
ror from the city of big shoulders and red lights. When I wrote the
first draft of this study, I was living in a neighborhood peculiarly sensitive to historical Chicago-bashing: Bridgeport, bastion of white machine politics and home of the Daleys, in the administration of the
black reform mayor, Harold Washington. When one of my neighbors
heard I was writing a history of Chicago politics, he had only one
question: "Is it favorable?"

Frankly, I'm not sure whether it's favorable; I leave that to the
reader. But this is not a story either of ethnic machine politics or of
political corruption. That was the key revelation to emerge from the
Council Proceedings Files. The documents showed a period in Chicago's history when its government was clean enough to satisfy even
the most fastidious of urban reformers, the self-consciously elitist
"structural reformers" of the late nineteenth century, the men who
compared cities to private corporations in order to condemn municipal governments as inappropriately democratic.[5] I call the government of this clean period, this elite reformer's dream of urban politics,
the "segmented system." I define this system from its particular administrative procedures and financial arrangements. From the perspective of American urban history, one of the most important
findings of this study is the nature of these procedures and instruments. They are quite different from those major American cities use
today as well as from those most urban historians have assumed for
the past. While I learned of these procedures and instruments from
the Chicago documents, however, they were not unique to Chicago.
Few historians have examined the surviving municipal records of
other cities that would confirm their ubiquitous use.[6] Yet indirect evidence clearly suggests it: nineteenth-century commentators, as I will
show in chapter 1, assumed the very things this study presents as
new contributions to our knowledge of American urban history.

These municipal procedures and instruments, moreover, reflected
the same kinds of political ideas that structured national-level debates
about the proper uses of government in nineteenth-century America.
The constitutional "strict construction" and "states rights" rhetoric
that was so important in national politics from the Jacksonian era

5. On structural reform, see esp. Martin J. Schiesl, *The Politics of Efficiency: Municipal
Administration and Reform in America, 1880–1920* (Berkeley: University of California
Press, 1977).
6. The key exception here is Eugene P. Moehring, *Public Works and the Patterns of
Urban Real Estate in Manhattan, 1835–1894* (New York: Arno Press, 1981).

through Reconstruction—seen in such issues as tariffs, internal improvements and, of course, slavery and the enforcement of its post–Civil War abolition—had urban counterparts in the strict construction of city charters and the localization of municipal finance, especially through the use of special assessments rather than property taxes for public works. While historians have long been familiar with these national concerns, their application to cities is a major finding of this study. American cities were "cities in the republic," not only in Bridges's sense of sharing a political culture influenced by an enfranchised working class, but also in their uses of government. Urban politics reflected McDonald's "consensus" on low taxes, but in ways that promoted localized rather than low-cost government. Cities were very successful in building public works, and they accomplished this by local and privatized strategies long before the triumph of the central coordination that Teaford describes. Finally, American cities were, as Warner argued, "private cities." Yet by nineteenth-century standards, this was their strength rather than their pathology. This book explores the impact of those nineteenth-century standards in Chicago and attempts to unravel their implications for the development of American city government.

IN DIRECT WAYS, this project was made possible by the Illinois State Archives. Director John Daly, Robert E. Bailey, Elaine Shemoney Evans, and Patrick Cunningham (who carried all those boxes) not only provided access to documents, guidance in their use, and an unbelievably congenial place to work, but they also helped me to learn from the laboratory of American politics that is Springfield, Illinois. John B. Jentz and Richard Schneirov introduced me to Chicago history and allowed me to use unpublished papers and census data from their Origins of Chicago's Industrial Working Class Project, NEH grant RS-20393-83, based from 1983 to 1985 at the Newberry Library. Archie Motley of the Chicago Historical Society helped with access to materials, as did the manuscript librarians of the University of Chicago Library, whom I thank for permission to quote from the Stephen A. Douglas papers. The Chicago Title and Trust Company kindly allowed me to use their ante-Fire plat books, and Historic Urban Plans, Inc., provided some of the illustrations. I also thank Cambridge University Press for allowing me to use portions of my "Civil War and Municipal Government in Chicago" in *Toward a Social History of the American Civil War: Exploratory Essays*, Maris A. Vinovskis, ed. (Cambridge: Cambridge University Press, 1990), 117–38, in chapters 5 and 6 of this book.

Amy Bridges, Michael Frisch, J. Morgan Kousser, Jon C. Teaford,

Susan Gray, Ellen Eslinger, and the members of the Social History Workshop at the University of Chicago criticized early drafts of parts of this study, helping me to clarify its arguments; Philip J. Ethington and Olivier Zunz provided extremely helpful critiques of complete drafts; and Eric Monkkonen, Louise Wade, and Barry Eichengreen generously assisted near the end with their specialized knowledge. The historians of the University of California, Berkeley, especially Lawrence Levine, Jon Gjerde, Paula Fass, James Gregory, and Harry Scheiber, offered a much appreciated and time-consuming mix of critical reading, encouragement, and stimulating conversation. I thank Nelson Polsby for these as well as for arranging financial assistance. Grants from the Berkeley Chancellor's Office, Institute for Governmental Studies, and the Regents Junior Faculty Fellowship facilitated the transformation of the manuscript into a book, in which Wendy Nicholson's research assistance was indispensable. Anneke Vonk of the UCB Geography Department created the maps, which speak for themselves.

My debt to the University of Chicago is enormous, and particularly to Kathleen Neils Conzen for supervising the dissertation, reading and dissecting its repeated drafts, and, at bottom, for my education in U.S. history. James Grossman and Edward M. Cook, Jr., raised key issues early, and the History Department and Social Sciences Division provided crucial financial aid. The division's award of the Marc Perry Galler Prize to the dissertation made its revision far easier to complete. Rima Schultz has influenced this project from its inception, as Chicago historian, teacher, and friend. Finally, it is pointless to attempt to isolate my parents' contributions, but I can dedicate the book to them, noting with awe and love their personal embodiments of the liberal public spirit in modern America.

I, of course, remain responsible for all errors of fact, interpretation, and style. None of these people could force me to take all their good advice.

1

From the Banks of Healy's Slough

HEALY'S SLOUGH was so disgusting that Chicago aldermen found it difficult to describe. A nuisance "of the vilest and most dangerous kind, which any civilized people ever had to contend with," this short, shallow ditch filled with meat industry wastes provoked one alderman to Shakespearean metaphor—it was "like Falstaff's buck basket 'a rank compound of villainous smells.'"[1] Other aldermen employed a detailed approach to convey Healy's squalor. On an inspection tour, they saw Healy's water "colored crimson" from blood that was pouring undiluted off the Milward company's packing floor, though even that sight paled next to the scene outside Nash's, where the aldermen watched "Boys collecting putrid grease from the surface of the Slough just as it had been run from that establishment."[2] In January 1866, having debated what to do about the mess at Healy's Slough for a full six months, aldermen heard "what we hope will be the final report . . . on this vexed question." On the recommendation of its "smelling committee," the council passed an ordinance that declared Healy's Slough a nuisance and ordered the city's Board of Public Works (BPW) to clean it by dredging it to a depth of 12 feet and a width of 55 (75 at the surface). The ordinance also ordered the BPW to bill the $29,450 cost of this project to the owners of "real estate chargeable for the removal of the nuisance"—the meat packers, slaughterers, and renderers who were polluting Healy's Slough.[3]

Mayor John B. Rice, former actor and impresario, vetoed the 1866

1. Chicago City Council Proceedings Files [hereafter CP], 1865/66:458.
2. Ibid., 1865/66:863.
3. Ibid., 1865/66:914.

ordinance. He agreed, he said, that Healy's Slough was a nuisance, that it should be cleaned, and that the packers should pay for the cleaning, but he doubted that the council, as the city's "legislative" branch, had the authority to decide how to clean it. That, Rice claimed, was a decision for the city's "executive" branch, either the BPW or the Board of Police Commissioners, though the mayor did not say which.[4] However clever it was—and it was clever, the first time any official ever had distinguished between legislative and executive authority in Chicago's government—Rice's abstraction hid other, more concrete objections to the ordinance. The corporation counsel (another "executive" officer) had told Rice that the city charter provisions dealing with special assessment (the procedure through which the packers would pay for the project) required that the enabling ordinance specify which pieces of real estate would be charged; because the Healy's ordinance did not do this, it was illegal. The BPW, meanwhile, wondered how, if it excavated the slough, it would dispose of "this slimy, half fluid stuff, [in such a way] that its deposit shall not create a greater nuisance than now exists." The board also saw a hidden agenda in the council's action: "Apparently," they informed Rice, "the work as ordered is designed for a canal or a slip."[5]

This last observation, as the BPW knew from political experience rather than technological inference, was the key. The police board had declared Healy's Slough a nuisance back in July 1865 and, pursuant to that report, the BPW had sent the council a plan to clean it by dredging it to a depth of 5 feet and a width of 30 (though the board urged delay, since "to stir up this mass of filth during the summer months, will so add to the present nuisance, that it seems to us that it will become intolerable, if not dangerous, to the immediate neighborhood"). The council responded by sending a smelling committee to inspect Healy's Slough and Bridgeport, its larger, equally filthy, neighborhood. "In our investigations," this committee reported on Healy's, "we examined a large number of the dwellers on the banks of that noble stream and the uniform testimony was that the locality was not unhealthy and if the testimony of some is to be relied upon, the peculiar chemical conditions of the atmosphere makes it a certain cure for consumption." Besides, the committee continued, "all will admit that the odor is much improved from last year & previous years" and, in any case, the BPW's 5-foot dredging proposal would

4. Ibid.
5. Ibid.

"remove only a small part of the conglomarate [sic] stenches of the place."[6]

The clincher, however, and the reason that aldermen rejected the BPW's 5-foot dredging plan, was a contention that Healy's Slough—which was connected to and drew its water from the South Branch of the Chicago River—once had been a navigable stream, though, presumably quite recently, accumulated filth had closed it to shipping. By law, a stream once navigable had to be kept navigable. Dredging Healy's Slough to a depth of 5 feet would be a positive governmental action that illegally closed a formerly navigable stream. If the city dredged Healy's at all, this argument went, it had to dredge deeply; it had to "return" Healy's to its "former" condition. The council passed a 12-foot dredging ordinance that summer, but Mayor Rice vetoed it after the BPW disposed of the navigable stream argument by searching the city's land records: Healy's had never been navigable and no government body ever had conferred "navigable stream" status upon it. The council made its next move in October, ordering the BPW to devise a plan to clean Healy's "at the least possible cost to, and the greatest possible advantage of the owners of property abutting said slough, or in other words, a plan the principal features of which shall be thoroughness, cheapness and utility." By "utility," of course, aldermen meant a navigable canal for the meat industry.[7]

The BPW reported two plans in November 1865. The city could clean Healy's either by dredging it or by filling it with earth. Although less effective than filling (getting rid of Healy's Slough altogether), dredging had the advantage of cheapness; a 5-foot trench would cost $27,000 compared with $35,000 for filling. Aldermen rejected both of these plans, demanding the 12-foot trench. Filling was useless because the ground around Healy's sloped down toward it (this assumed, of course, that the packers would keep dumping on the site), while the narrow and shallow dredge plan would only compound the nuisance: "any rational person can see that the first heavy rain would wash the contents of the twenty feet left on each side, into the channel and the process of dredging would have to be done over again and again, and the already filthy condition of the Chicago River would not be made less so by rec[e]iving the washings of the [Healy] Slough."[8] Now demanding deep dredging on sanitary grounds, aldermen sent out the smelling committee who found the boys skim-

6. Ibid., 1865/66:458.
7. Ibid., 1865/66:459, 468, 914.
8. Ibid., 1865/66:914.

ming grease and passed the 1866 deep-dredge ordinance that got Mayor Rice philosophizing on checks and balances in municipal government.

The city did nothing about Healy's Slough in 1866 or for the next five years. In 1872, however, 186 Bridgeport residents petitioned the council to clean it, making it quite clear that they were interested in cleaning rather than navigation. Closing Healy's once and for all would be "a tardy act of justice." This petition obviously emanated from the Bridgeport community. It had been taken door to door along Archer Avenue and other local streets and contained several "marks" for signatures. The petitioners would have none of the old dredging plan, which the packers (who probably employed many of them) then were urging.

> A few wealthy individuals owning property bordering on said slough
> have made strenuous efforts to have the same dredged, actuated only
> by motives of their own private aggrandizement. . . . To open and
> dredge said slough would be to perpetuate all the nuisances at present
> complained and add more to the number as also to entail a vast
> expense on the city for the building and maintaining bridges over
> the same without any public consideration therefor.

Healy's Slough had to be filled. Its "stench" had made its neighborhood uninhabitable "except by the slaughtering and rendering establishments that thrive along its banks—and contribute to its odor."[9]

The council sent yet another smelling committee, considered both filling and dredging, and did nothing except urge the city's Board of Health to enforce old regulatory ordinances that actually had banned dumping by the meat industry all along.[10] For their part, the packers, slaughterers, and renderers revived the navigable stream argument, continuing the battle until 1885, when they finally lost in the U.S. Supreme Court. The solution, meanwhile, began to seem inevitable as the Chicago *Tribune* demanded that the city not only dredge the slough (rather than fill it) but also compensate the packers and renderers on its banks for any losses they might suffer in the process. Regardless of the cost, the paper asserted, "the public will cheerfully pay the bill."[11] The packers had failed to transform Healy's Slough

9. Ibid., 1872/73:1346. See also Chicago *Tribune*, July 20, 1872, for allegations of the intimidation of packinghouse employees.

10. CP, 1872/73:1346.

11. *Joliet and Chicago Railroad Company v. Healy*, 94 Ill. 416 (1880); *Healy v. Joliet & Chicago Railroad Company*, 116 U.S. 191 (1885); Louise Carroll Wade, *Chicago's Pride: The Stockyards, Packingtown, and Environs in the Nineteenth Century* (Urbana: University of Illinois Press, 1987), 69, 131; *Tribune*, June 30, 1872 (quotation), July 12, 20, 1872 (I am

into a legally sanctioned canal, but they kept it open for dumping. It remained as disgusting as ever, doubtless appreciated in the neighborhood as a "certain cure for consumption." More than this, had the city dredged Healy's, subsidizing the waste disposal costs of the meat industry—and the city approved a plan that was shelved only because of the Great Fire—every property owner in Chicago would have paid for the project in his property tax bill. And every renter, including those in Bridgeport, would have picked up that part of the charge that landlords could shift into higher rents.

THE STORY OF Healy's Slough, with minor variations in detail, has been repeated innumerable times in the history of American cities and, no doubt, in the cities of every other civilization from the ancient to the postmodern world. Yet American urban history has been written, as it were, from the very banks of Healy's. From the moment historians "discovered" the American city early in the twentieth century, they have focused much attention on the endless series of Healy's Sloughs and the endless failures of city governments to clean them. How was it, many historians have asked, that American city dwellers could tolerate such gross abuse of their environments and such patent injustice to their neighbors who, solely because of poverty, had to smell Healy's Sloughs every day of their lives? It is a difficult question, but most urban historians have agreed that the answer is connected in some way to a more general inadequacy of American city government, especially in the late nineteenth- and early twentieth-century decades when Healy's Sloughs began to appear on a scale large enough to trouble even city dwellers who had to travel across town to smell them. At that crucial juncture, the argument usually goes, American cities were shackled by governments that were designed for weakness, rife with corruption, and staffed by electorates who could not have cared less. They were, in Bryce's famous phrase, "the one conspicuous failure of the United States."[12]

---

indebted to Louise Wade for these references). Note the railroad involvement in the litigation. Technically, it involved an effort to force the conversion of a railroad bridge into a drawbridge to "restore" the slough's navigable status. The courts found for the railroad.

12. James Bryce, *The American Commonwealth*, rev. ed. (2 vols.; New York: Macmillan, 1914), 1:642. There also has been a countertradition stressing a public or communal spirit inherent in urban life, which can be traced from Arthur M. Schlesinger, "The City in American History," *Mississippi Valley Historical Review* 27 (1940–41): 43–66, to Eric H. Monkkonen, *America Becomes Urban: The Development of U.S. Cities and Towns, 1780–1980* (Berkeley: University of California Press, 1988), though until recently this has been a distinctly minority viewpoint.

It is a dismal picture whose dominance was nearly complete until 1984, when Jon C. Teaford's *The Unheralded Triumph* provided the first major corrective. Comparing late nineteenth-century American city governments with their European counterparts, Teaford found that the U.S. cities delivered higher service levels at lower costs (especially to affluent neighborhoods) in every policy area but the maintenance of order—and fell short there only because democracy curbed a police presence like those of the more authoritarian European regimes.[13] Teaford may have gone a bit far toward erasing the Healy's Sloughs from the American landscape, though this is to be expected in a work challenging a century of interpretation to the contrary. Indeed, Teaford's book is important less for its rosy portrait of urban life than for its exploration of just what Americans wanted from municipal government in the nineteenth century. Teaford was not the first to ask this question; Sam Bass Warner, Jr., asked it in 1968 in *The Private City*, another pathbreaker of urban history. As Teaford notes, Warner assumed urban failure on the usual gargantuan scale, but he explained it in an important way, arguing that an ideology of "privatism" prevented Americans even from seeing their cities "as a public environment of a democratic society."[14] Lacking a conceptual framework for success, they could imagine no alternative to failure.

Yet, what if the Healy's Sloughs are not considered urban failures? What if Chicago's handling of Healy's Slough was considered successful by nineteenth-century standards that were very different from our own? What if the city was supposed to subsidize meat packers and lard renderers in their dumping and ignore rambling petitions from irrelevant people who happened to live nearby? What if, as many late nineteenth-century municipal reformers contended, city governments were business corporations that should be operated chiefly to benefit their stockholders, the property owners who had invested in urban real estate? What if these stockholders actually deserved to "vote" their "shares" in the city's corporate management decisions in proportion to their investments rather than by a universal manhood suffrage that the Citizens Association of Chicago declared in 1874 to

13. Jon C. Teaford, *The Unheralded Triumph: City Government in America, 1870–1900* (Baltimore: Johns Hopkins University Press, 1984). For police protection, see 277–78.
14. Sam Bass Warner, Jr., *The Private City: Philadelphia in Three Periods of Its Growth* (Philadelphia: University of Pennsylvania Press, 1968), 223; Teaford, *Unheralded Triumph*, 3. "Privatism" defined the city "as a community of private money makers" that, therefore, subordinated public to private goals in politics and government; Warner, *Private City*, x.

be the "immoderate fancy" of American politics?[15] What if Warner's "privatism" was less an expression of urban failure than a statement of American political philosophy? To use Teaford's terms, what if the "unheralded triumph" of American city government consisted in keeping the Healy's Sloughs open as long as their stenches did not befoul the neighborhoods of the city's major "stockholders"— including those who profited by polluting them? What if municipal government in nineteenth-century America wasn't supposed to be democratic at all?

To answer these admittedly alarming questions, urban historians have to step back from the banks of Healy's Slough. We have to place the slough in the larger contexts both of municipal government operation and the operation of government at other levels of the federal system. We have to ask just what government was for in nineteenth-century America and just how it was supposed to work. More directly, we have to ask how nineteenth-century American government did work. Historians too often have assumed answers to these questions instead of probing them directly. We have tended to assume, for example, that the central actors in the Healy's Slough story were the Bridgeport residents, though they entered the decision-making arena only once and exerted no discernible influence on the outcome. Clearly, it would be nice to believe that the Bridgeport residents were key players. It would be nice to be able to show that nineteenth-century American city government (or government at any level) was democratic. It would be nice to be able to agree with Samuel P. Hays that a ward-based "machine politics" in nineteenth-century American cities conferred power on the "lower and middle classes" because "each ward tended to select as representatives people who were like the majority of its inhabitants."[16]

But this is impossible. American city government not only was not democratic in the nineteenth century, but it was not even designed to be a democratic institution—one whose policies were guided by a majority of "universally" enfranchised voters (male citizens, or in many cities, white male citizens). True, cities held elections, often annually, and staffed elective positions by counting votes, declaring a winner when one candidate obtained a majority (or a plurality) of all

15. "Address by President Franklin MacVeagh, September 11, 1874," *Addresses and Reports of the Citizens Association of Chicago, 1874–1876* (Chicago: Hazlitt & Reed, 1876), 4–5. Also, Martin J. Schiesl, *The Politics of Efficiency: Municipal Administration and Reform in America, 1880–1920* (Berkeley: University of California Press, 1977).

16. Samuel P. Hays, "The Changing Political Structure of the City in Industrial America," *Journal of Urban History* 1 (1974): 14.

ballots cast. It also is true that by the mid nineteenth century many cities had councils whose members were elected from small wards—with boundaries drawn to reflect ethnic and class-based neighborhoods. It may even be true that each ward "select[ed] as representatives people who were like the majority of its inhabitants," though studies of municipal officeholding have left this open to doubt.[17] Yet it was only rarely true that these democratic elections structured city policies, especially those policies that involved money. Much taxing and spending in the nineteenth-century American city was isolated by law from the majoritarian, electoral arena commonly known as "politics." To borrow a distinction made by the late nineteenth-century reformers, financial decision making was a matter not of "politics," but of "administration." And city governments did not make "administrative" decisions by counting equally weighted ballots.[18]

Cities made financial decisions according to the wishes of those who had what Chicagoans called "direct personal and pecuniary interests" in their outcomes. The influence that these "interested parties" could wield in decision making, moreover, depended on the magnitude of their interests in the decision at hand. It depended, quite literally, on the value of the property likely to be taxed by the decision. To use the Healy's Slough example, aldermen ordered the BPW to devise a plan that maximized "thoroughness, cheapness and utility" not for the whole city or the Bridgeport residents, but for "the owners of property abutting said slough." These people were "interested" because they owned the "real estate chargeable for the removal of the nuisance." Because, in other words, the packers were supposed to pay for cleaning Healy's, they had the right to decide how to clean it, a right Bridgeport residents without "chargeable real estate" did not share. This is why every city official agreed to the dredging plan (though not the navigable stream). Dredging was the

17. Eugene J. Watts, *The Social Bases of City Politics: Atlanta, 1865–1903* (Westport: Greenwood, 1978); Edward Pessen, *Riches, Class, and Power before the Civil War* (Lexington: D. C. Heath, 1973), 281–301. Also Philip J. Ethington, "The Structures of Urban Political Life: Political Culture in San Francisco, 1849–1880" (Ph.D. diss., Stanford University, 1989), for evidence that the urban electorate itself was quite restricted.

18. L. Ray Gunn recently has made an analogous argument about state government in antebellum New York, noting the coincidence of democratizing changes such as the expansion of suffrage with changes in government that cut the other way: "A whole range of issues, mostly economic, had been either depoliticized or privatized. At the same time, the rise of administration and adjudication, almost by definition, imposed limits on the power of popular majorities. Together, these developments drained political participation of much of its substantive meaning"; Gunn, *The Decline of Authority: Public Economic Policy and Political Development in New York State, 1800–1860* (Ithaca: Cornell University Press, 1988), 257.

plan that the "interested parties" preferred. It seems obvious to modern sensibilities that the Bridgeport residents were the most "interested parties" of all. They were the ones who had to smell Healy's Slough. But if we are to understand nineteenth-century American city government, we must begin by defining "interest" as it was defined in the nineteenth century. It was not a democratic idea.

Two GROUPS of urban historians have scouted routes away from the banks of Healy's Slough in recent decades, distancing themselves from the "conspicuous failure" school of interpretation. One group, the "new urban historians" of the 1960s and 1970s and their "cultural Marxist" successors in the 1980s, has switched the focus of urban history away from politics and government entirely, searching instead for the social and economic bases of ethnic and class relations in nineteenth-century American cities. The other group, whose work Kathleen Neils Conzen has labeled a "post-new" urban history, has turned directly to city government, paying particular attention to public works provision and municipal finance.[19] While Teaford's book typifies the "post-new" approach to city government, Hays's view of ward-based democracy has inspired the approach to politics characteristic of much "new urban history," though especially of other studies influenced by the "new urban" findings.[20] These historians have said much that is important about nineteenth-century American cities. Yet they have not even begun to explain either the nature of power or the structure of its exercise in those cities. They have assumed rather than investigated the purpose of city government in the nineteenth century.[21] And, with a few exceptions, they have assumed that this purpose was democratic.

19. Kathleen Neils Conzen, "The New Urban History: Defining the Field" in *Ordinary People and Everyday Life: Perspectives on the New Social History,* James B. Gardner and George Rollie Adams, eds. (Nashville: American Association for State and Local History, 1983), 80–81.

20. Amy Bridges, *A City in the Republic: Antebellum New York and the Origins of Machine Politics* (Cambridge: Cambridge University Press, 1984); Steven P. Erie, *Rainbow's End: Irish Americans and the Dilemmas of Urban Machine Politics* (Berkeley: University of California Press, 1988); John M. Allswang, *Bosses, Machines, and Urban Voters: An American Symbiosis* (Port Washington: Kennikat, 1977). Hays's influence stems from his "The Politics of Reform in Municipal Government in the Progressive Era," *Pacific Northwest Quarterly* 55 (1964): 157–69. His 1974 "Changing Political Structure" was more a product of the new urban history.

21. This point is made in detail in Terrence J. McDonald and Sally K. Ward's introduction to *The Politics of Urban Fiscal Policy,* McDonald and Ward, eds. (Beverly Hills: Sage, 1984), 16–22. An important exception to this generalization about power—though not about the structure or purposes of its exertion—is a historical literature

The "new urban history" began in the 1960s with a populist faith. Part of the larger "new social history" movement, it combined a mission to rewrite history "from the bottom up" with the new technological capabilities of statistical software. With old microfilm readers and new computers, young historians plunged into the population history of the American city, transcribing reel after reel of manuscript census returns. It was a daunting job, but it promised a bountiful reward—history itself could be democratized.[22] Although the "new urban historians" paid little attention to politics, the more closely they examined the nineteenth-century city in general, the more democratic that city began to look. Studying urban "common men" (and sometimes even women), these historians easily adopted a political analysis that not only put their subjects at its center, but also seemed to endow those subjects with power. This analysis of nineteenth-century urban politics, whose origin reached back to the "functionalist" social science of the 1950s (or further), had stripped such phenomena as "bosses" and "machines" of all negative connotation, calling them the means by which "the people" wielded political power. The boss, in this analysis, was exactly what he always had said he was: a "poor man's friend" who cushioned the harshness of industrial capitalism with coal, turkeys, and patronage for its casualties. If the late nineteenth-century reformers disliked this boss, it was because they resented his empowerment of "the people." Because the reformers rejected democracy, "the people" continually rejected reform. Machine politics was democracy triumphant.[23]

---

influenced by the pluralist research strategy outlined by the community power debate in political science, esp. Watts, *Social Bases;* Carl V. Harris, *Political Power in Birmingham, 1871–1921* (Knoxville: University of Tennessee Press, 1977); David C. Hammack, *Power and Society: Greater New York at the Turn of the Century* (New York: Russell Sage, 1982). For pluralism and community power, see Nelson W. Polsby, *Community Power and Political Theory: A Further Look at Problems of Evidence and Inference*, 2d ed. (New Haven: Yale University Press, 1980). The most influential pluralist analysis was Robert A. Dahl, *Who Governs? Democracy and Power in an American City* (New Haven: Yale University Press, 1961). See Terrence J. McDonald, "The Burdens of Urban History: The Theory of the State in Recent American Social History," *Studies in American Political Development* 3 (1989): 20–21.

22. Kathleen Neils Conzen, "Quantification and the New Urban History," *Journal of Interdisciplinary History* 13 (1983): 653–77.

23. This view is explicit in Allswang, *Bosses*, and Erie, *Rainbow's End*, which appeal to new urban history findings for support. On the intellectual genealogy of the good machine, Terrence J. McDonald, "The Problem of the Political in Recent American Urban History: Liberal Pluralism and the Rise of Functionalism," *Social History* 10 (1985): 323–345. For influential good machines, see Oscar Handlin, *The Uprooted*, 2d ed. (Boston: Little, Brown, 1973 [1951]), 180–202; Alexander B. Callow, Jr., *The Tweed Ring* (New York:

Some "new urban historians," particularly the Marxists among them (also called "new labor historians," though this distinction was fine), avoided the embrace of "poor man's friends." Concerned by the fact that urban working-class majorities failed not only to overthrow, but even to challenge industrial capitalism in a significant way—despite both "universal" suffrage and an anticapitalist "producer ideology"—these historians blamed the boss. Party politics at state and national levels and machine politics in the city formed a "coffin of class consciousness" because they led American workers to trust in a democracy that was little more than mirage.[24] In the 1980s, however, labor historians regained their faith. Using the conceptual tools of "cultural Marxism," they began to argue that workers in the nineteenth-century American city actually exerted great power by forging an independent working-class subculture. Within this subculture, workers maintained autonomy from their employers by devising their own language to describe social and economic reality. Reaching a climax in Sean Wilentz's 1984 *Chants Democratic*, this view restored the old populist faith in America, though in a somewhat limited manner. Working-class politics was to be sought in "ritual behaviors" such as parades and theater riots, which became political acts every bit as significant as the elections that earlier historians had stressed. With "politics" thus redefined, workers could wield political power and the nineteenth-century American city looked democratic once again.[25]

Oxford University Press, 1966). Rooted in the kindly boss legend expressed in Edwin O'Connor, *The Last Hurrah* (Boston: Little, Brown, 1956), the good machine became social science in Robert K. Merton, *Social Theory and Social Structure: Toward the Codification of Theory and Research* (Glencoe: Free Press, 1949), and began to dominate historical writing with the 1960s elite reform reinterpretation of Progressivism, esp. Hays, "Politics of Reform" and James Weinstein, *The Corporate Ideal in the Liberal State, 1900–1918* (Boston: Beacon Press, 1968). For what might be called the inevitable machine, a near relation of the good machine, Seymour J. Mandelbaum, *Boss Tweed's New York* (New York: Wiley, 1965). Other historians have demanded that the very concept of machine politics be abandoned. See Jon C. Teaford, "Finis for Tweed and Steffens: Rewriting the History of Urban Rule," *Reviews in American History* 10 (1982): 133–49; David P. Thelen, "Urban Politics: Beyond Bosses and Reformers," *Reviews in American History* 7 (1979): 406–12. This seems to me a classic baby-with-the-bathwater proposition.

24. Alan Dawley, *Class and Community: The Industrial Revolution in Lynn* (Cambridge: Harvard University Press, 1976), 70; Ira Katznelson, *City Trenches: Urban Politics and the Patterning of Class in the United States* (Chicago: University of Chicago Press, 1981); Susan E. Hirsch, *Roots of the American Working Class: The Industrialization of Crafts in Newark, 1800–1860* (Philadelphia: University of Pennsylvania Press, 1978).

25. Sean Wilentz, *Chants Democratic: New York City and the Rise of the American Working Class, 1788–1850* (New York: Oxford University Press, 1984). For earlier formula-

Meanwhile, and with much less fanfare, another group of historians began to study municipal government, though in ways as abstracted from political power as the rhetoric of "cultural Marxism." Following in the path of Nelson Manfred Blake's 1956 *Water for the Cities*, these "post-new" urban historians tended to see the nineteenth-century American city much as today's city manager sees the city that he manages—as a set of "urban problems" waiting to be solved.[26] The more information these historians gathered on the work of public health specialists, landscape architects, and sanitary engineers, the more energetically nineteenth-century American cities appeared to have attacked their problems. The problems themselves were staggering. Dizzyingly rapid growth, epidemic diseases, overcrowding and overbuilding, and such physical challenges as swampy ground or distant water sources made even limited technological solutions seem heroic in retrospect. Every time one of these engineers devised a solution, moreover, someone in the city tried to block it in order to avoid higher taxes. Warner called this lack of public spirit "privatism." It remained for Teaford's comparative approach to make the problem-solving effort look successful after all. Yet one key insight emerged from all the "post-new" work, regardless of its judgments about success and failure: the construction of public works, of a physical infrastructure of streets, bridges, sidewalks, and sewers, was the single most important activity of American city government.

Only in the last few years have urban historians turned to finance; Terrence J. McDonald's *The Parameters of Urban Fiscal Policy* is the most complete study by far.[27] McDonald has staked important and chal-

tions, Bruce Laurie, *Working People of Philadelphia, 1800–1850* (Philadelphia: Temple University Press, 1980); Alan Dawley and Paul Faler, "Working-Class Culture and Politics in the Industrial Revolution: Sources of Loyalism and Rebellion," *Journal of Social History* 9 (1976): 466–80. For "cultural Marxism" in American historiography, Richard L. McCormick, *The Party Period and Public Policy: American Politics from the Age of Jackson to the Progressive Era* (New York: Oxford University Press, 1986), 98–115.

26. Nelson Manfred Blake, *Water for the Cities: A History of the Urban Water Supply Problem in the United States* (Syracuse: Syracuse University Press, 1956). For a review, Eugene P. Moehring, *Public Works and Urban History: Recent Trends and New Directions* (Chicago: Public Works Historical Society, 1982). Also Christine Meisner Rosen, *The Limits of Power: Great Fires and the Process of City Growth in America* (Cambridge: Cambridge University Press, 1986); Ann Durkin Keating, *Building Chicago: Suburban Developers and the Creation of a Divided Metropolis* (Columbus: Ohio State University Press, 1988). Harris, *Political Power in Birmingham*, is unique in mobilizing a concrete analysis of public works policy and municipal finance for a study of community power.

27. Terrence J. McDonald, *The Parameters of Urban Fiscal Policy: Socioeconomic Change and Political Culture in San Francisco, 1860–1906* (Berkeley: University of California Press, 1986). Also Alan D. Anderson, *The Origin and Resolution of an Urban Crisis: Baltimore,*

lenging ground. Quoting Schumpeter, he calls public finance "the skeleton of the state, stripped of all misleading ideologies" and promises, through fiscal analysis, to "put politics back" into urban history.[28] Among the ideologies to be banished, potentially, is the modern notion that American cities were democratic institutions designed to solve urban problems, though McDonald proceeds in another direction. *Parameters* is a multiple regression analysis of fiscal, social, economic, and political data from San Francisco, calculated in order to test two historical propositions about American city government: (1) that bosses spent more than reformers, especially to fund illegal welfare programs, and (2) that taxation and spending rose with urban growth, as more or less inevitable responses to physical needs. McDonald's analysis casts doubt on both propositions, even suggesting that reformers were the real urban big spenders (because they were "poor man's friends?"). *Parameters* is an ambitious work whose pioneering nature probably excuses a serious error in its methodology—McDonald's estimates of taxation and spending omit the costs of most of San Francisco's public works. Physical infrastructure, whose importance other "post-new" historians have demonstrated beyond question, is almost completely excluded from McDonald's analysis.[29]

1890–1930 (Baltimore: Johns Hopkins University Press, 1977); J. Rogers Hollingsworth and Ellen Jane Hollingsworth, *Dimensions in Urban History: Historical and Social Science Perspectives on Middle-Size American Cities* (Madison: University of Wisconsin Press, 1979); McDonald and Ward, *Politics of Urban Fiscal Policy*.

28. See McDonald, *Parameters*, x, and McDonald's historiographical essays: "The Problem of the Political," "The Burdens of Urban History," and "Putting Politics Back into the History of the American City," *American Quarterly* 34 (1982): 200–209. Joseph A. Schumpeter, "The Crisis of the Tax State" (1918), W. F. Stolper and R. A. Musgrave, trans., *American Economic Papers* 4 (1954): 6, quoted the "skeleton of the state" line from a work that is available in English as Rudolf Goldscheid, "A Sociological Approach to Problems of Public Finance" in *Classics in the Theory of Public Finance*, Richard A. Musgrave and Alan T. Peacock, eds. (London: Macmillan, 1964), 202–13. The Goldscheid piece should be required reading for political historians.

29. McDonald measures fiscal policy from San Francisco's General Fund and others including a Street Fund. These excluded most public works costs, as he recognizes: "Throughout the nineteenth century, the cost of grading and building streets was assessed directly to the adjacent property owners"; *Parameters*, 47–48. He then excludes them from his analysis, apparently because they were handled outside the citywide assessment and budget process (though he is inconsistent here, sometimes describing general fund cuts as cutting street work). If McDonald is analyzing the political economy of San Francisco, both these costs and the manner of their assessment would seem highly significant. Two historians have explicitly defined nineteenth-century street improvements as public goods: while Rosen, *Limits of Power*, is an economic analysis built on this assumption, Monkkonen, *America Becomes Urban*, 110, notes it in passing.

This error typifies the larger problem of urban political history that McDonald himself has done so much to explain and publicize: without knowing just how city governments worked in the nineteenth century, we have tended to assume that they worked in the same way they seem to work today. Because spending for public works in most large cities today is allocated from general funds (and because getting your potholes filled often depends on how your ward voted in the last election), it is easy to assume the same situation prevailed over a century ago, when "unreformed" politicians presumably ran cities under less scrutiny than most must endure today. Because much urban political debate today is focussed on the socially equitable distribution of public services (getting the streets cleaned and the garbage removed as completely from poor neighborhoods as from affluent ones), it is easy to assume that nineteenth-century city officials tried—or even said they tried—to distribute services in a socially equitable manner. But they didn't. American city government in the nineteenth century worked on the principle that the distribution of services was equitable when each city dweller got what he paid for, no more and no less. It worked on the principle that those who paid, those who owned "chargeable real estate," should control those services in which they were "interested," and control them in proportion to the value of the "interested property" that they owned. This market-based allocation rule might be considered "fair." It is not "democratic."

HEALY'S SLOUGH, it turns out, was a municipal failure after all. It was a failure, however, not because it remained an open sewer filled with meat industry wastes, but because when the city approved a plan to dredge it, every property owner in town was charged for the project, regardless of their "particular interests" in it. In the 1870s Chicago experienced many such failures. After almost two decades of "success" in giving property owners what they wanted to pay for—and only that—the city's government was transformed in the late 1860s into a mechanism for redistributing wealth in the city. There is a convention in political science that reserves the term "redistributive" for public policies that redistribute wealth downward, that take from the rich and give to the poor.[30] While this usage may be problematic for contemporary analysis, it would have been mean-

30. See, e.g., Theodore Lowi, "American Business, Public Policy, Case-Studies, and Political Theory," *World Politics* 16 (1964): 677–715. But see also James O'Connor, *The Fiscal Crisis of the State* (New York: St. Martin's Press, 1973), for an important economic analysis of upward redistribution.

ingless to nineteenth-century Americans. Few of them seem to have considered the possibility that government might be used to redistribute wealth downward, that a democratic political system might be used to offset the inequalities generated by a capitalist economy.[31] Eighteenth-century theorists, particularly James Madison in *Federalist X*, did worry about this; hence the argument that the plural factions of a large republic could safeguard property despite democracy. Yet by the nineteenth century, Americans seem to have worried more about the opposite problem, the upward redistribution that the Jacksonians called "monopoly." That is what almost happened at Healy's Slough: wealth redistributed upward toward "a few wealthy individuals."

General systems of taxing and spending tend to redistribute wealth by definition: revenues that have been assessed on one basis are spent to provide services that are allocated on another basis.[32] No matter how progressive or regressive the assessments and allocations are, they almost always differ from one another and, thus, redistribute wealth. Nineteenth-century American city governments were designed to minimize the redistributive effects of general funding by removing as many of their services as possible from the general funding process—keeping property taxes low and general budgets small. Street-building was the most successful removal, kept almost totally off-budget in special assessment systems controlled by "interested parties."[33] Yet many other "public services" in the nineteenth-century

31. Interestingly enough, the most aggressive nineteenth-century proponents of downward redistribution were the former slaves who demanded downwardly redistributive policies from the reconstructed southern state governments. See Eric Foner, *Reconstruction: America's Unfinished Revolution, 1863–1877* (New York: Harper & Row, 1988), chap. 8; Thomas Holt, *Black over White: Negro Political Leadership in South Carolina during Reconstruction* (Urbana: University of Illinois Press, 1977); J. Mills Thornton III, "Fiscal Policy and the Failure of Radical Reconstruction in the Lower South" in *Region, Race, and Reconstruction: Essays in Honor of C. Vann Woodward*, J. Morgan Kousser and James M. McPherson, eds. (New York: Oxford University Press, 1982), 349–94.

32. Richard A. Musgrave, *The Theory of Public Finance: A Study in Public Economy* (New York: McGraw-Hill, 1959), 3–27.

33. Thus, McDonald reports that San Francisco's Street Fund comprised only 6 percent of "total local expenditure" in 1880; *Parameters*, 47. San Francisco is an interesting case; its special assessment system not only was off-budget but was not even administered by the city. After the Board of Supervisors accepted a contractor's work, it issued him a voucher so that *he* could collect from property owners. By the 1860s, it was routine for contractors to sell their vouchers to brokers who then collected from owners or sued them. See *Taylor v. Palmer*, 31 Cal., 240 (1866), a landmark case in California special assessment law.

My argument here overlaps with McDonald's on the importance of a "low tax consensus," but this consensus applied to general property taxes rather than to all tax payments. It was not a consensus on fiscal conservatism (or, in McDonald's terms,

American city also were not particularly public. For police, cities supplemented small regular forces by deputizing private watchmen who were hired and paid by those with "particular interests" in police protection. For firemen, they relied on volunteers who received subsidies from neighbors who wanted fire protection. For poor relief, a case in which those who would benefit obviously could not also pay, they allowed the philanthropically inclined to provide or not as they pleased.[34] This was a "privatism" extending far beyond an ideological absence of public spirit. It was a system that literally "privatized" government to avoid redistribution.

In Chicago this privatization was most complete and successful in the two decades from about 1845 to about 1865. During this period, the city's government operated through what I call the "segmented system." The dates are approximate because Chicagoans both built and destroyed this system gradually, by piecemeal changes in law and administrative practice that introduced, strengthened, routinized, and then undermined the policies on which it was based. Of these policies, the financing of physical infrastructure through special assessment was by far the most important. In the 1850s, what can be called the heyday of segmentation in Chicago, a Healy's Slough never would have been dredged with general funds. It probably would not have been dredged at all but if it were, the cost would have been paid either by special assessments levied on owners of "chargeable real estate," or by others who cared enough for some reason to subscribe voluntarily. The views of people unable to pay, though they might have cared deeply, would not have entered the decision-making process. Such people were irrelevant in the segmented system. While in the 1870s the Bridgeport residents were ignored, in the 1850s they would not have been heard. They almost certainly would not have circulated a petition. If the right of petition is considered a basic prerogative of citizenship in the United States, the segmented system

---

"fiscal incrementalism") because "low taxes" did not mean low special assessments or, therefore, low public works spending; *Parameters*, esp. chaps. 5, 6, and 8.

34. A large literature describes these services and their private provision, esp. Philip J. Ethington, "Vigilantes and the Police: The Creation of a Professional Police Bureaucracy in San Francisco, 1847–1900," *Journal of Social History* 21 (1987): 197–227; John C. Schneider, *Detroit and the Problem of Order, 1830–1880: A Geography of Crime, Riot, and Policing* (Lincoln: University of Nebraska Press, 1980); Paul Boyer, *Urban Masses and Moral Order in America, 1820–1920* (Cambridge: Harvard University Press, 1978); M. J. Heale, "From City Fathers to Social Critics: Humanitarianism and Government in New York, 1790–1860," *Journal of American History* 62 (1976): 21–41.

limited urban citizenship to the owners of real estate, particularly when money was involved.[35]

Yet what made this system "segmented" rather than simply elitist was that a voice in decision making required the ownership of more than just any piece of real estate. It required the ownership of property that was "chargeable" or "interested" in the decision at hand. An owner had to show that he owned a lot that was liable to a particular special assessment before he could participate in the decision to levy that assessment. A special assessment is a payment by a property owner to defray the cost of a specific public works project. The assessment is levied on "interested" property in proportion to the benefit that the property will gain from the project, with benefit measured as a rise in land value. Thus, on the assumption that a paved street will raise the value of the property abutting it, the abutters pay to pave their own street. A staple of American municipal finance for a century, from its widespread introduction in the 1830s to its wholesale abandonment in the 1930s, special assessment is still used today, especially to finance public works in small cities and suburbs.[36] In the segmented systems of the nineteenth century, however, special assessment involved more than just a payment. In a segmented system, the abutters who would be liable to pay for a paving also decided whether to pave—and the power that each individual abutter exerted in making this decision depended on the proportion of the abutting property that he owned.

Rather than a way to disfranchise the propertyless, therefore, the segmented system must be understood as a way to distribute costs and decision-making power among the propertied. Its "segmentation" lay in the fact that it distributed costs and power geographically. Officials drew lines on the city's map and then assigned the costs and

35. Even had they circulated the petition, the charge that motives of "private aggrandizement" were somehow inappropriate—given that the aggrandizers would pay—would have been laughable. It should be noted that anyone could participate in nonfinancial debates about, say, public morals, the most important of which in the nineteenth century involved liquor and tavern regulation. See chap. 5.

36. Stephen Diamond, "The Death and Transfiguration of Benefit Taxation: Special Assessments in Nineteenth-Century America," *Journal of Legal Studies* 12 (1983): 201–40, is a crucial recent study. Also Victor Rosewater, *Special Assessments: A Study in Municipal Finance* (New York: Columbia University, 1898), 26–56; *Special Assessments and Service Charges in Municipal Finance* (New York: Tax Foundation, 1970); William O. Winter, *The Special Assessment Today, with Emphasis on the Michigan Experience* (Ann Arbor: University of Michigan Press, 1952), 3–6, 46–60. Donald C. Shoup, "Financing Public Investment by Deferred Special Assessment," *National Tax Journal* 33 (1980): 413–29, is a call to revive this taxation device.

power to the property owners on one side of any given line.[37] The lines took many forms. They delimited wards, lots abutting a street, the property within some distance of a proposed park, downtown property "interested" in fire prevention or street lighting, or all property in a larger area that would enjoy some major benefit relatively equally (e.g., a market house to serve the whole north side of Chicago). But regardless of the size of the districts enclosed by the lines, the owners of the property within them controlled their public works investments with hardly any interference from outside. Each district, drawn for each decision, was supreme. It was politically and financially isolated—segmented—from the larger city. The segmented system did disfranchise both the propertyless and many working-class homeowners in a significant way, denying them access to the physical infrastructure that is necessary for a safe and comfortable urban existence. Yet its purpose was broader. The system was designed to prevent all political redistribution of individual wealth: downward, upward, or horizontal.

Local control and the avoidance of redistribution together served yet another goal in the segmented system: they depoliticized municipal government. They reduced political decision making to an administrative process driven directly by "interested" property owners. When one group of property-owning neighbors desired a project and another opposed it, their alderman arbitrated the conflict by counting how much "interested" property each group owned, the only issue that was relevant. While the adoption of these rules was a political decision of great importance, however, it was also, in some sense, the last political decision. It settled the issue of power in public works decision making. Clearly, relatively wealthy owners benefited from this settlement: their wealth was not spent to benefit other, poorer city-dwellers. Some historians have suggested that poorer homeowners also gained a benefit: because they could limit their tax liabilities, working-class families could preserve their savings to finance the houses that were their chief aspirations.[38] It is questionable whether

37. Robert H. Wiebe, *The Segmented Society: An Introduction to the Meaning of America* (New York: Oxford University Press, 1975), 14–46, is an important conceptual discussion.

38. Roger D. Simon, *The City-Building Process: Housing and Services in New Milwaukee Neighborhoods 1880–1910*, Transactions of the American Philosophical Society, vol. 68, pt. 5 (Philadelphia, 1978), 35–45; Olivier Zunz, *The Changing Face of Inequality: Urbanization, Industrial Development, and Immigrants in Detroit, 1880–1920* (Chicago: University of Chicago Press, 1982), 152–76; Monkkonen, *America Becomes Urban*, 183–86. But see Harris, *Political Power*, 177–85; David R. Goldfield, *Urban Growth in the Age of Sectional-*

unhealthy neighborhoods lacking basic physical infrastructure ought to be called "benefits." Yet the unequal distribution of public works that was so obvious a feature of the nineteenth-century urban landscape, seems to have been considered a mere side effect of a system whose real importance lay elsewhere.

Rather than justifying the economic inequality of the public works distribution, nineteenth-century Americans could stress the political benefits of segmentation. By refusing to let government redistribute wealth, they also refused to let politicians use city money as a source of political power. By keeping taxes low, budgets small, and decision-making power in private hands, they denied aspiring "bosses" access to public patronage. Politicians who distributed few favors, who made few decisions that redistributed wealth, could do little to reward friends or punish enemies. They certainly could not build "machines."[39] Perhaps the most striking characteristic of Chicago's segmented system was its freedom not only from actual corruption, but even from accusations of corruption. The most corrupt act Chicago aldermen performed in the 1850s was to vote themselves gold-headed canes in 1855, and even then only after strenuous justification: meeting at night, they had to ward off physical assaults as they walked home.[40] Segmented government was squeaky clean. The Whig party bogey of Jacksonian spoils—and its inspiration, the British "Opposition" or "radical Whig" bogey of court-centered patronage—were banished. Officials who rarely decided "who got what, when, and how" from the city's government were neither tempted nor empowered to corrupt it. With politics reduced to administration, the city's "stockholders" could rule automatically.[41]

---

ism: Virginia, 1847–1863 (Baton Rouge: Louisiana State University Press, 1977), 150, for less optimistic interpretations. The Chicago Tribune, June 18, 1885, made a similar point: "To find the very poor you will not look in the little frame houses on unpaved streets, but in the tenement houses which by law and inspection are provided with sewer connections and sanitary provisions." Quoted in Keating, Building Chicago, 49.

39. This formulation has been influenced by the definition of machine politics in Raymond E. Wolfinger, "Why Political Machines Have Not Withered Away and Other Revisionist Thoughts," Journal of Politics 34 (1972): 374–75: "'Machine politics' is the manipulation of certain incentives to partisan political participation: favoritism based on political criteria in personnel decisions, contracting, and administration of the laws. A 'political machine' is an organization that practices machine politics, i.e., that attracts and directs its members primarily by means of these incentives" (emphasis in original).

40. CP, 1855/56:1893–94, 1925.

41. Thus, segmentation may offer a solution to the puzzle posed in Richard Oestreicher, "Urban Working-Class Political Behavior and Theories of American Electoral

ONE OF THE MOST dramatic instances of the urban growth that transformed American society in the nineteenth century, the early history of Chicago has received little attention from historians because most of the city's official records were thought to have burned in the Great Fire of 1871—until 1984, when the city council records on which this study relies turned up in a long-neglected warehouse. Yet similar collections for other cities have been available for many years, indexed for historians' convenience, and almost nobody has noticed either the special assessment process or the segmented system it shaped.[42] Part of the problem, as I have suggested, is that few historians have looked closely at municipal government. Another part, however, may just be the indexing; by allowing a historian to swoop in and read every document that illuminates a topic he has defined in advance, the indexing of city records has made it unnecessary for historians to wade through the mass of municipal paperwork that nineteenth-century politicians considered too routine, even too normal, to argue much about in the newspapers.[43] The Chicago

---

Politics, 1870–1940," *Journal of American History* 74 (1988): 1257–86: considerable evidence that "untapped class sentiment existed within the working-class electorate well before the Great Depression," but that it rarely surfaced in politics "at least in part because politicians and business elites consciously sought to prevent [its] expression." Oestreicher suggests that "the structure of political power, the way in which politics was conducted" blocked the politicization of working-class sentiments (pp. 1281–82). An understanding of segmented governance makes this hypothesis more concrete.

42. For modern studies noting the social, spatial, and economic importance of special assessment, see Simon, *City-Building Process*; Diamond, "Death and Transfiguration"; Zunz, *Changing Face*, 174; Harris, *Political Power*, 177–85; Goldfield, *Urban Growth*, 150; Mandelbaum, *Boss Tweed's New York*, 55; Joel A. Tarr, "The Evolution of the Urban Infrastructure in the Nineteenth and Twentieth Centuries" in *Perspectives on Urban Infrastructure*, Royce Hanson, ed. (Washington, D.C.: National Academy Press, 1984); Elizabeth Blackmar, *Manhattan for Rent, 1785–1850* (Ithaca: Cornell University Press, 1989). Two key studies, primarily of street building and the special assessment process, are Eugene P. Moehring, *Public Works and the Patterns of Urban Real Estate Growth in Manhattan, 1835–1894* (New York: Arno Press, 1981) and Clay McShane, "Transforming the Use of Urban Space: A Look at the Revolution in Street Pavements, 1880–1924," *Journal of Urban History* 5 (1979): 279–307. Nobody, however, has placed special assessment into the context of government operation and political ideology.

43. A clear example of this research style is Charles E. Rosenberg, *The Cholera Years: The United States in 1832, 1849, and 1866* (Chicago: University of Chicago Press, 1962). Two major exceptions are Moehring, *Public Works in Manhattan*, and Hendrik Hartog, *Public Property and Private Power: The Corporation of the City of New York in American Law, 1730–1870* (Chapel Hill: University of North Carolina Press, 1983). Diamond's "Death and Transfiguration," the only modern study devoted exclusively to special assessment, does not use city records at all, focussing on a period when special assessment was a subject of debate in the New York State constitutional convention and, therefore, in the newspapers of New York City and Brooklyn.

records were not indexed when I used them; I therefore had to scan every document that Chicago's city clerks filed between 1833 and 1872.[44]

An astonishing number of these documents concerned the process of special assessment. Knowing about nineteenth-century city government chiefly from the leading histories, I had to read dusty economics texts to find out just what this financial device was that generated about half the council's paperwork in the 1850s. When I stumbled onto E. R. A. Seligman's *Essays in Taxation*, I learned that special assessment not only "has long been firmly rooted in the revenue system," but that it was a uniquely American tax instrument. "No American who treats of public finance as a whole," Seligman declared, "can fail to be struck with the importance of special assessments in actual practice."[45] Because, as I saw in the Chicago documents, special assessment always involved extensive litigation, large sections of the major nineteenth-century legal treatises also were devoted to explaining it; Thomas M. Cooley's *Taxation* and John F. Dillon's *Municipal Corporations* examine the minute details of the special assessment case law that developed in each state.[46] Indeed, Seligman's main complaint about the literature on special assessment was not its paucity, but its domination by lawyers rather than economists (until Seligman's student Victor Rosewater wrote an 1898 treatise that is still the standard reference).[47] Special assessments clearly were important in nineteenth-century America.

Seligman's claim that they were uniquely American was intriguing.

44. The records are indexed now. *Chicago City Council Proceedings Files, 1833–1871: An Index* is available on microfiche from the Illinois State Archives.

45. Edwin R. A. Seligman, *Essays in Taxation* (New York: Macmillan, 1895), 282–83, 357. Seligman's major theoretical statement on special assessment was originally published as "The Classification of Public Revenues," *Quarterly Journal of Economics* 7 (1893): 286–321. Rosewater, *Special Assessments*, 14–25, attributes greater importance than Seligman to European instruments similar to special assessment.

46. Thomas M. Cooley, *A Treatise on the Law of Taxation* (Chicago: Callaghan & Co., 1876), 416–73; John F. Dillon, *Treatise on the Law of Municipal Corporations* (Chicago: James Cockcroft & Co., 1872), 566–617. See Edwin A. Gere, Jr., "Dillon's Rule and the Cooley Doctrine: Reflections of the Political Culture," *Journal of Urban History* 8 (1982): 271–98. For a suggestive analysis of the importance of courts in nineteenth-century American government, Stephen Skowronek, *Building a New American State: The Expansion of National Administrative Capacities, 1877–1920* (Cambridge: Cambridge University Press, 1982), esp. 24–46. For the assumption that special assessment would be the way cities financed even centrally drawn plans, Nelson P. Lewis, *The Planning of the Modern City: A Review of the Principles Governing City Planning* (New York: Wiley, 1916), chap. 19.

47. Seligman, *Essays,* 283. For the continuing influence of Rosewater's treatise, Jorge Macon and Jose Merino Mañon, *Financing Urban and Rural Development through Betterment Levies: The Latin American Experience* (New York: Praeger, 1977).

Perhaps special assessments were not only important in nineteenth-century America but also important to us as a way of understanding it. What does the prevalence of this policy say about the nineteenth-century American city or about nineteenth-century American politics in general? About the city it says, first, that municipal government in the nineteenth century was not designed as a democratic institution whose fiscal policies responded to the demands of voters. Other kinds of policies did respond to electoral pressure, especially those linked to liquor licensing, which may help to explain the stress recent studies have laid on ethnocultural politics at the local level.[48] Second, it says that the demand that cities be run as "corporations" by their propertied "stockholders" was far from a novel idea when it first appeared in the guise of reform in the 1870s. If the Chicago chronology was a general one, this elitist reform rhetoric—which historians have labeled the "structural reform" critique of machine politics—appeared at the very time a real stockholder model—the segmented system—was breaking down.[49] Most significant, the segmented model was being broken not by "lower and middle class" voters who elected "people who were like them," but by wealthy businessmen who could outmaneuver their fellow stockholders, especially in state legislatures and the courts, the typical targets of reformist anger.

This is why the prevalence of segmented policy tools requires a new narrative of the history of nineteenth-century American city government, and particularly of the preoccupation of generations of urban historians, "the rise of machine politics." Although disputing many of its details, most historians have agreed on one story line: an eighteenth-century neocorporate model of government (from the English "corporation of freeholders") yielded near the mid nineteenth century to a machine politics model that, in turn, lasted to the 1910s, when anti-machine Progressives won their first major victories.[50] His-

48. But see McCormick, *Party Period*, 29–63, for other explanations and a key critique of the ethnocultural interpretation. In chap. 5, I analyze the ways in which segmented government shaped the political expression of ethnocultural conflict in Chicago in the 1850s.

49. Evidence from Moehring, *Public Works in Manhattan*, and Edward Dana Durand, *The Finances of New York City* (New York: Macmillan, 1898), places New York's chronology twenty years ahead, with segmentation from the 1830s to the 1850s. Still, New York reformer Simon Sterne's famous formulation of the stockholder model, "The Administration of American Cities," *International Review* 4 (1877): 631–46, fits the Chicago timing.

50. On neocorporatism, Jon C. Teaford, *The Municipal Revolution in America: Origins of Modern Urban Government, 1650–1825* (Chicago: University of Chicago Press, 1975); Hartog, *Public Property and Private Power*. I use "machine politics" rather than "political

torians have named the systems in different ways and disputed whether the transition from neocorporatism to machine politics represented deterioration (conspicuous failure) or democratization (poor man's friend), but the idea that one replaced the other directly has gone unchallenged. In part for this reason, historians also have agreed on the basic causes of the shift, locating them in the social history of the city itself. From this perspective, the key difference between neocorporatism and machine politics has been that one was centralized and the other decentralized. The shift, therefore, was a decentralization of city government that was powered by a decentralization of urban society.[51] This story, which often also identifies decentralization with democratization, gains plausibility from the fact that Progressives, whether they opposed machine politicians with elitist ("structural") or populistic ("social") reform critiques, nearly always demanded the replacement of localized chaos by centralized control.[52]

The use of Progressive Era political evidence to explain a change in mid nineteenth-century politics has resulted in serious distortion, especially since it has been bolstered by temporally—though not necessarily causally—appropriate evidence of mid nineteenth-century

---

machine" to distinguish the loose "rings" of ward-based politicians in the late nineteenth century from more recent Richard J. Daley-style concentrations of power. Thus, my definition of "machine politics" follows that in Hays's articles "Politics of Reform" and "Changing Political Structure." In the language of M. Craig Brown and Charles N. Halaby, "Machine Politics in America, 1870–1945," *Journal of Interdisciplinary History* 17 (1987): 587–612, I am describing "factional" rather than "dominant" machines; in that of Martin Shefter, "The Emergence of the Political Machine: An Alternative View" in Willis D. Hawley et al., *Theoretical Perspectives on Urban Politics* (Englewood Cliffs: Prentice-Hall, 1976), 14–44, the pre-machine "era of rapacious individualism."

51. Hays's "Changing Political Structure" is the most important statement of this position, which remains a staple of urban history texts. See David R. Goldfield and Blaine A. Brownell, *Urban America: A History,* 2d ed., (Boston: Houghton Mifflin, 1990), 236–37; Howard P. Chudacoff and Judith E. Smith, *The Evolution of American Urban Society,* 3d ed. (Englewood Cliffs: Prentice Hall, 1988), 151–53.

52. For the distinction between these types of reformers, Melvin G. Holli, *Reform in Detroit: Hazen S. Pingree and Urban Politics* (New York: Oxford University Press, 1969), 157–81. They shared a common enemy—machine politics—but defined it differently. While structural reformers criticized machine politics for allowing men without property to spend city taxes they did not pay, social reformers blamed it for allowing antisocial elites and venal politicians to extort fraudulent prices for inadequate and unfairly distributed city services. Thus, while one group saw machine politics as too democratic, the other saw it as not democratic enough. Both, however, advocated centralizing reforms as solutions. See also C. K. Yearley, *The Money Machines: The Breakdown and Reform of Governmental and Party Finance in the North, 1860–1920* (Albany: State University of New York Press, 1970).

social history. In Chicago, the transition from a neocorporate (or, in its western variant, a "booster") model to machine politics had the segmented system as an intermediate stage.[53] The segmented system, based on special assessment and other privatizing policy tools, was radically decentralized, more so than either the neocorporatism that preceded it or the machine politics that followed. Thus, the rise of machine politics in Chicago was a centralizing rather than a decentralizing event. To make my position clear, I do not dispute the existence of any of the models in the standard story of American city government. I do, however, dispute the causal mechanisms of the story. If the rise of machine politics was centralizing—and in Chicago it clearly was—it simply cannot be explained by the bundle of forces that seem to have decentralized urban society, and particularly not by those to which historians have attributed a democratization of city government (through, in Hays's sketch, representation at the ward level). The decentralizing political change in Chicago created the segmented system, the "stockholder" ideal that elitist reformers would recall longingly even while they tried to restore it through centralizing "structural reform" strategies. Neither segmentation nor machine politics emerged as democratizing responses to social change.

Yet the municipal system structured by these local tax policies also has a larger, national significance. Consider Andrew Jackson's famous 1830 veto of the Maysville Road bill. Federally funded improvements, Jackson argued, quoting Monroe before him, should be " 'of a general, not local, national not State,' character" because "disregard of this distinction would of necessity lead to the subversion of the federal system."[54] By "subversion," Jackson meant more than a departure from legalistic constructions of federal authority. He was worried about "a scramble for appropriations that have no relation to any general system of improvement, and whose good effects must of necessity be very limited." The government should subsidize only projects whose benefits would be shared across the Union. When he criticized policies "ministering to personal ambition and self-

---

53. For the similarity of eastern neocorporate to western booster government, compare Teaford, *Municipal Revolution*, and Richard C. Wade, *The Urban Frontier: Pioneer Life in Early Pittsburgh, Cincinnati, Lexington, Louisville, and St. Louis* (Chicago: University of Chicago Press, 1959).

54. For all quotations in this paragraph, James D. Richardson, comp., *A Compilation of the Messages and Papers of the Presidents, 1789–1897* (10 vols.; Washington, D.C.: Government Printing Office, 1896–99), 2:486–87, 490. Recent studies of state government show that similar considerations also shaped policy making at that level: Gunn, *Decline of Authority*; Peter Wallenstein, *From Slave South to New South: Public Policy in Nineteenth-Century Georgia* (Chapel Hill: University of North Carolina Press, 1987).

aggrandizement," Jackson was referring to the ambitions not only of economic classes, but of groups that were defined on a geographical basis. This is why it mattered that the Maysville Road "is exclusively within the limits of a State . . . and even as far as the State is interested conferring partial instead of general advantages." Those who were not "interested" in a public works project "of a purely local character," should not be asked to pay for it. National wealth should not be redistributed geographically or, really, at all. The Jacksonian internal improvements debate at the federal level reflected the same logic as the public works decision-making process at the municipal level.[55]

This segmented logic, moreover, had a significance extending beyond even tax policy. It was what divided Daniel Webster and Robert Hayne in their Great Debate of 1830 and what, in 1858, defined the positions of the Illinois debaters Abraham Lincoln and Stephen Douglas. What was popular sovereignty—Douglas's strategy for avoiding divisive national debates about slavery—if not local control over local decision making? It is unnecessary to describe here the sensitivity of antebellum politicians to the connection between tax policy and slavery; a mere reference to the Nullification Crisis—South Carolina's 1832 threat to secede from the Union over a tariff—is sufficient to show this close link. Active federal policies, by extending federal authority within the states, always raised the threat of a federal government that could and perhaps would interfere with the "local institutions" of the southern states. Only these states were "interested" in protecting the institution that was "peculiar" to themselves. In this context, Lincoln's fear that the Union "no longer can endure half slave and half free," that it would become "all one thing, or all the other," could appear truly radical to southerners even as Lincoln himself saw the Dred Scott decision as the crucial radical step.[56] Both rejected the logic by which a line drawn across a map of the United States in 1820 had become a "natural" solution to the problem of whether some people could hold others in bondage. Stated in these terms, the Missouri Compromise sounds almost surreal. Yet nineteenth-century Americans had great faith in the power of cartography to settle political problems.

55. See esp. Carter Goodrich, *Government Promotion of American Canals and Railroads, 1800–1890* (New York: Columbia University Press, 1960), 39–48, 169–85.

56. Don E. Fehrenbacher, *Slavery, Law, and Politics: The Dred Scott Case in Historical Perspective* (New York: Oxford University Press, 1981), is a brilliant analysis of the process by which politicians' refusal to legislate about slavery forced the Court into the national ruling that made war inevitable. Also Fehrenbacher, *Prelude to Greatness: Lincoln in the 1850s* (Stanford: Stanford University Press, 1962), 70–95.

To return to Chicago, it is not a coincidence that the segmented government of this one American city broke down at the same time the national system segmenting slavery from freedom came crashing in on itself. American cities were, in Amy Bridges's phrase, "cities in the republic," constantly affected by the national community of which they were part.[57] The segmented logic, the faith that cartographers could prevent conflict if they could only draw their maps correctly, became unrealistic in Chicago soon after it became unrealistic in the nation. As Bleeding Kansas made a nightmare of popular sovereignty and the Taney Court, in the Dred Scott case, declared the law of slavery to be national, Chicagoans were struggling to preserve an embattled system of local control within their own city. By the end of the Civil War, with the emergence of newly powerful groups who could thwart segmentation by coercing subsidies from their fellow "stockholders," the system collapsed. The city began to redistribute wealth, to make public decisions without reference to the lines drawn on maps. Although the city—like the federal government in an era aptly named the "Great Barbecue"—redistributed this wealth in an upward direction, the fact of redistribution opened decision making beyond the small groups who had "interests" in particular decisions.[58] As the city became a more public institution it also, potentially, became a more democratic institution. By the 1870s, anyone could demand that the city clean Healy's Slough. It would be the twentieth century, however, before the city would even begin to listen.

THE STORY OF CHICAGO'S government begins long before anyone like the late nineteenth-century residents of Bridgeport voiced opinions about public policies. It begins in 1833, with the initial incorporation of Chicago by land speculators who hoped that an internal improvement project, the Illinois and Michigan Canal, would promote the growth of a great northwestern commercial center. That the construction of this canal also brought many propertyless laborers to the area rarely engaged the attention of these urban boosters, whose neocorporate government existed to enhance local land values. This account of Chicago's history begins with them, analyzing the "booster system" of government in the next chapter. Chapter 3 de-

57. Bridges, *City in the Republic*, 14–15.
58. For immediate expressions of post–Civil War policy making in the "public interest" at the federal level, e.g., Wallace D. Farnham, "'The Weakened Spring of Government': A Study in Nineteenth-Century American History," *American Historical Review* 68 (1963): 662–80; Margaret Susan Thompson, *The "Spider Web": Congress and Lobbying in the Age of Grant* (Ithaca: Cornell University Press, 1985).

scribes the abandonment of this system and the "segmentation" of Chicago's government amidst a national battle over federal improvement funds for the city. After chapter 4 explains the characteristic policy-making tools of segmented government, chapter 5 analyzes the impact of segmentation on key political issues including the temperance fight of the 1850s and the rise of the local Republican party. Chapter 6, in part a narrative of Chicago's experience of the Civil War, shows the connections between the war and the ways in which Chicagoans destroyed the segmented system as it raged. In the epilogue, after the Great Chicago Fire has destroyed the city itself, Chicagoans rebuild under the terms of a new, late nineteenth-century politics: the politics of machine politicians and "structural" reformers.

2

The Booster System of City Government

FOR THE FIRST fifteen years of Chicago's corporate existence the city's government operated on a booster model.[1] City government played an active role in promoting urban growth and, thereby, the fortunes of the businessmen who had staked their futures on Chicago's development. Members of the city's booster elite made policy directly. Even after the statewide abandonment of property qualifications for the suffrage in 1841, they held municipal offices and made policy decisions that recognized both their personal dependence on Chicago's growth and the ways in which government could be used to encourage that growth. Jacksonian partisanship structured municipal elections. Although Democrats won council majorities and the mayoralty in most years, elections featured spirited partisan campaigns. In the booster system, "public policy" had a meaning it later would lose in Chicago. Booster policy decisions were public because they were made on a citywide basis. The council ordered bridges built and streets paved only after they had determined which public works projects most effectively would promote the development of the city

---

1. For booster models, Richard C. Wade, *The Urban Frontier: Pioneer Life in Early Pittsburgh, Cincinnati, Lexington, Louisville, and St. Louis* (Chicago: University of Chicago Press, 1959); Daniel J. Boorstin, *The Americans: The National Experience* (New York: Random House, 1965), 113–68; Don Harrison Doyle, *The Social Order of a Frontier Community: Jacksonville, Illinois, 1825–70* (Urbana: University of Illinois Press, 1978); Carl Abbott, *Boosters and Businessmen: Popular Economic Thought and Urban Growth in the Antebellum Middle West* (Westport: Greenwood Press, 1981); Stanley Elkins and Eric McKitrick, "A Meaning for Turner's Frontier," *Political Science Quarterly* 69 (1954): 321–53. Compare these, especially Wade's, with the eastern colonial governments described in Jon C. Teaford, *The Municipal Revolution in America: Origins of Modern Urban Government, 1650–1825* (Chicago: University of Chicago Press, 1975).

as a whole. Elite officeholding, Jacksonian partisanship, and citywide decision making defined the booster system of city government in Chicago.

CHICAGO IN 1833 was a frontier village in which frame houses were just beginning to supplement log cabins. Most of the town's 350 residents boarded in taverns or lived behind their stores or workshops. Others lodged in the empty barracks at Fort Dearborn, the home of the federal Indian Agent who served also as town president.[2] Thousands of Potawatomi Indians converged on Chicago annually to collect annuities from the government; some 5,000 arrived in 1833 to negotiate the treaty in which they ceded much of northern Illinois to the United States.[3] Chicago's pioneer population of fur traders and fort sutlers were joined in the mid 1830s by a flood of young businessmen from the East, a top-heavy population of lawyers, commission merchants, and land speculators.[4] If the physical appearance of early Chicago "was not one to encourage the speculator in search of real estate bargains or the *pater-familias* seeking an inviting place in which to establish a prosperous business and a happy home," recent events suggested otherwise. Businessmen flocked to this "small village on the very outskirts of civilized life" because they knew that the federal and state governments were at work developing a city.[5]

In addition to removing the Indians from the Chicago area, the federal government was dredging a harbor at the mouth of the Chicago River. On July 1, 1833, its dredges began to dig away the sandbar that blocked access by lake vessels into the river. Two piers extending into Lake Michigan enclosed a channel that a natural freshet flooded in 1834. Over 200 ships discharged cargo in Chicago's harbor in 1836, though engineering problems necessitated repeated dredging. By 1838 Congress had appropriated almost $200,000 for the harbor and

2. A. T. Andreas, *History of Chicago* (3 vols.; Chicago: Andreas, 1884–86), 1:128–29; Edwin O. Gale, *Reminiscences of Early Chicago and Vicinity* (Chicago: Fleming H. Revell, 1902), 25–55; *Reception to the Settlers of Chicago Prior to 1840* (Chicago: Calumet Club, 1879), 62–63; James Ryan Haydon, *Chicago's True Founder: Thomas J. V. Owen* (Lombard, Ill.: Owen Memorial Fund, 1934).

3. Andreas, *History*, 1:117, 122–28; Gale, *Reminiscences*, 54, 107; Jacqueline Peterson, "The Founding Fathers: The Absorption of French-Indian Chicago, 1816–1837" in *Ethnic Chicago*, rev. and exp., Melvin G. Holli and Peter d'A. Jones, eds. (Grand Rapids: William B. Eerdmans, 1984), 300–337.

4. Deborah L. Haines, "City Doctor, City Lawyer: The Learned Professions in Frontier Chicago, 1833–1860" (Ph.D. diss., University of Chicago, 1986), 29–231; Chicago *Democrat*, August 17, 1836; Chicago *American*, December 31, 1836, May 20, 27, 1837.

5. Gale, *Reminiscences*, 25; Charles Cleaver, *Early-Chicago Reminiscences*, Fergus Historical Series, no. 19 (Chicago: Fergus Printing Co., 1882), 13.

FIG. 1 CHICAGO FROM THE LAKE, 1830

by the mid 1840s over a thousand lake vessels were reaching Chicago annually, carrying commercial goods and new migrants.[6] The Great Lakes transportation route, which linked Chicago to New York through the Erie Canal, was the younger city's commercial lifeline until railroads supplemented the water route in the 1850s. Federal aid for the harbor had been essential.

The harbor improvements formed only part of a more ambitious government plan for Chicago: the Illinois and Michigan Canal. An 11-mile portage at Chicago separated the Chicago River, and thus also Lake Michigan, from the Illinois, and thus also the Mississippi, river system. After the completion of the Erie Canal, therefore, a canal at Chicago promised to convey the farm produce of the upper Midwest via Chicago to either New York or New Orleans. Congress granted Illinois alternate sections of land along the proposed canal route in 1827 and the legislature created a board of canal commissioners in 1829, intending to finance the project by selling the grant. After a disappointing sale of farmlands in April 1830, the commissioners looked to town lots for greater returns. They platted Ottawa and Chi-

6. Andreas, *History*, 1:233–35; Bessie Louise Pierce, *A History of Chicago* (3 vols.; Chicago: University of Chicago Press, 1937–57), 1:79, 90–94; Glen E. Holt, "The Birth of Chicago: An Examination of Economic Parentage," *Journal of the Illinois State Historical Society* [hereafter *JISHS*] 76 (1983): 82–94.

cago and began lobbying Congress for harbor appropriations to boost Chicago land prices. After a second unremunerative sale in September 1830, and amid debate about whether the state should abandon the canal plan and build a railroad instead, the legislature abolished the canal board in March 1833.[7]

Expectations for the canal, however, already had encouraged interest in Chicago. Residents obtained a town charter and proceeded to sell school section lots for an average of $60 an acre, a huge advance on the $1.25 prices of 1830. Among the purchasers of school section property was the New York capitalist Arthur Bronson, who also drew other eastern investors into the Chicago market. Easterners flocked to Chicago, boosting the town's population from 350 in 1833 to 2,000 in 1834 and 3,264 in 1835.[8] Two local newspapers lobbied the state to start canal construction. The legislature authorized a $500,000 loan in 1835 and in 1836 created a new board of canal commissioners. In 1835 the federal government opened a land office and Illinois chartered a state bank, with a branch in Chicago to offer credit to real estate investors. Land prices spiraled, enabling the canal board to raise enough money in a single day of sales to start construction in July 1836.[9]

With a land boom in progress, new settlers and investors arrived daily. The state continued to fuel the boom, especially with a $4 million canal loan in 1837, and by 1839 Illinois had appropriated another $1.25 million for the canal. Many of Chicago's new businessmen worked as contractors on the canal project, while canal wages drew hundreds of Irish immigrants to Chicago as well as to shanty towns along the line of construction. When the Panic of 1837 called a halt to the land boom, the canal board continued to sustain contractors and workers. Canal scrip circulated in Chicago as currency in small denominations; canal funds were "the chief support of Chicago and the region" as the depression deepened. With the collapse of the state's finances in 1843, the canal board suspended construction, but they

7. Andreas, *History*, 1:165–68; Pierce, *History*, 1:118–19; George Joseph Fleming, Jr., "Canal at Chicago: A Study in Political and Social History" (Ph.D. diss., Catholic University, 1951), 39–83; Holt, "Birth of Chicago," 88–90; Haydon, *True Founder*, 47–48, 164–65; James William Putnam, *The Illinois and Michigan Canal: A Study in Economic History* (Chicago: University of Chicago Press, 1918), 1–22.

8. Haydon, *True Founder*, 164–65; Homer Hoyt, *One Hundred Years of Land Values in Chicago* (Chicago: University of Chicago Press, 1933), 19, 26; Arthur Bronson to Richard J. Hamilton, June 15, 1834, and List of Land Bought by Bronson in School Section, 1833, folder 35, Bronson papers, Chicago Historical Society; John Denis Haeger, *The Investment Frontier: New York Businessmen and the Development of the Old Northwest* (Albany: State University of New York Press, 1981), 89–90.

9. Putnam, *Illinois and Michigan Canal*, 22–34; Hoyt, *One Hundred Years*, 27–30.

resumed work in 1845, and in 1848 opened the canal for navigation.[10] The Illinois and Michigan Canal played a huge role in Chicago's early development as a basis for speculative investment by easterners. When the eastern money dried up in the depression, canal construction helped to sustain Chicago until prosperity returned.

THE EASTERN businessmen who moved to Chicago in the 1830s understood their dependence on government action. As classic nineteenth-century city boosters, they structured their political priorities around the effort to obtain government aid. Thus, although Chicagoans maintained a two-party system and debated national questions on party lines, their party affiliations blurred when aid to Chicago was at issue. Whigs predictably criticized Democrats for lackluster support of the canal but Democrats returned the same charge against Whigs. Although the parties agreed on the need for government aid for the economic development of Chicago, they disputed the forms such aid should take. In the columns of his Chicago *Democrat*, John Wentworth persistently asked the troublesome questions: who should benefit from state-supported economic growth and who should pay for it?[11] Active government policies required answers to these questions, whether the answers came as statements of ideology or as the practical shaping of policy.

Wentworth answered his own questions with a Locofoco, or producer-oriented, ideology that championed the rights of "the people" to participate in the opportunities of commercial development. He did not oppose state banking and internal improvements in general. Rather, he opposed statist development strategies that, in his view, taxed the "producing classes," chiefly farmers and mechanics, to benefit wealthy and especially nonresident speculators. Chicagoans, of course, depended on these speculators and could ill afford to discourage their investments. Wentworth and other Illinois Democrats searched, therefore, for formulas that would preserve local access to the profits engendered by state-sponsored development while continuing to attract capital from the East.[12]

The Illinois and Michigan Canal board's land sale policy illustrated

10. Andreas, *History*, 1:168–71; *American*, June 11, 1836; *Reception to the Settlers*, 53–54; Rima Lunin Schultz, "The Businessman's Role in Western Settlement: The Entrepreneurial Frontier, Chicago, 1833–1872" (Ph.D. diss., Boston University, 1985), 52; Fleming, "Canal at Chicago," 125–31.

11. Pierce, *History*, 1:374–75; Schultz, "Businessman's Role," 129–37; Don E. Fehrenbacher, *Chicago Giant: A Biography of "Long John" Wentworth* (Madison: American History Research Center, 1957), 26–28.

12. Schultz, "Businessman's Role," 29–30.

this effort. The legislature, dominated by Jacksonian Democrats, allowed the board to sell its land on liberal "canal terms" that required only one quarter down and three annual installments at 6 percent interest. Canal terms would enable small investors to share in the profits that canal land was expected to generate during the land boom. Yet the legislature's failure to cap the amount of land that individuals could purchase also enabled wealthy easterners to use canal terms to buy huge tracts with minimal cash outlays. Banking policy followed a similar logic. Democrats agreed on the need for a state bank but resisted setting up a bank that would be controlled by outside capitalists. The legislature created the second state bank in 1835, but limited its power to issue currency, established the personal liability of its directors in the event of default, and tried to disperse the ownership of its stock and the voting rights accorded its stockholders. That the populistic intentions of this legislation also were thwarted should not minimize the force of the intentions themselves. When Locofoco Democrats called for hard money and easy credit, they offered an alternative, though equally statist, strategy for western development.[13]

The complexity of the economic issues led the local parties to use shorthand references to their national ideological positions, particularly in municipal campaigns. Chicago's newspapers used a stress on cultural conflict in this manner. While Democrats decried monopoly and aristocracy, emphasizing their friendship toward working-class and immigrant voters, Whigs complained of "mobocracy" and offered nativist interpretations of local events. The Whig paper, the *American*, carried an article just before the town election of 1835 deploring the Democrats' hold on Irish voters in New York City and demanding a restrictive naturalization law for Illinois. The comparison was preposterous. The New York situation could have had little relevance for politics in a town of three thousand, even if the boosters' wildest projections of Chicago's growth are taken into account.[14] Yet for a population that had migrated west as young adults, such arguments tapped familiar rhetorical sources of partisanship.

Only scattered issues of the *Democrat* from 1836 to 1844 have survived. Because Democrats outran Whigs in Chicago elections, the *American* tended to downplay partisanship, calling for nonpartisan municipal elections. "The Whigs, as a party," the paper reported in

13. Ibid., 34–39; F. Cyril James, *The Growth of Chicago Banks* (2 vols.; New York: Harper & Bros., 1938), 1:85–89.

14. Pierce, *History*, 1:364–76; *American*, June 8, July 11, 1835; July 9, October 22, 1836; March 18, 1837; *Democrat*, July 15, 1835; May 18, July 6, 1836.

1843, "have made no nominations, well knowing that if they should, they would be rode over roughshod by overwhelming opposition." Yet the paper usually campaigned with vigor. In 1840 it urged voters to return Whigs to municipal office. It printed the city ticket, led by Benjamin Raymond for mayor, under the heading "Harrison, Raymond and Reform," claiming that the election would "have an important influence" on the presidential election later that year. When the Whigs lost, the paper blamed illegal immigrant voters. The *American* repeated this pattern in 1841 and both parties ran slates of candidates in most other years through 1847 for which newspapers survive.[15]

Newspapers provide a biased source for judging partisanship in city elections because city printing contracts gave them vested interests in party politics. Municipal election returns, however, also reveal evidence of partisanship. Each year Chicagoans elected a mayor and two aldermen per ward. Partisan majorities in the mayoral vote from the wards matched the party affiliations of aldermen elected in three-fourths of all aldermanic elections from 1837 to 1845.[16] Candidates of the abolitionist Liberty party ran for mayor in each year from 1842 to 1847. While they never came close to winning, these candidates must have seen city elections as opportunities to build party strength.[17] More direct evidence of partisanship appears in an 1844 council investigation of a contested election. Democrat Augustus Garrett, the incumbent mayor, defeated Whig George Dole by seven votes out of a canvass of 1,796. Whig charges of fraud in two wards prompted the council to hold hearings and, ultimately, to order a new election in which another Democrat unseated Garrett. The hearings provide a detailed picture of the electoral process in booster Chicago.

Whigs charged Democrats with buying votes, treating, changing the clocks in election places, and violating the secrecy of ballots in two wards, the Third and the Fifth. The council investigating committee, after hearing more than thirty witnesses give two weeks of testimony, ducked the main issues but ordered a new election be-

15. *American*, March 3, 1843; March 2, 1842; January 29, February 19, March 2, 4, 1840; February 26, 27, March 1, 10, 24, 1841.

16. Party affiliation was determined from the newspapers. For citation of election returns, see appendix 1. Aldermanic elections matched mayoral majorities in 72 out of 106 elections (6 wards × 9 years × 2 aldermen except for the first two elections, when two wards elected one alderman apiece). Nine aldermanic candidates could not be identified because of missing newspapers. Every ward split tickets in 1846; the Whig mayoral candidate took 66 percent of the vote but the Democrats won a 9-to-3 council majority. If this election is counted, 70 percent of the aldermanic elections for the decade matched the partisan mayoral vote.

17. Pierce, *History*, 1:421.

cause clerks in the wards had been unqualified to vote. In a minority report, an alderman who was about to lose his seat in the new election dissented: "Are we prepared to reject the voice of the People because of the disqualification of a clerk? For myself I am not."[18] Yet the evidence suggested that Democrats had engaged in questionable practices.

Most of the accusations involved Garrett, and the committee allowed him personally to examine witnesses who testified against him. Aside from a brawl that knocked over the ballot box after the polls had closed, little of interest occurred in the Third Ward. Whigs did, however, find a Norwegian immigrant who offered damaging testimony against Garrett. The Whig committee member asked Oren Overson whether Garrett had given him an election ticket or money for his vote. Overson said that Garrett had given him both but that the money was not for voting. At this point Garrett took over the questioning.

Q. Can you read English?
A. No.
Q. Did you open the ticket that Mr Garrett gave you, and did you read his name on it?
A. I did.
. . . .
Q. Was the ticket I gave you in English or Norwegian?
A. It was in English. I understand as much English as Mr Garrett's name.
Q. Does the paper now shown you "James Rossiter" written thereon, contain my name?
A. I don't understand it. (The name of Augustus Garrett being shown the witness in print, the witness says he recognizes the name.)
Q. Had you made up your mind to vote for me previous to your receiving the dollar for splitting rails [at an unspecified future date]?
A. Yes.
Q. Would you have voted for me whether you had received the dollar or not?
A. The dollar had nothing to do with my vote.[19]

In the Fifth Ward, Democrats had made more elaborate plans for the Norwegians. The election was held in the home of aldermanic candidate Elihu Granger. Although everyone denied having altered Granger's clocks, witnesses could not agree on what time the polls had opened. Whigs charged that the Democrats had opened the polls

18. Chicago City Council Proceedings Files [hereafter CP], 1844/44:1859.
19. Ibid., 1844/44:1907.

illegally early so that they could bring the Norwegians to vote before other voters arrived. Norwegian leader Andrew Neilsen admitted to meeting with Garrett, Granger, and Samuel Grier the night before the election but denied that they had planned to open the polls early. Election clerk George Brady, however, recalled another meeting that night, where he had "recommended having the Norwegians brought up to the polls first, to prevent any disturbance during the after part of the day." Samuel Grier also claimed credit: "There was an arrangement of this kind made—that when I understood that great threats had been made to prevent the Norwegians' voting, and even to knock me down to prevent my voting, that when the polls should be opened in the morning it was best to have the Norwegians vote early before any liquor got about and fighting and quarreling began."[20] Nothing was proved about the clocks. Brady and Grier insisted that the polls opened no earlier than 8:00, and Granger said he was out of the house. Still, the fact that Grier's explanation could be considered reasonable says much about the normal practice of conducting Chicago elections.

In his final defense, Garrett stressed just this point. He questioned Dole and Dole's attorney Grant Goodrich about their own electoral practices. "During the time Chicago has been a City," Garrett asked the Whigs, "has it been the custom for candidates for office to use their influence to get what votes they could and had it not been the practice of both the political parties to expend money for teams at the time of elections—and have not you . . . expended money at previous elections, for purposes of treating and hiring teams? And do you . . . know of any fraud or illegal proceedings on the part of myself at this last election?" Goodrich hedged on the treating question as "a cold water man," but admitted paying for teams, "which I do not conceive to exercise a corrupting influence upon the voters." Dole agreed that Whigs followed all of these "customs." Neither knew of any fraud on Garrett's part even though Goodrich had taken depositions before the official hearings began.[21] Municipal elections in the booster system were thoroughly partisan and hotly contested.

THE PARTISANSHIP of municipal elections rarely carried over into policy debates. The *American* taunted Garrett for making "ridiculous" arguments in opposing the construction of a bridge in 1840, but the paper never tried to link the pro- and antibridge factions to the

20. Ibid., 1844/44:1888.
21. Ibid.

Whig and Democratic parties.[22] The management of the school fund did polarize Chicagoans on party lines. Whigs charged that Democrats had squandered money that they would preserve because of their party's commitment to public education. Yet even this debate failed to generate alternative, partisan approaches to policy. The council, controlled by Whigs early in the national election year of 1840, took the school fund out of Democratic hands and appointed a Whig school agent with great fanfare. The issue even prompted speeches at a Democratic election rally. Yet Whig aldermen did not support their appointee when he tried to alter school fund investment policy.[23] In general, partisanship did not structure local debate. National issues—Jackson, Van Buren, the "monster bank," and, by the mid 1840s, slavery extension and the Mexican War—provided the content of the partisan dialogue.

The citizens of Chicago in the 1830s and 1840s had "learned" their politics elsewhere. Because most native-born Chicagoans had migrated from New England and New York State as young adults, most brought with them the party affiliations and understandings they had established in these places.[24] The city's leading Democrat, John Wentworth—the publisher of the *Democrat* and the only congressman to represent Chicago in the booster period—had learned his politics in New Hampshire, where his father was a state legislator and personal friend of the Jacksonian governor Isaac Hill, who helped launch the younger Wentworth's career. William B. Ogden, a native of New York, had been a state legislator in Martin Van Buren's political organization, the Albany Regency, before moving to Chicago. J. Young Scammon, a Whig, also had established his partisan identity in the East, where his father had served in Maine's state legislature and he had studied law and gained admission to the bar.[25] Since many of Chicago's immigrant residents probably also had spent time in the Northeast, either in port cities or along the line of Erie Canal construction, they too probably arrived with established partisan identities.

22. *American*, April 22, 1840. For municipal partisan debate as repetition of national arguments in Jacksonian New York, Amy Bridges, *A City in the Republic: Antebellum New York and the Origins of Machine Politics* (Cambridge: Cambridge University Press, 1984), 61–82.

23. *American*, February 19, 1840.

24. For the predominance of young adult males in the population, Haines, "City Doctor," 48. On "partisan education," see Jean H. Baker, *Affairs of Party: The Political Culture of Northern Democrats in the Mid-Nineteenth Century* (Ithaca: Cornell University Press, 1983), 27–70.

25. Fehrenbacher, *Chicago Giant*, 12–14; Andreas, *History*, 1:550, 617; Charles Butler in *As Others See Chicago: Impressions of Visitors, 1673–1933*, Bessie Louise Pierce, comp. (Chicago: University of Chicago Press, 1933), 50–52.

Congressman Wentworth rarely took part in municipal policy debates during the booster years. His newspaper's promotion of Democrats for city offices did not contain promises of policy agendas. Voters were instructed to elect Democrats to support the party by conferring patronage—not least on the *Democrat* itself—and by building and demonstrating party strength for the more important state and national contests. That candidates were affiliated with the Democratic party and nominated by its conventions provided sufficient reason for support. Conventions ratified their popular selection and the party guaranteed their ideological stance. Democrats could be trusted to manage public affairs because they were Democrats.[26]

Whigs used a similar rhetoric. Like the *Democrat*, the *American* coveted the city printing. It upbraided "the *Whig* Common Council" of 1839 for awarding the printing of a pamphlet of city ordinances to another firm. The editor knew he was walking a fine line in demanding patronage. Whigs, he admitted, were not supposed to deal in spoils. His newspaper, however, had contributed to electing the Whig aldermen. The printing was only its due.[27] Promoting the party's municipal slate in 1840, the *American* assumed that its readers knew why Whigs were preferable to Democrats: "We want the affairs, character, and dignity of our City protected and represented, by men of responsibility and character—who have some stake in the institutions and interest in the laws which they are called upon to maintain and create."[28] This was shorthand for the range of ideological distinctions that separated Whigs from Democrats.

Because the local parties rarely adopted conflicting positions on city-building strategies, those council debates that were partisan tended to be cultural. Yet regular partisanship minimized the disruption of moral and cultural debates. In almost a parody of moralistic politics, Whig alderman Grant Goodrich tried to convince his fellow aldermen in 1838 not to grant theater licenses because "the performances of modern theaters are grossly demoralizing. Shall we foster this vicious taste of the low & profligate," he demanded, "or shall we shut down the flowgate at the fountain?" Democrat Henry Rucker answered predictably, refusing "to enter into an enquiry of the morality of the Drama in general, or of its moral tendency in this community. The moral world," he explained, "has long been divided on the first proposition; and your [judiciary] committee have no doubt

26. Pierce, *History*, 1:365–71, 386–87.
27. *American*, January 6, 1840 (emphasis in original).
28. Ibid., January 29, 1840.

but that such performances are approved by a large majority of the Citizens of Chicago."[29] Democrats won on this issue, doubtless in part because the immorality of the theater was an extreme position even among Whigs. Yet the booster system could handle Goodrich's moralism in a way that the depoliticized government system of the 1850s would not.

Even liquor, the cultural issue that would paralyze Chicago's government in the 1850s, caused the boosters few problems. The city began granting liquor licenses in 1837, though enforcement was lax. In 1839 licensed grocers and tavern keepers demanded that the council either force their competitors to get licenses or refund their own payments. Enforcement had not improved by 1841; the marshall found 52 liquor retailers in the city but collected license fees from only 29, seventeen of which were hotels. A proposal to lower the fee in 1840 alarmed even Rucker, who thought fifty dollars "sufficiently low that a reduction would only tend to multiply houses of dissipation and idleness and greatly tend to debase public morals."[30] While in 1839 license requests required approval by the voters of the ward in which the licensee would sell liquor, this practice did not outlast the year. By the mid 1840s, with the rise of a prohibitory movement in the city, liquor licenses became more problematic, though not disruptive of the council. In 1846, Whig alderman Levi Boone, who had been trying to convince the council to ban liquor, urged his fellow temperance advocates to respect the proliquor policy sustained by party politics.[31]

BOOSTER BUSINESSMEN participated actively in city government. While the mayoralty conferred little power or patronage on its incumbent, the city's leading businessmen competed for the office. Of sixteen candidates for mayor from 1837 to 1846, occupations could be identified for fourteen. Of these, five had their primary business interests in Chicago real estate and a sixth was an auctioneer, mainly of real estate. Two were commission merchants, partners in major firms, and three had businesses related to construction. Of the remaining three, two were lawyers, one of whom was a director of the Chicago Hydraulic Company, and one was a dry goods merchant. Ten of the sixteen candidates (and seven of the eight mayors) were

29. CP, 1838/38:505, 520.
30. Ibid., 1840/40:976; also 1837/37:399, 1839/39:743, 847, 1840/40:983, 1841/41:1162.
31. *American*, May 18, June 28, 1839; CP, 1839/39:744–45, 1840/40:984, 987, 1846/46:3096.

assessed for more than $10,000 of locally owned property on the city tax rolls of 1849 and 1850.[32]

Aldermen were less likely than mayors to have numbered among the richest men of the city, though the council contained a substantial contingent of booster businessmen. Twenty-three percent of the men who served as aldermen from 1837 to 1846 owned over $10,000 of property in 1849 and 1850. Counting multiple terms served by individuals, these rich men served 20 percent of all council terms. Conversely, 19 percent of the richest Chicagoans in 1849 and 1850 had served in the council before 1847, an impressive proportion of a list that includes men who did not even live in the city for the entire period. Rima Schultz, analyzing the occupations and business affiliations of Chicago aldermen from 1837 to 1860, found that 70 percent of them had "predominantly booster-business interests" as merchants, bankers, commission men, lumber dealers, and real estate brokers. Sixteen percent were lawyers, "often involved in business," and 6 percent were artisans (though one, a blacksmith, opened a foundry and acquired valuable real estate holdings).[33] Business leaders such as Ogden, Dole, and Scammon participated actively in municipal government.

Few members of Chicago's booster elite enjoyed party politics. Ogden, a Democrat, called for nonpartisanship as early as 1840 in order to concentrate "all the good, moderate & honest men . . . into one patriotic party acting rationally & for the true interests and welfare of the whole people." Frustrated with his party's failure to represent the interests of the city's businessmen, chiefly on state banking, Ogden despaired of partisanship. He deplored hypocritical appeals to the "people" and grew "sick & disgusted with these blackguard contests to keep a certain set in power."[34] Real estate speculator Thomas B. Bryan explained a less instrumental facet of this attitude. "I should never make a politician," he wrote to a business partner, "I cannot belittle myself, nor request others to do it for me." James Curtiss, an attorney who found success in Democratic politics, was called a "demagogue" by his colleagues and all but read out of the legal fraternity. If, as Deborah Haines has argued, Chicago's professionals considered themselves a leadership class entitled to and responsible for community stewardship, they shared with the busi-

32. Craig Buettinger, "The Concept of Jacksonian Aristocracy: Chicago as a Test Case, 1833–1857" (Ph.D. diss., Northwestern University, 1982), 72–76, lists the 105 taxpayers assessed at $10,000 or more in 1849 and 1850.

33. Schultz, "Businessman's Role," 402.

34. Ibid., 143–46 (Ogden quoted on 144).

nessmen Ogden and Bryan a distaste for vulgar and demagogic electoral politics.[35]

Yet unlike the economic elites of eastern cities at this time, Chicago's businessmen and professionals played active roles in municipal government. In the late 1840s they managed to banish partisanship from city elections, aided by the collapse of the Whig party and divisions among the Democrats on banking and other issues, and they continued to run for and win city offices. While members of eastern urban elites turned their attention to building voluntary societies through which they could exercise social stewardship, Chicagoans still were pursuing basic city-building goals that required government aid at the city as well as the state and national levels.[36] Stewardship may have been a social ideal for Chicago's budding leadership class but it was not the reason they ran for municipal office. The stewardship ideal itself had little basis in the city's social structure. Booster Chicago was not yet a class society in which workers, a middle class, and an elite defined distinctive cultures and built organizational expressions of opposing worldviews. The city's booster elite was a frontier elite of men working their way up rather than an established class of local patricians.[37]

This is not to deny that Chicago's early business and professional leaders saw themselves as a social elite. Having learned in the East how the members of an elite were supposed to behave, they attempted to replicate in their frontier city the trappings of upper-class urbanity. As early as 1834 they threw full-dress balls and formal dinner parties. Charles Cleaver recalled that in the late 1830s "the only way two of our most fashionable young ladies from the North-Side could get to the Presbyterian Church . . . was by riding in a dung-cart, with robes thrown on the bottom, on which they sat."[38] Yet the Chicagoans persevered in their efforts to act as a social elite. They founded churches and philanthropic organizations and spoke grandly of their stewardship responsibilities. They adopted the upper-class

35. Thomas Barbour Bryan to Andrew Wylie, March 22, 1856, Bryan papers, Chicago Historical Society; Haines, "City Doctor," 159–61, 197–231. Bryan, it should be noted, ran for mayor in 1861 and 1863.

36. On the withdrawal of eastern elites, Edward Pessen, *Riches, Class, and Power before the Civil War* (Lexington: D. C. Heath, 1973), 251–301; M. J. Heale, "From City Fathers to Social Critics: Humanitarianism and Government in New York, 1790–1860," *Journal of American History* 63 (1976): 21–41.

37. Frederic Cople Jaher, *The Urban Establishment: Upper Strata in Boston, New York, Charleston, Chicago, and Los Angeles* (Urbana: University of Illinois Press, 1982).

38. Cleaver, *Early-Chicago*, 28.

attitudes of easterners in their disdain for politics and said particularly nasty things about Irish immigrants whom they meanwhile took great pains to attract to the city.[39] Chicago's boosters were very big fish in a very small pond. They did not constitute an upper class comparable to those of eastern cities.

FOR CHICAGO'S EARLY business leaders, municipal politics was part of a larger booster strategy. Whatever their particular occupations, Chicago's early leaders—by their very presence—were speculating on the future of the city. Most of them did this directly, investing in Chicago real estate, but all had migrated to Chicago as a gamble on the city's commercial future. "I did not . . . come here involuntarily," Grant Goodrich recalled, "but of set purpose." After studying maps of the waterways of the Northwest, Goodrich "hit upon Chicago, and reading all I could find upon the subject, resolved that when I should graduate [from law school] I would seek my fortune there." Although he romanticized the frontier spirit of the early boosters, Goodrich accurately recalled their "mutual dependence" on the city's growth. Chicago's pioneers "had faith in each other and faith in Chicago. Its future greatness became their theme of thought and conversation, and the inspiration of great plans and deeds."[40] With their own futures dependent on that of the city, Chicago's boosters marshalled any resources they could use to promote its development. City government was one of these resources.

The private strategies that Chicago's businessmen employed to attract settlers and capital to the city have been well documented. The boosters advertised Chicago in newspaper articles, bragged to eastern speculators of the windfall profits awaiting investments in Chicago real estate, and lobbied the state and federal governments for internal improvements. They promoted the agricultural settlement of northern Illinois to develop a hinterland for Chicago's commercial facilities and built highways and a railroad to bring the farmers to town.[41] They

39. Pierce, *History*, 1:199–200; Charles Fenno Hoffman in Pierce, *As Others See Chicago*, 71–74; Haines, "City Doctor," 196–231; Kathleen D. McCarthy, *Noblesse Oblige: Charity and Cultural Philanthropy in Chicago, 1849–1929* (Chicago: University of Chicago Press, 1982), 3–96; Rima Lunin Schultz, *The Church and the City: A Social History of 150 Years at Saint James, Chicago* (Chicago: Cathedral of Saint James, 1986). Cf. Wade, *Urban Frontier*, 105–17.

40. *Reception to the Settlers*, 63–64.

41. Abbott, *Boosters and Businessmen*, passim.; Patrick E. McLear, "The Galena and Chicago Union Railroad: A Symbol of Chicago's Economic Maturity," *JISHS* 73 (1980): 17–26; Patrick E. McLear, "William Butler Ogden: A Chicago Promoter in the Speculative Era and the Panic of 1837," *JISHS* 70 (1977): 283–91; Patrick E. McLear, "John

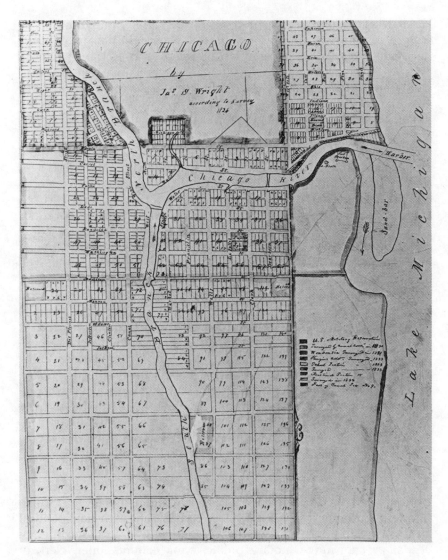

FIG. 2 CHICAGO IN 1834

managed the migration of capital through the medium of the land company. In this arrangement, Chicagoans including Ogden, Gurdon

Stephen Wright and Urban and Regional Promotion in the Nineteenth Century," *JISHS* 68 (1975): 407–20; Lloyd Lewis, *John S. Wright: Prophet of the Prairies* (Chicago: Prairie Farmer Publishing Co., 1941).

Hubbard, and John H. Kinzie invested the capital of syndicates of eastern investors in Chicago real estate. They held powers of attorney, paid taxes, and registered land purchases in their own names. They urged the sometimes reluctant easterners to invest in improvements not only to facilitate the profitable sale of particular lots but also to advance the development of Chicago as a whole. While the easterners might reap profits from the city's growth, their local agents absolutely depended on it.[42]

The boosters used municipal government as a tool to promote growth and commerce. While the construction of public works was the most important way in which government contributed to the city-building process (and will be described below), the boosters also used other local government resources, particularly the local school fund. Having originated from the 1833 sale of the federally dedicated school section in Chicago's congressional township, the school fund formally was intended to finance the development of public schools. The boosters applied the fund to schools, but they also used it for another purpose. The school fund was a source of loan capital for the local community. By lending the fund, municipal government served as banker for the city's businessmen. When the Panic of 1837 closed off private sources of capital, school fund lending assumed increased importance. City government helped to keep local businessmen afloat during the depression. No municipal policy more explicitly recognized the interdependence between the private fortunes of the boosters and the public good of Chicago's growth than the banking that the city performed with the school fund.

From the creation of Cook County in 1831 until 1839, the school fund was controlled by the county school commissioner, Richard J. Hamilton. Hamilton's career bridged Chicago's transition from a frontier town promoted by downstate politicians into a booster city of eastern migrants. A Kentucky native, Hamilton moved in 1820 to southern Illinois and established close connections with state political leaders. In 1831 he was appointed Cook County clerk, recorder of deeds, probate judge, notary public, bank commissioner, clerk of both the circuit and county courts, and school fund commissioner. Hamilton joined Indian Agent Thomas J. V. Owen, himself a well-connected downstater, in negotiating with local tribes during the Black Hawk War of 1832, and he witnessed the 1833 treaty that removed the Potawatomies to Kansas. After Owen's death in 1835, Hamilton worked closely with the new eastern migrants. He acted as

42. Schultz, "Businessman's Role," 17–43; Haeger, *Investment Frontier*, passim.

agent for nonresident speculators and used his many offices to help attract settlers, especially by employing young lawyers.[43]

Hamilton sold the school section at public auction in 1833. Although in hindsight the $38,865 proceeds from the square mile bounded by State, Halsted, Madison, and Twelfth streets looked paltry, Hamilton had good reasons to sell the land. After the abolition of the canal board, Chicago had a swelling land boom but no new land on the market, and towns throughout Illinois were busily alienating their school lands in a statewide speculative fever. The school law of 1833 encouraged commissioners to sell county school lands and then lend the proceeds to trustees who would build and operate schools. Hamilton also had received a petition from ninety-five Chicagoans—nearly one third of the town's entire population—asking him to make the sale, which was considered a great success. Unproductive land was converted into a cash fund that could earn interest on loan, increasing the fund for the future and enabling Chicago to establish schools.[44]

The laws allowed towns to spend only the interest from the school fund, preserving the principal as a permanent endowment. In 1835 the legislature authorized school trustees in Chicago to levy taxes to supplement an interest revenue that already was inadequate for the schools.[45] Hamilton, meanwhile, earned the Democrat's ire for his management of the fund. He was running for election to the recorder's office he had held by appointment for the past four years. The newspaper alleged that he loaned school money to his friends for real estate speculations (also giving them inside information as recorder of deeds), and used his lending powers for electioneering purposes.[46] Not until 1840, however, was Hamilton forced to open his records to public scrutiny. By then, the combined pressures of the depression and his lax lending policies had caused many school fund debtors to default on their loans. The principal itself was in danger.

Hamilton submitted his first semiannual report, required by the 1837 city charter, in January 1838. The entire school fund was loaned

43. Andreas, History, 1:143–44; Fleming, "Canal at Chicago," 70–80; Schultz, "Businessman's Role," 25–29; Richard J. Hamilton Letterbook, Chicago Historical Society; Thomas Hoyne, "The Lawyer as a Pioneer," Chicago Bar Association Lectures, Part One, Fergus Historical Series, no. 22 (Chicago: Fergus Printing Co., 1882), 63–104.

44. Hoyt, One Hundred Years, 26; Andreas, History, 1:133, 205–6; Haydon, True Founder, 164–65; Democrat, November 26, 1833; Illinois, Revised Laws, 1833, 562–66.

45. Illinois, Laws, 1835, 22–26, 161–63; Andreas, History, 1:208–9.

46. Democrat, August 5, 1835; American, July 18, August 1, 8, 1835.

at 10 percent interest but many of the debts were in arrears. As Hamilton explained it,

> since the greater part of the loans were made from the Fund, there has been as the Common Council know, a great change in the affairs and the fortunes of many persons; Many who were, a short time ago considered to be good and solvent men are not considered to be so now. And although no actual losses have occurred to the Fund that the Commissioner is aware of; yet it would not be astonishing if some few of the debts should be in jeopardy, considering the changes that have taken place, and the difficulty and pres[s]ure of the Times.[47]

A year later, Hamilton reported "no improvement" and admitted that "from present indications he cannot flatter himself that the receipts will be any better for some time to come." Of the $38,625 fund, he had renewed $10,000 of loans, filed suit for the recovery of $10,000 more, and planned to file suit for another $3,000. In July 1839, Hamilton reported that more than half of the fund's interest revenues had gone for legal fees rather than the teachers' salaries it was supposed to finance. Almost $15,000 was in suit and "it is to be feared that payments will not be made much more punctual for some time to come."[48]

Under increasing fire, Hamilton submitted to the council early in 1840 a list of the 136 loans into which he had invested the fund. The principal now amounted to slightly less than $38,000. Of this, $11,337 loaned on mortgage security had netted most of the interest due on it but $11,564 with only personal security had returned less than half of its accrued interest. Successful suits had gained judgments on the interest from $7,366, most of which remained unpaid. Finally, Hamilton was in the process of suing for $6,545, of which $5,845 had been loaned to the now bankrupt speculator Hiram Pearsons. One of two suits against Pearsons had been filed in 1834, before the depression, though Hamilton had loaned him an additional $5,000 in 1838, the largest single loan.[49] Hamilton included dates in his report for all loans but those for which he had gained judgments. Of 107 dated loans, 85 had been executed in 1838 and 1839, comprising almost 90 percent of the principal and three-fourths of the unpaid interest. Contrary to his earlier claim, Hamilton made "precarious" loans long after the "great change" had occurred in his debtors' fortunes.[50]

47. CP, 1838/38:526.
48. Ibid., 1839/39:766, 866.
49. Hamilton and Pearsons had been partners in laying out the town of Canalport in 1834; Andreas, *History*, 1:144.
50. CP, 1839/39:873.

There were other problems with Hamilton's management of the fund. In his 1838 report, which first noted the dangers to the principal, he revealed that 40 percent of his expenditures from the fund's interest revenue had gone into his own pocket as salary and fees. The council convinced county officials to reduce his salary and prevent him from charging the fund for executing its transactions. His 1840 loan list included a $4,000 loan to himself, made in 1839. He said he had secured his own loan with a mortgage and paid all of the interest, but this still was the only loan in 1839 for more than $1,000. While his report rendered a satisfactory account of the interest, it did not indicate the status of the principal. He noted only "that a number of the foregoing enumerated debts are considered precarious, some of them desperate and probably some of them may be lost."[51] This was not a sufficient accounting.

In March 1839, the legislature gave the council control of the school fund and in 1840 the council took it from Hamilton. They gave it to William H. Brown, whom they appointed school agent. Brown's quarterly reports were to contain "his opinion what notes may be in danger, and should be collected, and by suit or otherwise."[52] Brown refused the salary that the council offered him and within days uncovered a fraud. Hiram Pearsons had mortgaged a half section of land as security for his loan. According to Brown, the tract was valuable only for its timber, the rights to which Pearsons had sold to a third party who was "actively engaged in cutting & carrying off the same, in some instances to only a short distance over the line of the half section."[53] In 1842 Brown reckoned the nominal principal at nearly $43,000 but reported only $16,000 to be "so secured that the interest is promptly paid, and that a large portion of the balance is swallowed up in bad debts and unproductive real estate." In 1848 Brown was still trying to collect on Hamilton's loans, some from as far back as 1837, though legal victories had raised the "effective" fund back to $36,000.[54]

William H. Brown, by 1840, already had established a reputation as a conservative financier. A staunch Whig with a moralistic approach to both politics and investment, he would be remembered as one of the few Chicagoans to remain solvent when the land bubble burst in 1837, though he actually failed along with everyone else. Born in Connecticut, Brown had practiced law in territorial Illinois,

51. Ibid.; also 1838/38:526, 534, 638.
52. Ibid., 1847/47:3747 (the 1840 ordinance).
53. Ibid., 1840/40:876, 893.
54. Ibid., 1842/42:1286, 1845/45:2709, 2841, 2857, 2862, 1848/48:4241.

serving as clerk of the U.S. District Court until his 1835 appointment as cashier of the state bank brought him to Chicago. He made himself unpopular with his more speculative neighbors during the land boom by refusing to make loans he deemed unsound. In order to wrest the bank from him, local Democrats convinced the legislature temporarily to close the Chicago branch. A biographical sketch written during his lifetime described Brown as "cautious to a degree verging on excess. . . . He has entered into no rash speculations, nor made any desperate pushes for fortune. He takes care of what he has; and adds to it when he can do so with safety." Through such conservative strategies, he amassed a $500,000 fortune by 1857.[55]

Brown also was known for his commitment to education, as a man who would safeguard a fund that, as he put it, was "deemed sacred by every right minded man [and should be] restored to its rightful owners, the indigent children of our growing City."[56] Yet the council refused to let Brown abandon other, more immediate, objects. Soon after he took office, Brown began to receive petitions for new loans. When he tried to curtail local lending, aldermen defended the practice: "That inasmuch as said fund appears to have been created for the peculiar benefit of the inhabitants of said Township; and that the inhabitants of said Township are taxed for the support of the common schools therefore the benefits of said fund should be conferred upon those who support the burthen of the schools, at least so long as the funds on hand shall be unappropriated."[57] The "benefit" derived from the school fund involved more than education. Its investment served purposes remote from the generation of interest revenue to pay teachers. The school fund was a source of capital. On the council's insistence, Brown made new loans and in 1842 even used his opponents' rhetoric to defend the liquidation of Hamilton's loans, "so that a larger portion of the community may participate in the advantages of borrowing from [the school fund]."[58]

Brown's failure to transform school fund lending policy ratified Hamilton's booster strategy, if not his careless style. Brown remained

55. Andreas, *History*, 1:552–53; Schultz, "Businessman's Role," 54; Theodore Calvin Pease, *The Frontier State, 1818–1848* (Springfield: Illinois Centennial Commission, 1918), 82; *Biographical Sketches of Some of the Early Settlers of the City of Chicago*, Part 2, Fergus Historical Series, no. 6 (Chicago: Fergus Printing Co., 1876), 5–10; *American*, January 30, February 1, 4, 1840.

56. CP, 1850/50:5937.

57. Ibid., 1841/41:1090. For loan applications, 1840/40:1001, 1007, 1018, 1047, 1841/41:1074, 1180–81.

58. Ibid., 1842/42:1286, 1293.

school agent for thirteen years, until 1853, and once the policy issues were settled, his performance satisfied both Whigs and Democrats.[59] By the late 1840s private banking reduced the need for government loans to local businessmen. In 1849 aldermen rejected a plan to refer large loan applications to the council because it "would in effect be making the School Agent a cashier and the Council a board of Directors to decide upon loans."[60] Yet banking had been precisely the analogy to describe the boosters' use of the fund. By 1849 government lending simply had lost the urgency of the land boom and depression years. With the decline of the booster system and the depoliticization of city government in the 1840s, the lending continued quietly. Not until 1860, with the return of partisanship, did aldermen call a halt in order to remove the school fund from party politics. They invested it in city bonds.[61]

School fund lending did not exhaust the banking activities of booster government. The city also issued scrip after the banks suspended payments in 1837. This scrip, together with that issued by the canal board, helped to ease the currency shortage during the depression. The boosters apparently perceived few limitations on the power of municipal government to aid in the development, or in this case the survival, of the city. The city charters conferred no banking powers.[62] By the late 1840s Chicagoans began to adopt uniformly strict constructions of the charters, but in the booster system, loose construction prevailed. City government engaged in a variety of activities that expressed its purpose in the community: the general promotion of an urban growth on which all of the city's businessmen depended.

WHEN THE BOOSTERS reminisced about early Chicago, contrasting the frontier town with the industrial metropolis of the 1870s and

---

59. Ibid., 1852/53:1192, 1242; *The Constitutional Debates of 1847*, Arthur Charles Cole, ed. (Springfield: Illinois State Historical Library, 1919), 177.

60. CP, 1849/49:5084.

61. Ibid., 1859/60:849. The *Democrat*, March 3, 1849, made a class issue of large loans: "The money is loaned to a great extent to rich persons in large sums, who can thus reloan it again at great profits. This should not be. The money should not be loaned in sums of over $200; so that a number of hard working mechanics . . . might be accommodated; and not left the prey of sharpers who are more fortunate in being the possessors of large sums." Generally, however, the school fund debate had grown moot.

62. Pierce, *History*, 1:67, 357; CP, n.d./n.d.:100 (1842 or 1843 account of city scrip still in circulation). Illinois municipalities were specifically forbidden from issuing scrip in 1843. Edmund J. James, ed., *The Charters of the City of Chicago* (2 pts.; Chicago: University of Chicago Press, 1898–99), 117–18.

1880s, they almost always mentioned one aspect of the town's landscape: its lack of streets. "There was not even a wagon track upon any street in Chicago," John Dean Caton recalled,

> Everyone drove where he pleased across the prairie from one building to another. . . . It was early in the spring of 1834 that I found myself standing at the crossing of Dearborn and Lake streets looking west; and for the first time I could see where the street was by the line of buildings on either side of it. . . . Then for the first time I could fully realize that our little settlement was assuming the appearance of a town.

Edwin O. Gale remembered being especially struck in his first view of Chicago by "the entire absence of streets, of which, properly so called, there is not one, no, not even a ditch to mark the roads. Moreover, there is nothing to indicate where they ultimately will be, save the surveyors' stakes." Charles Cleaver emphasized the difficulty of navigating early Chicago's mud. "I remember, once, a stage-coach got mired in Clark Street, opposite the present Sherman House, where it remained several days, with a board driven in the mud . . . bearing this inscription: 'No bottom here.'"[63]

The centrality of streets in these recollections suggests the importance of physical infrastructure as an element of urban development. The boosters were trying to build a city and a city required streets, bridges, sidewalks, and other public works whose construction was the responsibility of municipal government. The *American* applauded an ordinance to number the houses on Lake Street in 1839 not only because of the "convenience and utility of having stores numbered" but because "a place looks more like a city for having its houses numbered." The editor prophesied an urban future for Chicago that would be expressed in "a continuous chain of numbered buildings from the Lake to the DesPlaines." Street numbering was a lower priority than actual street construction. Only the offer of J. W. Norris to notify building owners of their addresses for his 1848 city directory convinced the council to number buildings.[64] Physical infrastructure, however, affected the city's economy directly. It was a crucial dimension of the city-building process and one that required government action.

The depression, which lasted from 1837 until about 1845, limited the ability of Chicago's government to build infrastructure. The Panic

63. "John Dean Caton's Reminiscences of Chicago in 1833 and 1834," Harry E. Pratt, ed., *JISHS* 28 (1935): 8, 25; Gale, *Reminiscences*, 43; Cleaver, *Early-Chicago*, 28.
64. *American*, November 19, 1839; CP, 1847/47:3989, 1848/48:4670, 4718, 1849/49:5072.

of 1837 in Chicago was primarily a crash of land values that had reached artificial heights in a land boom usually described as a mad, speculative frenzy.[65] The panic brought an instant halt to the boom and bankrupted many of its local participants. Joseph Balestier recalled the depression as a time when the "more land a man had, the worse off he apparently was."[66] Because the city depended for most of its revenue on real estate taxes, low land values precluded ambitious plans for infrastructure during most of the booster period. Neither the city nor its property owners could afford to invest in public works. Still, some evidence of the public works decision process may be gleaned both from plans made before the panic and from the few projects that the booster council managed to implement.

Reflecting the mutual dependence of Chicago's boosters on the general development of the city, the booster system made public works decisions and financed public works projects on a citywide basis. The town charters of 1833 and 1835 provided for a Board of Trustees elected at large. This arrangement in itself guaranteed citywide decision making. It assumed a unity of interest in the electorate rather than a geographical differentiation of interests that might compete through ward representation. The trustees were authorized to pay for public works with general property taxes and the street labor of all adult male residents. General taxation, like at-large representation, implied a citywide process for decision making. Since all taxpayers contributed to the general fund and all performed street labor, all theoretically deserved a voice in the allocation of town funds for public works.

The 1833 charter contained one clause that foreshadowed the later segmentation of public works financing. It provided that when the trustees ordered the construction of a sidewalk, they had to collect at least half of the sidewalk's cost from the owners of abutting lots. This clause reflected the differential impact that public works exerted on land values. When financed from the general fund, public works projects augmented the value of some taxpayers' properties at the expense of the taxpaying community. The charter thus segmented the costs of sidewalks, removing them from the general fund and charging them directly to the property owners who benefited. The 1835 charter extended the segmentation of sidewalk work into the decision process. This law provided that "upon the application of the owners

65. See esp. Harriet Martineau, "Chicago in 1836" in *The Present and Future Prospects of Chicago*, Fergus Historical Series, no. 9 (Chicago: Fergus Printing Co., 1876), 37–38.
66. Joseph N. Balestier, *The Annals of Chicago*, 2d ed., Fergus Historical Series, no. 1 (Chicago: Fergus Printing Co., 1876), 4.

of two-thirds of real estate" on any particular street, the trustees could levy a special sidewalk tax on that street. Now the property owners who benefited from a sidewalk not only paid for it but also decided whether to build it. These laws are important for their anticipation of later, more comprehensive uses of segmented policy making; the town ordered few, if any, sidewalks.[67]

Town government seems not to have ordered much infrastructure at all, probably because of a simple lack of funds. While it levied a property tax, assessments could not keep pace with spiraling land values or inflated labor costs during the land boom.[68] The property tax, street labor, fines for the breach of ordinances, and the sidewalk tax were the only revenues specified in the 1833 charter. The 1835 charter added theater and billiard licenses, leases of town lands, and special assessments for eminent domain compensation, but neither charter allowed the Board of Trustees to borrow money. When the trustees borrowed $60 to drain a slough on Clark Street in 1836, the brokers required the town president to endorse their note personally. The trustees ordered that South Water Street be surveyed in 1833 and drained in 1834. In 1836 they ordered that State Street be opened, and that Clark, Canal, and Randolph streets be improved in a manner now unclear. These projects appear to have comprised the entire public works program of the four years of town government.[69]

The boosters supplemented these public efforts with private initiatives. After Gurdon Hubbard successfully petitioned the trustees in July 1835 for a tax abatement to reimburse his expenses in paving a block of LaSalle Street, other boosters tried their luck with the board.[70] Yet the trustees refused to allow more abatements. William B. Ogden's plea set the tone. He informed the trustees that he had "expended large sums of money and been at great expense at making improvements of a *public nature*." He had paved five streets and thought "that the public convenience required the above improvements to be made. At the time they were made the Corporation of Chicago had no funds which could be appropriated to the making of streets on the North side of the river; and that part of the town must have suffered in consequence, for the want of said improvements,

67. For charter provisions, James, *Charters*, 27, 32–34. The oldest surviving record of sidewalk work in the papers of Chicago's government dates from June 1837, after the adoption of the city charter the previous March. For early sidewalk orders, CP, 1837/37:393, 410, 450.

68. Andreas, *History*, 1:135–36.

69. James, *Charters*, 25–35; Cleaver, *Early-Chicago*, 29; Andreas, *History*, 1:192; CP, 1836/36:262.

70. CP, 1835/35:168, 1836/36:241–43, 246.

if the same had not been made by individual exertion."[71] Ogden claimed that he made his improvements in the belief the trustees would reimburse him. It was a belief the trustees did not share.

Ogden's stress on the "public nature" of his street projects masked the fact that he decided which streets to improve. His large north side holdings obviously benefited from the choices he made. When the town spent general tax money on street projects, the trustees, rather than individual property owners, decided which projects were of a "public nature." Because all projects except sidewalks were financed from the general fund, all had to pass the test of public utility as administered by the trustees. Individual owners' priorities were secondary to the public good of boosting Chicago. South Water, Clark, and Randolph streets were the commercial center of the town. By ordering the improvement of these streets, the trustees decided that they constituted the "public" improvements for which general fund spending was appropriate.

The city charter of 1837, copied from that of Buffalo, New York, granted Chicago's government greater power to raise money for public works. It enhanced the revenue potential of street labor by offering residents the option of paying cash, allowed the council to borrow money, added a variety of new license powers, and extended special assessment to all street improvements. The 1835 charter had authorized special assessment only in cases of eminent domain, so that those who reaped benefits from new streets would "contribute toward compensating the persons injured," but the 1837 law made it a revenue tool of general application. The council could levy special assessments for grading, paving, and repairing streets; laying sewers, drains, and aqueducts; or paving, fencing, and otherwise improving public squares. Where the 1835 charter granted its special assessment power in one short paragraph, the 1837 law devoted pages to detailed regulations for notices, hearings, and appeals.[72]

Special assessment implied a different form of public works decision making than did general fund financing, a form anticipated in the town charters' sidewalk clauses. In a special assessment project only those property owners "deemed to have benefited" from a given project paid for that project. They paid, moreover, in amounts proportional to benefits they would gain in the increased value that improvements conferred on their properties. Thus special assessment

71. Ibid., 1836/36:242 (emphasis in original).

72. James, *Charters*, 33–34, 50–61; Bayrd Still, "Patterns of Mid-Nineteenth Century Urbanization in the Middle West," *Mississippi Valley Historical Review* 28 (1941–42): 187–206.

dropped the assumption of citywide benefit. Its use assumed a competitive real estate market and allowed rival developers to decide for themselves what investments to make in streets or other improvements. While a low general tax limit may have reflected the Jacksonian preference for minimalist government, special assessment transcended the limit with a legal structure that allowed government to foster improvements at the same time that it refrained from intervention in the economy. By the mid 1840s, the use of special assessment would transform Chicago's government, replacing the citywide, booster system with a segmented decision-making process. Until then, however, the city did not exploit the segmentation that its charter allowed.

Chicago's government received its enhanced public works powers in March 1837. Two months later the New York banks suspended specie payments, starting the Panic of 1837. By July the depression had reached Chicago.[73] Plummeting land values meant plummeting tax revenues; the city was in no position to exercise its new powers, least of all special assessment. The few projects that the council ordered during the depression were financed with general funds. Chicago's street commissioners spent a total of $293 in 1837, $1,085 in 1841, and $1,600 in 1842. Their reports mention revenue from general taxes and street labor but not from special assessments.[74] Chicagoans struggled to maintain the city as a viable community in its first decade of existence. They pinned their hopes on the Illinois and Michigan Canal and the prosperity it promised. The depression probably lengthened the booster period by postponing the commercial success that later freed the boosters of the need for citywide cooperation.

THE MOST AMBITIOUS public works plan of the booster period involved the river. In 1835 the trustees promised to dredge the Chicago River within four years as compensation for "wharfing privileges," leases that required their holders to build wharves on the riverfront. The wharfing privilege decision was a disaster. Not only did the trustees fail to specify how they would pay for something as expensive as dredging the river, but they also created a mass of conflicting property rights that took fifteen years to unravel. The first petition for wharfing privileges reached the board in November 1833. Wharves, as Gurdon Hubbard explained, were "not more necessary as facilities for transacting business than to sustain the reputation of the place, and . . . they increase the value of all the property in or

73. Schultz, "Businessman's Role," 47–54; Pierce, History, 1:67.
74. CP, 1838/38:620, 1842/42:1278, n.d./n.d.:69.

near the Town." Wharfing privileges were needed because "holders of property . . . cannot be justified in making expendatures [sic] to construct w[h]arves without some assurance that they shall not be disturbed in the use of them." A month later the trustees offered five-year leases to the owners of riverfront lots.[75]

These leases were of questionable validity under the 1833 charter but the charter of 1835 explicitly allowed the trustees to lease the wharfing privileges, "giving to the owners, occupant or occupants of the lots fronting the river, the preference of such privilege."[76] In November 1835 the trustees announced a new offer: 999-year leases. In return for millennial wharfing rights, lessees had to construct docks of uniform height within two years and allow public access to tow and foot paths. The town, meanwhile, would dredge the river. The trustees announced this plan on Friday, November 20, with their intention to auction all unclaimed leases the following Monday morning. Claims from riverfront owners poured in during the weekend. The trustees also received papers on various land title disputes that complicated any simple disposition of the privileges.[77] On Saturday morning the *American* called a public meeting to discuss the trustees' action. Resolutions condemning the trustees failed to pass—because their supporters packed the meeting, according to the *American*—but another gathering that night organized a petition campaign against the 999-year leases.[78]

By Tuesday, the Whig opponents of the Democratic trustees had gathered more than 200 signatures on petitions that they sent to Springfield. The legislature responded with a charter amendment in January 1836 forbidding new wharfing leases longer than five years and reducing the town's taxing power.[79] While the *Democrat* condemned the amendment as an attack on Chicago's self-government and a "deadly blow" at its commerce, the *American* welcomed it. The legislature, "unlike our Trustees, was not *above* regarding a remonstrance signed by so many individuals—more especially when there was no counter-remonstrance." The paper reported that news of the 999-year leases "was received by the members of the Legislature with

75. Ibid., 1833/33:154; n.d./n.d.:33, 1833/33:155, 1834/34:158; *Democrat*, December 10, 1833.

76. James, *Charters*, 32. The "1833 charter" was a general incorporation law of 1831. The 1835 charter was a special law for Chicago.

77. CP, 1835/35:175; *Democrat*, November 18, 1835. For claims, CP, 1835/35:176–99; for titles, 1835/35:156, 171, 197, 200–201, 203–206, 208–209, 218–20, 234; for a wharfing privilege contract, 1848/48:4490.

78. *American*, November 21, 28, 1835.

79. Ibid., November 28, 1835; James, *Charters*, 36.

a universal burst of indignation. Away from the atmosphere of speculation, the wharfing privileges found but few advocates. The members of the Legislature looked upon the acts of the Trustees as being
not only illegal, but as evincing a desire to overreach." The new law
did not affect the 999-year leases that the trustees already had exe-
cuted. These went to court, where they were sustained.[80]

The property owners leasing wharfing privileges had four years to
pay for their leases. Thus, the Panic of 1837 hit Chicago before even
half the expected proceeds had been raised. The depression not only
prevented the lessees from paying, but it destroyed any prospect that
the city would dredge the river. Violated on both sides, the contracts
fell dormant. Only in 1844 did aldermen begin to investigate the
status of the wharfing privileges. In November the judiciary committee reported $41,860 plus accrued interest still due from the 1835 sale.
The committee complained that the lessees used the properties without paying for either the old or new contracts. "Individuals should
not be allowed to seize upon & occupy for nothing the property of
the city." If action were taken, the city could realize thousands of
dollars in revenue. A month later, the city attorney reported on the
wharfing lots. Many of the original leases had been transferred, most
with compensation. Other lots were vacant or occupied by squatters.
The original lessees who still held privileges refused to resume their
payments because the city had failed to dredge the river as stipulated
in the contracts.[81]

Early in 1846 the council ordered the city attorney to take legal
action to dispossess anyone occupying "wharfing privileges so called"
except those who had taken leases that year on water lots that had
not been included in the 1835 sale (because they had been outside the
town boundaries).[82] By the end of the year, however, it was clear that
the council could not solve the problem by fiat. In December they
asked for charter amendments and ordered penalties for those using
lots without leases "until some further settlement shall be made." In
February 1847 the legislature passed "An Act to adjust and settle the
title to the wharfing privileges in Chicago." The law vested title to all
wharfing lots in the council and required actions to settle the lease
issue to be approved by two-thirds votes. Wharfing privilege claim-
ants were to file suit, publishing notice of their action in three news-

80. *Democrat*, February 24, 1836; *American*, March 19, 1835 (emphasis in original);
CP, n.d./n.d.:71 (1837 or 1838). Pierce's description (*History*, 1:344–45) of the 999-year
leases as generally supported in Chicago but thwarted by an interfering state legislature
is misleading.

81. CP, 1844/44:2272; 1845/45:2866.

82. Ibid., 1846/46:2920.

papers. For the next three years, the council's committee on wharfing privileges developed compromises for a settlement. By mid 1850, lease rates, street locations, and a dredging plan had been accepted in articles of agreement signed by the property owners.[83]

The decision of the town trustees to grant 999-year leases in 1835 makes sense only as a citywide public works policy. The wharfing privileges simultaneously provided for the public dredging of the river and the private development of shipping facilities. The *American*'s criticism of the long leases as short-sighted missed the point.[84] The property rights conferred by the leases were transferable and wharfing rights, as the charter suggested, were legitimate perquisites to riverfront ownership. The leases required the construction and maintenance of docks; their long terms compensated this investment. Hendrik Hartog has described water lot grants in eighteenth-century New York as the "planning tools" of a political culture that eschewed direct government action, using grants of public property as incentives for private development.[85] Unlike colonial New York's wharfing grants, however, Chicago's included a promise of expensive public action. The city would dredge the river regardless of the income it received from the leases. Had the dredging proceeded, the city probably would have employed some general funds. Development of the riverfront was a public good, a citywide goal shared by the businessmen of Chicago. It was a booster imperative.

IF THE BOOSTERS understood their mutual dependence on the city's general development, they also competed with one another in their commercial and real estate ventures. This competition inevitably spilled over into public works debates. Because public works policy decisions were made by and for men whose major investments involved real estate, debates about them politicized the private competition of developers. Public works influenced both property values and the development potentials of particular tracts. This was espe-

83. Ibid., 1846/46:3531; Illinois, *Private and Special Laws, 1847*, 214–16. For the negotiations, CP, 1847/47:4081, 4144–45, 4131, 4147, 1848/48:4195, 4250, 4389, 4671–72, 4887, 4954, 1849/49:5153, 1850/50:5924, 5927.

84. *American*, November 28, 1835.

85. Hendrik Hartog, *Public Property and Private Power: The Corporation of the City of New York in American Law, 1730–1870* (Chapel Hill: University of North Carolina Press, 1983), 44–68. New York also distributed water lots incrementally instead of dumping them all on the market at once—and that during a land boom. Hartog argues that the high cost of dock construction acted as an economic brake on leasing, confining the desire for water lots to those who could afford the improvements. Eighteenth-century New Yorkers must have lacked the speculative spirit of nineteenth-century Chicagoans.

cially true of bridges over the river. "The question of the location of bridges in our city," noted the *American* in 1841, "has always been an embarrassing one, and productive of much ill feeling in different parts of the city."[86] The "bridge war" of the late 1830s resulted from two characteristics of booster Chicago: economic competition between the businessmen of the north and south sides and a governing process that required citywide decision making. Together, they could be paralyzing. The bridge war illustrated a fundamental weakness of the booster system of city government.

In 1837 Chicago had one bridge over the main river. The Dearborn Street drawbridge had been ordered by the trustees and constructed in 1834. Despite extensive repairs in 1835 and 1837, it remained unsafe and inconvenient—the street commissioner reported in 1838 that it could be raised and lowered only by six men working the chains of its draws. As chairman of a committee on the bridge, Alderman Henry Rucker described the council's options. They could repair the drawbridge again, place a "float" between its piers, or construct a new floating bridge not at Dearborn but at Clark Street (a floating bridge consisted of several scows tied together across the river). Rucker favored the float at Dearborn. Meanwhile, 150 petitioners, organized by William B. Ogden, asked for the bridge to be located at Wells Street, with the assurance that "interested" citizens would raise its cost by voluntary subscriptions. The council rejected this proposal and in 1839 ordered the destruction of the Dearborn Street drawbridge and its replacement with a ferry.[87]

The decision to destroy the bridge met enthusiastic support. "Many citizens were so afraid that the Council would rescind this action, that a large crowd gathered upon the river before daylight, the next morning, and going to work with a will, in a very short time, chopped the bridge to pieces."[88] With the destruction of the Dearborn Street bridge there was no convenient way to cross the river with large stocks of goods: the State Street ferry, a scow on a rope tow, could accommodate only one double-team wagon at a time. This, of course, was the objective of the antibridge group. Most of the grain that reached Chicago in the late 1830s came by "Hoosier wagon." While the Indiana farmers entered the city from the south, most of the grain warehouses were on the north side of the river. With no bridge to take the farmers across the river to the north side ware-

86. *American*, May 1, 1841.
87. Andreas, *History*, 1:198; CP, 1837/37:286, 348, 367, 1838/38:499, 501, 582, 612; Schultz, "Businessman's Role," 100.
88. Andreas, *History*, 1:198.

houses, they had to sell their produce to merchant middlemen on the accessible south side. Hence the bridge war. North siders worked hard to convince the council to authorize a bridge. The failure of Ogden's Wells Street plan, despite its provision for private subscriptions, confirms the fact that bridge decisions had little to do with the city's finances. The issue, as the newspapers phrased it, was "Bridge or No Bridge." The south side merchants wanted there to be no bridge at all.[89]

In the summer of 1839 the *American* predicted that the next municipal election would be fought on the bridge issue. The council had "decided the question divers times in divers ways, according as the board was full or not." The editor urged his readers not to politicize public works policy because if they did, "party will be swallowed up in self interest." In the spring 1840 campaign the paper stressed the virtues of William Henry Harrison, while the council debated about the bridge. In December, the *American* reported "that the Common Council last night *again voted* to erect a bridge over the Chicago River at the foot of Clark street," a compromise between the Wells and Dearborn locations.[90] South siders fought against it—Alderman Augustus Garrett even claimed it would jeopardize national defense in the event of a British attack from Canada—but the bridge survived these assaults. The 1840 ordinance authorizing it required property owners to subscribe funds for its construction. Ogden organized north siders to buy the bonds and fronted much of the money himself. Asking a fellow north sider for reimbursement, he explained that although it "was a heavy burden on me to build it, . . . I have the satisfaction . . . to know that it . . . has almost settled the vexed question of bridge or no bridge."[91]

Even so, the council continued to debate the matter. In the spring of 1841 south siders tried to get the bridge moved from Clark to Dearborn. A floating bridge at Wells also was constructed. In 1844, when a flood damaged the Clark Street bridge, Garrett again tried to have it removed, though north siders blocked this effort by repairing it themselves. A major flood in 1849 washed out all of the Chicago River bridges, but by this time the council had abandoned citywide decision making. Bridges were rebuilt by subscription: property owners

89. *American*, July 9, 1839; Andreas, *History*, 1:198–99. West siders also received wagon trade and opposed bridges; Gale, *Reminiscences*, 297–98.

90. *American*, July 9, August 26, December 3 (emphasis in original), December 5, 1839.

91. Ibid., December 3, 5, 1839, April 1, 15, 18, 22, 1840, May 1, 1841; Schultz, "Businessman's Role," 100–101; Ogden to Abner Wright, December 26, 1840, quoted on p. 101.

who raised money got the bridges they wanted. Subscription financing served a different purpose by the late 1840s. In the booster bridge war, subscriptions were a tool in policy debate, a concession that property owners made to forestall opposition to their public works priorities. Yet subscription offers did not guarantee council approval of a desired project. The booster council debated and decided issues of public works policy. By the late 1840s private subscription and special assessment replaced council public works debates. Decisions about physical infrastructure were moved to the private sector.

The booster system of city government lasted from Chicago's initial incorporation in 1833 until about 1847, when a charter revision introduced radical changes into the structure of the city's government. Partisanship on the national Jacksonian model, officeholding by the booster elite, and the citywide mode of public works decision making defined the booster system. Of these, only the high social status of officeholders survived into the 1850s. Local partisanship declined for reasons that will be explored in the next chapter. It was citywide decision making, however, that the 1847 charter was designed to supersede. The 1837 law had allowed Chicago's government to segment public works policy by using special assessments for infrastructure, but the boosters did not exploit this opportunity until the mid 1840s and the end of the depression. They retained citywide procedures despite the disruption that they brought to the decision-making process. The booster system rested on the central economic reality that faced Chicago's early entrepreneurs: their mutual dependence on an uncertain urban future.

3

The Introduction of Segmentation

THE CHICAGO RIVER and Harbor Convention of 1847 was a powerful symbol of change in the city. As the climax of fifteen years of aggressive boosterism, the convention announced to the nation that Chicago had arrived on the American urban scene. Ten thousand delegates from nineteen different states joined the 16,800 residents of Chicago to celebrate July 4, 1847. Visiting dignitaries brought home their impressions of, as New York delegate Thurlow Weed put it, an "infant city" that soon would "eclipse even its own past magic-like growth."[1] Democrats and Whigs in Chicago worked together to promote both the convention's demand for federal internal improvement appropriations and its advertisement of the city they had built. Chicago in 1847 was a different community from the one it had been ten years earlier. The River and Harbor Convention symbolized both the economic growth that had created a commercial city out of a frontier outpost and the political reordering that had undermined local competition under the Jacksonian party system. It also symbolized a central debate in antebellum political economy: how could government promote economic growth without redistributing wealth toward a favored class, party, or section? While Chicagoans resolved this debate differently on the national and local levels, their local resolution found expression in a new system of municipal government.

1. *Chicago River-and-Harbor Convention*, Fergus Historical Series, no. 18 (Chicago: Fergus Printing Co., 1882), 151–53; Mentor L. Williams, "The Chicago River and Harbor Convention, 1847," *Mississippi Valley Historical Review* 35 (1948–49): 607–26.

BY 1847 CHICAGOANS could look toward their city's future with confidence. The depression had lifted and evidence of recovery marked every area of the city's economy. The population had doubled in three years, from 8,000 in 1844 to 16,800 in 1847. While the city's wheat exports had doubled in the past two years, the total value of its commercial exports had tripled in the last three. Land values finally were rising again and more new buildings were constructed in 1845 alone than in the four years from 1838 to 1842. Machine shops, planing mills, breweries, and other manufacturing enterprises began to contribute an industrial component to the city's largely commercial economy. Construction on the Galena and Chicago Union Railroad was underway. The only one of Chicago's rail connections that would be financed primarily by Illinois residents, the Galena's tracks carried the first steam locomotive out of Chicago in November 1848. Most important, the Illinois and Michigan Canal was nearly finished. An 1845 deal between the state and the bondholders having made completion a certainty, the canal opened for navigation in April 1848.[2]

Chicago's growth in the mid 1840s was only a prelude to more rapid development in the next few years. The federal census of 1850 found 30,000 residents in Chicago, another near doubling in three years. Recovery in the land market had turned by the early 1850s into a second land boom that was accompanied by a burst of new construction. As eastern railroad lines approached the city, their directors began negotiating with the municipal government for rights of way and terminal locations, further stimulating the real estate market. Although the completion of the canal did not immediately affect the city's grain shippers, who continued to receive produce by wagon, the canal did generate rapid growth in the receipt of bulkier commodities, chiefly lumber and salt. The 1850 census revealed the extent of a still modest industrial development. The city's 247 manufacturing establishments employed 2,123 workers. Yet 40 percent of the 426 workers in Chicago's foundries, machine shops, and agricultural implement factories already worked in plants employing more than fifty workers apiece.[3] By the late 1840s, Chicago as

2. Homer Hoyt, *One Hundred Years of Land Values in Chicago* (Chicago: University of Chicago Press, 1933), 47–50, 474, 482; A. T. Andreas, *History of Chicago* (3 vols.; Chicago: Andreas, 1884–86), 1:557; Bessie Louise Pierce, *A History of Chicago* (3 vols.; Chicago: University of Chicago Press, 1937–57), 1:143; Patrick E. McLear, "The Galena and Chicago Union Railroad: A Symbol of Chicago's Economic Maturity," *Journal of the Illinois State Historical Society* [hereafter *JISHS*] 73 (1980): 17–26.

3. Hoyt, *One Hundred Years*, 53–67, 483; Charles H. Taylor, ed., *History of the Board of Trade of the City of Chicago* (3 vols.; Chicago: Robert O. Law, 1917), 1:139–40; U.S. Census of Manufactures, 1850, manuscript schedules.

a city no longer was a precarious economic venture. Through the River and Harbor Convention, the city's boosters sought to advertise this fact.

The River and Harbor Convention was a classic city-boosting event. Chicago boosters inserted into the convention's printed proceedings a twenty-page statistical appendix that celebrated the city's development. "A glance at the origin, progress, and present condition of the place," urged this piece, "will, perhaps, best illustrate [Chicago's] commercial importance and claims, in common with the other cities of the Union, upon the fostering care and protection of [the federal government]."[4] Cloaked in the convention's rhetoric of federal internal improvement appropriations, the appendix made a strong case for Chicago's private investment potential as well. The city's boosters had lobbied strenuously to convince eastern organizers to choose Chicago for the convention site. By drawing delegates from all over the country, the convention promised to focus national attention on its host city. Boosters in St. Louis thus also tried to attract the convention, hoping to use its advertising potential in their increasingly less successful economic rivalry with Chicago, but the Chicagoans won this symbolic victory as they later would win the booster rivalry itself.[5]

The Chicago boosters soon organized a citizens committee to make the necessary local arrangements. This 110-member committee included most of the important businessmen, professionals, and politicians in the city. Partisanship was subordinated to the general booster aspect of the project. Among Democrats the committee included Augustus Garrett, Henry Rucker, and Francis C. Sherman, while among Whigs Levi Boone, George Dole, and William H. Brown took part. The committee on the convention address showed the degree to which these boosters could work together to promote Chicago. Composed of three Democrats and three Whigs, the committee included the personal as well as political enemies, John Wentworth and J. Young Scammon. One member, the Democratic city attorney Patrick Ballingall, was at the time under investigation by Levi Boone's finance committee on charges of malfeasance that would result in his official censure by the city council.[6] When it came to inviting a na-

---

4. *River-and-Harbor Convention,* 178.

5. Ibid., 24; Pierce, *History,* 1:395–96; Carl Abbott, *Boosters and Businessmen: Popular Economic Thought and Urban Growth in the Antebellum Middle West* (Westport: Greenwood Press, 1981), 132–33.

6. Chicago City Council Proceedings Files [hereafter CP], 1847/47:3868, 3874, 3923, 1848/48:4416; John Wentworth to Edmund Stoughton Kimberly, June 26, 1848, Kimberly papers, Chicago Historical Society.

tional congress of political luminaries and potential investors to visit their city, however, these men worked together.

Many members of the citizens committee assumed that the city's government would help to finance the convention. In May 1847 the committee applied to the council for funds. Levi Boone, as finance chairman, approved an appropriation of $500, citing the convention's "entirely public & national character" and pointing out "that there must necessarily be considerable expenses attending the same which . . . ought not to be sustained by private citizens." This appropriation did not satisfy the leaders of the citizens committee. The $500 was "entirely inadequate . . . for the proper entertainment of so distinguished a body, and by no means worthy of the liberal spirit of the citizens of Chicago." The committee demanded that the council appropriate another $1,000. Boone refused to authorize the money and on June 4, with the convention exactly a month away, the council concurred in his decision.[7]

In refusing to appropriate the $1,000, Boone pointed to "the embarrassed condition of the City Treasury," a response generally employed to avoid policy debate, but he also went further. Boone informed the citizens committee that "some of our fellow citizens, who pay taxes, and give direction to public sentiment" thought that the council had no power to spend money for the convention.[8] Boone did not elaborate on either the sources of opposition or the reason that the council might lack the necessary authority. The "public" character of the event as a tool for boosting the city had provided ample justification for the initial appropriation. One-third of the city's aldermen also were members of the citizens committee. No difference in party affiliation separated members from nonmembers, both groups including twice as many Democrats as Whigs. Boone's championship of the antifunding position, however, as well as his allusion to leaders of "public sentiment," suggests that membership in the citizens committee did not structure the debate. The city's recognized leaders of "public sentiment," including Boone himself, were members of the committee.[9]

When the council again refused to appropriate the additional $1,000, the citizens committee expressed their outrage in the loftiest rhetoric of American politics. On June 18 aldermen received the following:

7. CP, 1847/47:3897, 3905.
8. Ibid.
9. For the roster of city officers, see Andreas, *History*, 1:184–85. Party affiliation was determined from newspapers.

> Resolved by the people of Chicago in mass meeting assembled that the refusal of the Common Council to grant the appropriation asked for by the Committee is against the wishes of a large majority of our citizens. . . .
>
> Resolved that we deem it the duty of the Common Council to obey the wishes of their constituents and believing in the doctrine of instruction, we have met for the purpose of instructing them to make the appropriation for $1,000 additional asked for by the Committee.[10]

Norman B. Judd, organizer of the mass meeting, also delivered the meeting's demand for $5,000 from the council should that amount prove necessary. An alderman who was not a member of the citizens committee suggested further negotiations by a council committee authorized to appropriate $1,200. The council sent this motion back to Boone's committee and refused further funding.[11]

Debate about the council's role in the convention died down during the event itself, doubtless to avoid advertising to the delegates the lack of harmony in the city. Horace Greeley's dispatches to the New York *Tribune* confirmed success in this effort. Greeley, a Whig, mocked the Chicagoans' assertions of nonpartisan support for the convention's goals. His reports marshalled evidence of Whig support and Democratic opposition to internal improvements. Yet Greeley apparently did not know that Chicago's predominantly Democratic city council had refused funding for the convention. His praise of the city's "grand parade" was effusive. The spectacle, he wrote, "was truly magnificent. The citizens of Chicago, of course, furnished the most imposing part of it—the Music, the Military, the Ships on wheels, ornamented Fire Engines, etc. I have never witnessed anything so superb as the appearance of some of the Fire Companies with their Engines drawn by led horses, tastefully caparisoned. Our New-York Firemen must try again: they have certainly been outdone."[12] As far as Greeley was aware, Chicago's municipal government had acted with the unanimous support for the convention that its "grand parade" implied.

After the delegates left, Boone audited bills submitted by the citizens committee. He approved $241 in costs beyond the $500 appropriation, selectively accepting particular items of expenditure. The city's annual finance report, released early in 1848, revealed that the council had spent a total of $1,300 on the convention.[13] The citizens

10. CP, 1847/47:3913, 3925.
11. Ibid., 1847/47:3925, 3930. Pierce, *History*, 1:396, incorrectly states that the council approved $10,000 for the committee.
12. *River-and-Harbor Convention*, 139–47.
13. CP, 1847/47:3965, 3987, 4020, 1848/48:4288.

committee ultimately received most of the money it had demanded. Yet the reluctance of Boone and a majority of the council to fund the convention raises important questions. The River and Harbor Convention was precisely the type of event that a government dominated by city boosters should have supported. Partisanship was irrelevant to the debate; Boone was a Whig and Judd, the loudest proponent of funding, was a Democrat. While the city charter that had gone into effect in February 1847 made no specific provision for convention expenditures, it did not outlaw them either. Clearly, by 1847 many Chicagoans no longer assumed that municipal government should participate in the general promotion of the city's growth, an assumption that had been central to the booster system of city government.

The citizens committee that organized the River and Harbor Convention was a voluntary association. Chicago's government participated only by assembling the "grand parade." St. Louis's bid for the convention also had emanated from a private source, that city's Chamber of Commerce. When Chicagoans set up their counterpart to this organization in 1848 by founding the Chicago Board of Trade, members of the citizens committee provided 38 percent of the new organization's members and 59 percent of its directors. Almost one-third of the citizens committee joined the Board of Trade.[14] Conspicuously absent from the board's roster, however, were the politicians who were so prominent in the citizens committee. Not only did politicians including Wentworth and Scammon remain outside the board, but only two of the city's sixteen aldermen in 1847 and only one in 1848 also were members of the Board of Trade. A full third of the 1847 council served on the citizens committee.

Thus, although the Board of Trade drew much of its membership from the citizens committee, it was a very different body. The board was set up as a lobbying group for Chicago's businessmen, chiefly those involved in the commodities trade. In 1856 the board would reorganize itself as an exchange and begin to regulate trading, but in its first few years it served general lobbying functions. Primary among the board's early projects was the passage of a free banking law by the state legislature. While the Illinois constitution of 1848 allowed the legislature to charter private banks, the legislature acted on this power only in 1851, after a major lobbying effort by Chicago's businessmen and their Board of Trade. The probank coalition in

14. For St. Louis's bid, *River-and-Harbor Convention*, 24. Thirty-one of the Board of Trade's 82 members and 16 of its 27 directors had been on the 110-member citizens committee. For the citizens committee, ibid., 25–26. For Board of Trade members and directors in 1848, Taylor, *Board of Trade*, 1:137.

Chicago also involved booster politicians who were not members of the board. While Democrat Francis C. Sherman shepherded the bank clause through the constitutional convention, Scammon, a Whig, drafted the bill that the legislature ultimately enacted. Wentworth's opposition to the bank law angered William B. Ogden, a Democrat who had joined the Board of Trade, but Wentworth could not stop a bill whose support among other Democratic boosters was overwhelming.[15]

The Board of Trade also lobbied the city council for river improvement. Dredging of the Chicago River had been stalled by the wharfing privilege debacle. As aldermen sorted the wharfing claims, the Board of Trade pressed for dredging. Aldermen were reluctant to spend citywide tax proceeds on the river because the project would benefit the few businessmen who shipped commodities much more than it would benefit the whole of the city's property taxpayers. The Board of Trade, not surprisingly, disagreed. In 1851 a committee of the council met officially with a committee of the Board of Trade to discuss the dredging issue. The board's committee insisted that dredging would benefit all of the city's property owners and that most therefore would accept the extra tax burden. The council committee considered the distribution of the benefits more complex and resisted general taxation.[16] Many more years would elapse before Chicagoans solved this problem, but it is important to recognize the new configuration of city politics that the river conference represented. An organized body of booster businessmen lobbied the council as outsiders, while the council proclaimed the existence of a public interest separate from that of the businessmen, an interest that a publicly financed river project would have betrayed.

The economic growth of Chicago in the mid 1840s created a business community in the city whose interests no longer could be subsumed under a citywide interest in boosterism. A variety of commercial ventures—commodities, banking, and manufacturing—now supplemented the real estate that had dominated the investment portfolios of the city's early boosters. The real estate market itself had matured to a point where the developers of different parts of the city competed with one another rather than depending, as in the 1830s, on the speculative value of the city as a whole. As their economic interests

15. Taylor, *Board of Trade*, 1:138–39, 145–46; Jonathan Lurie, *The Chicago Board of Trade, 1859–1905: The Dynamics of Self-Regulation* (Urbana: University of Illinois Press, 1979), 23–27; Rima Lunin Schultz, "The Businessman's Role in Western Settlement: The Entrepreneurial Frontier, Chicago 1833–1872" (Ph.D. diss., Boston University, 1985), 129–46.

16. CP, 1851/52:326. Also Thomas B. Dwyer to Stephen A. Douglas, February 10, 1853, Box 1, Folder 26, Douglas papers, University of Chicago Library.

diverged, the city's businessmen made competing demands on municipal government. Projects such as river dredging no longer seemed to confer equivalent benefits on all of the boosters simply because they promoted the growth of Chicago. There is a danger in overemphasizing the degree to which these businessmen had specialized by 1850; many of the most successful boosters still combined interests in several branches of the city's economy. Yet the Board of Trade represented a distinct segment of the booster community, a segment anxious, though unable, to present its interests as those of the entire city.

The River and Harbor Convention represented the climax of Chicago's booster era. Business, professional, and political leaders subordinated their differences to promote a national celebration of the city's growth. That very growth, however, had brought economic developments that undermined the rationale of citywide boosterism, leading to the almost incredible resistance of the city's aldermen to convention funding. Differentiation of interests threatened to restructure municipal government along lines of interest-group competition. In the bridge debate of the late 1830s the *American* had condemned such a politics as one in which "party will be swallowed up in self-interest."[17] If this image sounded unattractive in 1839, by the late 1840s the city's government had to adapt to a segmentation of the economy that reached deeper and affected more issues than the simple sectional competition of the bridge war.

THE RIVER AND HARBOR Convention was called to protest President James K. Polk's 1846 veto of an omnibus appropriation bill for western river and harbor projects. Polk's defense of strict construction of the Constitution, rejection of interest-group politics, and insistence on a locally based government that would minimize the redistribution of national wealth comprised the ideological position that Chicagoans and their guests assembled to attack. There were other, less lofty, factors involved in both the veto and the protest, but the debate that they reflected was a central one in Jacksonian America and one that applied to states and cities as well as the federal government. When a government's constituency became sufficiently complex, the sum of all "local" interests no longer added to a "public" interest, even if the government still could serve all of the local interests involved. Granting the public interest's primacy,

17. Chicago *American*, July 9, 1839.

legislators had to define that interest and find appropriate ways to pursue it.[18]

While Polk mentioned states' rights and the specter of heavy debts in his veto, he rested the case for strict construction on the "inevitable tendency [of an active government] to embrace objects for the expenditure of the public money which are local in their character, benefiting but few at the expense of the common Treasury of the whole."[19] He did not develop the antimonopoly critique of federal spending that this juxtaposition implied, recognizing that the federal largess might be distributed widely. Rather, he stressed the "disreputable scramble for the public money, by the conflict which is inseparable from such a system between local and individual interests and the general interest of the whole." Polk objected, at bottom, to a political system structured by interest-group competition. Interest-group politics not only was "disreputable" but also would "engender sectional feelings and prejudices [that would] destroy the harmony which should prevail in our legislative councils." Congressional politics would degenerate into the logrolling process that had placed forty separate projects into the 1846 river and harbor appropriation bill.

Economic development and western expansion raised the stakes of interest-group competition for federal internal improvement funds. "In a country of limited extent, with but few such objects of expenditure," Polk argued, "a common treasury might be used for their improvement with much less inequality and injustice than in one of

18. At the state level, L. Ray Gunn, *The Decline of Authority: Public Economic Policy and Political Development in New York State, 1800–1860* (Ithaca: Cornell University Press, 1988); Oscar Handlin and Mary Flug Handlin, *Commonwealth: A Study of the Role of Government in the American Economy, Massachusetts, 1774–1861,* rev. ed. (Cambridge: Harvard University Press, 1969); Louis Hartz, *Economic Policy and Democratic Thought: Pennsylvania, 1776–1860* (Chicago: Quadrangle Books, 1948); Harry N. Scheiber, "Government and the Economy: Studies of the 'Commonwealth' Policy in Nineteenth–Century America," *Journal of Interdisciplinary History* 3 (1972): 135–51; Peter Wallenstein, *From Slave South to New South: Public Policy in Nineteenth-Century Georgia* (Chapel Hill: University of North Carolina Press, 1987). At the urban level, Jon C. Teaford, *The Municipal Revolution in America: Origins of Modern Urban Government, 1650–1825* (Chicago: University of Chicago Press, 1975); Michael H. Frisch, *Town into City: Springfield, Massachusetts, and the Meaning of Community, 1840–1880* (Cambridge: Harvard University Press, 1972). For national politics, see esp. Richard L. McCormick, *The Party Period and Public Policy: American Politics from the Age of Jackson to the Progressive Era* (New York: Oxford University Press, 1986), chap. 5.

19. All quotations from the veto message in this and the following paragraphs are from James D. Richardson, comp., *A Compilation of the Messages and Papers of the Presidents, 1798–1897* (10 vols.; Washington, D.C.: Government Printing Office, 1896–99), 4:460–66.

the vast extent which ours now presents in population and territory." The expansion of the United States "proportionately increased" the number of "local objects demanding appropriations of the public money for their improvement." As the number of worthy projects increased, Congress increasingly would have to choose among them; "the treasure of the world would hardly be equal to the improvement of every bay, inlet, creek, and river in our country which might be supposed to promote the agricultural, manufacturing, or commercial interests of a neighborhood." Some constituencies inevitably would be disappointed, increasing sectional tension as each appropriation spent "the public money [to] confer benefits, direct or indirect, only on a section."

Strict construction would avoid the exacerbation of sectional conflict. Local governments, forced to spend local money for local projects, would limit their expenditures to those projects that they most needed rather than fighting for "extravagant" appropriations in logrolling that could "carry propositions . . . which could not of themselves, and standing alone, succeed." Local governments would not spend money on "comparatively unimportant objects" because the money that they spent was their own. They not only distributed benefits but also raised the entire amount of their funds from taxation of the local community that they governed. Localization of government spending would minimize redistribution of the national wealth among the sections of the country, thus also limiting conflict among the sections for shares of this wealth.

Polk's resistance to redistribution of the national wealth was not total. He contrasted the predominantly northern and "comparatively unimportant" objects of the river and harbor bill against the expenses of the Mexican War even though the war clearly promised disproportionate benefits to the South. More to the point, he agreed that some improvement projects legitimately claimed federal funds. He invoked Andrew Jackson's Maysville Road doctrine, requiring "public" improvements to be located within the territory of more than one state, and defined the word "harbor" to demand that federally funded projects be connected to either foreign commerce (by collecting tariffs) or national defense (by supplying the navy). These distinctions offered little hope to the West, and westerners greeted the veto with an outrage that found voice in the River and Harbor Convention.[20] In rejecting Polk's veto, however, westerners also had to reject his logic. They either had to show that their local improvement projects would confer

20. Mentor L. Williams, "The Background of the Chicago River and Harbor Convention, 1847," *Mid-America* 30 (1948): 219–32.

national benefits or they had to call openly for a westward redistribution of national wealth.

Whigs, both East and West, rallied to and organized the protest movement Polk's veto inspired. They interpreted the veto as a further demonstration of the Democratic party's opposition to internal improvements. Whigs could present both a coherent defense of redistribution, the general system of internal improvements envisioned by Henry Clay in his "American System" of 1824, and an attack on the Democratic South that emphasized the connection John C. Calhoun had drawn in the 1828 *South Carolina Exposition* between strict constructions of federal power and the defense of slavery. Thus the Chicago *Journal*, a Whig paper, attacked Polk: "Are not *millions* being squandered by this same James K. Polk for the invasion of Mexico and the extension of slavery? . . . Are not the Treasury doors unbarred whenever the '*open sesame*' is whispered by the slave-driver?" Polk, in the *Journal*'s critique, opposed improvements for the Northwest because "the slave-owner was jealous of the prosperity of the free States." Strict construction was merely a "Virginia abstraction" employed to protect "that idol of the South, negro slavery."[21]

For western Democrats, however, these positions were untenable. They could neither dismiss strict construction so easily nor launch an all-out attack on their southern party allies.[22] The Democratic party was the majority party in the West and the dominant party in Illinois. Democratic congressmen from northern Illinois, chiefly John Wentworth and Stephen Douglas, had fought hard to pass the river and harbor bill. The West depended on federal spending for the transportation routes that made western settlement viable. Chicagoans knew the key role that federal spending already had played in opening their harbor on Lake Michigan. They knew that the federal land grant for the Illinois and Michigan Canal had created their city. Western Democrats saw the veto as a betrayal. One Chicago Democrat wrote to Douglas of a "series of petty intrigues" in support of the veto that had weakened the party in Cook County by expressing "opinions adverse to the wishes of the community."[23] These Democrats had a tough decision to make.

21. *River-and-Harbor Convention,* 14–15 (emphasis in original). For the Whig response in terms of a national improvement policy, ibid., 107–21.

22. Letters of regret from Democrats stressed constitutional restraint even as they endorsed the convention's goals. None even hinted at an attack on the South. Ibid., 69–76.

23. Robert W. Johannsen, *Stephen A. Douglas* (New York: Oxford University Press, 1973), 134–36, 183–85; Don E. Fehrenbacher, *Chicago Giant: A Biography of "Long John" Wentworth* (Madison: American History Research Center, 1957), 65–68, 75–78; Glen E.

Douglas opposed the veto without either disputing the president's logic or questioning his good will. He called Polk's constitutional exegesis "sound and orthodox" and denied only its application to the particular items in the river and harbor bill, though he had to admit that some of them defied constitutional defense. He did not charge hypocrisy or point to the sectionalism of the southern wing of his party. Douglas insisted, then, on the national benefit defense of the bill. He refused to alienate his party's leaders, though he warned that "odious and unjust discrimination" against the West would threaten Democratic power there. Doug-

FIG. 3 JOHN WENTWORTH

las's failure to attend the River and Harbor Convention confirmed his continued allegiance to Polk.[24] But while Douglas did not yet either reside in or represent Chicago in 1847, John Wentworth did both. If Douglas conceded defeat after a short, futile attempt to override the veto, Wentworth carried the fight to the floor of the River and Harbor Convention. Wentworth thus took his first cautious step in the direction that would lead him a decade later into the Republican party.

Wentworth considered the defeat of the river and harbor bill a betrayal of the West not only by the southern leaders of the Democratic party, but by the South in general. Wentworth had supported the Mexican War, though he, like Douglas, had linked it to northern claims in Oregon. When Polk first abandoned the 54° 40' line in Ore-

---

Holt, "The Birth of Chicago: An Examination of Economic Parentage," *JISHS* 76 (1983): 82–94; Edmund S. Kimberly to Douglas, April 10, 1848, Box 1, Folder 6, Douglas papers.

24. Johannsen, *Douglas*, 184–85, 211.

gon (settling for a northern boundary at the 49th parallel) and then vetoed the river and harbor bill, Wentworth became convinced of southern antagonism toward the development of the Northwest. Southerners had opposed the river and harbor bill in both the House and the Senate. The veto was the final blow. Having supported the war, Wentworth registered his anger as the only Illinois Democrat to vote for the Wilmot Proviso (to ban slavery in territories acquired from Mexico) on its first introduction—five days after Polk's river and harbor veto. The veto, Wentworth argued, reflected neither constitutional scruple nor Democratic ideology. It was an aggression by southerners. "This harbor question," he wrote, "is one between north and south. The Southern Whig President of 1840, and the southern democratic President of 1844, both vetoed our harbor bills. So politics have nothing to do with the matter."[25]

Wentworth began to call for the election of "northern men" by the Democratic party and to urge that the party throw off its "southern yoke." He insisted on a purification of the party, a return to its first principles and to leaders such as the New Yorkers Martin Van Buren and Silas Wright. He likened the Wilmot Proviso to Jefferson's Northwest Ordinance, whose language it echoed, and by 1847 had made his Chicago *Democrat* an avowedly free-soil newspaper. After the Barnburner revolt of the Van Burenites split the Democratic national convention in 1848, Wentworth became the leading Barnburner Democrat in Illinois. He combined in the *Democrat* his new free-soil message with his longstanding Locofoco positions on banking and public lands. He described bankers as thieves, advocated land reform through a homestead bill, and attacked the monopolistic behavior of produce speculators who, "as they own and control vessels on the lakes, . . . have every means of regulating the markets to suit themselves. . . . they can raise or depress the prices of all articles of farmers' produce at their will and pleasure."[26]

The integral relationship between free soil and Locofoco economics in Wentworth's thinking would structure not only his own political course as the party system realigned but also that of his northern Illinois constituents. By 1848 Wentworth, through the *Democrat*, had been educating northern Illinois voters in his populist version of Jacksonian orthodoxy for more than a decade. In the summer of 1848 he prepared to support Van Buren's Free Soil bid for president and won

25. Chicago *Democrat*, November 10, 1846, quoted in Pierce, *History*, 1:394; *Democrat*, January 12, 1847; Fehrenbacher, *Chicago Giant*, 62–70; David M. Potter, *The Impending Crisis, 1848–1861* (New York: Harper & Row, 1976), 18–26.

26. *Democrat*, February 19, 1849, quoted in Taylor, *Board of Trade*, 1:145; Williams, "Chicago River and Harbor Convention," 232; Fehrenbacher, *Chicago Giant*, 72–82.

a fourth term in Congress, though in Chicago he ran behind Scammon, the Whig champion of free banks. By November, when party loyalty and skepticism about third-party politics had persuaded Wentworth to support the regular Democratic nominee Lewis Cass rather than Van Buren, Chicago voters gave Van Buren a plurality, though Cass narrowly carried the state. Wentworth had instructed his supporters in the congressional race to "put upon Scammon's back all the sins of the Whig party" and "to treat Scammon as the emblem of Old fashioned Hartford Convention federalism."[27] It was crucial that he distinguish his Democratic free-soil position from that of the hated Whigs. Jacksonian Democracy was for Wentworth a primarily economic ideology.

How, then, could Wentworth oppose Polk's veto of the river and harbor bill? How could he dispute the strict construction that Andrew Jackson himself had made a keystone of Democratic ideology? How could he join the Whigs to condemn a Democratic president for failing to authorize what looked suspiciously like a "general system" of internal improvements? The Democratic party, Wentworth insisted, never had opposed internal improvements. Old Hickory himself, though "remarkably scrupulous as to the extent to which the power to construct works of internal improvement should be exercised," had signed bills for eighty-nine improvement projects in 1836 and another fifty-nine in 1837. Jackson and Van Buren together had approved $7.8 million in river and harbor appropriations. In the Chicago address for the River and Harbor Convention, Wentworth flatly denied that internal improvements ever had "entered into any presidential canvass, since each party has always taken it for granted that the candidate of the other was above suspicion upon a matter of such preëminent importance."[28] Government power should be construed strictly on issues like banking, where monopoly posed a serious threat, but internal improvements were another matter entirely.

Like Douglas, Wentworth's Chicago committee tried to stress the national benefit defense of the bill. In language that would be repeated many times on the convention floor, they insisted that only ignorance of western geography could explain opposition. "It is a notorious fact," they asserted, "that statements, during the pendency of harbor and river bills before Congress, are made on the highest personal authority, which never would be made if the authors had any personal observation of the great inland waters of this country,

---

27. Wentworth to E. S. Kimberly, June 26, June 27, 1848, Wentworth to James Long, July 16, 1848, Kimberly papers; Fehrenbacher, *Chicago Giant*, 80–85.

28. *River-and-Harbor Convention*, 27–28.

or could realize the necessity of the millions whose lives and property are jeoparded by them." Yet the Chicago delegates also moved beyond claims of national benefit to a defense not only of redistributive government, but of interest-group politics to implement it. "For the past three years, petitions have been presented to Congress in vain: senators and representatives in Congress have spoken in vain. . . . Our bills have invariably been vetoed, and we have been unable to secure two-thirds of the popular branch." Having failed thus far to enact their sectional interests, the Chicagoans turned to the convention as a lobbying tool with which to educate legislators in the legitimacy of their demands.[29]

The River and Harbor Convention represented a decision about national public policy by westerners in general and Chicagoans in particular. Democrats and Whigs joined together to reject strict construction, demand a westward redistribution of national wealth, and affirm the propriety of interest-group politics. Whigs as much as Democrats had to sacrifice key concepts of party ideology to accept this formulation, chiefly the notion of a common good that legislators could pursue by "general system." It is easy to impeach the rhetoric of the convention by pointing to the obvious fact that westerners only could gain from redistributive policies. They lacked capital that could be raised in the East for western transportation projects. Yet Polk's position was hardly above such criticism; he did define the national interest in a manner that favored the South. The irony here lies not in the relative hypocrisy of the participants in the national debate, but in the simultaneous and opposite conclusion that Chicagoans drew when the wealth to be redistributed was their own. For all their unity in demanding that an active federal government pay for public goods, they could not even agree to fund the convention that so clearly was a public good for the city.

THE FARCICAL character of the River and Harbor Convention funding debate resulted, of course, from the trivial nature of the public good at issue. Chicagoans elevated $1,000 in hospitality expenses to a question of high political principle. They did not debate whether the convention was a public good—nobody ever questioned that—but whether their municipal government legitimately could apply its tax proceeds to that good. Leaders of "public sentiment" turned convention funding into a test of the purpose of municipal government in the community. While the advocates of funding claimed that the city's government should reflect the "liberal spirit of the citizens of

29. Ibid., 28–29.

Chicago," the opponents denied precisely that statement. Municipal government did not exist to implement any citywide "spirit" of its constituents. Nor did it exist to promote material interests that all citizens shared in the development of Chicago. The "mutual dependence" with which Grant Goodrich defined boosterism no longer seemed sufficient to mobilize the boosters around public purposes at the municipal level. If the River and Harbor Convention was the climax of city boosterism in Chicago, it also marked the end of both the booster era and the system of city government appropriate to that era.

Between 1845 and 1851 Chicagoans reorganized their municipal government along lines that assumed the validity of nearly every point in Polk's analysis of government spending. They replaced the booster system with a system designed to minimize conflict "between local and individual interests and the general interest of the whole." They implemented Polk's demand for a government that avoided "disreputable scrambles" and "sectional prejudices" by localizing municipal public works expenditures at and below the ward level. They recognized that because urban growth increased the number of "local objects demanding appropriations of the public money for their improvement," the citywide booster mode of decision making would lead either to delays caused by political infighting, as it had in the bridge war, or to "extravagant" programs developed through logrolling in the city council. While the opponents of convention funding employed a strict construction of the city charter to deny municipal authority for public goods, the new system of city government also rejected both the redistribution of wealth through improvement spending and the use of interest-group politics to make public works decisions.

The system with which Chicagoans replaced citywide boosterism had as its fundamental characteristic a segmentation of both the costs of physical infrastructure and the process by which the city government made public works decisions. Segmentation rested on the principle of local control of city-building decisions. Only those property owners whose real estate would be affected by a particular decision had a right to participate in making that decision. Only the owners whose properties reaped benefits from an improvement paid for that improvement. Notions of the public good all but disappeared from municipal policy debate as Chicagoans turned their attention to the rapid creation of physical infrastructure.

Chicagoans did not speak as eloquently about the introduction of the segmented system as they did about their national demand for internal improvements. In fact, they said very little at all about the local reorganization. They did, however, concretely transform their municipal government. They changed the laws that specified its organization and administration and they changed their uses of both government and politics within the city. Because they said so little about these changes, their intentions in most cases must be inferred from their actions.[30] Still, these actions appear to have been consistent, and Chicagoans did alter the rhetoric with which they debated particular city-building issues. How to finance river dredging, for example, hinged on whether the benefits of the dredging were "strictly local" or of value to the owners "of *all* the real estate within the City."[31] Most issues that confronted municipal government in the segmented system were reduced to two simple administrative questions: who would benefit and who, therefore, should pay. This was the rhetoric of segmentation.

That a radical transformation of municipal government could have taken place with so little comment suggests that to mid nineteenth-century eyes the change seemed normal. Indeed, Oscar and Mary Handlin argued long ago that economic growth and differentiation in Massachusetts led early in the nineteenth century to the abandonment of a "commonwealth" ideal of active government and its replacement by a "humanitarian police state" less directly involved in the state's economy. While commonwealth policies, like the booster system in Chicago, had rested on "the primordial concept of common interests," the police state "set up rules of judgment among individuals and aimed to assure equitable conditions of life and labor to all."[32] Jon C. Teaford has described a similar shift at the urban level. Commercial regulation by eighteenth-century "municipal corporations" gave way to physical development by nineteenth-century "city governments." Teaford locates the causes of this shift in both economic growth and ideological change: "By 1775 economic scarcity

30. Thus, the 1847 charter amendment, although adopted in public meetings, received scant newspaper coverage. The *Journal* printed drafts anonymously, made no editorial comments aside from publishing two vague letters to the editor (also anonymously), and covered the meetings with quasi-official minutes that noted instances of debate without specifying its content or the identity of debaters. The *Democrat* is missing for the week of the meetings, but its coverage of the charter's legislative progress two weeks later suggests little more interest. For the complete coverage, *Journal*, January 8, 12, 13, 15, 18, 20, 23, 28, 1847; *Democrat*, February 23, 1847.

31. CP, 1852/53:1094, 1096 (emphasis in original); Illinois, *Private and Special Laws, 1847*, 215–16 and *Laws, 1854*, 219. Also Eugene P. Moehring, *Public Works and the Patterns of Urban Real Estate in Manhattan, 1835–1894* (New York: Arno Press, 1981), 64.

32. Handlin and Handlin, *Commonwealth*, passim. The quotes are collected in Scheiber, "Government and the Economy," 136.

no longer dominated urban thinking, whereas economic growth did. . . . the ideal of regulated concord was yielding to an ideal of open competition."[33]

Robert Wiebe has gone further. Throughout their history, according to Wiebe, Americans have tended to "segment" rather than confront conflicts that threatened social stability. American history may be periodized, therefore, by its shifting lines of segmentation, since these reflected the salient conflicts of any given period. In the nineteenth century, Americans segmented social and economic conflict on a geographical basis. They drew lines on the map, the most dramatic being the Missouri Compromise line that separated the North from the South. "A properly ordered society" in the nineteenth century comprised "countless, isolated lanes where Americans, singly or in groups, dashed like rows of racers toward their goals." Government existed to "provide sufficient space for the parallel enterprises of all its citizens" and to "guarantee freedom within each lane" of enterprise. Law drew the boundaries separating the parallel lanes so that "charges of 'monopoly' were directed not at exclusive privilege itself but at the intrusion of someone else's privilege into a sphere that the accusers considered their own."[34] The segmented system of city government was an urban expression of this phenomenon.

The idea of parallel lanes found graphic expression in the ward map that Chicagoans introduced with their 1847 charter. The basis of the segmented system in the city, this law was written in January 1847 by many of the same men who, a few months later, would organize the River and Harbor Convention. Of twenty-three identifiable participants in the charter-writing sessions, fourteen would serve on Chicago's delegation to the convention and seventeen on the citizens committee. Only three charter drafters failed to join in convention activities. The 1847 charter was produced, in other words, not only by the same group of land-speculating businessmen and lawyers who had dominated Chicago politics throughout the booster period but by the very men who championed the goals of the River and Harbor Convention.[35] Although surviving reports are sketchy, the

33. Teaford, *Municipal Revolution*, 49, 100. See also Moehring, *Public Works in Manhattan*, 52–119; Frisch, *Town into City*, 32–49.

34. Robert H. Wiebe, *The Segmented Society: An Introduction to the Meaning of America* (New York: Oxford University Press, 1975), 14–46, quotations from 19–20. See also Wiebe, *The Opening of American Society: From the Adoption of the Constitution to the Eve of Disunion* (New York: Vintage, 1984), esp. chaps. 12–15.

35. *Journal*, January 28, 1847. There is no record of attendance at these meetings. Of 23 men named in the *Journal's* minutes, 9 were among the 105 Chicagoans with $10,000 or more real estate in 1849 and 1850. Of 9 members of a subcommittee that

charter writers seem to have disagreed with one another only on proposals that would have made the segmentation of the city's government more—rather than less—extreme. Thus, they rejected a proposal by J. Young Scammon to make the city's three "divisions" (the north, south, and west sides) into independent "municipalities" for public works and other fiscal purposes.[36] Once drafted, moreover, the charter was pushed through the state legislature by Chicago representatives who also had been active in the River and Harbor Convention: in the house by Francis C. Sherman and in the senate by Norman B. Judd, the champion of boosterism in the funding debate. Aside from one amendment that Sherman tacked onto the bill, the charter sailed through the legislature as written in Chicago.[37]

The 1847 charter drew a ward map that can be described only as a series of parallel lanes of development. Its nine wards consisted of seven narrow strips of land on the north and south sides of the city and two large tracts on the largely undeveloped west side. The north and south side ward boundaries extended from the main branch of the river all the way to the city limits—three blocks apart on the north side and only two blocks apart on the south side. (See maps 1 and 2.) While this map was not, like that of 1837, a simple geographical split of the city, neither did it attempt to reflect the social composition of neighborhoods. This map, adopted in the charter meetings "without any amendment or dissent," bore no relation to communities that might have existed within the city.[38] Rather, it bounded economic groups whose only shared interest was the real estate that fronted on particular streets.

---

wrote the main draft, 5 (3 of them former mayors) made the $10,000 list and all 9 participated in the River and Harbor Convention, 7 as delegates. Partisanship was identified for 18 attenders (13 Democrats, 5 Whigs) and 7 subcommittee members (5 Democrats, 2 Whigs). For the $10,000 list, Craig Buettinger, "The Concept of Jacksonian Aristocracy: Chicago as a Test Case, 1833–1857" (Ph.D. diss., Northwestern University, 1982), 72–76.

36. *Journal*, January 20, 28, 1847. Part of Scammon's proposal was implemented in 1849, when Cook County organized itself into townships for some local government functions, and in the 1851 charter, which provided that general tax revenues had to be spent in the division in which they were collected "for all purposes strictly local."

37. Illinois, Senate, *Journal* (1846), 190, 207, 229, 261; Illinois, House, *Journal* (1846), 327, 379. The amendment was not trivial: it exempted a costly lakefront project from segmented financing, a move reversed in 1851. Sherman nevertheless urged passage on the grounds that the charter "had been acted upon by the citizens of Chicago in a public meeting"; *Democrat*, February 23, 1847. See Robin L. Einhorn, "A Taxing Dilemma: Early Lake Shore Protection," *Chicago History* 18 (1989): 46.

38. *Journal*, January 28, 1847. For a demographic analysis of the ward boundaries, see appendix 2.

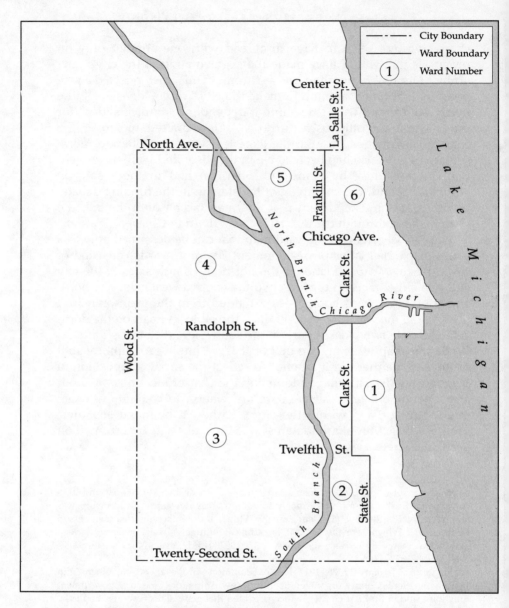

MAP 1 CHICAGO WARDS IN 1837

The 1847 ward map diffused the representation of other interests that Chicago's boosters might have wanted government policies to reflect. It divided the banks of the main river among seven different wards, five of which included long stretches of property with no river access. While warehousemen and commodities shippers had begun

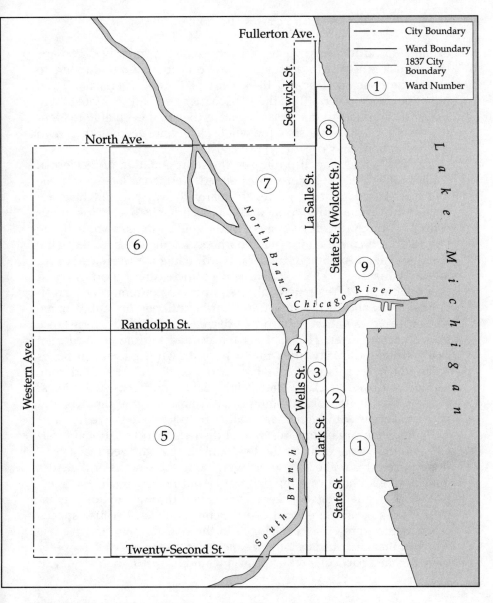

MAP 2 CHICAGO WARDS IN 1847

by 1847 to spread their operations to the South Branch, most such activity in 1847 still was located on the main branch near the Lake Michigan harbor. If fourteen of the city's eighteen aldermen—each ward elected two—represented what might be called the river interest, none represented that interest exclusively, though as shipping expanded southward, two would represent it primarily.[39] Perhaps this diffusion helped to persuade Chicago's commodities shippers to found the Board of Trade in 1848. Perhaps they felt gerrymandered out of political power. While the 1837 charter also had separated them from one another, in the booster system they had been able to identify their interests as those of the whole city. Now, needing their own representation, they organized privately.

The 1847 ward map also diffused the representation of residential communities that in eastern cities already formed a locus of ethnic and class-based political power.[40] Clearly this map could have reflected such communities only if they were organized as strips. Interestingly enough, the development of the south side lake shore in the late 1840s did create a strip neighborhood for the city's Yankee elite along Michigan Avenue in the First Ward, while the riverside Fourth acquired the social characteristics of its increasingly port-oriented economic activity. Yet in general, the wards cut randomly across residential areas and included within their boundaries the entire range of a property valuation pattern that decreased steadily with distance from the main river. Had Chicagoans wanted to draw a ward map that reflected ethnicity, they might have drawn the irregular boxes with which they later (1863) bounded neighborhoods. Had they wanted it to reflect class, they might have drawn east-west lines. These would have isolated commercial from industrial districts and separated areas with higher land values from less expensive tracts.[41]

Rather than organizing residential districts or occupational interests into municipal politics, the 1847 ward map organized real estate. It organized this real estate, moreover, along the lengths of the city's longer streets, those running in a north-south direction. The real estate ward map facilitated street improvement through an administrative process based on special assessment financing. Because special assessments were easily challenged in the courts, their effective use required that city officials build a consensus among affected property owners that a particular street project would be worth their money. If

39. Andreas, *History*, 1:579–80; Pierce, *History*, 1:130. But see also John Wentworth to Robert Schuyler, January 3, 1851, Illinois Central Archives, Newberry Library, in which Wentworth notes the political influence of "the six river aldermen."

40. Amy Bridges, *A City in the Republic: Antebellum New York and the Origins of Machine Politics* (Cambridge: Cambridge University Press, 1984), esp. 147–54; Ira Katznelson, *City Trenches: Urban Politics and the Patterning of Class in the United States* (Chicago: University of Chicago Press, 1981).

41. On the land values, see Hoyt, *One Hundred Years*, 70–72. For evidence that Chicagoans knew they could represent class by drawing east-west lines on the north and south sides, see the next chapter's discussion of fire limit boundaries.

the property owners agreed that they wanted an improvement, they would be more likely to pay the assessment levied for it without mounting legal challenges. Wards in the segmented system of city government were jurisdictions for public works decisions that required a spatial organization of policy consensus. The real estate ward map maximized the segregation into wards of the property liable to special assessment for the improvement of any particular street. It created in the real estate market a series of parallel lanes whose separation was guaranteed by government policy.

WHILE THE REAL ESTATE ward map illustrated and organized the segmented system of city government in Chicago, special assessment formed its policy-making core. A special assessment is a one-time payment by a property owner to defray the cost of a specific improvement project. The assessment is levied on the owner's property in proportion to the particular benefit that accrues to his property as a result of the project, generally measured by an expected rise in land value.[42] A special assessment, then, bills the cost of a physical improvement to and only to those property owners whom it benefits "particularly." It is, in economist Dick Netzer's words, "a halfway house between the property tax and a user charge."[43] A rigorous use of special assessment minimizes the redistribution of wealth among property owners that otherwise would result from public works construction. It avoids the expenditure of general property tax proceeds on projects that benefit only a portion of the taxpaying community.

Special assessment was a staple of American municipal finance from the 1830s to the 1930s. "No American who treats of public finance as a whole," as E. R. A. Seligman noted in 1895, "can fail to be struck with the importance of special assessments in actual practice."[44] Scholars who have studied special assessment generally attribute its decline to a reckless expansion of urban subdivision financed by a distorted version of special assessment in the 1920s and the collapse in the Great Depression of the anticipation bonds issued to finance this expansion. The collapse of the bonds threw the entire system into disrepute, leading most large cities to abandon it.[45] Many

---

42. Edwin R. A. Seligman, *Essays in Taxation* (New York: Macmillan, 1895), 304.

43. Dick Netzer, *Economics of the Property Tax* (Washington, D.C.: Brookings Institution, 1966), 213.

44. Seligman, *Essays*, 283.

45. For the origins, see Stephen Diamond, "The Death and Transfiguration of Benefit Taxation: Special Assessments in Nineteenth-Century America," *Journal of Legal Studies* 12 (1983): 201–40; Victor Rosewater, *Special Assessments: A Study in Municipal Finance* (New York: Columbia University, 1898), 26–56. For the collapse, see William O.

small cities and suburban jurisdictions in the United States still use special assessments and in the 1950s and 1960s, when American cities and their suburbs expanded rapidly, urban economists became interested in special assessment as a user charge that could help to control urban sprawl if the legal distortions of the 1920s were corrected.[46]

The potential of special assessment to control urban sprawl rests on the same economic property that structured its use in the nineteenth century: if public works are financed only by the owners of real estate that they benefit, these owners will resist premature and unnecessary expansion of a city's infrastructure. By making public works private rather than public goods, municipal governments can take the politics out of public works decision making, avoiding the expansionary effects of public works patronage on the physical growth of cities.[47] The advocates of a renewed use of special assessment appear to comprise a small group of economists. Most new urban and suburban subdivision today is done by developers who extend entire service packages—streets, sidewalks, water, sewers, gas, and electricity—to their developments, capitalizing the costs of these improvements into the prices of the houses they sell. As Ann Durkin Keating has shown, this "developer's alternative" to municipal extension of public works began to shape the housing market in the Chicago area in the 1870s.[48] This privatization of public works was a logical extension of the concept of special assessment.

Another objection to a return to special assessment financing lies in the changed nature of public works spending once a city has built its basic infrastructure. After most streets have been paved, for example, spending is redirected from construction to maintenance. While the benefits of an initial paving may be assessed on abutting property with

---

Winter, *The Special Assessment Today with Emphasis on the Michigan Experience* (Ann Arbor: University of Michigan Press, 1952), 3–6, 46–60; Glenn W. Fisher and Robert P. Fairbanks, *Illinois Municipal Finance: A Political and Economic Analysis* (Urbana: University of Illinois Press, 1968), 158.

46. Walter Rybeck, "The Property Tax as a Super User Charge," *The Property Tax and Local Finance*, Proceedings of the Academy of Political Science, vol. 35, C. Lowell Harriss, ed. (New York, 1983), 133–47; Donald D. Herrman, *The Special Assessment in Oak Lawn* (Carbondale: Public Affairs Research Bureau, Southern Illinois University, 1962); Donald C. Shoup, "Financing Public Investment by Deferred Special Assessment," *National Tax Journal* 33 (1980): 413–29.

47. Wilbur R. Thompson, *A Preface to Urban Economics* (Baltimore: Johns Hopkins Press, 1965), 324–25; Edward Dana Durand, *The Finances of New York City* (New York: Macmillan, 1898), 142–45.

48. Ann Durkin Keating, "From City to Metropolis: Infrastructure and Residential Growth in Urban Chicago" in *Infrastructure and Urban Growth in the Nineteenth Century* (Chicago: Public Works Historical Society, 1985).

some logic—paving enhances values by making property accessible and directing commercial traffic toward it—maintenance confers less obvious benefits. Now the street's actual users, the owners of vehicles that travel on it, are the chief beneficiaries. These users and the city government, which will be sued when accidents result from poor maintenance, comprise a broader population than the owners of the abutting lots.[49] The shift from initial construction to maintenance helped to undermine the logic of special assessment in the late nineteenth century. In part because of the unmeasurable benefits that street maintenance conferred on travelers, cities combined special assessments with increasing proportions of general revenue for repavings, thus defeating the resistance to unnecessary spending built into a pure special assessment system.[50]

This distortion of the special assessment system was a major prop of machine rule in Tweed era New York City. While a legal structure resembling special assessment had existed in New York from the 1650s, that city started to levy special assessments in earnest in the 1830s, when it began to extend and improve streets on a large scale. In the 1850s, however, legal controls on the system began to slip away. A state law of 1852 introduced special assessment anticipation bonds, allowing city officials to pay contractors before they collected special assessments—thus undermining the control that property owners exerted over contractors' activities through the threat of nonpayment. In 1869 New York's government gained the power to charge half of the cost of all street improvements to the general tax fund, the results of which included the premature opening of new streets, excessive damages awarded to cronies in eminent domain proceedings, and intentional errors that caused the courts to void the special assessments charged to favored property owners.[51]

Such distortion of the special assessment system, however, loomed relatively far in the future for Chicagoans in the late 1840s. Meanwhile, they adopted the system in a rigorous fashion and redesigned their municipal government in order to facilitate its operation. Yet

49. Repair might also benefit abutters, but today many consider traffic more a nuisance than benefit. See William W. Vickrey, "General and Specific Financing of Urban Services" in *Public Expenditure Decisions in the Urban Community* (Washington, D.C.: Resources for the Future, 1963), 72–73.

50. Diamond, "Death and Transfiguration," 218–22.

51. Durand, *Finances*, 58–59, 107–9, 142–45; Moehring, *Public Works in Manhattan*, 52–82; Diamond, "Death and Transfiguration," 203–24. See also Richard T. Ely, *Taxation in American States and Cities* (New York: Thomas Y. Crowell, 1888), 248. Ely argued that property owners still controlled the improvement process and that they, rather than the working class, were therefore to blame for spiraling municipal debts.

it is important here to note the definition of corruption in a rigorously segmented special assessment system. Special assessment rested on control by property owners of the improvement process; corruption consisted of any action by a city official that usurped this control, particularly by presuming to make an improvement decision himself. Independent planning decisions by city officials, as a Chicago alderman argued in 1855, made "an absolute farce" of the special assessment system. "This mode of assessment is an *ultimatum* . . . The *Edict* is make any improvement your fancy may dictate, figure up the cost, compel the payment. This in the opinion of your Committee is not the intent, nor the meaning of the [city charter]."[52] The charter surrounded the special assessment system with procedural controls designed to preserve the sovereignty of property owners in the improvement process. Any violation of these controls opened the doors to corruption.

It was the meticulous detail of these procedural controls that made special assessments vulnerable to legal challenge. The charter specified nearly every step in the assessment process, elevating administrative practices to legal imperatives. From the improper delivery of any of the four separate types of notice that the charter required the council to serve on property owners to the failure, as of an Illinois supreme court decision of 1859, to place dollar signs in front of the numbers on assessment rolls, all procedural lapses could threaten the legal validity of special assessments. Because these administrative details were specified in the city charter, moreover, council debates about them easily mushroomed into debates about the basic character and fundamental purpose of municipal government. This was strict construction with a vengeance, though continuous amendments to the charter left increasingly little for officials to construe.[53]

MORE IMPORTANT than the rhetorical exaggeration with which both the council and the courts discussed the details of special assessment, was the effect of property owner sovereignty on the character of municipal government. If independent decision making by an alderman was considered corruption, the office could confer little power on its incumbent. Aldermen were elected to expedite the im-

52. CP, 1855/56:1868 (emphasis in original).
53. Cf. Moehring, *Public Works in Manhattan*, 59. For the charters, Edmund J. James, ed., *The Charters of the City of Chicago* (2 pts.; Chicago: University of Chicago Press, 1898–99), 51–61 (1837); Illinois, *Private and Special Laws, 1847*, 85–89; James, *Charters*, 160–75 (1851); Illinois, *Laws, 1857*, 901–5. See also *Morris et al. v. Chicago*, 11 Ill. 650 (1850); *Canal Trustees v. Chicago*, 14 Ill. 334 (1853); *Chicago v. Rock Island Railroad Company*, 20 Ill. 286 (1858); *Gibson v. Chicago*, 22 Ill. 567 (1859).

provement projects that their constituents asked for by petition. A petition was a declaration by property owners that they would be willing to pay a special assessment for the improvement they requested, though petitions had no legal standing when assessments went to court. While the petition requirement was inserted formally into the charter only in 1861, when a Board of Public Works took infrastructure administration away from the council, aldermen depended from the beginning of the segmented system on petitions from the owners of affected real estate in order to make improvement decisions. They counted the proportions of affected property that advocates and opponents of a particular project owned and made their decision by majority rule—majority of property rather than majority of owners. Any other course was corrupt.[54]

Edward Pessen has argued that in New York and other eastern cities members of the economic elite began to shun participation in city councils in the 1840s because of the "limited and prosaic nature" of the tasks they would have to perform. The wealthiest men in these cities made sure they participated in important efforts such as rewriting city charters and often ran for mayor, since "for all of the weaknesses built into the office, [it] permitted a man of force and stature . . . to place his own imprint on it."[55] They did not, however, serve as aldermen with the frequency that they had in previous decades. In Chicago the boosters continued to comprise a significant portion of the council as the segmented system emerged. Between 1847 and 1851, the years in which the system was established, 24 percent of the city's aldermen were among the 105 Chicagoans assessed at $10,000 or more real estate on the city tax rolls of 1849 and 1850.[56] While this figure is slightly higher than that of the booster years and the figure for total number of council terms served by these men is an identical 20 percent, this latter calculation probably represents a greater concentration of wealthy men in the council, since it measures wealth at the time of service rather than in the future.

The wealth of aldermen becomes more difficult to measure in the 1850s; a retrospective calculation based on the 1849 and 1850 lists probably would be worth little given the dynamic nature of the city's economy in these years and the emergence of a new group of wealthy men whose assets extended beyond real estate. Yet Rima Schultz has argued not only that members of Chicago's booster elite continued to

54. This process is described in detail in the next chapter. Also, Moehring, *Public Works in Manhattan,* 55–64; Illinois, *Laws, 1861,* 118–52.

55. Edward Pessen, *Riches, Class, and Power before the Civil War* (Lexington: D. C. Heath, 1973), 291.

56. Buettinger, "Concept of Jacksonian Aristocracy," 72–76.

serve in the council but that in the late 1840s they actually consolidated their control of the city's government. The vehicle by which the boosters assumed control, according to Schultz, was nonpartisan municipal elections.[57] Whigs, as the last chapter noted, had been calling for nonpartisan city elections for years, chiefly because of the weakness of their party in the city. The rhetoric of apolitical public service, moreover, appealed to Chicagoans who fancied themselves members of a patrician elite. In the late 1840s, however, the nonpartisan movement gained new power from dynamics within the Democratic party, particularly the antibank, antispeculative positions championed by the party's leader in the city, John Wentworth.

Wentworth's demands for a populist approach to western development, as Schultz has shown, became increasingly annoying to Chicago's businessmen as they built the economic structures of modern commodities trading and private banking. If public regulation of the commodities market soon would become a major issue in Illinois politics, producing antimonopoly Granger legislation after the Civil War, banking was the economic issue of the 1840s and 1850s. Not only did the boosters need legislative authorization for "free banks," but they faced huge opposition in the legislature from downstate Democrats. Wentworth appeared to be siding with the enemies of Chicago's development, and he controlled the local Democratic party.[58] The national nonpartisanship so loudly proclaimed in the River and Harbor Convention by the Chicago committee that Wentworth led, had a local counterpart in the probank coalition that Wentworth fought. His *Democrat* criticized the state constitutional convention of 1847 for failing to prohibit banks altogether even though most of Chicago's booster Democrats—not to mention the Board of Trade—had worked to avoid bank prohibition.[59]

The Whig party stopped running municipal candidates after 1846. In 1847 Democrat James Curtiss, a regular member of Wentworth's party, narrowly won the mayoralty over John H. Kinzie. A Whig, Kinzie was popularly identified with Chicago's frontier origin; his father had been among the first white settlers. In 1837, when Kinzie lost the city's first mayoral election to William B. Ogden, the Whig paper had promoted Kinzie by calling Ogden a mere "transient speculator." While Kinzie never became a major player in Chicago's economy, he remained a living symbol of its development. He therefore was an

57. Schultz, "Businessman's Role," 147–58.
58. Ibid.
59. Ibid., 151; Arthur C. Cole, ed., *The Constitutional Debates of 1847* (Springfield: Illinois State Historical Library, 1919), 519–21, 640–47, 654–73.

obvious choice for Chicagoans trying to revive the crumbling ideals of boosterism in the electoral arena.[60] City officials would call upon Kinzie often in the 1850s to lend his prestige to the special assessment process by serving as an assessor of damages and benefits. Kinzie stood not only above politics but also above many of the economic rivalries that divided the city's major businessmen. After Kinzie failed to beat Curtiss in 1847, a bipartisan coalition united in 1848 around the probank Democrat James H. Woodworth, who had lost his party's nomination to Curtiss.

Woodworth's 1848 victory—he carried every ward on the south and west sides but lost all three of the disproportionately immi-grant and working-class north side wards—inspired a celebration of the nonpartisan resolution that the businessmen had brought to municipal politics. At a meeting chaired by Charles Walker, first vice president of the Board of Trade, the boosters claimed to see the election as "no partisan triumph, but as a renewed testimony in favor of the ability of the People for self government. . . . in our municipal elections, neither the chasm of party caucuses, nor the tyrranous [sic] demagogues shall bend us; but we will make such se-lections, and cast our votes irrespective of party politics."[61] In 1849 neither the Whigs nor the Democrats held a party caucus for the city election. From 1849 to 1854 mayoral and aldermanic elections re-mained nonpartisan.

This nonpartisanship was total. The partisan newspapers reported no ward meetings, ran no municipal slates on their mastheads, and printed city election returns without comment. Candidates an-nounced their availability in uninformative notices placed in the clas-sified columns of the various papers. The *Democrat* explained to voters in 1850 that it had printed ballots "of all kinds and combina-tions imaginable . . . and if it does not puzzle the judges and clerks of election to canvass them, we shall lose our guess."[62] The *Journal*

60. Andreas, *History*, 1:97–98; Jacqueline Peterson, "The Founding Fathers: The Absorption of French-Indian Chicago, 1816–1837" in *Ethnic Chicago*, rev. and exp., Melvin G. Holli and Peter d'A. Jones, eds. (Grand Rapids: William D. Eerdmans, 1984), 311–34; *American*, April 29, 1837, quoted in Pierce, *History*, 1:376.

61. Quoted in Schultz, "Businessman's Role," 152–53. For election returns, appen-dix 1. See also Taylor, *Board of Trade*, 1:137; Deborah L. Haines, "City Doctor, City Lawyer: The Learned Professions in Frontier Chicago, 1833–1860" (Ph.D. diss., Uni-versity of Chicago, 1986), 400–401.

62. Chicago *Journal*, February 26, March 2, 1849; March 6, 1850; March 2, 1852; March 6, 8, 1854; March 5, 1855; *Democrat*, March 6, 1849; March 5, 1850; February 19, March 4, 1851. Haines, "City Doctor," 401–7, cites the rhetoric of some of these no-tices, candidates saying they were forced to run by popular demand, as evidence that the nonpartisan resolution ratified a service ideal. Such rhetoric more likely was a cam-

reported an intense, though personal, campaign in 1851. "Candidates for the people's choice, for all the city offices, multiply each day as the election approaches, and the contest promises to be quite exciting, and as none of the political parties, have party candidates in the field, a good opportunity will be afforded to tell, after the election, who has the most friends." The *Democrat* agreed. "It is a desperate guerilla contest—every man fighting on his own hook and for himself." Three- and four-way races for alderman became common in the absence of organized nominations.[63]

The *Democrat* resigned itself to the nonpartisan resolution, citing the "common consent" of the parties not to politicize the 1849 election. Unable to resist a plug for aldermanic candidate Charles McDonnell, who "has been a working man in the Council, and we never knew him to go for any measure which did not contemplate the right of the masses," the paper concluded by admitting that McDonnell's opponents also were "very good men." By 1851 the *Democrat* had to "confess we do not like the [nonpartisan] system. The old convention system, though perhaps not without its evils, we regard as much preferable to it."[64] The Democratic party's strength in the city meant that nonpartisan elections deprived the *Democrat* of the easy access to city printing contracts that party politics would have ensured. The *Journal* favored nonpartisanship, though its Whig editor really seems to have wanted a complete end to electioneering. The *Journal* urged voters in 1852 to ignore "the brawling of demagogues who are seeking place and power, merely for a sight at the public plunder. . . . Select from among the candidates the men whom you would soonest trust with your own private affairs."[65]

This was apt advice for a system of government in which aldermen processed public works projects in response to petitions. Aldermen were indeed trustees of the "private affairs" of their propertied constituents. In the only aldermanic race of these years to inspire newspaper debate, the point at issue was the candidate's fitness to perform this trustee function for the property owners of his ward. A First Ward voter accused Thomas Richmond of running for alderman in that ward to gain benefits for property he owned elsewhere. Richmond defended himself: "The gentleman intimates that I am inter-

---

paign tactic. It appeared rarely; notices usually stated just candidates' names and the offices they sought.

63. *Journal*, February 27, 1851; *Democrat*, March 4, 1851. For election returns, appendix 1.

64. *Democrat*, February 6, 1849, March 4, 1851.

65. *Journal*, March 1, 1852.

ested in lands in the 6th ward, west of the river, and want to use an election in the first ward to favor rail road depot locations on the west side. Upon this subject I only have to say that my interest in real estate is about equal in the 1st, 2d, 6th and 8th wards, being nearly equal in the three general divisions of the city."[66] Richmond did not deny that his own real estate interests motivated his campaign. He and his critic agreed that the relevant issue was the location of the real estate that he wanted to benefit. Richmond assured his First Ward neighbors that they could count on his self-interested efforts to promote the ward's real estate, though the election returns registered their disagreement.

While the tasks of municipal government in the segmented system were indeed both limited and prosaic, they exerted a huge impact on the value of property. Whether an alderman could and would move a public works project quickly through the council made a great deal of difference to the property owners who wanted that project. The enormous amount of paperwork involved in special assessments and the importance of competent handling of the rules governing their use made service in the council worth the time of the city's leading businessmen, especially those who owned much real estate. If they made few independent decisions, aldermen organized activity of major importance to the value of their own properties. If special assessments required the development of consensus among the owners of neighboring property, who better to develop that consensus than one of the major property owners involved? If party politics had frustrated the boosters' attempts to manage the improvement process in the council, the nonpartisan resolution may indeed have marked a consolidation of their power.

WHILE CHICAGO'S municipal government had gained the power to levy special assessments in the city charter of 1837, it did not use them during the depression. Unable to collect even its small general property tax levies, the booster council performed only those tasks necessary to maintain the city as a viable community until prosperity returned. By the mid 1840s, with the depression over, the city's government finally could turn its attention to public works. The real estate market had recovered and commerce was booming. Only the city's physical infrastructure lagged behind: Chicago had few if any planked streets, an insufficient supply of water provided by an inadequately capitalized private company, and, after a flood in the spring

66. *Democrat*, February 24, 27, 1851.

of 1849, no bridges over the river.[67] With capital now available, Chicago's boosters wanted public works. They wanted planked streets, sidewalks, bridges, gas lights, drainage, and water. As New Yorkers had done some twenty years earlier, Chicagoans turned to special assessment to finance an ambitious public works program.[68]

The council began this program in 1845 with three large projects. Proceeding under the special assessment rules of the 1837 charter, they ordered Lake Street planked, a lake shore breakwater built, and a series of drainage aqueducts constructed on the south side. It is unclear whether property owners petitioned for Lake Street or the aqueducts, but the collection of assessments for them proved difficult. After a three-year court battle over the Lake Street assessment, the judiciary committee reported in 1848 that they "are not advised of the reasons or causes why the assessment was not legal or enforced; but believing that it is well understood that some defect exists," the city would refund payments that had been made. The aqueduct assessments also encountered opposition. Property owners resisted these by claiming poverty and arguing that their properties did not benefit from particular aqueducts. One owner demanded that his tenant be charged half of his assessment since the tenant's buildings received the benefits. By 1848, with the new charter in place and greater sophistication among Chicagoans about the use of special assessment, objectors argued that the aqueduct assessments had been levied illegally in the first place. This was the best way to evade a special assessment.[69]

Although the lake shore protection had been initiated by petition, its assessment faced similar obstacles. Property owners offered many objections: their own assessments were too large, many who benefited from the improvement were not assessed, public property (a

67. Andreas, *History*, 1:192, 200–202; Pierce, *History*, 1:336–44; Louis P. Cain, *Sanitation Strategy for a Lakefront Metropolis: The Case of Chicago* (DeKalb: Northern Illinois University Press, 1978), 39–41.

68. The property tax rate dropped sharply after 1842. From 6 percent of valuation in 1841 and 1842, it dropped to 0.6 percent in 1843 and continued to drop, to 0.35 percent in 1850. While this reflected rising land value, the rate inched up slowly in the 1850s despite a boom in public works construction, topping 1 percent in 1856 and 2 only in 1863. The property tax measured per capita fluctuated more widely. It remained below $3.00 from 1845 to 1855, jumping to between $4.00 and $6.00 from 1856 to 1859. Computed from Chicago, Department of Finance, *Annual Statement, 1877* (Chicago: Hazlitt & Reed, 1878), 172–73.

69. For Lake Street, then Chicago's main commercial strip, CP, 1845/45:2535, 1846/46:3367, 1848/48:4220, 4908, 5048. For the aqueducts, 1845/45:2790, 1846/46:3072, 3227–28, 1847/47:4094, 4107, 4109, 1848/48:4512, 4596, 4663, 4672, 4716, 4734, 4738, 4762.

park on the lake shore) benefited from the project, the assessment had been made illegally, the total amount assessed was too high, and special assessments were unconstitutional in any case. To complicate matters further, the city had employed general financing for a previous breakwater in 1840.[70] In 1846 the council began refunding the assessments collected for the lake shore protection. The park on the lake shore would continue to plague efforts to segment the project's cost, though in 1852 the effort prompted a ringing defense of special assessment by an alderman from the riverside Fourth Ward. Faced with objections from lake shore property owners, Amos Throop asked: "How would these gentlemen relish an assessment to repair the banks of the South Branch, or for planking streets a long distance from them?"[71] Clearly they would not. Long lists of objections became an integral part of the assessment process in the 1850s, but as the Illinois supreme court developed a special assessment case law and the charter provisions grew more detailed, many of the objections lost their force.

The constitutional argument was quashed by the supreme court's 1851 decision in *Canal Trustees v. Chicago*. This case, which involved an assessment for widening an alley, prompted the first definition of special assessment by the Illinois court. The trustees of the Illinois and Michigan Canal had sued the city for assessing canal property, claiming that as state property it was exempt from taxation. The distinction between special assessments and taxes also was important because the 1848 state constitution required that taxation be uniform and universal. Special assessments clearly could be neither.[72] The court held, therefore, that a special assessment

has none of the distinctive features of a tax. It is imposed for a special purpose, and not for a general or public object. . . . The improvement is made for the convenience of a particular district, and the property there situated is required to bear the expense in the proportion to which it is benefitted. The assessment is precisely in the ratio of the advantages accruing to the property in consequence of the improvement.

70. For more on the lake shore protection, Einhorn, "A Taxing Dilemma."
71. CP, 1845/45:2799, 2813, 2817, 1852/53:418; *American*, September 19, October 3, 1840.
72. For the "uniformity and universality movement" in state property taxation, see Sumner Benson, "A History of the General Property Tax" in George C. S. Benson et al., *The American Property Tax: Its History, Administration, and Economic Impact* (Claremont, Calif.: College Press, 1965), 11–81. A tax is "uniform" if assessed at the same rate on all property and "universal" if levied on all forms of property, personal as well as real. Special assessments are levied only on real estate and assessed in proportion to benefit rather than at a single, uniform rate.

> It is but an equivalent or compensation for the increased value the property derived from the [improvement].[73]

The canal trustees had to pay special assessments when canal property gained special benefits. More important, the court laid a legal foundation for special assessment in Illinois and undercut challenges based on constitutional arguments. This decision remained the basis of special assessment case law in the state even as the court modified its strict distinction between special assessments and taxes.

Lake Street, the aqueducts, and the lake shore protection were poor choices for projects with which to establish a system of special assessment. Large projects conferring widely distributed benefits, they involved too many people and too much money for a system whose very legitimacy had not yet been established in the city. More troubling for the aqueduct project was the central planning involved. The champion of aqueducts in the council was Elihu Granger, chairman of the committee on streets and bridges. Granger not only insisted on special assessment financing, instead of the general financing that a citizens committee urged, but he also redesigned the aqueduct plans several times, raising their cost. While other aldermen considered the aqueduct system a technological experiment and argued that "all experiments which are to be made by the City should be made at the general expense of the whole City, and not by a special tax," Granger successfully defended both the technology and the segmentation of its cost.[74]

Elihu Granger was well qualified to lecture his fellow aldermen on engineering technology, though his lengthy reports sometimes strained their patience. A mechanic, Granger had moved from New York to Chicago in 1836 to build the city's first flour mill for a local firm. He worked on canal contracts until 1839, when he opened a

73. *Canal Trustees v. Chicago*, 12 Ill. 406 (1851); *McBride v. Chicago*, 22 Ill. 574 (1859); *Chicago v. Larned*, 34 Ill. 203 (1864). Debate waged in many nineteenth-century state courts centered on whether special assessments were taxes or exercises of eminent domain. The relationship between special assessment and eminent domain rested on the use of the former to finance damage awards in the latter when property was taken for streets. This link was weakened by the use of special assessment for projects that did not involve takings. See Diamond, "Death and Transfiguration," 206–10; Rosewater, *Special Assessments*, 88–130.

74. CP, 1845/45:2749, 1846/46:2945, 2947, 2963, 2970. Granger supervised the project as the chairman of a special committee on aqueducts. Use of the term "special tax" rather than "special assessment" shows unfamiliarity with these instruments. A special assessment is levied proportionally on benefited property, but a special tax is levied uniformly on property in a benefited jurisdiction. By 1851 Chicagoans no longer confused these terms.

machine shop on the north side.[75] While his election as Fifth Ward Democratic alderman in 1844 did not survive the canvass held after the fraud hearings, Granger entered the council in 1845 and in 1846 hosted the Fifth Ward poll at his furnace. By 1850 Granger already outranked his fellow aldermen in seniority and he continued to serve on and off in the council until 1856, when he became superintendent of public works. If his technological lectures annoyed other aldermen, his emotional responses to shoddy work by street contractors and, when partisanship returned to municipal politics, his inability to understand the stakes of urban-level party conflict may have shortened his tenure as superintendent.[76] In addition to being a qualified engineer of the preprofessional variety (he had great trouble with written English), Granger was a Jacksonian ideologue. He called steadfastly for minimalist government, led the council opposition to nativist legislation in 1855, and perceived threats to popular rule in a wide variety of government policies.

If Granger erred with the aqueduct project, he was an ardent defender of segmented finance—though for reasons different from those of many of his council colleagues. His artisan occupation, abrasive personality, and long council tenure made Granger an unusual Chicago alderman anyway. He participated in the 1847 charter meetings, but did not join the River and Harbor Convention committee and never invested heavily enough either in real estate or anything else to draw much attention from the authors of biographical collections. In fact, Elihu Granger emerges for the historian only in the role he seems to have taken so much more seriously than many of his fellow aldermen, his participation in municipal government. His alienation from the projects of the booster elite lend his frequent ideological pronouncements a standing above the openly personal interests with which most of them evaluated government policies. Granger defended segmentation not because of its neutral effects on the real estate market but because it allowed the city to build infrastructure without committing the Jacksonian sins of high taxes or, especially, monopoly.

75. Andreas, *History*, 1:567.
76. CP, 1845/45:2486-A, 2535, 1855/56:1243, 1245, 1856/57:1923, 1857/58:73, 90, 105. After chairing the streets and bridges committee for several years, Granger moved to fire and water, where he made a major issue of firemen's refreshments at fires; 1847/47:3811, 1849/49:5788, 1850/50:6071. He also objected to "special fire wardens," an elite group that took an even more amateur interest in firefighting than the regular companies; 1847/47:3562, 1849/49:5512, 5575. Firemen addressed him contemptuously as "Old Plug" and at a fire in 1846 he physically threatened a fireman who took a break to clear the smoke from his eyes; 1846/46:3498. For Granger's political fate after the return of municipal partisanship, see chap. 5.

When the newly chartered Chicago Gas Light and Coke Company asked for a contract to light the city streets in 1849, Granger was quick in urging the council to guard "against any unreasonable monopoly which such Companys [sic] are sometimes disposed to exersise [sic] if they have the power." That the company's engineer, George F. Lee, also was involved in other facets of the city's financial management heightened the potential danger—Lee was a major creditor of the city and was then negotiating a complex transaction through which it acquired a public square.[77] In the spring of 1850 Lee erected ninety street lamps according to a plan that he designed and the council approved. The city then paid Lee by issuing bonds on the general fund.[78] This procedure invited abuse. If Granger's warning was to be heeded, decisions about how to expand the street lighting system clearly could not rest with the gas company itself. Yet if Lee did not design the lighting plan, who would? The council could make lighting decisions, though this would allow aldermen an easily abused discretion and encourage them to rely on Lee's technical advice.

The solution lay in segmenting the costs of street lighting by a process similar to special assessment. In November 1850, finding "no law to assess the benefits of street lighting," the council suspended all further lighting until private citizens raised subscriptions to cover half of the cost of each individual lamp. "When the sum of 7 1/2 Dollars is subscribed for any one lamp by the Citizens they shall designate the lamp they wish lighted, and deposit the money in advance for 6 [months]." These rules placed an automatic brake on expansion of the lighting system by giving decision power to the individuals who would bear the cost. Yet they also threatened to involve the city in unmanageable paperwork and to ignore the technological basis of gas lighting: the lamps had to be connected to gas mains laid by the company. Two weeks later the council repealed this order and authorized general funding of street lamps until the city could get charter amendments "to authorize lamp districts in the City and to make local assessments for the expenses incurred in street lighting."[79]

The legislature granted this power in the charter amendment of 1851, which the city's aldermen had drafted themselves. The city now

77. Ibid., 1849/49:6885. For Lee's dealings with the city, 1850/50:6174, 6259, 6324, 6395, 6411, 6414, 6429, 6451, 6453. Lee, a Philadelphian, tried to build a gas works in Milwaukee in the same year. Bayrd Still, *Milwaukee: The History of a City* (Madison: State Historical Society of Wisconsin, 1948), 246.

78. CP, 1850/50:6900–6902, 6908–10, 1851/52:543. On Lee's suggestion the council also created a committee on gas lights to confer with the company and make decisions on all matters relating to lighting; 1850/50:6363, 6911.

79. Ibid., 1850/50:6912, 6915.

could create lamp districts and levy special property taxes to cover three-fourths of the cost of the lighting, provided that "the money thus raised shall be exclusively expended for such purposes in the district paying the same."[80] Gas lighting, then, would be financed by special taxes, uniform property taxes levied on benefited jurisdictions, rather than by special assessments levied proportionately on particular tracts of benefited real estate. Property owners who wanted street lamps near their properties petitioned the council first for the creation of a lamp district and then for the erection and lighting of lamps in the district. The charter did not prescribe the size of lamp districts. The city tax levies of 1852 and 1853 specified half mill taxes for lighting only "in the lamp district of the south division."[81] Since only the south division, and perhaps only part of it, paid the lamp tax, street lighting appears to have been limited to the downtown commercial area.

That this outcome resulted from Lee's original plan should not obscure the effects of lamp districts on the decision-making process. First, the downtown property owners whose streets were lit paid most of the cost of the lighting. They did not gain this benefit at the expense of the rest of the city's taxpayers. Second, the system made lighting more of a private than public good. Property owners within a lamp district might resist the system's expansion rather than pressing unconditionally for increased lighting. Finally, the system set the property owners' interests in opposition to those of the gas company. Not only would they resist its demands for expansion, but neither the company nor politicians subject to its influence would make these decisions. The threat of "unreasonable monopoly" was reduced. Late in 1852 a company official submitted a list of lamps that he claimed were "wanted" (he did not say by whom). The committee on gas lights reported that they had "uniformly declined to recommend the errection [sic] of additional Lamps except in cases where they were petitioned for by . . . owners of property residing in the district."[82] Segmentation set up a countervailing political power to oppose that of the gas company. It was a system that could satisfy even Elihu Granger.

Street lighting was a special case in the segmentation of city government. Most public works did not involve a private company with

80. James, *Charters*, 158; CP, 1851/51:6702, 6750, 1851/52:300, 350. See also Moehring, *Public Works in Manhattan*, 102–6, for a lamp district system established in New York in 1833.

81. George Manierre, ed., *The Revised Charter and Ordinances of the City of Chicago* (Chicago: Daily Democrat, 1851), 63–65.

82. CP, 1852/53:900.

monopolistic power, though segmentation exerted a similar discipline on street contractors by encouraging property owners to monitor their activities. Lamp districts and special taxes also avoided the need to compute which property benefited from any particular lamp, a process required in special assessment projects. If special assessment was a "halfway house" between the property tax and a user charge, a special tax stood between the property tax and special assessment. Useful for improvements whose benefits could not be apportioned even with the limited precision of special assessment—Schumpeter called the assessment of benefit "something like an attempt to load a sack of flour on the shadow of an ass"[83]—special taxes were another tool with which the city's government segmented the costs of its public works.

Special taxes also were useful for large public works projects. The 1851 charter, in addition to authorizing the lamp districts, made the city's three divisions jurisdictions for special taxes. Applied to parks, market houses, and another attempt to build the lake shore protection, special taxes would have been helpful for the aqueduct system. Levied uniformly on all south division property, a special tax would have sidestepped property owners' individual judgments about the particular aqueduct for which they should have been assessed. Special taxes rested on the assumption that all property within a jurisdiction benefited similarly from an improvement. While special assessment depended on petitions from individuals, the charter required that special taxes gain the approval of a majority of aldermen elected from the division to be taxed. Special taxing jurisdictions could consist of existing political units, such as the divisions, or could be created in the charter for a specific improvement, as with the lamp districts.[84]

In a sense, most property taxes in Chicago in the 1850s were special taxes on the divisions. Property tax proceeds under the 1851 charter had to be spent in the division in which they were collected, "for all purposes strictly local." The property tax financed police protection, the fire department, and emergency situations such as the cholera epidemic of 1849, when the city paid physicians to treat indigent patients and set up a quarantine hospital to confine them.[85] As the next chapter will show, the property tax also helped to finance two large public works projects whose costs could not be

83. Joseph A. Schumpeter, "The Crisis of the Tax State" (1918), W. F. Stolper and R. A. Musgrave, trans., *American Economic Papers* 4 (1954): 23.
84. See James, *Charters*, 157–58.
85. Ibid., 156–59; CP, 1849/49:5527, 5644, 1852/53:688.

segmented, though aldermen did not implement these projects directly. In 1849, when Cook County organized itself into townships, the north, south, and west sides of the city not only became jurisdictions for the assessment of state property taxes but also acquired independent authority for some local government functions, causing an intergovernmental confusion that would plague the city into the twentieth century. The towns of North Chicago, South Chicago, and West Chicago also embraced territory outside of the city limits. The township law was the origin of the proliferation of special taxing districts that remains a feature of local government in Illinois.[86]

BY 1851, SEGMENTED financial instruments had replaced the city-wide property tax that the booster system had applied to public works. The legitimacy of special assessment was established by judicial decision and repeated use. As Chicagoans grew more comfortable with special assessments and special taxes, they used them more appropriately. They also combined them in varying proportions both with each other and with subscriptions. The point was to make as close a match as possible between the benefits and the costs of physical improvements. A close match would avoid redistributing wealth among property owners and ensure that the public works decision process remained free of paralyzing interest-group competition. If the location of real estate usually provided an adequate proxy for benefits that enhanced individual wealth, some projects defied such measurement. Voluntary subscriptions thus remained important for the financing of bridges, whose value to commuters and the firms to which they commuted made the link to particular tracts of real estate tenuous. As aldermen organized the special assessment process, private individuals organized the subscription process, though these often were the same people.[87]

The segmented system created a series of parallel lanes in the urban real estate market whose isolation city government protected. The city did not exert its power to favor development in any one of the lanes. It maintained an impartial stance among competing real estate developers at the same time that it provided the public works essential to their development plans. It allowed a government that was active in the local economy to avoid interest-group politics, log-

86. On the township law, see James, *Charters*, 125–29; Fisher and Fairbanks, *Illinois Municipal Finance*, 18–26; Charles Edward Merriam, Spencer D. Parratt, and Albert Lepawsky, *The Government of the Metropolitan Region of Chicago* (Chicago: University of Chicago Press, 1933).

87. Richard J. Hamilton to W. G. Ewing, March 24, May 10, 1849, Hamilton Letter-book, Chicago Historical Society; CP, 1847/47:3869, 1849/49:5203, 5288, 5742.

rolling, and charges of favoritism in the allocation of government funds. If municipal government remained neutral among its constituents, however, the segmented system defined this constituency in a particular manner. Aldermen represented real estate and served it with the public works that its owners demanded. The demands that other constituencies might have made were redistricted out of city politics by the real estate ward map. While the decision not to redistribute wealth among property owners appears to have been neutral and equitable—and the segmented system an ingenious method of accomplishing it—the system also represented a decision not to redistribute wealth among the citizens of Chicago. It represented, in other words, a decision about the class interest that municipal government would serve.

At the River and Harbor Convention, Chicagoans demanded that the wealthy states of the East subsidize internal improvement projects for western states that lacked enough capital to develop themselves. They promised that a developed West eventually would return this investment but presented themselves in the meantime as needy members of the national community whose very need justified downwardly redistributive national policies. They wanted the federal government to take from the wealthy East and give to the capital-starved West. The segmented system of city government prevented precisely this form of redistribution at the urban level. Chicagoans avoided outright vetoes and rousing protest meetings by designing a system that made the very articulation of downwardly redistributive public works demands impossible. Yet the segmented system also avoided upward redistribution, toward the wealthy. As it controlled the monopolistic power of the gas company, it also frustrated the shippers' attempts to get the city to finance river dredging in the 1850s through the general property tax. The segmented system neither took from the rich to give to the poor, nor took from the poor to give to the rich. It attempted to avoid all governmental redistribution of individual wealth.

The segmented system avoided political conflict by avoiding politics. It worked automatically and reduced politics to administration without intervention by the experts and trained administrators who later would make this their rallying cry as reformers. The tasks that aldermen performed were tedious but simple. Any man with business experience could guide special assessment projects through the council, though the courts presented other problems. Nonpartisan city elections prevented party leaders, particularly Democratic party leaders, from using their partisan appeals to organize a working-class constituency to make demands on the city's government. Nonpartisanship, however, also helped to curb the power that the wealthy later would exert through financial contributions to party coffers and outright bribes to city officials. Electioneering was individual, inexpensive, and based on candidates' claims of fidelity to the real estate interests of their wards. In the segmented system of city government, property owners reigned supreme. If the owners of larger tracts wielded disproportionate power in the decision process, they also bore disproportionate expenses not only through their higher property tax bills, but also through the segmented financial instruments.

Chicago was hardly a typical American city, and its implementation of the segmented system may have been extreme—especially in the combination of segmentation with nonpartisanship. Yet Chicagoans always had borrowed their laws and ordinances from the eastern cities whose models they respected. When aldermen tried to impeach Mayor James Curtiss in 1850 for failing to account for the fines collected in his police court, they taunted him in a manner that assumed this dependence: "Was he to go to Buffalo to see what the receipts of the Police Court were there when he wanted to know what they were in Chicago?"[88] The central administrative feature of the segmented system, special assessment financing of public works, was borrowed from the East, particularly from New York, but this borrowing did not determine Chicagoans' use of the system. They borrowed the legal structure in 1837 and ignored it for nearly a decade, until their own needs prompted them to use it. Chicagoans borrowed the tools of segmentation, but the system they created was their own.

New York's ward map, for example, bore little resemblance to the narrow strip design that Chicagoans adopted. As early as the 1830s, wards in New York seem to have been communities with dense networks of social and political institutions. As Amy Bridges has emphasized, New York politics by mid century reflected well-articulated class divisions in that city. By the 1850s, New York's workers had been struggling for political power for decades. They seem to have gained it locally in the regime of Fernando Wood, whose resistance to street contracting and "scandalous" charity program distributed employment and alms to workers during the decade's depressions. The "scandal" of Wood's policies, of course, lay in the very fact of their downward redistribution of wealth. New York's elite, meanwhile, turned its attention to a higher level of government—the federal level

88. CP, 1850/50:6503; Bayrd Still, "Patterns of Mid-Nineteenth Century Urbanization in the Middle West," *Mississippi Valley Historical Review* 28 (1941–42): 187–206.

that the Chicago boosters were unable to influence—and withdrew from formal participation in city government.[89] One result of their inattention by the 1860s was corruption in the special assessment system as politicians took control of the decision process and assessed property owners for the padded costs of unnecessary projects. New York's elite was a cosmopolitan elite whose interests extended beyond the boundaries of either New York City or New York State. Chicago's elite still depended on the growth of Chicago, however sanguine they had become about the prospect of that growth.

Neither could other western cities establish a segmentation quite as rigorous as Chicago's, though they borrowed from the same eastern models. These western cities needed a public good that Chicago was lucky enough to get for free. The importance of railroad connections for commercial development and urban growth encouraged many cities, particularly in the West, to invest public funds in railroad bonds. Milwaukee used its general taxation and borrowing powers to buy the bonds of eight separate railroad companies in the 1850s.[90] Chicago made no public railroad investments; the railroads fought one another for rights of way to enter Chicago. Mayor Thomas Dyer boasted in 1856 that "Chicago, as a city, has not invested one dollar in railroads. She stands, at present, the recipient of all their immense trade, wealth and business, and yet does not hold one dollar's worth of stock in them."[91] Chicago's ability to attract the railroads without offering them its tax proceeds allowed its city government to abandon citywide boosterism in a way cities such as Milwaukee could not. Chicago in the 1850s had the luxury of a rigorous segmentation.

Nevertheless, considerable evidence from both eastern and western cities suggests the general influence of segmented policy making. For New York in the 1830s (rather than 1850s), Stephen Diamond and Eugene P. Moehring have shown the importance of special assessment, while Moehring has documented a deference by aldermen to property owners in public works decision making every bit as rigorous as that of segmented Chicago.[92] Analyzing the government of Springfield, Massachusetts, in the 1850s, Michael H. Frisch has

89. Bridges, *City in the Republic*, 126–54.
90. George Rogers Taylor, *The Transportation Revolution, 1815–1860* (New York: Harper & Row, 1951), 92–94; Carter Goodrich, "The Revulsion against Internal Improvements," *Journal of Economic History* 10 (1950): 145–69; Douglas E. Booth, "Transportation, City Building, and Financial Crisis: Milwaukee, 1852–1868," *Journal of Urban History* 9 (1983): 335–63.
91. CP, 1856/57:1; John S. Wright, *Chicago: Past, Present, Future* (Chicago: Horton & Leonard, 1868), 28–29.
92. Diamond, "Death and Transfiguration"; Moehring, *Public Works in Manhattan*.

stressed privatization and decentralization. "In a real sense," according to Frisch, "the business of government was thus not public at all. . . . people generally accepted the principle that policy was the concern of those most directly involved, and of limited interest to others."[93] To cite a western example, the privatization of street work in San Francisco was spelled out in the first special assessment case to reach the California supreme court. In this 1857 decision, the court not only demanded that special assessment revenues be kept in separate accounts for each project (rather than aggregated into a general, public street fund) but interpreted the petition-based decision process as an essential component of the system.[94] Even Milwaukee, despite its railroad investments, had a government whose policy-making procedures reflected a stark enough privatization for the city's "urban biographer" to call the antebellum decades the "subscription stage" of Milwaukee's municipal history.[95]

The segmented system as implemented in Chicago was an ideal type of mid nineteenth-century American city government. Specific local conditions in the late 1840s—prosperity, an undeveloped class structure, a dormant party system, and the ability to attract private transportation investments—allowed Chicagoans to build a government system that expressed both their needs and their aspirations. By the late 1850s, this resolution no longer worked with the automatic character it assumed in the 1840s. By the late 1860s, it no longer worked at all. Before analyzing the decline of the segmented system, however, it is necessary to probe its successful operation for the nature of that success.

93. Frisch, *Town into City*, 43. Massachusetts, however, did not authorize Boston to levy special assessments (called "betterments" in that state) until 1866 and even then they raised little revenue. Charles Phillips Huse, *The Financial History of Boston* (Cambridge: Harvard University Press, 1916), 73, 154–55, 307–308.

94. *Lucas, Turner & Co. v. San Francisco*, 7 Cal. 463 (1857). In California, special assessments were called "street assessments."

95. Still, *Milwaukee*, 230, 251–53. For later developments, Roger D. Simon, *The City-Building Process: Housing and Services in New Milwaukee Neighborhoods, 1880–1910*, Transactions of the American Philosophical Society, vol. 68, pt. 5 (Philadelphia, 1978).

4

The Mechanics of Local Control

EVALUATED ON ITS own terms, the segmented system was one of the major success stories of urban political history. In the amount of public works constructed, the absence of corruption, and the responsiveness of officials to the demands of their constituents, the system worked more effectively and with less political conflict than almost any imaginable alternative. The segmented system channelled private capital into public works through privatization, by ensuring that local groups of property owners controlled those aspects of the improvement process that affected their own holdings. In a rapidly growing city, the system enabled real estate developers to plan localized growth with only minimal interference from outside. It expressed the American commitment to "privatism" in a pristine form.[1] Yet, as urban historians have shown, this privatized success story also made the American urban landscape a physical expression of political inequality. Visible in macadam, plank, and mud and recorded in the high death rates in working-class neighborhoods, this landscape was another product of privatized government.[2] That segmented city-building policies formed the primary busi-

1. Sam Bass Warner, Jr., *The Private City: Philadelphia in Three Periods of Its Growth* (Philadelphia: University of Pennsylvania Press, 1968).

2. Eugene P. Moehring, *Public Works and the Patterns of Urban Real Estate in Manhattan, 1835–1894* (New York: Arno Press, 1981); Olivier Zunz, *The Changing Face of Inequality: Urbanization, Industrial Development, and Immigrants in Detroit, 1880–1920* (Chicago: University of Chicago Press, 1982); Roger D. Simon, *The City-Building Process: Housing and Services in New Milwaukee Neighborhoods, 1880–1910,* Transactions of the American Philosophical Society, vol. 68, pt. 5 (Philadelphia, 1978); Carl V. Harris, *Political Power in Birmingham, 1871–1921* (Knoxville: University of Tennessee Press, 1977); Christine Meisner

ness of Chicago's government in the 1850s had important consequences for the nature of that government and its role in the community. That the details of segmented administration absorbed the attention of officials who were committed—unquestioningly—to local control makes a grasp of these details crucial to understanding the system itself.

ON MARCH 12, 1849, a flood washed out all five of the bridges spanning the Chicago River and destroyed nearly 100 vessels that had been locked in the river's suddenly mobile ice. Carried by water rushing toward the lake, the former components of wharves and ships smashed into each bridge in sequence, adding the iron and wood of the bridges themselves to the destructive power of the current. By 1853 the city had eight new bridges over the river, most of substantially better quality than those the river had claimed.[3] Bridges were necessary for Chicago's commercial life. Chicagoans had planted the core of their settlement along the banks of the river's three branches in order to capitalize on its connection to both Lake Michigan and the Illinois and Michigan Canal. They used the river for transportation as well as for water supply and sewerage, with the latter combination exacerbating a public health problem that took decades to overcome.[4] The river's location in the center of the city, however, also formed a physical obstacle to social and commercial intercourse. Bridges were essential components of the city's infrastructure and public goods that its government had to provide.

Bridges had been a problem for Chicago's government in the booster years. Citywide decision-making procedures had turned bridge debates into political free-for-alls as proponents of bridges clashed with opponents and the partisans of various locations tried to block one another's plans. After the flood, however, the city built eight bridges in four years. The key to this success was subscription financing that transformed bridges from public goods into private in-

Rosen, *The Limits of Power: Great Fires and the Process of City Growth in America* (Cambridge: Cambridge University Press, 1986). These studies document vast inequality in the distribution of public works and link that inequality to special assessment financing.

3. A. T. Andreas, *History of Chicago* (3 vols.; Chicago: Andreas, 1884–86), 1:200–202.

4. See Louis P. Cain, *Sanitation Strategy for a Lakefront Metropolis: The Case of Chicago* (DeKalb: Northern Illinois University Press, 1978); James C. O'Connell, "Technology and Pollution: Chicago's Water Policy, 1833–1930" (Ph.D. diss., University of Chicago, 1980).

vestments.[5] Two weeks after the disaster, the council offered a reward for the best bridge design and floated a $6,000 loan to spend on bridge reconstruction, provided that private citizens raised the balance of bridge costs by subscription. The adopted design turned out to be a patent infringement, causing some delay, but late in April aldermen ordered two temporary bridges thrown over the river "in the cheapest manner that will admit of the passage of teams, and in as short time as possible." Using materials from destroyed bridges and ferries, they built a temporary bridge over the South Branch for $110 and a similar structure over the main branch.[6]

The temporary bridges removed the sense of emergency from decisions about bridge reconstruction. By responding quickly to the public demand for river crossings, aldermen gave themselves room to maneuver in negotiating for subscriptions to finance more durable and permanent structures. They began this process in April with a threat. Property owners who wanted the Randolph Street bridge replaced were given two weeks to raise one-third of its cost. If they failed to subscribe this amount, the council would move the bridge to Washington Street, where, aldermen hinted, funds could be raised immediately. The Randolph Street partisans raised the money. Subscribers also paid part of the cost of the other replacement bridges and raised the entire cost of three new bridges.[7] Citywide revenues financed two-thirds of the costs of the replacement bridges. While the flood seems in hindsight to have been a public calamity that demanded a public response, Chicagoans actually justified this general funding differently. Aldermen defended general fund contributions for replacement bridges by pointing to the private subscriptions that had financed the original structures. These subscriptions were relevant because of the manner in which Chicagoans defined bridges and other public works in the 1850s.

Chicagoans understood bridges less as public facilities than as capital improvements tending to raise the value of real estate. Rather than public goods, whose costs would have been public responsibilities, bridges were investments that enhanced the value of privately

5. In economic theory, a public good is an indivisible commodity whose supply and demand are regulated politically, rather than by economic processes that match individual calculations of demand to market determinants of supply. Rosen, *Limits of Power*, is a historical application of the theory.

6. Chicago City Council Proceedings Files [hereafter CP], 1849/49:5204, 5237, 5286–87, 5301–3.

7. Ibid., 1849/49:5288, 5543, 1850/50:5941. The Randolph Street owners opted for a cheap bridge that soon had to be rebuilt; 1849/49:5681, 5696, 5770, 1850/50:5891. For the other bridges, 1849/49:5203, 5287, 5468, 5743, 1852/53:594, 1855/56:1821.

owned land. By subscribing funds for the bridges they wanted, property owners conferred capital gains on their own properties. Those who wanted bridges paid for them, while those who opposed such investments did not. Chicagoans thus avoided citywide debates that might have entangled bridge decisions in the competition of rival developers, the state of the city treasury, the equitable distribution of public services, or the property tax rate. When the flood created a public need for bridges, aldermen acted quickly to ensure that permanent structures could not be construed as public goods by property owners attempting to resist the cost of subscription. They modified their strict reliance on subscription for the replacement bridges because, by subscribing for the original bridges, owners already had paid for gains long since capitalized into their property values.[8] Nevertheless, "interested" property owners raised at least one-third of the cost of each replacement bridge.

Chicagoans explicitly and repeatedly insisted on land value enhancement as the basis of public works financing. Property owners seeking public funds for a new bridge in progress at Lake Street in 1852 met resistance from aldermen who knew that Lake Street property "has advanced very much in value in anticipation of the Bridge" and insisted that Lake Street landholders therefore should bear its cost.[9] Four years later, when other property owners asked for public bridge funding, aldermen again denied public responsibility:

> Your Special Committee do not know of any Bridge that is *not* a City thorough-fare—nor have they a doubt but the present Bridge at Chicago Avenue was built by the then owners of the real estate in its vicinity for the purpose of enhancing the value and facilitating the sale of the same—and as such end was undoubtedly accomplished, your Committee cannot see any good reason to deviate from the general rule, which requires the property owners more immediately benefited to pay a proportion of the expense.[10]

Chicagoans debated about particular public works policies not only in terms of private land value accretions but with a clear understanding of the manner in which improvements were capitalized into land value. Governmental procedures based on the benefits accruing to real estate were implemented by men who knew the real estate market.

Aldermen in the segmented system of city government worked to

8. Ibid., 1852/53:594.
9. Ibid. See also 1851/52:1457–58, 1852/53:843.
10. Ibid., 1855/56:1821 (emphasis in original). For a similar argument about capitalization in a street project, see 1857/58:1236.

build consensus on improvement demands among the property owners in their wards and to translate this consensus into construction.
Subscriptions measured the demand for public works directly; those
property owners who wanted a project raised the cash for it. Yet subscriptions did not correlate the desire for a project with the distribution of its actual economic benefits. The city could threaten not to
build a bridge without some aggregate private contribution, but property owners had to apportion this total among themselves. Thus Richard J. Hamilton mobilized his neighbors to subscribe for the Clark
Street bridge. "In reference to the bridge," he wrote to an absentee
owner, "I have been able to get along with a hundred dollars from
you[;] if we could have followed your suggestions we should no
doubt have done better, that is to make an equitable assessment on
all alike, but property holders more remote and whose benefits are
more indirect would not consent to any such arrangement knowing
there were others that would have the bridge at all events and thus
by such meanness avoid giving any thing."[11] Subscription financing,
as Hamilton understood, suffered from two weaknesses as a tool for
capital mobilization: a lack of equitable assessment and the free-rider
problem. Special assessment solved both of these, though at the price
of an individual-level articulation of demand.

Special assessment made contributions from the property owners
who benefited from an improvement project mandatory and enforce-
able. Special assessors first estimated the distribution of benefits that
a project would confer and then assessed its cost on the owners of
the benefited property in sums proportional to this distribution. Nobody pretended that these estimates reflected the distribution of
benefits in a precise manner. Assessors, after all, estimated benefits
that would accrue to properties in the future, though anticipatory
capitalization eased their task. Chicagoans searched for assessment
methods that would ensure the legitimacy of special assessments.
They even developed shortcuts that were designed to sacrifice precision to the appearance of equity.[12] The system's legitimacy rested less

11. Richard J. Hamilton to W. G. Ewing, May 10, 1849, Hamilton Letterbook, Chicago Historical Society.

12. See esp. CP, 1858/59:52, 966-A. The 1861 charter mandated assessment by front-
foot and on abutters only. The Illinois supreme court ruled this unconstitutional,
though other state courts accepted it. Illinois, *Laws, 1861*, 123; *Chicago v. Larned*, 34
Ill. 203 (1864); Stephen Diamond, "The Death and Transfiguration of Benefit Taxation:
Special Assessments in Nineteenth-Century America," *Journal of Legal Studies* 12
(1983): 201–40; Victor Rosewater, *Special Assessments: A Study in Municipal Finance* (New
York: Columbia University, 1898), 29–56, 67–68. Modern studies urge the use of complex assessment formulas not because they are precise, but because daunting mathe-

on its mathematical precision than on its procedural safeguards and the personal reputations of assessors. Special assessors had to be impartial, careful, and knowledgeable about the city's real estate market. Property owners had to trust that they competently could and faithfully would judge the effects of a public works project on the value of the real estate in its vicinity.

The key concept in special assessment was the "particular" benefit that certain property owners derived from an improvement. Chicagoans recognized that public works actually were public goods. They knew that a physical infrastructure of streets, bridges, sidewalks, and sewers not only would make the entire city more healthful, convenient, and attractive but also would promote the growth of population and commerce that was essential for victory in the intercity booster rivalry—Chicago in the 1850s still lagged well behind St. Louis. Chicagoans knew, as city attorney Elliott Anthony argued in 1858, that "it does not follow because property happens to be situated off from a public street which is being improved that it may not be benefited—& that the individual occupying the same may not also be benefited, that in a great city like this, no man can live within himself—he cannot always travel on the street that lies before his door."[13] Chicagoans may also have known that even the propertyless gained benefits from walking on paved streets and crossing the river by bridge, though there is no evidence that any concern for the interests of the propertyless—either in costs or in benefits—graced the public works debates of the propertied.[14] Yet propertied Chicagoans definitely knew that individual public works projects benefited some of them more than others. In addition to their public benefits as usable infrastructure, they conferred "particular" benefits to land value. If projects were financed from the general property tax, city officials would have to apportion these "particular" benefits through a political process subject to delay, logrolling, and, possibly, corruption.

Special assessment projects formed a major component of the business handled by Chicago's city council in the 1850s. The detailed rules governing their use meant that special assessments generated a great

---

matics gives the appearance of scientific expertise. Jorge Macon and Jose Merino Mañon, *Financing Urban and Rural Development through Betterment Levies: The Latin American Experience* (New York: Praeger, 1977), 87–93; William A. Doebele, et al., "Participation of Beneficiaries in Financing Urban Services: Valorization Charges in Bogotá, Colombia," *Land Economics* 55 (1979): 89–90.

13. CP, 1858/59:52.

14. Cf. Elizabeth Blackmar, *Manhattan for Rent, 1785–1850* (Ithaca: Cornell University Press, 1989), 168.

FIG. 4 CHICAGO FROM THE LAKE, 1853

deal of paperwork, most of which required action by aldermen. Of all the documents passing through the council in the 1850s (including such routine matters as official oaths), special assessments generated a quarter in 1851 and 1852, between a third and half from 1853 to 1856, and slightly more than half in 1857 and 1858, after which their incidence fell because of public works cutbacks during the Panic of 1857. Aldermen, who met only one or two evenings a week, clearly spent much of their official time in the 1850s on special assessments.[15] The predominance of special assessments in council business, however, reflected more than their paper-generating power. Chicagoans used special assessment to finance an explosion of public works construction in the 1850s. The city's 3 miles of planked street in 1849 grew to 27 by 1854, when property owners began to replace the plank altogether with macadam and Nicholson (wooden brick and tar) pavements. Hundreds of miles of sidewalk, several new bridges, the water works, and the sewerage system expressed Chicagoans' financial commitment to public works in the 1850s.[16]

15. Computed from Robert E. Bailey, et al., eds., *Chicago City Council Proceedings Files 1833–1871: An Inventory* (Springfield: Illinois State Archives, 1987). City officials did not compute the annual aggregate cost of special assessments until 1862. The city's general tax rate inched upward in the 1850s, from 0.35 percent of assessed valuation in 1850 to 0.76 percent by 1855 to a high of 1.57 percent in 1857. It dropped back to 1.01 percent in 1860. Computed from Chicago, Department of Finance, *Annual Statement, 1877* (Chicago: Hazlitt & Reed, 1878), 172–73. This gradual rise in the general tax rate may be contrasted with the sharp increase in time that the council allocated to special assessment.

16. Homer Hoyt, *One Hundred Years of Land Values in Chicago* (Chicago: University of Chicago Press, 1933), 64; Ann Durkin Keating, "Governing the New Metropolis: The

The city's property owners could afford this burst of public works construction because Chicago was in the midst of a second land boom. Values rose precipitously after 1848, and investment in new buildings soared. Unlike the 1830s boom, which had been fueled by pure speculation, the land value rise of the 1850s rested on palpable evidence of city growth. As railroads entered the city, they stimulated both commerce and industry and carried thousands of migrants to Chicago. The city's population more than tripled, from 30,000 in 1850 to 109,000 in 1860. Rising demand for housing and business facilities spurred new construction. The total assessed valuation of Chicago's land and buildings grew from $5.7 million in 1850 to $21.6 million in 1855 and $31.2 million in 1860.[17] The city's wealthier businessmen directed their capital into real estate, especially commercial property. Craig Buettinger has found that two-thirds of Chicago's 37 leading landlords in 1857 had retired from other occupations at a mean age of 46 to devote their full attention to real estate development. After closing their stores, banks, or professional offices, announcing that they had "retired from active trade," they pursued real estate operations that became less risky and more profitable as the city grew.[18]

Chicago's developers were an aggressive lot. Men like William B. Ogden and Richard J. Hamilton did not wait idly for their lands to appreciate. They developed their holdings with buildings, especially the brick buildings known as "business blocks." Most had erected brick structures on their downtown lots by 1857.[19] They also predominated among the property owners sending public works petitions to the council, though a precise measurement of their representation must await further research. Their investments in street projects complemented their investments in buildings. Both were part of a development strategy, as John Wentworth explained to David Davis in 1852. Davis, Wentworth noted, was "now the only obstacle" to a project that would raise the value of his own property. "Like you, Judge," he continued, "I am holding upon mine for the rise, but I have always gone in for streets, & so have Ogden, Jones, Scammon

---

Development of Urban and Suburban Governments in Cook County, Illinois, 1831 to 1902" (Ph.D. diss., University of Chicago, 1984), 63–93. Also Ann Durkin Keating, *Building Chicago: Suburban Developers and the Creation of a Divided Metropolis* (Columbus: Ohio State University Press, 1988).

17. Hoyt, *One Hundred Years*, 62–73, 483, 487.

18. Craig Buettinger, "The Concept of Jacksonian Aristocracy: Chicago as a Test Case, 1833–1857" (Ph.D. diss., Northwestern University, 1982), 44–56, 97–98.

19. Ibid., 10–18, 88–94.

& all our successful speculators."[20] Wentworth made a similar argument in his newspaper, hoping that "property holders will see that it is in their interest to improve as fast as practicable the streets upon which their lots lie."[21] Unlike the construction of buildings, however, public works projects required the owners of neighboring property to work together. As Hamilton mobilized his neighbors for the Clark Street bridge, Chicago's developers organized through the special assessment system to build other kinds of infrastructure.

While these developers did not own all of Chicago's real property, they owned a large portion of it. Buettinger found that the wealthiest 1 percent of Chicago's adult males in 1849 and 1850 owned 52 percent of the city's total wealth, a more concentrated distribution even than those of the major eastern cities. While the richest fourth owned all of the wealth on the tax rolls, however, federal census takers found fairly widespread ownership of small parcels of real estate among skilled and even unskilled workers. Less than one-fifth of the adult males in Chicago were property owners in 1850, though this figure rose to one-fourth by 1860 and, when only household heads are considered, to almost one-third in both census years.[22] Most property owners, of course, owned small amounts of property: in 1850, 36 percent of the owners reported holdings valued at $500 or less, and 64 percent reported $1,000 or less. By 1860, perhaps because of generally rising land values, only 10 percent of the owners had holdings of $500 or less, but 54 percent still had $1,000 or less. In 1850, when 22 percent of Chicago's skilled workers and 14 percent of its unskilled workers owned at least some property, the wealthiest 10 percent of the property owners owned an estimated 82 percent of the property reported on the census. In 1860, when 27 percent of the city's skilled

20. Wentworth to Davis, May 22, 1852, folder 33, David Davis papers, Chicago Historical Society. Wentworth also argued that landowners had to heed public demand outside the city limits: "Besides, if we do not make these streets to suit the people, the Jurisdiction of the city will be extended over us so as to not only compel us to make the streets but also to pay City Taxes."

21. *Democrat*, January 5, 1852. "Wherever the streets have been planked," the paper claimed, "there the greatest appreciation in the value of property, other things being equal is visible."

22. Craig Buettinger, "Economic Inequality in Early Chicago, 1849–50," *Journal of Social History* 11 (1978): 414–15; John B. Jentz and Richard Schneirov, "Class and Politics in an Antebellum Commercial Boom Town, Chicago, 1848–1861," Working Paper, Origins of Chicago's Industrial Working Class Project, Newberry Library. The census figures reported in this and the next paragraph are analyzed in more detail in appendix 2 below, which also describes the data set on which they are based. Eric H. Monkkonen, *America Becomes Urban: The Development of U.S. Cities and Towns, 1780–1980* (Berkeley: University of California Press, 1988), 199, suggests that "the mid-century era may have had the lowest urban home owning proportions in U.S. history."

and 18 percent of its unskilled workers owned property, the wealthiest 10 percent of the owners still owned about 74 percent of the property.

Appendix 2 presents a more complete analysis of the census figures, but it is important to establish the heterogeneity of the population of property owners. Almost every owner was a man, almost all of them over the age of 20, but the population of property owners was not markedly different from the population of adult men as a whole. In 1850, 66 percent of Chicago's adult men were immigrants (21 percent from the German states and 26 percent from Ireland) and 63 percent of the property owners were immigrants (though while 29 percent were German, only 17 percent were Irish). These figures are similar for 1860, when immigrants comprised an even larger proportion of the population: 72 percent of the men were immigrants (29 German and 27 Irish), and 73 percent of the owners were immigrants (33 German and 25 Irish). The overrepresentation of German immigrants among the propertied is clear and, as historians also have found in other nineteenth-century American cities, it cut across lines of occupational class: German men had high rates of ownership despite the fact that 54 percent of them were skilled and 29 percent unskilled workers in 1850. Only 37 percent of native-born men were skilled and only 13 percent unskilled; the rest had white-collar occupations (the Irish were 28 percent skilled and 57 percent unskilled).[23] Thus, while native-born men with high-level white-collar occupations (chiefly in commerce and the professions) were overrepresented in the owning population—and owned a majority of the property—the Ogdens, Hamiltons, Scammons, and Wentworths shared their status as property owners with many other men very different from them.[24]

23. The federal census did not tabulate home-ownership directly until 1880, but the high immigrant and working-class rates for real property resemble the home-ownership rates revealed by a state census in Buffalo, New York, in 1855 as well as those historians have found for the period after 1880. Thus, Zunz, *Changing Face*, 152–56, found that German and Polish immigrants were more likely to own their homes than native-born whites in Detroit in 1900. As Zunz summarizes the findings of his and other studies, "owning one's home was more an ethnocultural phenomenon than one of class," and was not in any sense an emblem of middle-class status (p. 153). In Milwaukee in 1850 and 1860, however, the native-born were more likely than Germans to own property; Kathleen Neils Conzen, *Immigrant Milwaukee, 1836–1860: Accommodation and Community in a Frontier City* (Cambridge: Harvard University Press, 1976), 77. For Buffalo, Michael B. Katz, Michael J. Doucet, and Mark J. Stern, *The Social Organization of Early Industrial Capitalism* (Cambridge: Harvard University Press, 1982), 146–47.

24. The high white-collar group constituted 10 percent of the adult men and 14 percent of the property owners in 1850; they were 7 percent of the men and 15 percent

In 1850, 47 percent of Chicago's property owners were skilled and 22 percent unskilled workers; in 1860, these figures were 40 and 25 percent, respectively.

Wealthy developers, middle-class homeowners, and workers who owned only houselots or just houses built on leased land had different public works priorities. Roger D. Simon has shown the reluctance with which working-class owners in Milwaukee paid special assessments in the early twentieth century, sacrificing pavements, piped water, and sewerage to their struggles for home-ownership. Olivier Zunz found much the same thing in Detroit in the 1880s.[25] Ann Durkin Keating, meanwhile, has described the improvement strategies with which Chicago's suburban developers attracted residential buyers as early as the 1860s. Developments aimed at workers included only houses, those intended for middle-class buyers included some improvements, while those built for the wealthy contained larger ranges of services.[26] Decision procedures that had to arbitrate these variable demands could have generated enormous political conflict. If, on the one hand, public works were conceived as general public goods whose distribution would be determined by need, or by the politics of numbers at the polls, wealthy developers might have found themselves asked to subsidize streets and sidewalks for the mass of poorer owners, the far larger mass of nonowners, or perhaps just for neighborhoods with unusual political clout. If, however, public works were generally financed but distributed by some other measure of influence—say, to campaign contributors or those paying large bribes—then poorer owners might have found themselves asked to subsidize the aggressive development plans of the wealthy. In either case the result would have taken the form of the conflict and bargaining of competing groups that characterizes modern urban politics, that is, subsidies for downtown redevelopment in return for pothole repairs in the neighborhoods.[27]

In the 1850s, municipal politics in Chicago did not take this form.

---

of the owners in 1860. The high white-collar owners owned an estimated 73 percent of the property in 1850 and 61 percent in 1860.

25. Simon, *City-Building Process,* 35–45; Zunz, *Changing Face,* 174.

26. Ann Durkin Keating, "Infrastructure and Urban Growth in the Nineteenth Century," *Essays in Public Works History* 14 (December 1985): 15–18. Simon, *City-Building Process,* contains similar evidence from Milwaukee. For a theoretical analysis of this phenomenon, Charles M. Tiebout, "A Pure Theory of Local Expenditures," *Journal of Political Economy* 64 (1956): 416–24.

27. I am not claiming that everyone does or can win in the modern system of interest-group competition, but only that the pluralist contest is the form that modern decision making generally takes.

In fact, it is difficult to imagine how it could have. Even the ludicrously narrow dispute in the 1830s between the handful of north side warehouse owners who wanted a bridge and the handful of south side grain merchants who did not was "settled" by axe-wielding vigilantes. By the 1850s, with Chicago's leading developers anxious to build lavishly and the city's overall population of owners more diverse, potential conflicts over public works policy making became a good deal more complicated. If Chicago's "booster" developers could not even settle public works disputes among themselves, a citywide decision-making process involving the whole property-owning population was unthinkable. These developers, then, needed a public works decision-making process that avoided not only their competition with one another but also the resistance that less investment-oriented owners might have raised to the high taxes that an aggressive and publicly financed improvement program would have required. Despite their collective dominance of the city's wealth structure, these developers lacked the economic power that would have enabled them either to ignore the city's government or to coerce it to grant public subsidies. George Pullman, who would build his industrial model town without government interference, and the meat-packing giants, who would threaten to destroy Chicago's economy if the city did not finance public works for them, loomed relatively far in the future in the early 1850s.[28] Even the wealthiest Chicagoans still depended on government to manage public works financing.

Yet management was different from subsidy. What the developers needed was help in their local consensus building: a formal process that could mobilize neighbors to invest in the public works that would benefit them collectively but not involve the owners of any other properties that would not share in such benefits. They needed a process that ensured—or at least assumed—that public works were not public goods whose merits could be debated citywide. They needed direct control of the improvement of their own holdings, the power to plan local development locally, and they were willing to pay for this power by bearing the costs of their improvement projects on the same local basis. This arrangement, implemented most directly through the special assessment system, rested on certain assumptions about the nature of political equity. In particular, the vast majority of poorer owners and nonowners accepted the physical

28. On Pullman, see Stanley Buder, *Pullman: An Experiment in Industrial Order and Community Planning, 1880–1930* (Chicago: University of Chicago Press, 1977); Keating, "From City to Metropolis," 20. The packers' demands are analyzed in detail in chap. 6 below.

consequences of privatized government. Freed from the costs of subsidizing the developers' plans, none of them seems to have considered the possibility of demanding subsidies for themselves. It seems never to have occurred to anyone, in fact, that the city might have a "public interest" in the attractiveness, the convenience, or even the health of neighborhoods that could not purchase these benefits on their own. While the wealthy paid for their control of policy making in high special assessment levies, therefore, the poor paid for their low tax costs in voicelessness, in a governmental decision-making process based directly on wealth rather than, either directly or indirectly, on the power of numbers of ballots.

THE SPECIAL ASSESSMENT process in the segmented system consisted of a rigorously defined administrative procedure and a highly stylized rhetoric. Each stage in the policy-making process had rules that regulated both the eligibility of participants and the arguments that these participants could make. Thus, although the process elicited constant bargaining and contention, it also set strict limits on the range of admissible debate. The obvious character of these limits is an artifact of hindsight, of the fact that the boundaries enclosing debate in the segmented system are different from any analogous boundaries that may circumscribe urban political debate today.[29] The segmented limits stand out because the conflicts waged within them were waged in a rhetoric that sounds strikingly foreign to the observer holding more modern assumptions about politics. There is no evidence to suggest that anyone ever challenged the basic rules of the public works game in the 1850s. There is overwhelming evidence, however, that many Chicagoans understood both the rules and the best ways to manipulate them to advantage. Within the boundaries, in other words, the city's diverse population of property owners (ownership was the basic eligibility requirement) pursued their interests with sophistication. This can be appreciated only in the context of the rules and procedures that structured their efforts.

The special assessment process began with a petition, which described a physical improvement that its signers wanted the city to make. This project could range in scale from a single block-face of sidewalk to several blocks of street planking or macadam to the acquisition and improvement of a park. Rather than advancing any particu-

29. For a concise, though hostile, review and critique of efforts to delineate modern boundaries, Nelson W. Polsby, *Community Power and Political Theory: A Further Look at Problems of Evidence and Inference*, 2d ed. (New Haven: Yale University Press, 1980), chap. 11.

lar reasons why this project was desirable, petitioners argued only that they had developed a consensus in favor of the project among the owners of the property that would be assessed for it. While petitioners always claimed that this consensus existed, they sometimes also buttressed the claim by listing the lots that each signer owned. No laws before 1861 specified a necessary degree of consensus, but property owners and the aldermen who read their petitions generally understood that the consensus should include the owners of at least half of all property that would be liable for the assessment (that is, half of the total value of the property that would appear on the assessment roll). At this stage of the process, neither the owners nor their alderman knew precisely which property the assessors ultimately would include in the assessment. Not until 1859 did the council formally limit assessment liability in street projects to abutters, thus determining in advance which properties would be charged. Nevertheless, because assessment commissioners usually did charge abutters, petitioners listed their holdings in numbers of abutting front-feet.[30]

When the petition reached the council, the city clerk sent it to the alderman sitting on a streets and alleys committee who represented the ward in which the improvement would be made (each ward elected two aldermen for staggered two-year terms). In 1847, when the council began to use special assessment on a large scale, they replaced the single committee that had examined all public works proposals in the booster system with three streets and alleys committees, one for each division. While all other council committees (except the one sorting the wharfing claims) consisted of three aldermen appointed at the mayor's discretion, council rules required the mayor to appoint one alderman from each ward to a divisional streets and alleys committee. Thus from 1847 to 1857 the South Division committee (SASD) had four members, the West Division committee (SAWD) had two, and the North Division committee (SAND) had three; as the ward map changed, these numbers grew. Committee reports concerning special assessment projects almost always were unanimous because committee members left these decisions to the aldermen of the affected wards.[31]

30. For the limitation of assessment liability, CP, 1858/59:966-A. The 1861 charter was the first to require petitions, but it also created a Board of Public Works that took the public works decision-making process out of the council; Illinois, *Laws, 1861*, 125.

31. CP, 1846/46:3058, 1854/55:1503; George Manierre, ed., *The Revised Charter and Ordinances of the City of Chicago* (Chicago: Daily Democrat, 1851), vii, 23–24. The divisions were the basis of special taxes, which required approval by a majority of aldermen from the division to be taxed. After 1849, the divisions also belonged to separate townships for state tax purposes. The wharfing privilege committee had five members.

In addition to petitions, the aldermen on streets and alleys committees often received remonstrances. These documents tended to say that while the signers had "heard" that their neighbors were circulating an improvement petition, the circulators had not consulted them about the proposed project. Remonstrants usually wanted to block a project to avoid its assessment, though some used this tactic to influence project specifications, generally in ways that reduced cost. Like petitioners, remonstrants avoided substantive debate about the project itself. They claimed only that they, rather than the petitioners, owned a majority of the affected real estate (sometimes listing their holdings) and that they opposed the project. Remonstrants also tried to impugn the claims of petitioners to the ownership of affected property. While remonstrants charged that petitioners really were street contractors hoping to be awarded work or railroad promoters attempting to force local owners to pay for projects that benefited distant properties (i.e., by providing access to a nonabutting depot), petitioners responded that remonstrants were tenants rather than owners or ineligible for some similar reason to participate in the decision.[32]

Aldermen solved conflicts between petitioners and remonstrants by counting the amounts of affected real estate owned by each. Influences and priorities besides the wishes of "interested" property owners had no place in the public works decision process, as petitioners, remonstrants, and aldermen argued repeatedly. The skewed nature of property ownership in Chicago, of course, meant that these decisions might involve both a few owners of large tracts and many owners of small ones. That the large landowners tended more readily to favor improvements suggests a coercive aspect of the special assessment process. The system was stacked against small-scale owners unless their streets contained only (or chiefly) small holdings, in which case fewer improvement petitions would have been circulated in the first place. A systematic study of nineteenth-century special assessment rolls would help to determine the degree to which large- and small-scale property owners actually mingled on improved streets at different points in time, thus contributing to a more precise notion of the economic incidence of special assessment, the correlation between magnitude of property holding and demand for public works, and the economic structure of neighborhoods. It might also add a policy-based dimension to our understanding of residential segregation in the nineteenth century: the segmented decision process may have created additional incentives for working-

32. CP, 1855/56:1998, 2204, 1860/61:94.

class and immigrant homeowners (but not necessarily renters) to choose neighborhoods where they were protected against the large public works demands and proportionately greater policy-making influence of the wealthy.[33]

In any case, public works debates did not always result in all-or-nothing decisions. While aldermen had to accede to the wishes of property owners, they could build a consensus for an improvement project by modifying its specifications. Thus, after debate between petitioners and remonstrants, neither of whom owned a majority of the property liable to assessment for the planking of Ringgold Place and Cottage Grove Avenue in 1856, aldermen conciliated the remonstrants by ordering the use of a narrower plank than the petitioners had requested, thereby cutting the project's cost.[34] Projects that crossed ward boundaries were more complex, in part because they involved more than one alderman. When a petition to widen Twelfth Street between Michigan Avenue and the South Branch encountered opposition, SASD split the project into two parts so that its supporters could have their portion while its opponents defeated or delayed theirs. That they split the project at State Street, the ward boundary, suggests the importance of individual aldermen as consensus builders in the assessment process. While the First Ward portion of Twelfth Street was widened immediately, the Second Ward part of the project was delayed for several months.[35]

Once a streets and alleys committee approved a project, the council ordered a street commissioner to estimate its cost. If the project involved opening a new street or widening an existing one, the council also applied to the county court for a writ of condemnation and ordered the city surveyor to survey the property to be taken. The surveyor generally was a professional, elected on the mayor's ticket in elections that used party tickets. Street commissioners, on the other hand, were elected by the divisions and tended to be immigrant political leaders. The political roles of street commissioners will be described in the next chapter; it is important here to note only that they controlled some public works patronage through the street labor system (for routine repairs) but took no part in the decision-making process. After 1856 the council appointed a superintendent of public

33. See appendix 2. For suggestive discussions of the economics of special assessment, Simon, *City-Building Process;* Moehring, *Public Works in Manhattan;* Harris, *Political Power,* 176–85; Zunz, *Changing Face,* 174–76; Clay McShane, "Transforming the Use of Urban Space: A Look at the Revolution in Street Pavements, 1880–1924," *Journal of Urban History* 5 (1979): 283–85.
34. CP, 1855/56:2204.
35. Ibid., 1855/56:602, 1856/57:26, 202, 253, 1120.

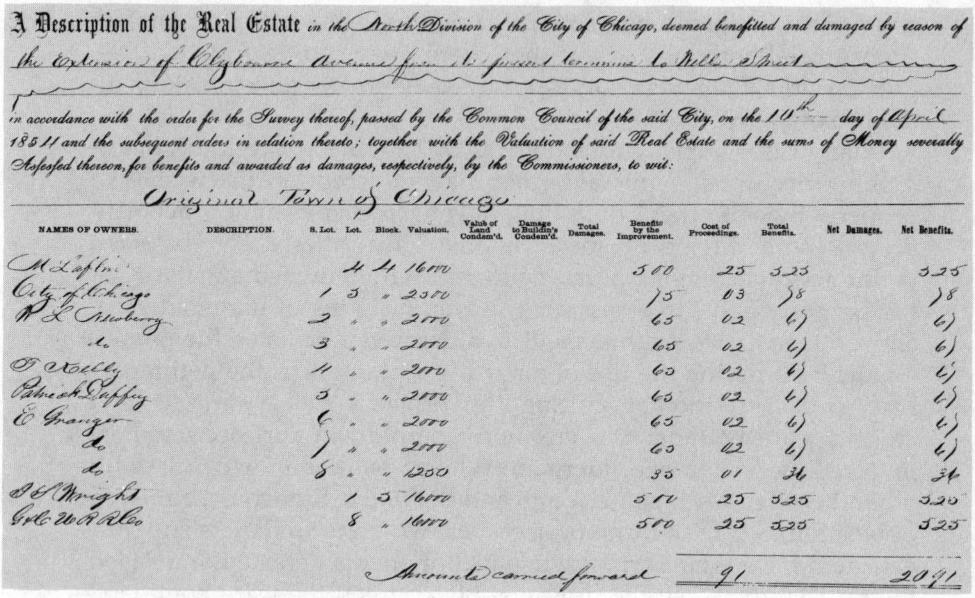

A Description of the Real Estate in the North Division of the City of Chicago, deemed benefitted and damaged by reason of the Extension of Clybourne Avenue from its present terminus to Wells Street

in accordance with the order for the Survey thereof, passed by the Common Council of the said City, on the 10th day of April 1851 and the subsequent orders in relation thereto; together with the Valuation of said Real Estate and the sums of Money severally Assessed thereon, for benefits and awarded as damages, respectively, by the Commissioners, to wit:

Original Town of Chicago

NAMES OF OWNERS.	DESCRIPTION.	S. Lot.	Lot.	Block.	Valuation.	Valu of Land Condem'd.	Damage to Buildin's Condem'd.	Total Damages.	Benefits by the Improvement.	Cost of Proceedings.	Total Benefits.	Net Damages.	Net Benefits.
M Laflin			4	4	1600				500	25	525		525
City of Chicago			1	5	2500				75	03	78		78
W L Newberry			2	"	2000				65	02	67		67
do			3	"	2000				65	02	67		67
T Kelly			4	"	2000				65	02	67		67
Patrick Duffy			5	"	2000				65	02	67		67
E Granger			6	"	2000				65	02	67		67
do			7	"	2000				65	02	67		67
do			8	"	1250				35	01	36		36
J S Wright			1	5	1600				500	25	525		525
G & C U R R Co			8	"	1600				500	25	525		525
Amounts carried forward										91			2091

FIG. 5 SPECIAL ASSESSMENT ROLL

works to make estimates and supervise construction. Elihu Granger, the first man to fill this post, strove to keep assessments down through rigorous inspection of the work of contractors. Granger's successor, another scrupulous official, objected on one occasion that "his discretion should not be taxed" to decide whether to build even a single block-face of sidewalk. These officers left decision making to the aldermen who represented the owners of assessed property.[36]

Once they had the street commissioner's estimate, the council passed an ordinance to effect the project and elected three assessment commissioners. The charter required these assessors to be "disinterested freeholders," a characteristic not expected of the aldermen who managed the decision-making process. Assessment commissioners usually were wealthy real estate developers who knew the city and had reputations for honest dealing. While they were elected separately for each project, the council actually relied on a small group of men, particularly Thomas Church, long-time South Division general tax assessor, for south side projects and John H. Kinzie, a north sider

36. Manierre, *Revised Charter*, 26, 30; Illinois, *Private and Special Laws, 1847*, 85; CP, 1856/57:1923, 1857/58:73, 90, 105, 1858/59:322, 403. The 1851 charter dropped the condemnation writ, though property owners still could take all eminent domain judgments to court early in the process.

Newberrys Addition to Chicago

NAMES OF OWNERS.	DESCRIPTION	S. Lot.	Lot.	Block.	Valuation.	Value of Land Condem'd.	Damage to Building's Condem'd.	Total Damages.	Benefits by the Improvement.	Cost of Proceedings.	Total Benefits.	Net Damages.	Net Benefits.
	Amounts brot forward									91			20 91
W L Newberry		1	1	2350				28 30	14	2 29 92			29 92
do		2	"	18/5				2) 00	1	85 28 35			28 35
do		3	"	18/5				2) 00	1	35 28 35			28 35
do		4	"	18/5				2) 00	1	35 28 35			28 35
do		5	"	18/5				2) 00	1	35 28 35			28 35
do		6	"	18/5				2) 00	1	35 28 35			28 35
do		7	"	18/5				2) 00	1	35 28 35			28 35
do		8	"	18/5				2) 00	1	35 28 35			28 35
do		9	"	18/5				2) 00	1	35 28 35			28 35
German Church		10	"	18/5				2) 00	1	35 28 35			28 35
do		11	"	2400				28 30	14	2 29 92			29 92
W L Newberry		1	2	2350				25) 5	1	28 2) 03			2) 03
do		2	"	18/5				24) 5	12	) 26 02			26 02
do		3	"	18/5				24) 5	12	) 26 02			26 02
do		4	"	18/5				24) 5	12	) 26 02			26 02
do		5	"	18/5				24) 5	12	) 26 02			26 02
do		6	"	18/5				24) 5	12	) 26 02			26 02
	Amounts carried forward							23 53					49 3 03

whose name was identified with the city's frontier origin, for north side projects. The assessors gave notice in the corporation newspaper of the time and place of their meeting and proceeded to view property to estimate the damages and benefits that would result from the proposed project. Damages included the value of property taken for, say, a street widening, the injury to buildings that would have to be moved or destroyed, and less tangible aspects of property value such as the damage a lot might sustain simply because it was made narrower. Benefits consisted of expected increments to land value as a result of the project, plus prorated costs that compensated the assessors.[37]

After they had estimated damages and benefits for all of the affected real estate, the assessors added the sum of all damages and

37. Manierre, *Revised Charter*, 26–28. An 1854 charter amendment created a superintendent of special assessments who served as a permanent commissioner with two others appointed for each project. F. A. Bragg, about whom little is known, held this post for most of the decade. During a heated partisan struggle in 1856, aldermen elected Douglasite Samuel Ashton to the job. Ashton resigned his council seat, informing the mayor that he would "hold the city . . . responsible for the fees in all assessments," but aldermen resisted such politicization of the assessment process and reelected Bragg a month later, leaving Ashton with no city job. Illinois, *Laws, 1854*, 218–19; CP, 1856/57: 487, 647, 806, 1075.

costs to the street commissioner's construction estimate and assessed this total on the property they deemed benefited. They entered this information on an assessment roll that offset damage awards against benefit assessments and costs for each individual lot. The council then gave notice in the newspapers that they would hold a confirmation hearing, at which property owners could dispute the assessors' judgments and correct any errors in the assessment. Although confirmation hearings were supposed to concern only the assessments themselves, property owners who had failed to block a project at the decision stage might renew their objections at this point. The council's committee on local assessments managed the confirmation process. The aldermen who sat on streets and alleys committees were likely to have personal interests in the outcome of confirmation hearings and at this stage, when the policy consensus presumably had been developed, "interested" aldermen disqualified themselves from decisions. Even so, special assessors resisted council meddling that would "make any assessment offered by us perfectly nugatory." [38]

Assessment rolls generally underwent slight modifications before confirmation. Beyond correcting such things as the spelling of names, the accuracy of computations, and the identification of lot owners, however, aldermen made few changes in assessments except in cases where property owners could demonstrate clear violations of the segmented standards. [39] Thus, in an assessment for the extension of the diagonal Clybourn Avenue through a densely settled north side neighborhood, aldermen annulled the assessment and abandoned the project soon after confirmation when property owners made a convincing case for damages in addition to the eminent domain takings awarded by the assessors. According to its opponents, the extension of Clybourn (designed to make far north side tracts held by speculators more accessible to downtown) would divert traffic from established commercial strips, damaging their nonabutting commercial property. These owners could not participate at the decision stage because, as nonabutters, they were not expected to be liable for the assessment, and their actual absence from the assessment roll had prevented them from participating in the confirmation hearing. Unlike a simple paving project, the extension of Clybourn threatened to have a large negative impact on the value of nonabutting property. The council ultimately decided that the owners of this property had a

38. Manierre, *Revised Charter*, 32–33; CP, 1855/56:1534, 1895.
39. See, e.g., CP, 1857/58:470, 904.

legitimate claim to participate in the decision and, on their urging, called a halt to the project.[40]

Even in complicated assessments, aldermen usually did not overrule the decisions of assessment commissioners. One very complex assessment involved the planking of Lumber Street, a short river-access road on the west side of the South Branch. At one end of Lumber Street stood railway depots, grain elevators, and stockyards that, while not facing the street, must have made use of it. When the assessors charged only the abutters, aldermen received an angry protest. Remonstrants argued not only that the businesses on the depot grounds should have been assessed, but that riverfront lots benefited more from the project than lots on the other side of the street. The committee on local assessments agreed, returning the roll to the assessors. The assessors explained that they had indeed assessed the water lots more heavily than those on the inland side, and defended their exemption of the nonabutters on the grounds that "not long hence Lumber Street will probably be extended, and then the [businesses on the depot grounds] will not only have to pay for improvements on the street, but also for opening the same." After placating the remonstrants by correcting computational errors, the assessors returned the roll and the council confirmed it with no further changes. Aldermen had raised the tricky issues, but they left the decisions to the assessors.[41]

After confirmation, the council issued a collection warrant and ordered the start of construction. If the assessment included damage awards, the city had to pay the damages before taking possession of condemned property. Because damages could be paid only from assessment proceeds, construction in these cases had to await at least partial collection. Even where no damages were involved, however, there were good reasons to delay construction until the assessment had been collected, not least because the city could pay street contractors only out of assessment proceeds.[42] When the council awarded a contract before collection, the contractor agreed to make his fee contingent on the successful collection of the assessment. Now

40. Ibid., 1855/56:1998, 2099, 1856/57:199, 469. This incident will be analyzed in more detail below.

41. Ibid., 1857/58:1041.

42. While the committee drafting the 1847 charter had considered a clause to postpone construction on any project until three-fourths of its assessment had been collected, an 1852 ordinance required the collection of at least half before contracts were awarded or work commenced. *Journal*, January 28, 1847; Manierre, *Revised Charter*, 29; CP, 1852/53:175.

the process might reach a new level of complexity. Property owners who had opposed the project all along, those who were aggrieved by the assessment itself, and others who took their first notice of the proceedings only after the collector's visit had two remaining options. They could try to pressure aldermen to vacate the assessment and abandon the project or they could challenge the assessment in the courts, pointing to any technical deficiencies or procedural errors that may have marred the process.[43]

Awarding contracts before collecting assessments was bad but attractive policy. If winter was approaching, further delay would push the start of construction to the next spring, antagonizing petitioners who already had endured a lengthy decision process. In theory, the elaborate consensus-building procedure to this point would ensure smooth collection. If it did, the project was completed, the assessment collected, the contractor paid, and the proceedings concluded. If it did not, however, the premature award of a construction contract changed the balance of power between the council and recalcitrant property owners. The council lost the leverage of an uncompleted project, meanwhile subjecting itself to pressure from contractors who demanded payment for their completed work. As one alderman described this situation,

> A petition is presented and referred, and is detained for weeks for consideration[;] a report is then made and published . . . after frequent extension of the time the Commissioners report to the Council and they are paid, considerable valuable time is now required of the Clerk to put the assessment in respectable shape and it goes to the Collector, said officer advertizes it again and calls upon the parties for payment. Now for the first time (after all the labour and expenses are made) it is discovered that the improvements are to be a useless expenditure, a remonstrance is got up, the work stops, and the expenses are turned over to the *tax payers* and the whole proceedings of the Council turns out a perfect farce.[44]

43. For these practices during the Panic of 1857, see chap. 5.
44. CP, 1854/55:1782-E (emphasis in original). It is in this context of the relative power of owners and contractors that the San Francisco practice of making contractors collect, after completing their work, is interesting. It is no wonder that San Francisco contractors sold their vouchers at discount to brokers, who assumed the risk of collection and the costs of suing owners. In Chicago, because the city assumed these costs (the contractor's chief risk was delay), voucher brokers were not important. For the San Francisco practice, *Taylor v. Palmer*, 31 Cal. 240 (1866); *Gaffney v. Gough*, 36 Cal. 104 (1868); *Shepard v. McNeil*, 38 Cal. 72 (1869); *Himmelmann v. Reay*, 38 Cal. 163 (1869). In the Panic of 1857, Chicago aldermen stuck contractors rather than taxpayers with the costs of abandoned projects.

Turning the expenses "over to the tax payers" represented a defeat of the entire special assessment process. It was precisely what the system was designed to avoid.

Other refinements in the special assessment rules reinforced the segmentation of improvement costs and the control exerted by "interested" owners. These goals clearly informed the manner in which the system handled cost overruns. If a street contractor (or the city in case no contract was awarded) came in under the construction estimate, excess assessment revenue was refunded to assessed property owners in proportion to their contributions. If, however, the contractor spent more than the estimate, a second assessment was levied to recover the balance.[45] Because small groups of property owners had direct interests in economical construction, they paid close attention to the activity of contractors. Cost overruns were not general charges that could pass unnoticed into the property tax rate. If the Clybourn Avenue assessment was at all representative, major developers had powerful incentives to monitor construction. While this assessment roll included 110 different property owners, the top 11 were responsible for 62 percent of the assessed benefits. These owners were all leading developers in the city, men who not only participated in many assessment projects simultaneously, but for whom special assessments were a normal business expense. They would not pay an inflated assessment quietly.[46]

The special assessment process was remarkably free of corruption in the 1850s. Local control and segmented financing made it difficult to conceal kickbacks or padded costs from the owners who would be asked to pay for them. Definition of the word "corruption" to include any manifestation of independence by city officials in the decision-making process also controlled potential abuse. Aldermen would not authorize an improvement "against the wishes of those at whose expense it would be built." Neither would they "delay any needful improvements especially where the *Property holders* are willing to bear the burden therefrom."[47] There were exceptions when, for example,

45. Manierre, *Revised Charter*, 33.
46. CP, 1855/55:2099. This assessment was larger and involved more property than most. Although its inclusion of undeveloped land raised the participation of major developers, its location in an immigrant (German) neighborhood made it include many owners of single lots. That the top 11 owners were awarded nearly all the condemnation damages ($30,983 out of $31,033) suggests their role in designing the project. They also owned 73 percent of the real estate value involved, ensuring dominance in the decision process.
47. Ibid., 1860/61:84, 1855/56:352-A (emphasis in original).

the city invoked public safety arguments to force owners to rebuild dangerous sidewalks, but these exceptions were rare and did not involve high costs. Property owners protected their interests at each stage in the process, interfering when they did not like the costs, the materials, or the quality of workmanship of the projects they financed.[48] In the segmented system, "interested" owners made public works decisions and monitored their implementation. The aldermen who represented the owners worked to build consensus among them and to convert that consensus into infrastructure that enhanced the value of privately owned real estate. Chicagoans fought and bargained at every stage of the process, but only within its strict boundaries of eligible participation and legitimate rhetoric.

WHILE LOCAL CONTROL in the segmented system obviously would have undermined official attempts to plan Chicago's growth, it gave the private developers of tracts within the city substantial power to plan the kinds of development they wanted. When several developers had to cooperate to make a plan work, the special assessment process helped them to build a consensus on that plan by apportioning its costs in a manner all could deem legitimate. The establishment of Union Park, on the city's west side, involved just such consensus building. Developers in this area wanted to build a fashionable residential district and thought that a park would help to lure wealthy residents away from the lakefront, "across the mud bottoms of West Chicago." In late 1853, Samuel S. Hayes offered to sell the city an 11-acre tract and circulated a petition among neighboring owners asking that the council accept his offer. After some haggling over what proportion of the price the property owners should pay, the council agreed in 1854 to buy the land, levying one-third of its cost on the benefited property through a special assessment and two-thirds on all west side property through a special tax. They issued $60,000 in bonds, bought Union Park from Hayes, and ordered a $20,000 special assessment.[49]

There was a legal defect in this assessment, which remonstrants soon pointed out. While the bonds would not mature for twenty years, special assessment revenue could be spent only on the object for which it had been collected. There would be no legal use for the

---

48. For exceptions, ibid., 1857/58:1257, 1858/59:402, 1860/61:94–95. For owners' interference in technical details, 1855/56:590, 808, 866, 1534, 2127.

49. Ibid., 1853/54:1235, 1237–39, 1816, 1854/55:145; Henry L. Hammond, *Memorial Sketch of Philo Carpenter* (Chicago: Fergus Printing Co., 1888), 12.

proceeds of the assessment for twenty years.[50] Meanwhile, Hayes and his colleagues petitioned the council to grade the new park and to improve it with ornamental trees and footpaths. They were "quite willing to pay the entire expense that may be incurred [and] only ask to have the amount of that expense equitably distributed among them by an assessment." They promised not to take the land assessment to court if the city improved the park. Yet the developers' need for improvements—a vacant lot would not have served their purpose— gave the council the stronger bargaining position. Aldermen refused to improve the park until the property owners paid the land assessment.[51] When the courts later voided this obviously illegal $20,000 assessment, the city had to refund only $375. Most of the owners paid despite the legal defect because they were using the system to mobilize capital into a development plan. It worked. Union Park remained a wealthy neighborhood into the 1870s.[52]

The Clybourn Avenue assessment also involved a development scheme. Developers including Ogden, Jones & Co., Chicago's single largest landowner, and Sheffield & Co. recently had platted huge tracts of vacant land at the city's northern edge. By extending Clybourn diagonally through gridded blocks closer to downtown, they hoped to cut the travel time from these properties, boosting their value to residential buyers. The problem with this plan, however, was that it lacked sufficient segmentation. To extend Clybourn, the developers had to involve the property owners in the area near the point of extension. These owners, most of them German immigrants with very small holdings, had no interest in the accessibility of distant tracts and no part in the developers' speculation. Indeed, the Clybourn project involved such a large range of property that the council waived its normal referral rules and sent the assessment to a special committee composed of all of the north side aldermen. Remonstrants refused to bear a "serious tax upon our property & labour" for a project that was of no "service to the community at large." Even without the extension, "the Public [had] easy access" through their neighborhood (along, of course, its established commercial strips). The Clybourn Avenue extension project was debated as a public good. Once it was defined this way, it could be defeated by political pressure; it

50. CP, 1853/54:1816, 1854/55:145, 745, 870, 873, 1530; Manierre, *Revised Charter*, 22–25.

51. CP, 1854/55:1118, 1855/56:352-A.

52. Ibid., 1855/56:352-A, 1856/57:1700, 1857/58:894, 989; Richard Sennett, *Families against the City: Middle Class Homes of Industrial Chicago, 1872–1890* (New York: Vintage, 1970), 9–35. See also the Fifth Ward census data in appendix 2 below.

no longer was a "local" improvement or a segmented development plan.[53]

The Clybourn Avenue project, in fact, would have wreaked havoc on the working-class neighborhood it was intended to cross, slicing through four densely built blocks. It was, on a less extreme scale, like cutting an expressway through a neighborhood today. Yet the Clybourn neighbors knew (or quickly learned) how to manipulate the resources of segmented decision making to thwart it. Wealthy developers could do what they wanted in areas where they owned all or most of the property, as in Union Park—even imposing the special tax on the whole west side—but when they tried to disrupt the Clybourn neighborhood they met resistance. They almost won there too; the power of their larger landholdings enabled them to beat the neighborhood's abutting remonstrants easily. Signed by 22 German immigrants, the first remonstrance against the project complained that the cost of the assessment "might compel some of us to lose all we have saved after years of industry & economy." Aldermen rejected this, however, pointing out after the assessment roll had been completed that few of the remonstrants appeared on it "and that there [sic] aggregate assessment for Benefits is about one forty-ith of the whole amount." The developers lost their project only after the damaged nonabutters of the neighborhood widened the issue. The second remonstrance against the project had 145 signers, made the argument about the commercial strips, and even enrolled some of the wealthiest native-born landowners of the north side. The German immigrants had figured out how to use the system to protect their neighborhood.[54]

Local control in the segmented system also extended beyond the special assessment process altogether, conferring direct planning power in a neglected precursor of modern zoning regulation—the fire limit. Using the fire limit, property owners were able to zone certain neighborhoods to prohibit the construction of new wooden buildings within them. A fire limit marked a boundary around a city's center

53. CP, 1855/56:1998, 2099, 1856/57:469; Ante-Fire Subdivision Plats, Book A, pp. 10, 34, 54 1/2, 74, Chicago Title and Trust Company.

54. CP, 1855/56:1998, 2099, 1856/57:469. While regrouping for the second remonstrance, the German abutters requested a three-month extension on their assessment payments ("That owing to the scarcity of money," an immediate collection "would greatly distress and ruin your Petitioners") and, a week later, the native-born owners joined in, having noticed errors on the assessment roll ("The reason this was not attended to before, was, that our property was so remote from the improvement, that we did not suppose it would be assessed, and did not look at the assessment"). In another month, the project was quashed. Ibid., 1856/57:25, 199.

within which all new buildings had to be constructed of brick or stone. While the fire limit's formal purpose was fire prevention, property owners had many different reasons for wanting fire limit coverage. As a Chicago alderman argued after the Great Fire of 1871: "Insurance Companies and their satellites . . . know exactly how we should build and where we shall locate our businesses. Others have strips of land they want to have benefitted. . . . Others owning frame buildings with a vacant lot alongside wants [sic] everybody to build with brick. Brewers in the heart of the city want all other brewers kept out of town."[55] The fire limit could have a powerful effect on local land values not only by forbidding cheap construction, but also by determining land use. If, in legal theory, modern zoning grew out of nuisance regulation while fire limits developed into building codes, in practice, mid nineteenth-century Chicagoans used the fire limit as a tool for land-use control.[56]

American cities had used fire limits for some time before Chicago enacted its first fire limit ordinance. Philadelphia had established a fire limit by 1796, and both Pittsburgh and Cincinnati had done so by the mid 1820s. Chicago's city charter of 1837, copied almost verbatim from the 1832 charter of Buffalo, allowed the council to set a fire limit, though aldermen did not set one until 1845, proclaiming then that "the time has arrived when the dangers from fire have rendered such an ordinance necessary."[57] The notion that a time for fire limit coverage could "arrive" remained central to fire limit debates in Chicago. Property owners opposed extending the fire limit to areas that were not yet "valuable enough to warrant permanent brick buildings." They argued that the fire limit was "not needed" until property was "valuable for business purposes" and premature where "whole blocks [contained] very few buildings."[58] These were peculiar arguments with which to challenge a fire prevention measure that applied only to new construction. The fire limit was extended only over areas that already had high concentrations of older wooden buildings. It was applied only after the risk of damaging fires had been allowed to

55. Ibid., 1872/73:181-B (file 5). See the epilogue.

56. Mel Scott, *American City Planning since 1890* (Berkeley: University of California Press, 1969), 75–76, 152–56.

57. CP, 1845/45:2344; Charles R. Adrian and Ernest S. Griffith, *A History of American City Government: The Formation of Traditions, 1775–1870* (New York: Praeger, 1976), 93; Richard C. Wade, *The Urban Frontier: Pioneer Life in Early Pittsburgh, Cincinnati, Lexington, Louisville, and St. Louis* (Chicago: University of Chicago Press, 1959), 293; Bayrd Still, "Patterns of Mid-Nineteenth Century Urbanization in the Middle West," *Mississippi Valley Historical Review* 28 (1941–42): 190.

58. CP, 1851/52:638, 1855/56:648, 1858/59:287.

grow great, and even then it did not address the presumed sources of fire risk, the old wooden buildings.[59]

In practice, fire limits had little to do with the prevention of fires. Brick buildings were desirable not because they were fireproof (which they were not), but because they were expensive, and thus enhanced the value of neighboring real estate. If they were less inflammable than frame buildings, they nevertheless burned with alarming frequency. Chicagoans postponed fire limit coverage until property was "valuable for business purposes" because brick buildings in the 1850s were commercial buildings, often of imposing scale and design.[60] By extending the fire limit, real estate developers effectively zoned property for commercial use and lavish construction. In a real estate market in which no single investor wielded sufficient power to determine the direction of development, the fire limit allowed the builders of brick "business blocks" to expect (indeed, to require) their neighbors to make similar investments. The fire limit reduced the risk of poor site selection for the developer of commercial property. Still, unlike special assessment, which rested on a forthright logic of property value, the fire limit ostensibly was a public safety measure. Only by invoking this overriding public good could the city's government justify such interference with private property rights.[61]

This interference, however, remained under strictly local control. Chicagoans tinkered endlessly with the fire limit in the 1850s, changing its boundaries almost every year and sometimes more than once in a year. These revisions might involve a single block whose owners agreed that they wanted or did not want the fire limit; on the south side the limit inched southward one half-block at a time. Aldermen demanded only that the complete limit bound a single, contiguous tract. They refused "to spread the fire limits over an isolated block" because such an action, as the dependable Elihu Granger rushed to explain, "would appear like especial and partial legislation." In fact, such an extension would have undermined the public safety rationale that gave the fire limit its legitimacy. This incident was the only case between 1845 and 1861 in which aldermen balked at a fire limit extension (or repeal) that affected owners requested, and this particular

59. Fire limit ordinances did prohibit moving or improving wooden buildings and repairing them if fires destroyed half of their value.

60. Buettinger, "Concept of Jacksonian Aristocracy," 10–18.

61. For modern zoning as a collective property right that allows neighbors to subordinate individual property rights to neighborhood characteristics, William A. Fischel, *The Economics of Zoning Laws: A Property Rights Approach to Land Use Controls* (Baltimore: Johns Hopkins University Press, 1985); Robert H. Nelson, *Zoning and Property Rights: An Analysis of the American System of Land-Use Regulation* (Cambridge: MIT Press, 1977).

request had a problem besides noncontiguity. It involved posh Michigan Avenue residential property whose owners wanted to restrain a neighbor from renting to undesirable tenants. When, two years after the original request, the fire limit was extended over the now contiguous block, the extension ordinance exempted present owners from its restriction on moving wooden buildings. This ordinance was an abuse of the fire limit, much as exclusionary zoning is an abuse of the municipal zoning power today.[62]

Aldermen relied on the owners of affected property to make fire limit decisions. The council referred fire limit petitions and remonstrances to its committee on fire and water, who looked for a local consensus. They took "much pains to ascertain the feelings of the property owners," refusing to change the fire limit "unless by an expressed wish of those interested & effected [sic] thereby," but committee members never specified whether they were counting the number of affected owners or the extent of their property.[63] They relied in practice on the tenacity with which neighboring owners (and sometimes even tenants) badgered them for an extension or repeal of fire limit coverage. The committee also decided on petitions for individual exemptions from fire limit rules, again relying on the opinions of neighbors. Exemption requests usually claimed that a proposed improvement to a wooden building would reduce the fire risk posed by the building. While many exemption petitions included the signatures of consenting neighbors, others prompted remonstrances from neighbors who had heard that they were pending. A request with a cover letter from a leading businessman that described the petitioner's poverty and asked his alderman "to engineer for him a little" met a quick rebuff.[64]

62. CP, 1851/52:1639, 1853/54:1581, 1613. This also was the only extension that exempted present owners. The Michigan Avenue neighbors did a lot of bargaining in 1854. Many of them signed the fire limit petition, aimed against the Society of the New Jerusalem Church, until J. Young Scammon and other trustees of the church remonstrated that the petition had been "secretly and through misrepresentation gotten up by Mr. [George G.] Grubb who lives in an aristocratic edifice adjoining said lot." Most of the petitioners then signed a new petition claiming they had misunderstood the original and asking that the church be exempted. The organizer of this second petition, a church trustee, noted that Grubb was obstinate and urged that if he refused to sign, "we'd better carry it over his head if we can." The exemption of existing wooden buildings was a compromise. Nobody seems to have considered it bad taste for these wealthy leaders of Chicago society to complain about the "aristocratic edifice" of their neighbor.

63. Ibid., 1854/55:203, 1856/57:36.

64. Ibid., 1857/58:160. Aldermen showed more favor to safety arguments in granting exemptions than to pleas of poverty or ignorance of the ordinance. Yet acceptance

Fire limit debates were planning debates in which neighbors argued about alternative strategies for local development. Owners and tenants on Randolph Street protested against fire limit coverage in 1848 because "the present business of said Street requires a cheap class of buildings for the reason that the business of the occupants residing on the street is not sufficiently lucrative to pay the expense of that class of buildings called fire proof—they having sought this refuge of cheap rents, having been driven from those streets w[h]ere rents are dear."[65] West siders argued for years about whether the fire limit should be extended so they could ban lumber yards that discouraged "good substantial brick buildings . . . adding to the beauty & real wealth & business of this portion of the City." While the lumber dealers opposed the limit, demanding that their trade be recognized as "the *principal business* on the west side," other west siders insisted on using the fire limit to banish them:

> nearly all of the unimproved property . . . in the said Fire Limits is owned by speculators . . . who never improve or build; but who are satisfied to allow their Lots, which are the largest, most central and Elligable [sic] for business purposes . . . to remain unimproved while they can lease them temporarily for the use of Lumber Dealers at rates that will pay Interest & Taxes and thus indefinitely retard the improvement of the West Division . . . not only so far as their own unimproved property extends; but to the extent of much of the adjoining property which will never be improved while permitted to be surrounded by Lumber Yards.[66]

This was a planning debate. Unable to reach a local consensus, the west siders petitioned and remonstrated until the fire and water committee could think of no solution short of a call by the mayor "for a mass meeting of all those who feel deeply interested in this Great and important matter, and there to take such action . . . as they shall deem proper."[67]

The safety rationale for fire limit coverage was essentially a sham.

---

of a safety argument involved another contradiction in the fire limit's rationale: improved wooden buildings would last longer, postponing the day when an area would contain only "fireproof" buildings. See, e.g., 1847/47:3606, 1848/48:4709, 4787, 1852/53:69, 1857/58:58.

65. Ibid., 1848/48:4579. Randolph was included two years later.

66. Ibid., 1855/56:648, 1856/57:1586 (emphasis in original), 1853/54:230. For the rest of the west side debate, 1852/53:1279, 1855/56:592, 1404, 1857/58:485, 520, 618.

67. Ibid., 1857/58:485. At its largest, the west side limit extended from Randolph to Madison and from the river to a half-block west of Des Plaines, plus one other block west of Des Plaines along Randolph itself. This was a total of 9 city blocks.

The west side proponents of the limit began their agitation by citing a destructive fire, but clearly had other goals in mind. The safety rationale was a nineteenth-century version of today's comprehensive plan which, while it may be a pretense or an afterthought, is essential to the legitimacy of modern zoning regulation. The council's committee on fire and water functioned much like a zoning board of appeals in seeking neighbors' input on exemption requests. The fire limit provided Chicagoans with a zoning tool to regulate urban growth. It differed from modern zoning chiefly in its application to commercial rather than residential property. When fire limits were extended over entire cities (as Chicago's fire limit was in 1874), they became building codes; they no longer marked the boundaries that had been the basis of their zoning power. Modern zoning would find other precedents and another logic in the law of nuisance.[68] Yet the fire limit was an important precursor of zoning regulation. That mid nineteenth-century Chicagoans could use government for this purpose illustrates the local planning power that property owners enjoyed in the segmented system of city government.

TWO OF THE MOST important city-building projects of the 1850s could not be segmented with the rigor of street projects or fire limit rules: water and sewerage systems required central planning and large initial investments. While decisions about the overall design of these systems clearly could not rest with small groups of property owners, neither could large parts of their costs be assessed as benefits to particular parcels of real estate. Yet Chicagoans did not simply abandon segmented government in pursuing these projects. Resistance to citywide expenditures led to the adoption of sewerage plans that, while less costly in the short run, posed expensive problems for the future. The city also privatized all water and sewerage costs that it could through special assessments and user charges; the more rapid expansion of the water than the sewerage system may have resulted in part from a greater privatization of water financing. Moreover, once the initial costs had been incurred, pressure mounted to end general financing for the further expansion of both systems. Finally, the segmented nature of council representation in the 1850s may have contributed to the administrative strategy of delegating these projects to independent boards. Aldermen who represented the interests of particular tracts of real estate may have been unable to implement citywide policies on such a grand financial scale.

Several historians have described urban water and sewerage sys-

68. See *Village of Euclid v. Ambler Realty Co.*, 272 U.S. 303 (1926).

tems as public goods whose creation was spurred by widespread calamities such as epidemics and whose technical complexity required central administration by professionals with citywide visions of planned urban growth. Clearly, the engineers, sanitarians, and landscape architects who grappled with the unhealthy environments of nineteenth-century cities saw them as integrated communities whose public problems demanded public responses. As clearly, they met powerful opposition at every point where their plans impinged on the "privatist" preferences of individual property owners.[69] The triumph of some degree of political centralization in American cities by the late nineteenth century, however, would depend more on the collapse of the segmented system than on the persuasive power of such visionary professionals. Nor did the engineers that these boards employed create "baronies of power" outside the normal political process.[70] Their expertise was harnessed and their recommendations subordinated to the local interests of Chicago's property owners.

In most American cities in the nineteenth century, state legislatures delegated the power to construct water systems to private companies or to independent commissions. There were several reasons for this. First, such delegation expressed what by then was a traditional American administrative practice: chartering private corporations to perform public tasks in return for monopoly privileges.[71] The Illinois legislature chartered the Chicago Hydraulic Company in 1836 to provide Chicago with water in return for a monopoly on the city's water business. The company built its waterworks in 1842, but the water was dirty and as late as 1850 the company served only one-fifth of Chicago's population, having failed to expand beyond the city's south side.[72] Second, independent boards could borrow funds that were not

69. Warner, *Private City;* Jon C. Teaford, *The Unheralded Triumph: City Government in America, 1870–1900* (Baltimore: Johns Hopkins University Press, 1984); Charles E. Rosenberg, *The Cholera Years: The United States in 1832, 1849, and 1866* (Chicago: University of Chicago Press, 1962); Nelson Manfred Blake, *Water for the Cities: A History of the Urban Water Supply Problem in the United States* (Syracuse: Syracuse University Press, 1956); Stanley K. Schultz and Clay McShane, "To Engineer the Metropolis: Sewers, Sanitation, and City Planning in Late-Nineteenth Century America," *Journal of American History* 65 (1978): 389–411; Jon A. Peterson, "The Impact of Sanitary Reform upon American Urban Planning, 1840–90," *Journal of Social History* 13 (1979): 83–103; Alan I. Marcus, "The Strange Career of Municipal Health Initiatives: Cincinnati and City Government in the Early Nineteenth Century," *Journal of Urban History* 7 (1980): 3–29.

70. Teaford, *Unheralded Triumph,* 139.

71. Blake, *Water for the Cities;* Oscar Handlin and Mary Flug Handlin, *Commonwealth: A Study of the Role of Government in the American Economy, Massachusetts, 1774–1861,* rev. ed. (Cambridge: Harvard University Press, 1969).

72. O'Connell, "Technology and Pollution," 10–11.

subject to municipal debt ceilings. Chicago's Board of Water Commissioners, created in 1851, floated $440,000 in water bonds on the city's credit in 1852 alone. The city's municipal debt ceiling, meanwhile, was a mere $100,000 and the legislature had allowed the private company to amass only $250,000 in capital stock.[73] Finally, independent commissions allowed city governments to centralize the construction of necessarily citywide projects without sacrificing local control of the rest.

The decision to build a large-scale water system was a public one. After a cholera epidemic in 1849, Chicagoans held public meetings to mobilize pro-water opinion and applied to the state legislature for the creation of a water board. There was opposition to the board from aldermen and others who had investments in the Chicago Hydraulic Company, especially while the board and company negotiated a buyout, but the council supported the board's legislative requests for expanded debt limits and approved its bond issues with little debate or delay.[74] The water commissioners brought a nationally known civil engineer, William J. McAlpine, to Chicago, but submitted his waterworks plan to the city's voters before acting on it even though their charter included no referendum requirement. The response was overwhelming—an 84 percent pro-water vote with 79 percent in the least enthusiastic ward. Chicagoans clearly wanted a publicly financed water system capable of serving the whole city. Construction of the waterworks proceeded rapidly and the board pumped its first water early in 1854. They laid 24 miles of water pipe in 1854 and another 48 in 1855. By 1856 four-fifths of Chicago's dwellings were connected to the system, and by 1861 nearly the entire city was supplied, despite the huge growth in its population, from 66,000 in 1854 to 120,000 in 1861.[75]

The Board of Water Commissioners financed its central pumping station, lake intake tunnel, and main pipes from bonds (and the council levied a "water tax" for its debt service), but the rest of its financing was privatized. It levied special assessments for the pipes laid in particular streets and, more important, assessed user charges: one-time

73. Ibid., 11–12; Cain, *Sanitation Strategy*, 39–41; CP, 1852/53:332, 454, 518, 641–42, 926, 961, 1010, 1061.

74. O'Connell, "Technology and Pollution," 11–12; Keating, "Governing the New Metropolis," 65–70; CP, 1851/52:393, 1532, 1593, 1852/53:42, 1853/54:1584, 1611, 1854/55:333. For the politics of the buyout, Cain, *Sanitation Strategy*, 42; *Democrat*, January 1, 7, 10, 17, February 7, 1852; CP, 1853/54:1080, 1086, 1112–14, 1144.

75. O'Connell, "Technology and Pollution," 16–17; Keating, "Governing the New Metropolis," 70–75; Keating, *Building Chicago*, 190; Hoyt, *One Hundred Years*, 483. See CP, 1851/52:1626–34 for the referendum returns and 1851/52:1593 for the authorization. The referendum probably was a ploy in the buyout negotiation.

tap fees to connect buildings and annual water rents graded by building size and expected water usage.[76] Its lucrative user charge revenues allowed the board to operate as though it were a profit-making (or at least self-supporting) utility company. In the early 1850s, the board installed public water hydrants to serve building owners on whose streets pipe had yet to be laid, as well as those who could not afford (or did not want to pay) the fees for connection. The board could try to coerce building owners to connect by levying special assessments on owners near hydrants who chose not to connect to completed pipes, though it is not clear that they actually levied these assessments. As soon as it became physically possible to connect most buildings, however, the board acted against its "free riders." In 1855 the commissioners were empowered to charge water rents to all buildings that could be connected, whether actually connected or not, and in 1856 they began to remove the public water hydrants. Ann Durkin Keating has attributed the removal of the hydrants to Chicagoans' changing perception of the value of water service. From a public health imperative in 1849, water by 1856 had become a "personal amenity" for which takers were expected to pay user charges.[77]

The water commissioners laid pipe according to a central plan that designated the order in which properties would gain water service. They marked a water district in 1851 that included the city's most heavily settled area plus major thoroughfares outside of that area. In 1854 the commissioners reported that they had "been frequently petitioned . . . for the extension of the water pipes to supply the wants and protect the property [from fire] of those citizens not now in the water districts, and to which they would have gladly complied if they had had the necessary means to purchase the pipe and pay for the labor."[78] These petitions did not determine the commissioners' construction activity in the same way that they guided the council's special assessment process, though as the board implied, they might have been taken more seriously had they been backed, as special assessment petitions were, by the promise of money. The water district was expanded in 1857, only after all piping in the original district had

76. Illinois, *Private Laws, 1851,* 214–17; O'Connell, "Technology and Pollution," 16–17. The water board technically was a quasi-private corporation called the Chicago City Hydraulic Company.

77. Keating, *Building Chicago,* 39–40; Illinois, *Private Laws, 1851,* 214–16, and *Private Laws, 1855,* 565. The perception of water service as a private commodity is clear, but the degree of change in this perception in the early 1850s is debatable.

78. Board of Water Commissioners, *Seventh Semi-Annual Report* (1854), quoted in Keating, "Governing the New Metropolis," 71.

been laid. While individual connection to the water system had an "amenity" value to which building owners responded, the property value enhancement of the piping could not be segmented into a leap-frogging pattern. While there was no reason that paving or sidewalks had to be uniform from one street to another, water piping in a densely settled area had to proceed in a reasonably orderly fashion.

Thus, while the water board, rather than local groups of property owners, decided when to extend service to particular streets, the importance of this centralization should not be exaggerated. Viewing their system more as a business venture than a public service, the commissioners watched their user charge revenues closely and attempted to link their supply decisions with economic demand, that is, demand that would raise revenue for the system. By 1864, the Board of Public Works (created in 1861 to consolidate public works administration) had accomplished this linkage. They required neighboring property owners to advance them the costs of new pipe-laying in areas where they did not expect tap fees and water rents to yield profits, making such advances a condition for extending water service to those areas.[79] In neighborhoods outside the downtown water districts, therefore, property owners subscribed for water pipes much as they had subscribed for bridges a decade earlier. Local groups of property owners decided whether and when to invest in water piping for their neighborhoods, and the individual owners of buildings decided whether and when to invest in connection. Property-owning neighbors paid collectively for the piping and individually for the service. And by 1864 there were no more public water hydrants in Chicago.[80]

Like its water system, Chicago's sewerage system originated as a public project, again as a citywide response to disease. Six consecutive years of cholera, typhoid, and dysentery epidemics—including an 1854 cholera outbreak that killed over fifteen hundred Chicagoans—seemed clearly linked to the city's filth and poor drainage.[81] The council had drained part of the city with Elihu Granger's aqueducts in the 1840s, but the aqueducts served only the downtown and grew more obviously inadequate even there once large amounts of water began

79. Keating, *Building Chicago*, 40. The creation of the BPW is described in the next chapter.

80. Ibid.

81. O'Connell, "Technology and Pollution," 21–22; Cain, *Sanitation Strategy*, 23; Gregg Wolper, "Winning the Battle but Losing the War: Building-Raising and Sanitation in Mid-Nineteenth-Century Chicago" (seminar paper, University of Chicago, 1983), 8.

to be piped into Chicago daily. After conducting preliminary research for "a general and uniform system of sewerage for the city," the council asked the state legislature to create a sewerage board on the water commission model in 1855. The legislature responded immediately.[82] Unlike the water board, however, the sewerage board never was conceived as a quasi-private company conducting a profit-making operation, perhaps because the sewerage system was planned from the start as an investment in innovative technology. No American city had yet built a "combined" sewer system—one that drained rainfall from streets and household wastes from buildings simultaneously— and European engineers differed on their preferred sewerage designs. The Board of Sewerage Commissioners hired Boston's city engineer, Ellis S. Chesbrough, and, after adopting his initial proposal, sent him to Europe on a research trip.[83]

Chesbrough has become something of a hero to urban historians. A talented problem-solver, he was active in the emerging national profession of engineering in the late nineteenth century and in the diffusion of technical knowledge that gave the profession its identity. In Chicago, his work as chief engineer for the sewerage board and then for the Board of Public Works, which he served until 1879, included major technological achievements. It was Chesbrough who, in the 1860s, reversed the flow of the Chicago River and built the world's longest underwater tunnel in Lake Michigan, and it was Chesbrough who, in the 1850s, figured out how to drain a city built where nature had intended a swamp.[84] The problem was topographical: low, flat, and on soil that absorbed little moisture, Chicago lacked natural means of drainage. Rainfall sat in stagnant puddles that bred mosquitoes and, according to mid nineteenth-century medical theory, the "noxious vapors" that caused cholera. Unable to design underground sewers sufficiently steep to empty their contents (the weakness of Granger's aqueducts), Chesbrough decided to lay his sewers close to the ground and then raise the street levels to cover them. A seemingly simple solution, this plan won easy acceptance from the sewerage board and the council: neither seems to have noticed a cost that Ches-

82. CP, 1851/52:720, 1853/54:520, 1854/55:1519–20, 1723.

83. Where the water board had its quasi-private corporate title, the sewerage board's official name was Board of Sewerage Commissioners; Illinois, *Private Laws, 1855*, 93–96. See also Joel A. Tarr, "The Separate vs. Combined Sewer Problem: A Case Study in Urban Technology Design Choice," *Journal of Urban History* 5 (1979): 308–9.

84. Louis P. Cain, "Raising and Watering a City: Ellis Sylvester Chesbrough and Chicago's First Sanitation System," *Technology and Culture* 13 (1972): 353–72; Teaford, *Unheralded Triumph*, 139; Schultz and McShane, "To Engineer the Metropolis," 393.

brough failed to mention, that of raising existing buildings to the higher street grade.[85]

Most attention focused instead on the outlets for the new sewers, a problem Chesbrough addressed by presenting the sewerage commissioners with four ways to dispose of Chicago's sewage. They could dump it directly into Lake Michigan, dump it into the river and thus indirectly into the lake, deepen the Illinois and Michigan Canal in order to reverse the river so that it carried the sewage away from the lake, or collect the sewage to convert it into fertilizer. High cost estimates damned the latter two options, though Chesbrough predicted that the canal eventually would be deepened and thought this the optimal solution. Direct discharge into the lake appeared to be more expensive than discharge into the river because, as the water commissioners had found, storms made lake tunneling difficult. The river plan also seemed less likely to contaminate the city's water supply. Chesbrough thought that the river could dilute the sewage before it reached the water intake located in the lake and planned to ensure dilution by building two flushing conduits between the lake and points on the North and South branches that were far from the river's mouth. He recommended the river dumping option. The sewerage board agreed but dropped his flushing conduits from the plan. Thus, not only did they choose the cheapest solution, but they also removed the device that Chesbrough had designed to protect the city's water supply.[86]

The sewerage board followed the water commission's example in mapping a service district, combining bond revenues with special assessments for pipe-laying within the district, and charging one-time fees to connect buildings to the system, but they could levy no continuing charges like the water rents. Some building owners resisted sewer connection, moreover, because it would have required them to install plumbing fixtures as well, though the board was

85. Cain, *Sanitation Strategy,* 27–30. Wolper, "Winning the Battle," 14–15, 42–43, shows that the sewers were not built, as some have suggested, "in the air." They were built underground but not far enough underground to cover sufficiently without raising the streets. The cost of building-raising was entirely privatized, which is interesting because it hit wealthy owners the hardest. While wooden buildings could be raised on stilts, brick "business blocks" presented a technological challenge and a significant cost. The technological solution appeared in the person of a young engineer named George Pullman, who could raise stores and banks without disrupting their business. Many poorer owners left their buildings below grade, adding stairs to climb down from the street. See also Rosen, *Limits of Power,* 99–100.

86. O'Connell, "Technology and Pollution," 25–27; Cain, *Sanitation Strategy,* 23–26.

empowered to force owners to drain property "which in their judgment requires it."[87] The sewerage system expanded more slowly than
the water system. The sewerage board laid only 6 miles of sewers in
1856 and 5 in 1857. By 1861, the city had 95 miles of water pipe but
only 54 miles of sewers; where nearly 7000 buildings had water taps,
only 2200 had drains. Both systems expanded dramatically in the
1860s, but the waterworks stayed far ahead. In 1870 there were 272
miles of water pipe and 132 miles of sewers; over 35,000 buildings had
water taps and almost 20,000 had drains.[88] The slower expansion of
the sewerage system probably reflects the less specifically personal
benefits of sewage disposal. While the health benefits of clean water
derived from its individual use, sewerage affected health in a more
public manner: a healthy neighborhood was one in which everyone's
properties drained. Because it was unable to raise "amenity" revenues, moreover, the sewerage board relied on bonds that became difficult to market in the late 1850s (the board actually went bankrupt
in 1861).

No surviving data indicate the proportional roles played by general
revenue and special assessment in financing either of the systems;
not until 1862 did any city officer even keep track of the aggregate
special assessment levies scattered among individual project accounts. General funding, however, clearly financed the bulk of the
sewerage project in the 1850s. In the next decade, as the Board of
Public Works began to demand subscriptions for water pipe extension, they also attempted to reduce the city's public commitment to
sewerage. Between 1867 and 1871 the board tried three times to persuade the council to approve a shift from general debt funding to
special assessment for sewers. They argued that while the sewering
of the downtown had been a matter of public health and a "general
benefit to the whole city," sewers in outlying neighborhoods would
serve only local interests. General funding would provoke "opposition from the sewered portion of the City" and "constant strife as to
where [sewer funds] should be expended." As the corporation counsel explained the dilemma, there was no "fixed rule" to guide general
spending for sewers. Aldermen who represented unsewered areas—
the 1863 and 1869 ward maps distinguished downtown (sewered) from
outlying (unsewered) neighborhoods—successfully resisted the introduction of special assessments after Chicago's most valuable property
already had been sewered with general funds. In 1871, after the state

87. Illinois, *Private Laws, 1855*, 100.
88. Keating, *Building Chicago*, 192.

constitution of 1870 barred the city from issuing new sewer bonds, the outlying wards won a citywide property tax for sewerage.[89]

Sewer extension remained a generally funded public good in Chicago until 1890, after a mass annexation of service-hungry suburbs changed the political issue considerably (Chicago grew from 43 to over 168 square miles in 1889).[90] One result of public funding is evident from the 1873 map of sewers and pavements, drawn by economist Homer Hoyt. Comparing Hoyt's map with ward-based data from the 1870 census shows that the neighborhoods of poorer property owners were more likely to have sewers than pavements. Wealthy wards had both, but the wards that had widespread ownership of small amounts of property—wards with high rates of working-class ownership—had more extensive sewerage than pavement. Although most of these areas lacked both improvements, public financing may have put sewers into neighborhoods that otherwise would have been unable to afford them.[91] This evidence is not conclusive; if the working-class owners had had to pay for sewers as well as pavements, they might have deemed sewers the higher priority. Yet studies of public works provision in the 1890s in Detroit and Milwaukee, where special assessments financed both services, show that working-class homeowners did indeed delay both types of improvement in order to marshall their resources for their mortgages. The results in Milwaukee's Fourteenth Ward in 1910 were extensive working-class home-ownership and the highest mortality rate in that city.[92]

The waterworks and sewerage system were major public triumphs for a government designed to reflect "privatism." They were the most expensive projects of the 1850s and the cost of building them comprised the largest component of the city's public debt. By 1864, Chicago's total debt of $3.5 million included over $2 million in water and sewerage bonds.[93] The men who borrowed these vast public funds,

89. CP, 1866/67:940, 942, 1031, 1868/69:1310, 1869/70:1351, 1870/71:205, 371, 561; Keating, *Building Chicago*, 42–43; Bessie Louise Pierce, *A History of Chicago* (3 vols.; Chicago: University of Chicago Press, 1937–57): 2:331.

90. Keating, *Building Chicago*, is a study primarily of the politics of annexation in the Chicago area. For the 1889 annexations, see pp. 103–16.

91. Hoyt, *One Hundred Years*, 92. Hoyt's map also appears in Cain, *Sanitation Strategy*, 33, and Rosen, *Limits of Power*, 173. For the 1870 census data, see maps 9 and 10 in appendix 2 below.

92. Zunz, *Changing Face*, 174; Simon, *City-Building Process*, 40–41. Also Roger D. Simon, "Housing and Services in an Immigrant Neighborhood: Milwaukee's Ward 14," *Journal of Urban History* 2 (1976): 435–58. Milwaukee's Fourteenth Ward homeowners paved their streets before sewering them.

93. Cain, *Sanitation Strategy*, 147; Pierce, *History*, 2:510.

the water and sewerage commissioners, were similar to those who served as aldermen, though William B. Ogden, the city's first mayor and wealthiest developer by far, brought his prestige to the sewerage board as a commissioner. The engineers were different. McAlpine and Chesbrough arrived in Chicago with no interests in the value of particular tracts of its real estate. They designed projects that their employers and the council (and in McAlpine's case the voters) approved in a wholesale rather than piecemeal fashion, free from the local consensus building of the special assessment process. Still, the engineers had little impact on distributional decisions, on who got which services when. Those decisions were "public" in only a limited sense because, like aldermen considering street projects, the boards relied on user charges and special assessments for decision making as well as financing. Sewer extension, though not individual connection, was an important exception in segmented government, the only improvement for which all of Chicago's property owners paid collectively for "particular" benefits. It was the only project without "fixed rules" for decision making.

The fixed rules of segmented government built a gatekeeping mechanism at the process of policy formation. Each decision enrolled a well-defined group of participants: for initiating a special assessment project, those likely to be assessed; for confirming an assessment roll, those actually assessed; for revising the fire limit, those in the relevant boundaries; for connecting to the water and sewerage systems, those paying tap and drain fees. Only an "interested party" had a voice in decision making and only a property owner could be "interested." With participation dependent on property ownership and influence weighted by property value, the segmented system translated economic power directly into political power, counting wealth rather than numbers of citizens. And the translation worked automatically. No politician refused to provide services to poor neighborhoods because no politician made decisions framed in those terms. Aldermen denied that they were decision-makers at all. Yet, although the fixed rules barred the propertyless—three-fourths of the adult men in Chicago—from any role in policy making, they also set limits on the degree to which wealthy owners could exploit those with more modest holdings. The rules protected poorer owners against taxes and gave them political resources with which to challenge development schemes that could threaten their properties.

For wealthier property owners, the rules provided automatic access to the physical improvements that enhanced the appearance, convenience, and value of real estate. These owners could count on their aldermen to defer to their wishes, to expedite projects they wanted and refrain from considering others. They could count on a political process based directly and entirely on their expressly articulated demands. As long as they designed their projects with consensus in mind, trying not to involve opponents with extensive holdings, they could count on autonomy in the development and even planning of a city that was growing explosively. Government built consensus among local owners to mobilize capital for improvements. Through its many separate decisions, the segmented system produced a physical infrastructure for urban growth with little political conflict or public accountability. This was the triumph of "privatism."

5

The Politics of Segmentation

IF THE "FIXED RULES" of segmented decision making gave much of the activity of Chicago's government an apolitical and static character, this description did not extend to any other aspect of the city's history in the 1850s. Its party system was in constant realignment from 1854 to 1863 as Chicagoans recast their political loyalties in response to national events. Its economy, which had grown rapidly for a decade, suffered a major reversal in the Panic of 1857. These pressures exacerbated the social conflicts of a polyglot city, forcing them onto the agenda of a government designed to avoid rather than solve political problems. Through it all, however, Chicagoans rejected efforts to reshape their city government into an active policy-making institution. They clung to segmented privatism as the proper way to govern the city. They defended segmentation against party politics, social conflict, and economic disruption, demanding that their government represent property interests organized on a segmented basis. They insisted, in other words, that there was no such thing as a public interest that city government could pursue citywide. And their understanding of municipal government mirrored their understanding of the national conflicts that would lead the United States into the Civil War.

THE ALDERMEN, state legislators, and "interested" citizens who designed the segmented public works process in the late 1840s also applied the principle of local control to other kinds of policy. By privatizing city services such as police and fire protection, they removed potentially divisive issues from the council's agenda and extended the segmented system's ideological compromise between

Whiggish economic promotion and Democratic laissez-faire. Like the segmented public works process, this further privatization allowed Chicago's government to provide services to property owners without redistributing their wealth. Unlike the public works process, however, other privatist strategies had social and moral implications that became entangled with temperance, an issue so divisive that the nonpartisan council tried to avoid even debating it. The liquor conflict, which reached a violent climax in 1855, not only helped to undermine nonpartisan elections, but also outlined the limits of the segmented ideological compromise with a new clarity. Before turning to the liquor fight, however, it is necessary to sketch the mechanics of segmented policy making outside the public works process and to explore the meaning of "reform" as Chicagoans used the term in the 1850s.

When David Walsh, Chicago's bridewell keeper, sought council authority to set up a system of prison labor in 1855, he did not present his proposals directly. Walsh had devised a program in which convicts could earn labor credits for work that they performed in addition to their mandatory tasks. Each prisoner would decide whether to convert his credits into a shortened prison term or a cash payment. Thus, Walsh would encourage industrious behavior and finance a period of job-hunting for convicts who otherwise would leave the bridewell penniless. The key to this system was a task for the convicts to perform, and Walsh had decided they could crush stone for macadam. In November 1855 Walsh and forty-two of his neighbors sent the council a remonstrance against its recent order to pave Wells Street. Having hired a private contractor who furnished them with an estimate for paving Wells that was roughly half of that on which their assessments had been computed, they accused the city superintendent of fraud. The council, anxious to prevent corruption in the assessment process, appointed a committee to investigate their charges. Walsh then sent this committee his prison labor plan, noting that it would placate the Wells Street remonstrants by cutting the cost of macadam. The committee agreed, dropping its investigation of the superintendent without comment. The convicts began making macadam.[1]

Several days later, Walsh asked aldermen to formalize this arrangement. He unveiled his full labor credit plan and requested the police committee to amend the bridewell ordinance now that its central problem—a task for the convicts—had been solved. The police com-

---

1. Chicago City Council Proceedings Files [hereafter CP], 1855/56:2023, 2127, 1856/57:322, 662. Chicago *Times*, November 1, 1855, treats the fraud charge seriously.

mittee declared the plan a legal question and passed it to the judiciary committee, who refused even to consider it. Aldermen apparently did not object to convict labor; macadam production at the bridewell proceeded with such vigor that the city soon had a surplus on hand. Rather, they refused to discuss a necessarily citywide and potentially divisive issue. Although the charter allowed them to authorize convict labor, they neither debated nor voted on it. Walsh's sole authority for macadam production was a second Wells Street assessment based on its reduced cost.[2] Walsh had been clever to enroll his neighbors on the remonstrance. By taking advantage of the council's responsiveness to the local interests of property owners, he had sidestepped aldermen's reluctance to address a citywide issue. He was naive, however, in assuming that this decision, once made, would be extended into policy. In the segmented system, the council carefully avoided such decisions and molded policy making to fit its segmented requirements.

The 1847 charter amendment that created the real estate ward map and bolstered the special assessment process also segmented the provision of police services through decentralization. While in the booster years the police force had consisted of an elected marshall plus constables that the council appointed as patronage employees, the 1847 law directed that each of the segmented wards elect its own constable. Aldermen could add special constables "when any emergency, or the public interest, may require it," but they exercised this power with caution for two reasons.[3] First, the constables' chief duties involved not street patrol or the arrest of criminals, but process–serving and the collection of licenses, fines, and civil warrants. Since their incomes depended on the fees they earned from these activities, elected constables resisted competition from specials and pressured the council to keep its appointed force small. Second, special constables cost money. Because, as Terrence J. McDonald has shown, nineteenth-century American city governments operated under the constraints of a "low tax consensus" independent of party politics, Chicagoans kept their general property taxes low in part by limiting the costs of policing.[4]

2. CP, 1855/56:2023, 1856/57:662, 1859/60:133; George Manierre, ed., *The Revised Charter and Ordinances of the City of Chicago* (Chicago: Daily Democrat, 1851), 20.

3. John J. Flinn, *History of the Chicago Police from the Settlement of the Community to the Present Time* (New York: AMS Press, 1973 [1887]), 53–58; CP, 1844/44:2154, 2271, 1845/45:2776; Illinois, *Private and Special Laws, 1847*, 84.

4. CP, 1852/53:58, 162; Manierre, *Revised Charter*, 12; Terrence J. McDonald, *The Parameters of Urban Fiscal Policy: Socioeconomic Change and Political Culture in San Francisco, 1860–1906* (Berkeley: University of California Press, 1986), esp. 117–57.

The role of special constables was never clear. The council appointed a bill collector to the post in 1847 after his petition stressed his occupational needs; he was paid more promptly when he had police status. In 1854 the council hired a special for the north side because none of its elected constables spoke German and added two specials for south side residents who lived over a mile away from their elected constable's office. While the south side petition stressed protection from crime, the north siders seem to have wanted a German-speaking civil officer.[5] In actions more closely related to law enforcement, aldermen deputized private watchmen who "would be much more serviceable to their employers and beneficial to the city if invested with police powers" but also would cost the city nothing and similarly deputized the city's bridge tenders and ferrymen, who already drew salaries and, presumably, witnessed crimes from their posts. Before appointing a constable to patrol the city's rail depots in 1852, aldermen obtained subscriptions from the railroad companies to cover his salary, and in 1854 a theater license required the licensed impresario to "employ at his own expense such police force as may be necessary".to maintain order in his theater's vicinity.[6]

The charter did not specify how Chicago's police force should be paid and placed no cap on the council's hiring of specials, watchmen, or other policemen. Yet, although aldermen could appoint as many as they wanted, they actually appointed few. Even the night watch—which did not compete with elected constables for fees—grew slowly. By 1855, Chicago's 80,000 residents were served by forty individuals who could be called policemen. This total seems to have included the elected constables, specials employed either by the city or private concerns, and watchmen who worked for the city. Of these, only the night watchmen and a tiny day watch gave their full attention to public order. Owners of valuable stores and warehouses, generally located in the downtown area, provided for their own protection by hiring private watchmen either with or without the arrest-making authority that came with special constable status. The council occasionally appropriated small "secret service funds" for the mayor to spend

5. CP, 1847/47:4013, 1854/55:758–59.

6. Ibid., 1852/53:192, 1854/55:57, 664, 1855/56:611, 623. For specials in western cities, Philip J. Ethington, "Vigilantes and the Police: The Creation of a Professional Police Bureaucracy in San Francisco, 1847–1900," *Journal of Social History* 21 (1987): 204; John C. Schneider, "Riot and Reaction in St. Louis, 1854–1856," *Missouri Historical Review* 68 (1974): 177. For eastern comparison, Roger Lane, *Policing the City: Boston, 1822–1885* (Cambridge: Harvard University Press, 1967), 34–35, 59–84; James F. Richardson, *The New York Police: Colonial Times to 1901* (New York: Oxford University Press, 1970), 23–50.

in catching burglars and rewarded private detectives such as Allan Pinkerton for apprehending counterfeiters. Yet in general, aldermen spent little time and little money on the maintenance of public order.[7]

In 1855, as part of the liquor debate then at a crisis point, some Chicagoans demanded police reform: a large, centralized, uniformed force under the mayor's control. In addition to making ethnocultural attacks on Irish policemen who did not enforce the liquor laws, however, reformers also stressed Chicago's public interest in effective policing. They claimed that Chicagoans as a group needed protection against transients who caused "nineteen twentieths" of the city's crime. Forty policemen, moreover, who could not patrol even the downtown effectively, provided no service to the outlying areas where most Chicagoans lived. Finally, as the city became a convention center, its guests would demand "to conduct their deliberations unmolested by unauthorized visitors, and to receive those civilities for the transaction of their business, for which other cities have been so justly praised." Privatized policing promoted none of these public objectives. "To obtain good government," the reformers insisted, "there must be some system pursued . . . and your [police] Committee only regret that they have been compelled from Economical Considerations to present a less Extensive Organization of this department than in their judgment is required."[8]

The Chicago opponents of police reform never met these arguments directly, relying instead on ethnocultural appeals and attacking the "Know Nothing gentry" who supported reform.[9] In Detroit, however, a similar reform program linked to burglaries rather than temperance was proposed at about the same time. After analyzing the Detroit debate, John C. Schneider concluded that the public nature of the proposed reform proved its chief obstacle. While the service of "a municipal agency, publicly funded" would have to be distributed in a geographically equitable manner, crime was a downtown problem. The Detroit critics of police reform defended privatization directly. As that city's newspapers explained, privatized policing left "to the wealthier and more dense portions of the city the care and expense of protecting their own interests in some measure at their own exclusive cost." Even within the downtown, a "public police would cost

7. Manierre, *Revised Charter*, 19. The night watch totalled 14 men in 1852 and 25 by late 1853; CP, 1852/53:13, 1853/54:57-B, 976. The day police totalled 9 in 1853 and 11 in 1854; see 1853/54:130, 1854/55:466. For secret service, 1851/52:683, 1852/53:282, 1856/57:391, and for rewards, 1847/47:4063, 1854/55:946, 1855/56:2119, 1857/58:589, 1858/59:303.

8. CP, 1855/56:294; *Tribune*, June 26, 1854, February 1, May 4, 1855.

9. *Times*, February 21, March 18, May 10, 1855.

less to individuals, but would be far less serviceable, as no attention is paid to particular private interests in such a system."[10] This was precisely what made special assessment an attractive way for Chicagoans to build infrastructure: the "interested" property owners who paid for a service controlled the manner of its provision.

Reform of Chicago's fire department also was entangled with the temperance conflict. Reformers wanted to replace what had become a chaotic system of volunteer companies with a centralized, salaried, steam-powered department. Again, opponents emphasized ethnocultural issues, adding a class rhetoric as well. Reform was a scheme to purge the city's Irish and German firemen, who had "an equal privilege of working at fires without pay, to save the property of 'Americans,' as the Americans themselves. . . . Then these firemen make such a noise! they are so rough; they are mostly mechanics and laboring men, who cannot understand the genius of our free institutions [as nativists did]—particularly those institutions issuing worthless Cherokee currency."[11] The advocates of fire department reform also used ethnocultural arguments. After a trip to Cincinnati to inspect the nation's pioneer steam department, a group of Chicago aldermen not only praised the greater efficiency of steam over hand-driven engines (though they watched one explode during the demonstration, killing a fireman), but also repeated the boasts of Cincinnati officials that steam engines had improved the morals of Cincinnati firemen: "they ought to be termed Evangelists instead of Steam Fire Engines."[12]

While Chicago's police force had remained small, the fire department included over 500 volunteers in its twelve separate companies by 1853. The charter subjected the department's three salaried positions, one chief and two assistant engineers, to citywide election, but firemen controlled this process. Before each election, the fire companies held a convention to nominate a "fire ticket" that then ran unopposed.[13] Company officers, with support from the elected chief engineer, lobbied aldermen for buildings and apparatus financed from general revenue, though the companies owned some of their equipment and real estate. In return for volunteer service, firemen

10. John C. Schneider, *Detroit and the Problem of Order, 1830–1880: A Geography of Crime, Riot, and Policing* (Lincoln: University of Nebraska Press, 1980), 62–63, 81–82.

11. *Times*, March 19, 1855.

12. CP, 1855/56:2002; David D. Dana, *The Fireman: The Fire Departments of the United States*, 2d ed. (Boston: James French, 1858), 92–94.

13. CP, 1852/53:1235. Fire tickets ran unopposed from 1841. See the election returns, appendix 1, and, e.g., *American*, March 3, 1841, *Democrat*, March 6, 1844, *Journal*, March 8, 1848.

gained exemption from jury duty and the city street tax. The Firemen's Benevolent Society, a privately chartered body, aided disabled firemen and their families, financing its operations by collecting a 2 percent tax on all Chicago fire insurance premiums paid to companies incorporated outside of Illinois. This organization exemplified the manner in which state legislatures mixed public and private goals in the nineteenth century: a private body levied a tax that not only took care of the city's firemen, but also gave local insurance men an edge on their "foreign" rivals.[14]

Chicago's fire companies were "rowdy" in the 1850s, but they were neither the ethnic gangs that terrorized eastern cities nor the partisan clubs so prominent in eastern politics.[15] When the firemen sought additional "inducements" for volunteering, they always stressed the danger of recruits who would "discredit" the city. Perhaps because of the "paltry" incentives the city offered to volunteers, the fire department contained many very young men. The chief engineer described a bucket company of "twenty boys who have conducted themselves as well as could be expected" in 1850, but he found it useless in 1851 "owing to the Material of which it has been composed." When another company not only lapsed in its paperwork but also managed to lose its fire engine, aldermen attributed its problems to "a boyish instability of mind, one of the consequent evils of forming fire companies out of to[o] many minors, and persons that are wholly irresponsible." The companies sometimes raced to fires and bet on their comparative speed. One went on strike in 1854 for a new engine house, but even the chief engineer could not defend this. After two hose companies came to blows at a fire in 1855, the council limited the further enrollment of minors in the department.[16]

Fire companies maintained close contacts with the property owners they served. The council formed new companies in response to the petitions of local owners who wanted protection, while the owners often signed firemen's petitions for building and equipment re-

---

14. CP, 1849/49:5104, 1850/50:6530, 1859/60:426; Illinois, *Laws, 1852,* 65–66. The 1863 charter transferred the insurance tax to the city and divided it so that one-eighth went for firemen's relief and seven-eighths for fire-fighting equipment. The Benevolent Society must have been a profitable operation. See Illinois, *Private Laws, 1863,* 98–99, 126–27. The *Times,* January 23, 1863, estimated its revenue to date at $40,000 to $50,000.

15. George D. Bushnell, "Chicago's Rowdy Firefighters," *Chicago History* 2 (1973): 232–41; Schneider, *Detroit,* 65; Lane, *Policing the City,* 33; Richardson, *New York Police,* 149–50; Bruce Laurie, "Fire Companies and Gangs in Southwark: The 1840s" in *The Peoples of Philadelphia: A History of Ethnic Groups and Lower-Class Life, 1790–1940,* Allen F. Davis and Mark H. Haller, eds. (Philadelphia: Temple University Press, 1973), 71–87.

16. CP, 1850/50:6098, 1851/52:1391, 1854/55:848–49, 1855/56:1177, 1213, 1511, 1642.

pair. They also may have subscribed funds for the acquisition of property that the companies owned.[17] Fire department reform was to some extent a challenge to this local control by the less geographically based interests of insurance companies. Class and ethnic appeals clouded this issue. Whereas support in the council for police reform mirrored the alignment on liquor, fire department reform did not, despite the ethnocultural rhetoric. Leaders of both groups, including both Levi Boone and Elihu Granger, united on the fire reform program. Nevertheless, while police reform succeeded in 1855, fire department reform failed, perhaps because its advocates could not work together. Between 1857 and 1860, with the liquor issue settled, the council professionalized the fire department. It purchased steam engines, paid firemen to run them, and forced hand-engine companies to yield to steam companies at fires. These policies finally goaded the volunteers to quit because there was "no Honourable Competition left for them."[18]

As has been suggested, police and fire department reform were closely linked with the most explosive program for the reform of northern society in the 1850s, the prohibition of liquor. In the years of the booster system, the council had handled calls for temperance legislation in a partisan manner. Since Whigs supported strict liquor laws and Democrats opposed them, the council's normally Democratic majorities stifled prohibition and kept liquor license fees low. Antiliquor aldermen accepted this political resolution of the issue, condemning the extralegal pressure tactics of their less patient allies. Through an informal political compromise of 1846, antiliquor aldermen chaired a new council license committee on the condition that they agreed to issue licenses, though they could use this position to regulate compliance with the license provisions by refusing either to remit fines for violations (selling liquor to minors or women, allowing gambling on licensed premises, etc.) or to renew licenses that had been suspended on these grounds. Thus Levi Boone, who opposed "the issuing of licenses to any person at any price," routinely approved new license requests, adding always that he had "no objections other than such as are common to all such applications."[19]

17. Ibid., 1851/52:1240, 1854/55:1419.

18. Ibid., 1855/56:1801, 1857/58:791, 1858/59:18, 367, 463, 557–58, 663, 759–60, 872, 1859/60:257, 426.

19. Ibid., 1846/46:3068, 3096–97, 3114, 3122, 3126, 3144–45, 3149, 3224, 1847/47:3876, 3956, 1849/49:5253–54, 5266, 5292, 5307, 5346, 5391, 5408. License fees, chiefly but not only from liquor licenses, comprised one-fourth of general revenue in 1848 and one-tenth in 1853; Faith Fitzgerald, "Growth of Municipal Activities in Chicago, 1833 to 1875" (M.A. thesis, University of Chicago, 1933), 254.

By 1850, this partisan resolution of the liquor issue had begun to break down for two reasons. First, a national temperance movement that would adopt a uniform program in the comprehensive Maine liquor ban of 1851 gave Chicago's temperance men both a concrete goal and a new confidence that success was possible. Through a network of Maine Law Alliances, they worked with temperance groups that were strong in many of Illinois's northern counties to lobby the legislature to copy the Maine enactment. In response to their pressure, the legislature in 1851 prohibited the sale of liquor in amounts less than a quart and stripped local governments of their license powers but did not provide enforcement mechanisms. If this law failed to stop liquor sales anywhere in Illinois, Chicago aldermen went so far as to pass a new license ordinance four days after it went into effect. An 1852 license ban that the legislature aimed specifically at Chicago was equally useless. Not only did the council continue to issue licenses, but because the law made license fees difficult to collect, it thwarted even the limited tavern regulation that licensing made possible. In 1853, when the legislature remedied this situation by restoring local license powers, the state's antiliquor groups united on the Maine Law as the only feasible solution to the liquor problem.[20]

In 1854, moreover, the Illinois legislature had a different composition. With the state's Democratic party split over the Kansas-Nebraska Act, anti-Nebraska candidates won seats throughout the northern parts of Illinois ("pro-Nebraska" Democrats followed Illinois senator Stephen Douglas, author of the Kansas-Nebraska Act, while "anti-Nebraska" Democrats demanded that their party disavow the law's extension of slavery into new northwestern territory).[21] Historian Ar-

20. Arthur Charles Cole, *The Era of the Civil War, 1848–1870* (Chicago: A. C. McClurg, 1922), 205–7; Illinois, *General Laws, 1851*, 18–19 and *Laws, Second Session, 1852*, 219–20; CP, 1851/52:1509, 1666, 1852/53:441, 665, 1091. The *Democrat*, February 19, 1851, claimed Chicago was exempt from the license ban because the new charter, passed after the liquor law, contained a blanket clause asserting that the city retained all powers granted in previous charters.

21. The Kansas-Nebraska Act organized two territories, Kansas and Nebraska, and allowed Kansas to develop into a slave state if, at the time it applied for statehood, a majority of its voters favored slavery. An attempt to implement Douglas's policy of "popular sovereignty" as a solution to the problem of national conflict about slavery in the territories, Kansas-Nebraska also repealed the Missouri Compromise of 1820 by allowing slavery in a territory north of the 36° 30′ line drawn by that compromise. This description of the Kansas-Nebraska Act (repeal of the Missouri Compromise) dominated anti-Nebraska rhetoric. Thus, it is possible to see the real significance of Kansas-Nebraska in its violation of the national practice of segmenting decisions about slavery. This violation, with others such as the Dred Scott decision, made the Civil War

thur C. Cole described the complexity that the Kansas-Nebraska Act suddenly brought to Illinois politics. The 1854 state election, according to Cole, was "more than an anti-Nebraska victory, it was a reform triumph, a temperance victory. The new legislature was a strong anti-Nebraska temperance body, anxious to secure the enactment of the Maine law."[22] While the political impact of this link will be explored in more detail below, it is important to establish here the partisan nature of the liquor fight. The legislature ordered a referendum for June 1855 in which the effort to ban liquor through a Maine Law failed, losing both in Chicago and statewide. In his ecological regression analysis of the state vote, William Gienapp found that while two-thirds of Illinois's Whigs and Free Soilers voted for the law, nearly every Democrat—including anti-Nebraska Democrats—voted against it. Because those Whigs and Free Soilers who opposed the Maine Law tended to abstain rather than cast negative ballots, the anti–Maine Law tally was an almost exclusively Democratic vote. In other states, all three parties tended to split on the Maine Law. In Illinois, however, and for reasons that are not altogether clear, liquor was a partisan issue.[23]

If the statewide result of 1855 resembled the Chicago liquor splits of the 1830s and 1840s, when aldermen had acted on strict party lines, it also suggests the second reason that the council no longer could resolve liquor issues politically. The compromise that gave the license chairmanship to Boone (Whig), Henry Smith (Liberty party), and Amos Throop (a Whig who would chair the Cook County Maine Law Alliance) assumed that these men would respect partisan majority rule, which they did by issuing licenses. By 1850, however, the council no longer reflected party organization or discipline. Aldermen who were elected on the basis of their ability to process public works requests lacked clear mandates to act on a partisan issue. Now, when the council approved new licenses by voice vote, the license chairman resigned rather than issue them "at variance with opinions conscien-

inevitable. See Don E. Fehrenbacher, *Slavery, Law, and Politics: The Dred Scott Case in Historical Perspective* (New York: Oxford University Press, 1981). The best introduction to the act itself still is Roy F. Nichols, "The Kansas-Nebraska Act: A Century of Historiography," *Mississippi Valley Historical Review* 43 (1956–57): 187–212.

22. Cole, *Era*, 209.

23. William E. Gienapp, *The Origins of the Republican Party, 1852–1856* (New York: Oxford University Press, 1987), 46–47, 488. For an attempt at ethnocultural analysis, Stephen L. Hansen, *The Making of the Third Party System: Voters and Parties in Illinois, 1850–1876* (Ann Arbor: University Microfilms International, 1980), 63–66.

tiously entertained by myself upon that subject." In 1852, when the committee demanded a Maine Law, declaring themselves "willing to be judged" by this position, the council "accepted" their report to avoid concurring in, rejecting, or tabling it; any of which might have required a formal roll call.[24] Except for those who had personal commitments, most aldermen simply refused to take open positions on liquor.

Yet the arguments with which antiliquor aldermen defended high-license and no-license policies after 1850 suggest a Whig influence that extended well beyond the affiliations of Boone and Throop in the 1840s. When an antilicense petition with one thousand signatures described aldermen as "guardians of public morals," a sympathetic license committee ignored this, emphasizing instead the number of signatures—they had counted them—and the effects of drinking on property. Not only did the "poverty, crime & wretchedness" caused by liquor raise taxes, but taverns also depressed property values because it was "impossible to establish good neighborhoods in the midst of this business." The antiliquor forces exploited the segmented style of decision making by counting the signatures and hinting at the property interests they represented; many of Chicago's major real estate owners had indeed signed the petition. The committee also explicitly rejected the class argument of the city's tavern owners, that a high license would allow only the rich to sell liquor or, for that matter, to buy it (everyone understood that this tax was shifted to consumers in drink prices). The committee stressed instead "the interest of the City" in temperance, arguing that a petition "signed by our most respectable citizens . . . called loudly for a reform."[25]

What was reformist about the antiliquor program, and what distinguished it from segmented services to property, was its citywide nature. Chicagoans had established the segmented system in the 1840s in a national political atmosphere structured by a Whig call for internal improvements in the public interest and a Democratic reluctance to redistribute wealth through the political system. They had compromised these positions within the city in a government structure that fostered improvements on a local basis. When the antiliquor group, therefore, argued that the defense of property required citywide action, that it was an all-or-nothing proposition that could not be evaded through decentralization, they revealed that the segmented ideological compromise actually was less a compromise than a Demo-

24. CP, 1850/50:6641, 1852/53:1091.
25. Ibid., 1851/52:253, 402–3.

cratic victory. When, in his 1854 inaugural address, the proliquor mayor Isaac Milliken, a Democrat, coupled his pride "that it is to the laboring classes principally, [that] I am indebted for the position I now occupy" with a promise to keep divisive and partisan issues out of the debates of the segmented council, the limits of the compromise could not have been more clear.[26]

Nonpartisan elections and the council's refusal to vote on liquor guaranteed a prolicense policy. Like privatized policing and rowdy volunteer fire companies, this policy denied the kind of service to property that could be effected only through reforms predicated on the existence of a public interest. Milliken's inaugural may have been frightening in its omission of the city's property owners from the list of those to whom he felt "indebted." By 1855, however, Chicagoans also could compare this aversion to divisive debate with a national Democratic rhetoric, Stephen Douglas's call for popular sovereignty. When the liquor conflict exploded in 1855 at the polls, in the streets, and finally on the council floor itself, aldermen made their citywide decision and, in the end, rejected antiliquor reform. As they struggled with this decision, they also watched the logic of popular sovereignty unfold in Kansas, where Douglas's "solution" to divisive debate had degenerated into a proxy war between guerrilla armies.[27] Because Chicago's final showdown on liquor was shaped as much by the reorganization of party politics as by the limits of the segmented ideological compromise, the showdown must be embedded in the local dynamics of party realignment in the mid 1850s and the collapse of municipal nonpartisanship.

WHILE MANY ASPECTS of the segmented system depended on some combination of law and custom, nonpartisan elections rested on custom alone. In 1848, with Chicago's Whigs doomed to permanent minority status and its Democrats split over state banking, the parties reached a formal agreement to stay out of city elections. If Democrats

26. Ibid., 1854/55:4. Milliken also eulogized the city's immigrants. Nobody seems to have suggested that the liquor fight be resolved through a ward-based local option like that used in 1839, perhaps because the 1847 ward map would have made the term "local" meaningless in this context.

27. For an introduction, James A. Rawley, *Race and Politics: "Bleeding Kansas" and the Coming of the Civil War* (Philadelphia: Lippincott, 1969). On the importance of the Kansas warfare for northern politics, William E. Gienapp, "The Crime against Sumner: The Caning of Charles Sumner and the Rise of the Republican Party," *Civil War History* 25 (1979): 218–45; Bernard A. Weisberger, "The Newspaper Reporter and the Kansas Imbroglio," *Mississippi Valley Historical Review* 36 (1949–50): 633–56.

left more reluctantly than Whigs, both refrained from campaigning until the mid 1850s, when the pull of national politics and the intervention of national party leaders enmeshed city elections in the realignment that created the Republican party. The realignment was a powerfully politicizing experience. Northerners took stands on slavery, temperance, and nativism not only at party caucuses, rallies, and the polls, but in church, at the theater, in commercial bodies and trade unions, and at home. In an environment that politicized every American institution to some extent, a government that held annual elections could hardly remain aloof.[28] Yet it could remain segmented. If a majority of Chicagoans came to agree with Abraham Lincoln that the United States had to become "all one thing, or all the other" in regard to slavery, they continued to reject an integrated approach to municipal government.

The nonpartisan pact of 1848 was made by two well-defined political forces that represented their views in Chicago's two daily newspapers: the Whig *Journal* and John Wentworth's *Democrat*. By 1855 the city had eight partisan dailies in addition to a host of weeklies promoting religious affairs, abolitionism, temperance, nativism, and other causes. Yet it was the partisan press that best reflected the political distance Chicagoans travelled in these years. By 1852 the *Journal* and *Democrat* had been joined by two dailies that would remain important in local politics: the antislavery Democratic *Illinois Staats-Zeitung*, published by forty-eighter émigrés, and the *Tribune*, probank but otherwise nonpartisan. After several ownership changes and a brief career as a Free Soil party organ, the *Tribune* became officially Whig in 1852, when its Democratic partner sold out to start the *Democratic Press*, a free-soil daily known for its commercial coverage. In its Whig phase, the *Tribune* emphasized temperance, nativism, and "the anti-republican character of the Romish church." It also criticized nonpartisanship because without organized nominations, the mayoralty was "scrambled for by hungry, needy and ambitious *little* men" who courted the city's Irish voters.[29]

28. Jean H. Baker, *Affairs of Party: The Political Culture of Northern Democrats in the Mid-Nineteenth Century* (Ithaca: Cornell University Press, 1983); William E. Gienapp, "'Politics Seems to Enter into Everything,': Political Culture in the North, 1840–1860" in *Essays on American Antebellum Politics, 1840–1860,* Stephen E. Maizlish and John J. Kushma, eds. (College Station: Texas A&M University Press, 1982), 14–69; John R. McKivigan, *The War against Proslavery Religion: Abolitionism and the Northern Churches, 1830–1865* (Ithaca: Cornell University Press, 1984).

29. "A Voter," *Tribune*, February 24, 1854 (emphasis in original). On the press generally, A. T. Andreas, *History of Chicago* (3 vols.; Chicago: Andreas, 1884–86), 1:377–412. On the *Staats-Zeitung*, Andrew Jacke Townsend, "The Germans of Chi-

The "ambitious little" object of the *Tribune*'s ire was the native-born Isaac Milliken. A blacksmith, Milliken was indeed Chicago's only mayor before 1869 who, in Bessie Louise Pierce's words, "had not attained enviable standing in the business life of the city." Yet Milliken was not an outsider. When he ran against Amos Throop in 1854, both had served four years in the council, playing by the rules of nonpartisan segmentation. The *Tribune* not only endorsed Throop but campaigned actively once a Maine Law convention nominated him, predicting that the nomination would help Throop to defeat his three "independent" opponents. It urged Chicago's "solid men" to vote for a "moral triumph" on the road to prohibition. On election day, with the field narrowed to Throop and Milliken, the *Tribune* alleged that Milliken would divide the school fund between public and Catholic schools (Milliken denied this in his inaugural) and listed Irishmen in position to "plunder" the city, though it cited no actual plundering. "Let no one omit voting," it called. "Vote early too. Toward the close of the day there is no doubt that the polls in many wards, will be blockaded by a bleary-eyed, drunken rabble, who will try to prevent all ingress or egress by any decent persons."[30]

The other papers ignored the *Tribune* in 1854, printing paid electoral notices and the returns without comment. The *Tribune*, however, only escalated its attacks on "the system of Priestcraft and delusion which is at present recognized under the name of the Catholic church." As the 1855 election approached, it fabricated a story about rioters who shouted "Death to the Know Nothings" and beat native-born victims until the snow was red with their blood. "Ruled as we are by drunken Irishmen," it asked, "what safety is there to life or property?" Under the headline "How Long Must We Endure This?" it claimed that Irish crowds routinely harassed Protestants on their way out of church services and soon revealed a "grog sellers" conspiracy to "put down" the city's nativists "if they had to wade knee-deep in blood to do it."[31] The other papers again tried

---

cago" (Ph.D. diss., University of Chicago, 1927), 30–33. On the *Tribune*, Thomas M. Keefe, "The Catholic Issue in the Chicago Tribune before the Civil War," *Mid-America* 57 (1975): 227–45 (quote from 230).

30. Bessie Louise Pierce, *A History of Chicago* (3 vols.; Chicago: University of Chicago Press, 1937–57), 2:305; *Tribune*, February 6, March 6, 7, 1854; CP, 1854/55:4.

31. *Tribune*, March 20, 1854, quoted in Keefe, "Catholic Issue," 232; *Tribune*, February 1, February 21, 1855; *Tribune*, March 3, 1855, quoted in Bruce McKitterick Cole, "The Chicago Press and the Know-Nothings, 1850–1856" (M.A. thesis, University of Chicago, 1948), 59.

to ignore the campaign. While the Whig *Journal* predicted that the *Tribune's* "heartless and unprincipled conduct" would provoke riots, the *Democratic Press* repeated the normal nonpartisan advice: vote for the best men "without reference to nativities or creeds."[32] Between the 1854 and 1855 elections, however, the political landscape had undergone a dramatic change—Congress had passed the Kansas-Nebraska Act.

This legislation provoked outrage across the North, but two local circumstances increased its volatility in Chicago. First, its author, Stephen Douglas, was the state's leading politician. While President Franklin Pierce made support for Kansas-Nebraska the standard of Democratic party loyalty throughout the North, Douglas saw the anti-Nebraska Democrats of his own state as personal traitors.[33] Second, even as most Chicago Democrats opposed Kansas-Nebraska, they still were divided on banking. Historians generally have attributed the early Republican party's silence on economic policy both to divisions between the party's former Democrats and Whigs and to the obsolescence especially of the national bank debate. In Illinois, however, banking was a current issue in the mid 1850s before the Panic of 1857 revived it nationally. In 1860 Chicago's Republicans were divided so bitterly—by both banking and simple personality conflicts—that Norman B. Judd, the former probank Democrat who would nominate Lincoln at the 1860 Republican national convention, was suing John Wentworth, then Chicago's Republican mayor, for libel. A year later, the former Whig and now Republican lawyer and banker J. Young Scammon brought another libel suit after Wentworth's *Democrat* urged Chicago's laborers to "arouse" against bankers who "are fattening upon your blood."[34]

Every Chicago newspaper condemned the Kansas-Nebraska Act. Not only did the Whig *Tribune* and *Journal* oppose Douglas, but the three Democratic papers, *Democrat*, *Press*, and *Staats-Zeitung*, also repudiated his leadership. Lacking a reliable press organ in his home

32. *Journal*, March 5, 1855; *Democratic Press*, March 6, 1855, quoted in Cole, "Chicago Press," 60.

33. Robert W. Johannsen, *Stephen A. Douglas* (New York: Oxford University Press, 1973), 447–61.

34. Rima Lunin Schultz, "The Businessman's Role in Western Settlement: The Entrepreneurial Frontier, Chicago, 1833–1872" (Ph.D. diss., Boston University, 1985), 160–66, 172–78; Eric Foner, *Free Soil, Free Labor, Free Men: The Ideology of the Republican Party before the Civil War* (New York: Oxford University Press, 1970), 168–76; Gienapp, *Origins*, 353–54; Don E. Fehrenbacher, *Chicago Giant: A Biography of "Long John" Wentworth* (Madison: American History Research Center, 1957), 170–72, 188, 192 (quote from the *Democrat*). Also Don E. Fehrenbacher, "The Judd-Wentworth Feud," *Journal of the Illinois State Historical Society* [hereafter *JISHS*] 45 (1952): 197–211.

town, Douglas convinced James W. Sheahan, a Washington journalist, to start the Chicago *Times* in September 1854 and financed the venture directly. A year later, Douglas men added the *National Demokrat* to compete with the *Staats-Zeitung*. Although Douglas advised Sheahan to portray the *Tribune, Democrat,* and *Press* as allied organs of the "great abolition Party," Sheahan sized up the Chicago situation accurately enough to paint anti-immigrant Know Nothings, rather than abolitionists, as the chief enemies of the Democratic party. Sheahan also tried to respect nonpartisan city elections. As the *Tribune*'s support of openly nativist candidates for the March 1855 contest grew increasingly apparent, the *Times* meekly listed several candidates who "will be supported by those citizens . . . who are in favor of the free enjoyment of civil and religious liberty." This was closer to an endorsement than the *Democrat, Press,* or *Journal* came, but it was not a Democratic party slate.[35]

Although Chicago's newspapers often exaggerated the strength of the local Know Nothing organization for unrelated partisan purposes—accusations of nativism were effective smears in a city two-thirds of whose residents were immigrants—the secret nativist order was an undeniable local presence by early 1855, with the *Tribune* as its unofficial press organ. While, as Gienapp has shown conclusively, Know Nothings reaped the initial gains from anti-Nebraska disaffection in many states, in Chicago they also profited from Whig impotence and the Democratic bank quarrel. No other party could appear to champion temperance, antislavery, or "reform." The nativist appeal, however, was temporary. The antiliquor and free-soil groups who joined the Know Nothings' Native American party rarely shared, as Cole phrased it, "any strong conviction that nativism was the dominant issue of the day." Within six months, when the Maine Law's defeat ended the antiliquor crusade and two stormy state Know Nothing conventions revealed the limits of nativist support for free soil, most of these men left the party. And they left in the summer of 1855, almost a year before the first state Republican convention—still calling itself anti-Nebraska—launched the new party in Illinois.[36]

At the same time that the Know Nothings courted antislavery and temperance men, they also attracted an even more politically homeless group: southern Whigs. Among the most prominent Chicagoans to join the Know Nothing order, Levi Boone had split his First Baptist

35. Johannsen, *Douglas,* 448–49, 533; *Times,* February 21, 26, March 3, 1855.

36. Gienapp, *Origins,* 103–66; Cole, *Era,* 138; Keefe, "Catholic Issue," and Thomas M. Keefe, "Chicago's Flirtation with Political Nativism, 1854–1856," *Records of the American Catholic Historical Society of Philadelphia* 82 (1971): 131–58.

Church in 1843 by lecturing on the scriptural defense of slavery, and in 1853 he bought and shut down the antislavery Baptist *Watchman of the Prairies*. Not himself a teetotaler, Boone probably supported prohibition as an anti-Catholic measure. If he had adopted the reform approach to property value by the mid 1850s, he also had been the 1847 council finance chairman reluctant to fund the River and Harbor Convention. By 1858, Levi Boone was a Democrat. Although less than 4 percent of native-born Chicagoans were southerners, both Boone and Buckner Morris (Whig mayor in 1838, Native candidate for governor in 1856, open Copperhead during the war) had come from Kentucky. Except for his attendance at the national American party founding convention in 1845, no biographical information is available about William W. Danenhower, who led the Illinois Know Nothings and published the daily *Native Citizen* in Chicago for a year beginning late in 1855 (after the *Tribune* abandoned the cause). Yet Danenhower and Boone both tried—and failed—to prevent the mid 1855 state Know Nothing meetings from adopting free-soil resolutions.[37]

In Chicago's nonpartisan elections, candidates had announced their availability in paid advertisements that began to appear in the newspapers several weeks before each contest. Not so in 1855. Two weeks before the March 6 election, with few paid notices in the press, hostile partisan rumors surfaced as the *Democrat* and *Times* printed Know Nothing tickets and the *Tribune* announced the ticket of "the Irish, Jesuitical, Foreign Domination and American Proscription Party" headed by Milliken for mayor. The *Journal*, which opposed the Know Nothings, vainly protested this politicization, endorsing a Democrat for one city office in order to validate its nonpartisan credentials. On election day the *Press* noted the lack of paid notices, reporting that the "canvass has been conducted in private," but interpreted this situation through a patently false history of the city's elections. "Ordinarily the occasion is one of great interest from the issues involved—issues pertaining to the good government and substantial welfare of our city. Today, however, there is no such issue before the people." There was an issue before Chicago's voters in 1855, though it was announced officially only on election day, when the *Tribune* unveiled a Law and Order ticket led by Levi Boone for mayor.[38]

37. Andreas, *History*, 1:319–20, 402, 426–27; Pierce, *History*, 2:481; Keefe, "Chicago's Flirtation," 133, 143–47; Weston A. Goodspeed and Daniel D. Healy, eds., *History of Cook County, Illinois* (2 vols.; Chicago: Goodspeed Historical Association, 1909), 1:376.

38. *Tribune*, February 8, 26, 27, 28, March 1, 5, 6, 1855; *Journal*, March 5, 1855; *Times*, February 19, 21, 26, March 3, 1855; *Democratic Press*, March 6, 1855, quoted in Keefe, "Chicago's Flirtation," 140–41; Cole, "Chicago Press," 57–60.

In 1854, when Milliken beat Throop for the mayoralty, the city's ward races had remained unorganized. Aldermanic candidates had followed the nonpartisan procedure, buying press notices "on their own hooks." Of nine aldermanic contests, six had featured three or more viable candidates, while in a seventh the winner ran unopposed. In 1855, however, all ten council races (Boone vacated his seat to run for mayor) were one-on-one contests that pitted a Law and Order nominee against a single opponent. Even though no formal tickets had been printed, only one ward split its vote, delivering a majority for Milliken but electing a Law and Order alderman. Boone and his ticket for the citywide offices (attorney, collector, treasurer, surveyor, and three police court justices) squeaked past Milliken and his allies with 51 percent of the vote, a major improvement over the 40 percent that Throop had won a year earlier. Law and Order men also took seven of the ten open council seats, losing only in the heavily immigrant wards of the north side.[39] Of the ten new aldermen, only three, two of them north siders, had any previous council experience, making this council the least experienced since 1848, the first year of municipal nonpartisanship.[40]

In his inaugural address, Boone interpreted the result as a mandate for prohibition. Sharing a platform with Danenhower and Throop, he called for either an end to liquor licensing or a hike in the license fee from $50 to $300. The sixfold fee hike would be combined with a shortening of the licenses' terms from a year to three months so that they would expire when the Maine Law referendum, scheduled for June, declared Illinois dry. Boone would enforce his prohibitive ordinance using a reorganized and native-born police force. He also pledged fire department reform and "consecrate[d] my talents, my property, and, if need be, my life" to defeat "a powerful politico-religious organization . . . bound under an oath of allegiance to the temporal, as well as the spiritual supremacy of a foreign despot."[41] Because aldermen served staggered two-year terms, however, the seven Law and Order aldermen elected with Boone did not themselves constitute a council majority. To pass, the antiliquor program would require unanimity among the Law and Order aldermen and

39. Election returns cited in appendix 1. While 34 percent of Chicago's adult male residents in 1850 and 28 percent in 1860 had been born in the U.S., only 21 percent of the city's north side men in 1850 and 18 percent in 1860 were native-born. See appendix 2 for more detail.

40. Experience calculated from council rosters in Andreas, *History*, 1:184–85.

41. Keefe, "Chicago's Flirtation," 141–42; Richard Wilson Renner, "In a Perfect Ferment: Chicago, the Know-Nothings, and the Riot for Lager Beer," *Chicago History* 5 (1976): 163–64.

the cooperation of at least two holdovers from the 1854 nonpartisan contest. In the event of a tie, Boone could cast the winning antiliquor vote.

Wrangling within the new council began immediately. Elihu Granger—the abrasive Democrat who, a decade earlier, had helped to build the special assessment process and who now was the most experienced alderman by far—soon emerged among Boone's chief opponents. The *Times* classified Granger and another proliquor holdover with the Know Nothings, however, because they voted to award the city printing contract to Wentworth's *Democrat*. Yet this vote was a proliquor victory; neither the *Tribune* nor the more moderately antiliquor *Journal* won the printing. Boone then claimed the right to vote on every issue before the council rather than only in ties (aldermen rejected this illegal maneuver), and the Boone forces defeated an equally invalid proliquor demand to scrap the results of the police justice election because some of the ballots read "police justice" and others "police magistrate." Meanwhile, Boone hired 80 native-born special policemen, swelling the total to 120, and put the force in uniform, "the mark of their degradation," in the *Times'* view; "he intends to have his American officers dressed up in fantastic style, like prize cattle."[42] Then, on March 26, the council turned to the $300 license ordinance.

The high license fee passed by a vote of 13–5. It won not only the seven Law and Order votes, but also those of five holdovers, one a north sider, and a new north side alderman, James L. Howe, who actually had beaten a Law and Order nominee in the election. When this vote is compared with the Maine Law referendum result, aldermen's failure to represent their constituents on the liquor issue becomes clear. Seven aldermen whose wards would reject the Maine Law voted for the $300 license: three Law and Order men, three holdovers, and Howe. When they voted on it after the referendum, however, every north sider except Howe opposed the high license, while Howe and two Law and Order men from anti–Maine Law wards abstained. One Law and Order alderman rejected his ward's proliquor decision, causing a 7–7 tie that allowed Boone to sustain the $300 license, but even he changed his vote six weeks later to support a reduction to $100 rather than $50.[43] Had aldermen voted their constituents' preferences, the prohibitive license fee would not have passed. As it was, however, the high license and Boone's "American"

42. *Tribune*, March 10, 12, 13, 16, 1855; *Times*, March 16, 17, 19, April 5, 1855.
43. For the votes, CP, 1855/56:93 (March 26), 712 (June 25), 938 (August 13).

police force—which also began to enforce an old Sunday closing law—provoked a riot.

Boone's police had begun arresting tavern owners under the Sunday law immediately after the election. Organized protest, however, awaited the April 1 expiration of the previous year's $50 licenses. Although Irish immigrants had been the main objects of attack by the nativist press, it was the city's German community that mobilized. Led by brewer John Huck, six hundred Germans met in the north side market hall on April 4 to raise legal defense funds. Sunday trials proceeded in the police courts with the new city attorney, John Thompson, handling the prosecution and the previous incumbent, Patrick Ballingall, the defense. Isaac Milliken, now a police justice, dismissed several of these cases, but Henry L. Rucker, now also a police justice, issued convictions. Still, Sunday cases were less important than those concerning unlicensed sale, the number of which mushroomed when the $50 licenses expired. On April 14, after Milliken convicted a tavern keeper under the $300 ordinance, Thompson and Ballingall agreed to try a test case in Rucker's court. Ballingall planned to argue that the 1852 law stripping the city of its license power nullified the $300 ordinance.[44]

On Saturday, April 21, a large crowd, complete with fife and drum corps, assembled to support the defendants. With the courtroom overflowing, the corridors filled, and the streets outside blocked by demonstrators, Mayor Boone ordered the city marshall to clear the area, which was accomplished by noon with nine arrests and little violence. On the north side, however, a crowd of armed men decided to rescue the prisoners. Boone deputized 150 more special policemen, raising the total to 270, and ordered the Clark Street drawbridge raised to prevent the north siders from crossing the river to storm the courthouse. When the crowd reached the bridge, they threatened and tried to bribe the bridge tender, but he waited for instructions from Boone. At about 4:00, Boone ordered the bridge lowered and the rioters surged across, only to be met by a solid phalanx of policemen blocking Clark Street. Boone, watching from his office window, declared martial law as rioters and policemen began shooting outside. By 5:00, militia companies had arrived and the "lager beer riot" was over. One rioter had been killed, a policeman lost his arm, and other fatal casualties were rumored, if not quite confirmed, by a series of mysterious funerals on the north side. Among some sixty rioters ar-

44. Renner, "Perfect Ferment," 164–65; Tribune, March 26, 30, April 2, 7, 14, 17, 1855.

rested was one Stephen D. LaRue, a whiskey wholesaler who would parlay his notoriety into a council seat in a north side by-election four months later.[45]

The liquor debate paralyzed the council. In lowering the fee to $100, aldermen accepted a compromise whose proponents demanded any solution that would restore "the harmony and peace" of the council itself so that "*many* matters of vital importance to the City now neglected would receive attention." The council, in other words, had been neglecting its public works responsibilities. But the liquor fight continued as aldermen debated whether to order the dismissal of suits that were still pending against tavern owners under the $300 ordinance. Boone met this with outrage: the council might as well "pass a general order releasing every poor victim of intemperance from the Bridewell . . . and dismissing the entire police of the City, and let all parties do as they please!" This he could not allow and it lost by his casting vote.[46] Meanwhile, still listening to Boone defend his declaration of martial law, the council passed his police reform ordinance in an 8–7 vote close to the new liquor split. Every north sider opposed it, Elihu Granger "in a rather warm and excited manner." Although it was a constant object of attack by the *Times*, the new police force did have one desirable effect: it disbanded Boone's army of nativist specials.[47]

In their 1856 municipal election, Chicagoans dropped all pretense of nonpartisanship, making the contest a referendum on the Kansas-Nebraska Act. The Douglas forces organized ward clubs and, in the first major party convention since 1848, nominated a full slate led by Thomas Dyer for mayor. For Douglas, the 1856 city election presented an opportunity to purge anti-Nebraska Democrats, and especially John Wentworth, from the Democratic party. Every local observer agreed that although Chicago's German voters would oppose Douglas on Kansas-Nebraska, they would vote for the proliquor municipal candidates in 1856, particularly after the riot. Thus, Douglas could purge his anti-Nebraska opponents in a contest his party was bound to win on the liquor issue. "The *Times*," as Sheahan explained this strategy to Douglas, "is now the organ of the party. Dyer's nomination forces the *Democrat* over to the fusion party against our *nominees*, and at once, it will cease to exercise any control over the counsils [*sic*] of the party." Douglas had stumped the state against the Maine Law,

45. Renner, "Perfect Ferment," 165–69; Flinn, *Chicago Police*, 76–79; *Tribune*, April 24, 26, May 17, 1855; *Times*, August 30, 1855.

46. CP, 1855/56:938 (emphasis in original), 1114, 1133.

47. Ibid., 1855/56:294; *Tribune*, May 2, 17, 1855; *Times*, May 3, 10, November 1, 1855.

prompting the *Tribune* to predict a conversion by the presumably pro-liquor Wentworth for the sole purpose of opposing Douglas on yet another issue.[48]

Wentworth said little during the liquor fight, however, and by the time of the 1856 election, the *Tribune* had new owners who were equally anxious to avoid the issue. Joseph Medill, a Whig editor from Cleveland, had watched temperance frustrate anti-Nebraska fusion in Ohio. His partner, Charles H. Ray, had been a Democratic editor in Galena, Illinois, before breaking with Douglas on Kansas-Nebraska. Medill and Ray bought the *Tribune* in the summer of 1855, toned down its nativism to criticize only Catholics, and soon made the paper the organ of a local fusion movement that united former Whigs with Democrats who were both probank and anti-Nebraska. The *"Tribune* clique" of what would be the Republican party offered little welcome to the stridently antibank John Wentworth, despite his equally strident opposition to Kansas-Nebraska. Yet Wentworth's popularity among immigrant Democrats, especially the Germans whose votes Republicans needed, forced the *Tribune* group to maintain Wentworth's support. Not until after the 1860 presidential election could the Republicans even attempt what Douglas achieved in 1856, purging Wentworth from the party. Meanwhile, the *Tribune* alternately attacked and applauded him, enabling the *Times* to taunt "that John Wentworth is the only Republican in Chicago who can carry the city."[49]

The anti-Nebraska fusion group nominated Francis C. Sherman for mayor without naming an aldermanic ticket, and every newspaper except the *Times* endorsed him. When the Know Nothings nominated not just Sherman, but also aldermanic candidates for six of the city's nine wards, the *Tribune* and *Journal* both rejected their slate. "The test," the *Journal* proclaimed, ignoring the Douglas ticket, "is to be

48. Sheahan to Douglas, January 29, 1856, box 2, folder 8, Stephen A. Douglas papers, University of Chicago Library (emphasis in original); Buchanan and Breckenridge Club, West Chicago, folder 4, Henry Greenebaum papers, Chicago Historical Society; *Tribune*, April 20, 25, 1855. See also James Manning Bergquist, "The Political Attitudes of the German Immigrant in Illinois, 1848–1860" (Ph.D. diss., Northwestern University, 1966), 325–51; Bruce Carlan Levine, "Free Soil, Free Labor, and *Freimänner: German Chicago in the Civil War Era" in *German Workers in Industrial Chicago, 1850–1910: A Comparative Perspective*, Hartmut Keil and John B. Jentz, eds. (DeKalb: Northern Illinois University Press, 1983), 163–82.

49. *Times*, February 10, 1860; Tracy Elmer Strevey, "Joseph Medill and the *Chicago Tribune* during the Civil War Period" (Ph.D. diss., University of Chicago, 1930), 7–20; Gienapp, *Origins*, 180; Jay Monaghan, *The Man Who Elected Lincoln* (Indianapolis: Bobbs-Merrill, 1956), 14–52; Keefe, "Catholic Issue," 236; Fehrenbacher, *Chicago Giant*, 162–89.

upon the Mayor alone, leaving all other offices to be filled on the individual merits of the different candidates."[50] The mayoral candidates, Sherman and Dyer, were quite similar. Both were wealthy businessmen who had lived in Chicago since the mid 1830s. Sherman had made his fortune in brick-making and quarrying and had been mayor of the city in 1841, while Dyer was a commission merchant and railroad promoter who had been the first president of the Board of Trade. Not only had Sherman and Dyer both been active probank Democrats for two decades, but Sherman would return to the Democratic party in 1858 (perhaps because Douglas broke with President Buchanan over the fraudulent, proslavery Lecompton constitution for Kansas). Unlike Wentworth, who remained a loyal, if isolated, Republican, Sherman would serve as Chicago's Democratic mayor during the Civil War.[51]

It was a rowdy campaign. Douglasite Thomas Hoyne, the U.S. district attorney, and *Journal* editor Charles Wilson fell through the plate glass window of the Illinois State Bank building in a pre-election brawl. Election day brought more violent incidents, though one Democrat did "not think there was any more violence than there usually is around the [north side] 7th ward poll." The immigrant vote, German and Irish, materialized as expected. While the citywide vote was 46 percent heavier than that of 1855, the north side vote rose by 71 percent, prompting anti-Nebraska leaders to charge fraud. Dyer took 53 percent of the citywide total—but nearly three-fourths on the north side—and two pro-Nebraska Germans (including Michael Diversy, a brewer who would edit the *National Demokrat*) entered the council. The *Times* labelled five of the nine new aldermen "Nebraska men." With Douglas now actively campaigning for president, his followers informed the nation of the unlikely result: Chicago had ratified the Kansas-Nebraska Act. Although Chicago voters really had ratified a low liquor license fee, Samuel Ashton, the Douglasite registrar of the U.S. Land Office, now an alderman, gloated to the senator that "'Wentworthism, Know-Nothingism, Nig[g]er-ism, anti-Nebraska-ism and all the other Isms' in this city is dead, never again to be resurrected."[52]

While the March 1856 election was a setback for fusion, Ashton's verdict was premature. In May, with the conspicuous participation

50. *Journal*, February 12, 1856; Sheahan to Douglas, February 19, 1856 (misdated 1855), box 2, folder 2, Douglas papers; Keefe, "Chicago's Flirtation," 149–50.

51. Andreas, *History*, 1:620–22; Goodspeed and Healy, *Cook County*, 1:375.

52. Ashton to Douglas, March 5, 1856, box 2, folder 13, Douglas papers; Pierce, *History*, 2:214; CP, 1855/56:2157; *Tribune*, April 5, 1855; *Times*, March 6, 1856; Johannsen, *Douglas*, 505–12. For election returns, appendix 1.

of anti-Nebraska Democrats, especially Germans, a state Republican party was launched and in November, Republican presidential candidate John C. Frémont took 55 percent of Chicago's vote.[53] In 1857, over the *Tribune*'s objections, John Wentworth won the mayoralty as a Republican with strong German support and declared the "Nebraska" council's restoration of the $50 liquor license to have "satisfactorily adjusted" that issue. After his flagrant abuse of power as mayor—he particularly abused the police force, deploying it to harass anyone who displeased him—forced Wentworth to step aside in 1858, he retook the mayoralty in 1860, boasting to Abraham Lincoln that none of his *Tribune* clique enemies "*can afford* to have me beaten, however much they might desire it." After another stormy term as mayor, however, Wentworth was all but finished in politics and the *Tribune* group in control of the local party.[54] More important, after 1856 Chicago's municipal elections remained organized contests between Democratic and Republican tickets. Republicans kept the mayoralty and council majorities until 1862, when Sherman led the Democrats to victory, but the fortunes of both were linked to state and national voting patterns. The era of municipal nonpartisanship had ended.

One casualty of the new municipal politics was Elihu Granger. Still calling himself a Democrat, he bolted the Douglas ticket and lost in 1856, bolted the Democratic ticket and lost in 1858, and in 1859 bolted and lost yet again. When the *Times* rebuked him for his irregularity, Granger defended himself in a manner that only emphasized his irrelevance. If his party nominated him,

> I should answer it with a *Platform* of my own, which should ignore any political issue, and relate *solely* to the wants and interests of my own *ward*. . . . I have no desire to attend to the duties of an alderman; but, in common with the voters and property owners of the ward, I have a deep interest in the improvements of the ward. [I am running for] the benefit of those who have a *stronger* desire for the good of our own ward than for a *political fight*.[55]

Granger had been less a creator than a beneficiary of nonpartisanship. Never influential in political circles, he made his contributions to segmented policy making rather than to nonpartisan competition.

53. Cole, *Era*, 141–52; Pierce, *History*, 2:509.
54. *Tribune*, February 22, 1857; *Democrat*, March 10, 1857; Wentworth to Lincoln, February 19, 1860, folder 48, David Davis papers, Chicago Historical Society (emphasis in original). For German voting, Bergquist, "Political Attitudes," 349–50, and for Wentworth as mayor, Fehrenbacher, *Chicago Giant*, 143–47.
55. *Times*, February 24, 25, 1858 (emphasis in original).

The symbolic value of a partisan city victory was lost on Granger, who wanted only to promote "improvements" through the segmented system he had helped to build.

This system survived him. The more significant casualties of the new politics were the widened notion of property value and the idea of a public interest. The case for antiliquor reform had rested on a demand that one group of Chicagoans subordinate their interests to a public interest that another group claimed the right to define. That the groups, as many historians have shown, were divided along lines of ethnicity and class—Yankees against immigrants, Protestants against Catholics, businessmen against workers—rather than along the geographical lines that structured national internal improvement and municipal public works debates should not obscure the analogous manner in which the issues were resolved.[56] Insisting that there was indeed a public interest, the temperance men forced a political showdown on its definition. They lost, though only after the return of partisanship enabled aldermen to represent their constituents' political views. Not until the 1870s would reformers again attempt temperance, by then in an atmosphere of open class conflict. Meanwhile, the Republicans and Democrats who now comprised the council tacitly agreed to leave the public interest undefined while they promoted "improvements" through the segmented system.

When Stephen D. LaRue, of beer riot fame, lectured his fellow aldermen on deference to property owners in the segmented public works process, his antiliquor enemies marvelled at "what wonderful sounds the basest metal may sometimes give forth when properly struck." When Samuel Ashton threatened to politicize the assessment process from an appointive position, the council fired him notwithstanding its "Nebraska" majority.[57] Both the "Law and Order" and "Nebraska" councils rebuffed David Walsh, the erstwhile prison reformer. Yet the persistence of segmentation may be seen most clearly after 1857, as Chicagoans confronted a near collapse of the special assessment system and responded with the first significant charter amendments in a decade. Partisanship ensured that charter reform would be political, especially when it touched on such clearly partisan issues as the ward map. But the locally based sovereignty of

56. The ethnoreligious basis of antebellum liquor conflicts has been a staple of the ethnocultural interpretation of voting, esp. Ronald P. Formisano, *The Birth of Mass Political Parties: Michigan, 1827–1861* (Princeton: Princeton University Press, 1971). For a class analysis, see Ian R. Tyrrell, *Sobering Up: From Temperance to Prohibition in Antebellum America, 1800–1860* (Westport: Greenwood Press, 1979).

57. CP, 1855/56:1868, 1856/57:487, 647, 806, 1075.

the city's property owners was not a partisan issue. From 1857 to 1861, Republicans and Democrats both worked to preserve the segmented system, though not very amicably.

ON JANUARY 19, 1857, seven months before the collapse of the Ohio Life Insurance and Trust Company triggered the national Panic of 1857, the Chicago *Tribune* proclaimed "The Panic Over." If, as James L. Huston recently has argued, the national panic owed much to the end of the Crimean War in March 1856 and the consequent reduction of European demand for American grain, a 50 percent drop in wheat prices from May 1855 to December 1856 hit the Northwest's chief grain market especially hard. Early in 1857, the council took the unprecedented—and unrepeated—step of appropriating money for poor relief, a responsibility normally left to the county and private philanthropic agencies. While the aldermen who distributed the relief boasted of the thoroughness with which they searched paupers' homes, "much to the annoyance of the inmates," they spent $1,500 on food and firewood.[58] The real depression, however, did not begin until 1858 and it took another year for the crisis to affect land values. Between 1857 and 1860, property outside of the downtown area lost half its value. By 1861, downtown values had fallen by half and outlying property by three-fourths.[59] Chicago's second land boom and the aggressive public works construction it had encouraged were history.

Even before land values began to fall, Chicagoans saw that the segmented public works process was in disarray, weakened by a decade of its own success. With no central coordination, it had allowed local groups of property owners to build a huge amount of physical infrastructure without integrating their efforts over either space or time. Nobody seemed to care that the sidewalks contained stairs because neighbors had built their individual portions at different heights. Nor did it matter that, as the streets were raised to accommodate the sewer system, some buildings remained as much as 8 feet below

58. *Tribune,* January 19, 1857; James L. Huston, *The Panic of 1857 and the Coming of the Civil War* (Baton Rouge: Louisiana State University Press, 1987), 5–34; Homer Hoyt, *One Hundred Years of Land Values in Chicago* (Chicago: University of Chicago Press, 1933), 74; CP, 1856/57:1610, 1885, 1913. The committee boasted of finding liquor and food "in plenty under beds and other out-of-the-way places while the cupboard would show a case of extreme want." In one house they found "the nice sum of $178.45" in silver, gold, and bank bills "ingeniously quilted in strips of cloth and hidden in a chest of clothes." 1856/57:1913.

59. Hoyt, *One Hundred Years,* 75–76.

FIG. 6 SIDEWALKS IN CHICAGO

grade, still a common sight in Chicago's older neighborhoods.[60] But Chicago's property owners did mind the financial costs of decentralization. The same street might be paved, dug up for water pipes, paved, dug up for sewers, paved, and then dug up by the gas company, which, it was hoped, would pave it again soon. Not only did all this digging make streets impassable for long periods, but it cost property owners money because it was figured into the estimates for projects financed by special assessment. The city's property owners needed a board of public works that could coordinate street work on a citywide basis.[61] And the urgency of coordination increased as the economy deteriorated.

The dangers of reform were obvious. If a centralized board were to coordinate the public works process, whom could Chicagoans entrust with such power? What if a coordinator became a planner, authoriz-

60. Harold M. Mayer and Richard C. Wade, *Chicago: Growth of a Metropolis* (Chicago: University of Chicago Press, 1969), 94; Ann Durkin Keating, "Governing the New Metropolis: The Growth of Urban and Suburban Governments in Cook County, Illinois, 1833 to 1902" (Ph.D. diss., University of Chicago, 1984), 90; Gregg Wolper, "Winning the Battle but Losing the War: Building-Raising and Sanitation in Mid-Nineteenth-Century Chicago" (seminar paper, University of Chicago, 1983).

61. CP, 1858/59:787, 1859/60:614.

ing only those projects that he decided were in the public interest? Or worse, only those from which he himself profited? If a coordinator determined the mode and timing of public works projects, local control and property owner sovereignty might be jeopardized. Reading about eastern public works scandals, such as the 1855 indictment of New York City officials in a kickback scheme, some Chicagoans looked at their own municipal politics and wondered whether local control would survive the return of party.[62] Could property owners trust in the encouraging words of "Rot-gut" LaRue? Even if he was innocuous in the council, what if he controlled the whole public works process? These were the concerns with which Chicagoans had segmented their government in the first place. Through decentralization, they had eliminated the citywide competition for public goods that might have corrupted politicians with the power to distribute them. In fact, property owners could trust LaRue. Nevertheless, Chicagoans demanded that reform in the public works process preserve local control.

Charter amendment also was problematic. In each legislative session from 1857 to 1861, private "citizens committees" drafted reform charters. Aldermen opposed these efforts, defending what had been the council's prerogative since the city's founding. It is tempting to interpret these battles as a form of class conflict by contrasting either venal politicians and crusading reformers or ward-based democrats and downtown elites. Indeed, the antiliquor reformers were the first to violate the council's initiative in charter amendment, asking the legislature to ban licensing after the council had refused to do so. In the late 1850s, however, aldermen and citizens committees agreed on the proper constituency for the city's government. Both championed the property owners' interests in reform. Conflict arose because politicians—in both the council and the citizens committees—tried to attach reform to executive offices and ward maps designed for partisan advantage. When Democrats controlled the council, Republicans organized citizens committees and vice versa.[63] Their battles had nothing to do with class conflict. Instead, they delayed reforms that both parties favored.

Thus, in 1857, when a citizens committee proposed a board of public works, a new ward map, and a host of additional executive agencies, aldermen applauded their "many valuable suggestions" but

62. *Times*, November 1, 1855.

63. Chicagoans debated the actual composition of the 1857 citizens committee. I am using a list of those who tried to bill the city for their services; CP, 1857/58:591. See also 1856/57:1611; *Tribune*, January 23, 1857, January 29, 1861.

condemned the secrecy of their meetings.[64] In 1859, a Democratic committee linked a board of public works to an extension of the city limits over the heavily Irish Bridgeport meat-packing district. Aldermen rejected this by a straight party vote, Democrats for and Republicans against. Despite their partisan motives, the council's theoretical objection to citizens committees, written in this case by a Republican, is revealing:

> 1st. The public are taken by surprise in this movement. There has been no meeting called to consult on the propriety of a change in our Charter—everything has been done clandestinely—and when the interests of millions of property are involved, the property owners justly claim some voice in the propriety of the thing.
>
> 2d. Any change in our municipal laws, when not emanating from the public, should proceed from the Board of Aldermen, who represent the popular will in this department, and are supposed from experience to be capable of judging the merits of any alteration.[65]

If the manner in which amendments could "emanate from the public" was not clear, the identity of the "public" was. It was "property owners" who could "justly claim some voice" in decision making. Reform stalled completely in 1859. In 1857, however, aldermen had written their own charter amendment and introduced an important element of centralization into the city's government, though not the needed board of public works.

The 1857 charter amendment was the council's response to the coordination problem. It created a comptroller to "exercise such supervision over all the interests of said city, as in any manner may concern or relate to the city finances, revenues or property." Appointed by the mayor for an indefinite term, he controlled all of the city's financial documents and could compel testimony under oath when he doubted the validity of a claim against the city.[66] The charter also strengthened the mayor, providing that his veto could be overridden only by a two-thirds rather than simple council majority. It altered the ward map conservatively. While the citizens committee drew a radically new map that distinguished central from outlying wards, the council's version added only one ward on the city's southwest side with a straight-line boundary from the South Branch to the city limit. (See map 3.) The new and predominantly Irish Tenth Ward would elect only Democrats and was carved from a Fifth that already was

64. CP, 1856/57:1642; *Tribune*, January 31, February 13, 1857; *Times*, December 30, 1856.

65. CP, 1858/59:870.

66. Illinois, *Laws, 1857*, 893–97.

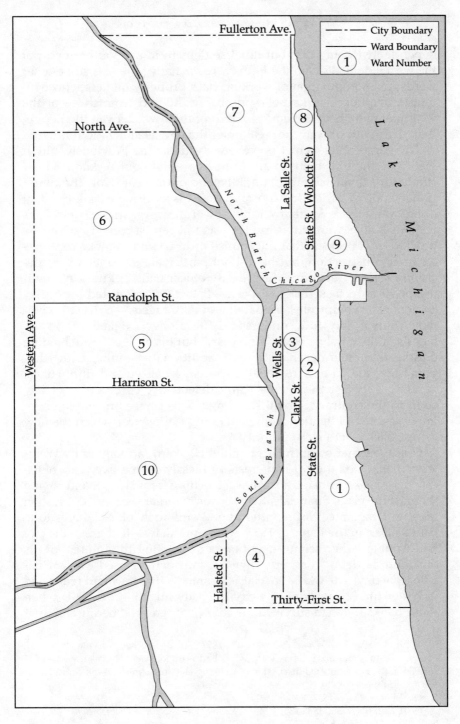

Legend:
— · — · City Boundary
——— Ward Boundary
(1) Ward Number

Fullerton Ave.

Lake Michigan

North Ave.

7

8

6

La Salle St.

State St. (Wolcott St.)

9

North Branch

Chicago River

Randolph St.

Western Ave.

5

Wells St.

3

Clark St.

2

Harrison St.

South Branch

State St.

10

1

Halsted St.

4

Thirty-First St.

MAP 3 CHICAGO WARDS IN 1857

dependably Republican, but rapid settlement in the southern part of the west side had given the Fifth twice as many voters as some other wards and a population of working-class property owners whose interests in public works policy probably differed from those of the wealthier owners in the northern part of their ward. Even the Republican *Tribune* approved the creation of the new Democratic Tenth.[67]

The comptroller's chief power involved claims. Previously, aldermen had audited them on an ad hoc basis without reckoning their cumulative financial impact until the end of the year. Now the comptroller audited all claims centrally and his decisions on individual claims were final. Aside from this power, however, the comptroller's responsibilities were advisory. He was to keep "a correct list" of the public works projects that the council ordered and to make contracts for their construction, but he did not participate in public works decision making. Yet before this, no city officer had kept track of pending projects, a task that had been left to the "interested" property owners. The comptroller prepared annual budgets "so that the common council may fully understand the money exigencies and demands of the city for the ensuing year," but his budgets were binding only in that aldermen had to cover additional spending with additional revenue. The charter also "expressly legalized and affirmed" all pending special assessments, "any defect, decree or order of any court to the contrary notwithstanding." This clause prevented ongoing assessment litigation from generating claims over which the new comptroller would lack authority.[68]

Chicago's first comptroller, Samuel D. Ward (appointed by Wentworth), guarded the city's interests ruthlessly during five years of fiscal crisis. He scrutinized all claims, searching for ways to avoid paying them. If the city's financial situation was disorganized in 1857, it soon became desperate. Six months after Ward took office, many local banks failed in the Panic of 1857. As the municipal debt grew, the city had trouble either selling new bonds or meeting the interest on its outstanding debt.[69] Property owners, meanwhile, used every available legal device to evade special assessments that they had requested in better times, involving the city in costly litigation. In 1861, when those banks that had survived the 1857 panic crashed because of their

67. Ibid., 892–93; *Tribune*, February 13, 1857. For the number of voters, see poll books cited in appendix 1. Some west siders had wanted a new ward since 1854; CP, 1853/54:1559. For a detailed discussion of working-class ownership in the Tenth Ward, see appendix 2.

68. Illinois, *Laws, 1857*, 894–97, 911.

69. CP, 1861/62:36, 188, 336; F. Cyril James, *The Growth of Chicago Banks* (2 vols.; New York: Harper & Bros., 1938), 1:262–70.

dependence on depreciated southern securities, the city could salvage its deposits only at 65 cents on the dollar.[70] On top of this, the sewerage board went bankrupt, in part because its treasurer Sylvester Lind (an old booster whose reputation had "precluded any idea of danger") embezzled $69,000, only a fraction of which the city could recover because those who had underwritten his official bond now defaulted on it.[71] Ward, with the support of elected officials, made Chicago's response to this fiscal crisis a crusade for segmented financing.

The crusade had one goal: to prevent the general fund from subsidizing the private benefits of public works. By maintaining the integrity of the special assessment system, the city not only could keep the general fund small and the tax rate low but could preserve the nonredistributive character of the segmented system. Early in 1858, John C. Haines, the Republican mayor who succeeded Wentworth, urged aldermen to slow the street-building boom. Many property owners, he reported, were complaining about "improvements heretofore ordered for which they say they did not ask and for which during these stringent times they do not feel able to pay."[72] Because when they resisted assessments property owners always denied that they had initiated them, Haines was right to be skeptical. Yet he recognized the threat the resistance posed. The council had advanced $30,000 in general funds to be refunded from assessments that litigation had delayed; in 1859 they also granted mortgage guarantees to property owners whose damage awards were tied up in the fifty lawsuits brought against a single assessment.[73] These were risky actions. As litigation made assessment revenue increasingly precarious, the likelihood of refunding diminished. Loans from the general fund might redistribute wealth.

The city implemented a retrenchment policy. The council followed Haines's advice "to order no improvement until a majority of the property holders in interest ask for [it] and even in such cases not until after a careful examination," and Ward refused to sign contracts for projects whose assessments were likely to be challenged. Street work ground to a halt, at least in theory. In practice, property owners

70. After withdrawing the deposits, the council ordered the treasurer to put the city's money in a vault under his personal guard. This "solution" lasted over a year. See CP, 1861/62:20, 35, 63–64, 137–38, 187, 1862/63:5, 161; James, *Chicago Banks*, 1:279–86.

71. CP, 1861/62:84, 1863/64:324.

72. Ibid., 1858/59:249. See also 1857/58:1021, 1859/60:533.

73. Ibid., 1856/57:1672, 1857/58:660, 662, 1859/60:174, 487, 1862/63:85. In the mortgage guarantee case, the city finally paid more than $30,000 from the general fund.

who wanted projects got them by dealing directly with street contractors. In this arrangement, the property owners designed their project, hired a contractor, and negotiated a price. The contractor began work immediately, while the property owners petitioned the council to order the project and levy an assessment—even though the project was complete.[74] Private contracts had two advantages for property owners. First, because special assessments generated over half of the council's annual paperwork but were concentrated in May and June to accommodate the construction season, every project encountered long delays between petition and construction. Second, because many owners wanted to cut back on public works spending during the depression and the council heeded this caution with the retrenchment policy, those who wanted projects faced arduous struggles in the consensus-building process.[75]

Retrenchment was a citywide response to what Haines, Ward, and the council viewed as the interest of the city's property owners. Retrenchment in the general fund, as McDonald has shown in his analysis of San Francisco's "low tax consensus," was a policy of almost unanimous popularity in the mid nineteenth century. This was why Chicago aldermen created the office of comptroller. Retrenchment in the special assessment system, however, was more complicated. It substituted a single decision by city officials for the many local decisions that property owners otherwise would have made for themselves.[76] If most property owners favored a retrenchment of public works spending, some opposed it. Like the citywide effort to serve property by banning liquor, citywide public works retrenchment failed, though without comparable drama. It was defeated by property owners who made private street contracts and then petitioned the council for retroactive—and therefore illegal—special assessments based on them. Aldermen followed the owners' directions at every stage of this process. The illegal assessments finally forced officials to choose between the competing claims of property owners who resisted assessments and street contractors who wanted to be paid for their work. Not surprisingly, they chose the property owners.

74. Ibid., 1858/59:249. For private street contracts, see 1857/58:548, 705, 1858/59:103, 223, 345, 1859/60:169.

75. *Tribune*, January 28, 1861. Special assessments generated 52 percent of council paperwork in 1857 and 1858. Computed from Robert E. Bailey, et al., eds., *Chicago City Council Proceedings Files, 1833–1871: An Inventory* (Springfield: Illinois State Archives, 1987).

76. McDonald, *Parameters*, passim.

From the owners' perspective, one desirable feature of the seg-mented system was the weak position in which it placed street con-tractors. Because neither corruptly inflated estimates nor honest cost overruns were diffused into general taxes, property owners super-vised contractors closely. The most damning objection an owner could raise against a proposed assessment was that its petition had been "got up" by a contractor who wanted the job. In his pioneering 1898 study of New York City, Edward Dana Durand argued that de-lays built into the special assessment process by the 1840s made street contracts accessible only to a few powerful firms. "To remedy this evil," New York began to issue assessment anticipation bonds in 1852. Yet, on Durand's evidence, these bonds actually illustrated the clout of street contractors in New York. By allowing city officials to pay contractors before collecting assessments, anticipation bonds re-distributed power in the assessment process. Property owners no longer could bully contractors with the threat of nonpayment. In Chi-cago, street contractors were paid only from assessment revenue. They either took loans or sold their vouchers at discounts while they waited for the owners to pay. They therefore had direct interests in the smooth consensus building and strict legality that would encour-age the owners to pay quickly.[77]

This distribution of power structured Chicago's experience with private street contracts. Most of these contracts obligated contractors to take their payments from special assessments. Thus, instead of avoiding the consensus-building stage of the assessment process, pri-vate contracts merely postponed it. Owners who had not been in-volved in the private contract still could oppose the project. Since those who had been involved already had received their physical im-provement, moreover, the contractor was the only one with any interest in levying an assessment. Remonstrants charged fraud: they, rather than contractors, were supposed to decide whether to levy as-sessments on their own properties. Clearly, no contractor should have signed private contracts. But, during the depression, they were the only contracts. Aldermen, who must have suspected the legal status of retroactive assessments, should never have levied them. As a city attorney complained, they made the city's government into "a sort of collecting agency for the contractors and in this way only un-

77. Edward Dana Durand, *The Finances of New York City* (New York: Macmillan, 1898), 107–9; CP, 1860/61:327. In San Francisco, where street contractors collected from property owners directly, they had even greater interests in legal assessments. See esp. *Taylor v. Palmer*, 31 Cal., 240 (1866).

dertaking to have them paid."[78] By levying the illegal assessments property owners requested, the council shifted a disagreeable task to the courts.

After the Illinois supreme court voided a private-contract assessment in 1859 as "an arbitrary order for assessing that sum for the purpose of raising money to pay one John McBean," a street contractor, city officials showed just how far they would go to preserve segmented financing. Since he could not be paid from the assessment, McBean asked to be paid from the general fund. Comptroller Ward refused arbitration, "believing [McBean] had no claim on the City to arbitrate, but [I] have requested him if he felt that he had, to commence suit in order that it might be shown in Court." McBean said he could not afford "a season of littigation [sic] which may last for years" and charged that the city attorney had betrayed him in the original suit against the property owners, "at the same time receiving large sums of money from me under false pretences." When a city claims commission recommended in 1861 that McBean be paid from the general fund, basing their opinion on grounds of fairness, aldermen agreed but Mayor Julian Rumsey vetoed their appropriation. Rumsey also agreed that McBean, "having done the work on the streets ought to be paid," but he refused to let the city's general fund subsidize the benefits of a small group of property owners. He was willing to sacrifice McBean's legitimate claims to the integrity of the special assessment system.[79]

All of Chicago's contractors, of course, were not as weak as McBean. One firm had superb political connections and tried to exploit them. William Colby and his partner Albert C. Ellithorpe both became aldermen in 1855, winning election on the Law and Order ticket. Ellithorpe retired from the council after one term but remained sufficiently active in politics to default in the sewerage embezzlement as an underwriter of Sylvester Lind's bond. Colby had lost a reelection bid in 1857 but, after moving to another ward, won in 1860. The partners paved the street next to their quarry in 1858. The council first ordered and then rescinded a retroactive assessment for this paving, and in 1861, with Colby back, they levied another, again illegally. When Ward refused to pay Colby from the general fund, Colby called for the comptroller's impeachment on the basis of an affidavit alleging fraud that was such a blatant forgery that the council investigated Colby instead. Mayor Rumsey called his fellow Republican a swindler

78. CP, 1862/63:123.
79. *Peck v. Chicago*, 22 Ill. 579 (1859); CP, 1860/61:327, 1862/63:123.

in front of one hundred spectators. Colby sued for libel, appealed to the state supreme court, and lost. Colby's failure to get general funds—the impeachment demand was only part of his effort—put John McBean in powerful company.[80] If by the 1850s in New York, anticipation bonds enabled corrupt officials to cover fraud with illegal assessments refunded from the property tax, in Chicago it was street contractors who paid for illegal assessments, whether they were fraudulent or not. In Chicago, property owners were supreme.

The 1857 charter had created a mechanism for controlling the general fund. Ward could report the contents of the city treasury at any time, a feat nobody could have performed before, and he instructed elected officials on the connection between a healthy special assessment system and a small general fund. This was inadequate. The special assessment process itself required reform. The city attorney reported over $100,000 in assessments pending before the courts in 1860, and Rumsey announced in 1861 that the figure had doubled.[81] While part of this litigation could be blamed on the depression, part also reflected a less permissive attitude by the Illinois courts. In 1858 the supreme court held "with reluctance" that the city could not levy special assessments for deepening the river because the charter specified the power only to "widen" it. In an 1859 decision that voided assessment rolls solely because they lacked dollar signs, the court warned that it would tolerate no informalities. In the chief private-contract case, the court invited property owners to challenge assessments on the basis of "any substantial irregularity in the mode of assessing [them]" without defining the word "substantial." "Less than this," the judges added, "would be but a mockery of justice."[82]

The city needed an agency that could check the legality of assessments, monitor their progress in the courts, and ensure that they ultimately were collected. Neither aldermen who served two-year terms—unpaid—nor mayors elected annually could do this. City attorneys, also elected annually, rarely could handle their routine caseloads, much less provide legal histories in complex special assessment cases. After experimenting with the collection procedure, Chicagoans saw that no collector could compel payment when property

80. CP, 1861/62:151, 165; Colby v. Rumsey, Supreme Court of Illinois papers, case file 15073, Illinois State Archives.

81. CP, 1860/61:200, 1861/62:1.

82. *Wright et al. v. Chicago*, 20 Ill. 252 (1858); *Gibson et al. v. Chicago*, 22 Ill. 567 (1859); *Pease v. Chicago*, 21 Ill. 500 (1859). In response to the 1858 *Wright* case, the 1861 charter authorized special assessment "to widen, deepen or dredge out the Chicago river"; Illinois, *Laws, 1861*, 124.

owners raised legal objections.[83] The comptroller had his hands full with general fund business. No city officer even computed the total cost of assessments levied by the council annually, not to mention those levied by the independent water and sewerage boards. Then, there was the physical problem, the continuous digging that the 1857 charter addressed only with the comptroller's "correct list" of projects—and it is not clear that Ward kept this list. If partisan conflict had stalled plans for a board of public works before, the political situation now included John Wentworth's second mayoral term and his ongoing feud with the "*Tribune* clique." That the mayor's enemies were the city's state legislators did not bode well for charter amendment.

There was one more street-related problem. The city financed repairs through a street tax that could be paid in three days of labor or $1.50 in cash. The tax was collected and spent by three street commissioners, elected by the divisions. Unlike aldermen, who represented property owners, street commissioners represented the laborers they hired. They tended to be ethnic community leaders. While some moved on to top police and fire jobs and one served as a park commissioner, none ever entered the council, became mayor, or held a state-level office. The street tax became increasingly regressive in the 1850s. As one street commissioner explained in 1858, the city paid hired laborers 75 cents per day. Since it took three days to work off a street tax, the tax cost $2.25 if paid in labor but only $1.50 if paid in cash. During the depression, moreover, when street commissioners could hire only one-tenth of the applicants for regular 75 cent jobs, some Chicagoans hired unemployed men to work off their $1.50 street taxes, paying them only 50 cents per day. The street commissioners pointed to the exploitation in this practice and demanded that the council adjust the tax to two days of work. Aldermen refused—the three-day rate was written into the charter—and when the commissioners tried to pay 75 cents anyway, the council rejected their payrolls.[84] The charter would have to be amended.

The Illinois legislators who convened in January 1861 knew from their opening day that partisan issues of unparalleled importance would dominate the legislative session. Nationally, South Carolina had seceded from the Union and three more southern states would follow that week. On the state level, the Republican majority planned

83. On the attorney, CP, 1860/61:200, 1862/63:143. On the collectors, *Chicago v. Colby*, 20 Ill. 614 (1858). This case did not involve William Colby.
84. CP, 1858/59:516, 1859/60:1, 172–73, 546, 1860/61:160, 1861/62:120, 122. Street commissioners were identified from election returns; see appendix 1.

to reapportion Illinois's legislative and congressional districts to conform to the 1860 census (and, of course, the interests of the new majority party) and to reorganize the state militia in preparation for an increasingly likely war against the South. Democrats opposed militia reform and hoped to reverse the Republican apportionment by calling a state constitutional convention for 1862.[85] The Chicago delegation, meanwhile, had their own agenda. Led by J. Young Scammon, whose libel suit would force John Wentworth to give up the *Democrat* a few months later, they took the police force away from the mayor by creating an independent police board appointed initially by Republican Governor Richard Yates, an ally of the *"Tribune* clique" Republicans of Chicago. Wentworth, who had used the police force as his personal army, retaliated at the 1862 constitutional convention as one of only three Republican delegates to sign the antibank and antirailroad as well as antiwar, antiblack, and anti-Republican constitution. On his demand, the convention mandated Chicago's first home rule referendum, but a nearly unanimous vote "For the City of Chicago electing its own officers" was moot when state voters refused to ratify the constitution itself. It was in this political context that Chicago's property owners finally got their Board of Public Works.[86]

While the police board law illustrated a familiar pattern in urban history—administrative centralization aimed at weakening a popular party politician—the creation of the Board of Public Works (BPW) demonstrated something else: public works policy could be isolated from politics even in the extreme situation of the winter of 1861. As in 1857 and 1859, two city charter drafts reached Springfield, one from the council and one from a citizens committee. Legislators sent both, along with the police bill, to the Cook County delegation. Both drafts included a public works board along with partisan clauses. While the council would have written the $50 liquor license into the charter, the *Tribune* group supported a new ward map. Wentworth, fearing treachery, tried to circumvent the city's delegation by sending the council's draft directly to the house speaker, but legislators cen-

85. David M. Potter, *The Impending Crisis, 1848–1861* (New York: Harper & Row, 1976), 490–98; Cole, *Era*, 257–59.

86. Fehrenbacher, *Chicago Giant*, 186, 193–95; O. M. Dickerson, *The Illinois Constitutional Convention of 1862*, University Studies, vol. 1, no. 9 (Urbana: University Press, 1905). Frank L. Klement, "Middle Western Copperheadism and the Genesis of the Granger Movement," *Mississippi Valley Historical Review* 38 (1951–52): 679–94, and Stanley L. Jones, "Agrarian Radicalism in Illinois' Constitutional Convention of 1862," *JISHS* 48 (1955): 271–82, ignore the convention's racism—it banned black migration to Illinois and black suffrage. Voters ratified these articles, which were submitted separately from the constitution itself.

sured the mayor for doubting his delegation's "impartiality" and treating them "with disrespect." Rather than postpone the board yet again, however, Scammon and his colleagues met with several aldermen to develop a compromise. As passed, the charter created the BPW in a mandatory section and lumped divisive provisions from both drafts into a section subject to ratification by Chicago voters.[87]

The BPW consisted of three commissioners, elected by division for staggered six-year terms. It took the authority for special assessments and fire limit exemptions from the council, the water and sewerage systems from the independent boards, the street tax from the street commissioners, the estimation of public works costs from the superintendent, and the assessment of damages and benefits from the special assessors who previously had been appointed for each individual project. The charter abolished the independent boards, street commissioners, superintendent, and special assessors and left the council with only a rubber stamp over public works decisions that now would be made at the BPW. It solved the legal and physical coordination problems by locating central authority with public works officials who served long, overlapping terms and devoted their full-time, professional attention to the city's infrastructure. It solved the street tax problem not by adjusting the rate—which remained three days or $1.50—but by abolishing the one city office whose incumbents had represented laborers. It preserved local control in the assessment process by elevating the petition requirement from custom to law and by requiring the owners of three-fourths of all affected property to approve special assessments, a stricter consensus-building rule than the customary half of the 1850s.[88]

Chicago voters rejected the optional part of the charter, including a Republican ward map that would have replaced the ten segmented wards with twenty-three irregular boxes, doubtless gerrymandered to ensure a Republican council. Campaigning for it, the *Tribune* claimed that smaller wards would improve council representation: "When the wards are reduced to the proposed size, an Alderman will know personally nearly the whole people whom he represents, and they will know him. He can vote and act more understandingly as to their wants and necessities." There was a certain logic to the idea that aldermen now should represent "the whole people" of their wards; with the BPW managing the consensus building of the public works process, it may have been less important that aldermen represent par-

87. Illinois, House, *Journal* (1861), 158, 162–63, 216, 267, 393, 429–31, 465, 655–56, 788. The Senate made no changes. Illinois, *Laws, 1861*, 118–48.

88. Illinois, *Laws, 1861*, 118–25, 132.

cels of property. When the optional charter provisions lost, the *Tribune* celebrated anyway, pointed to a Democratic clause that would have annexed Bridgeport, and denied that the Republicans had suffered defeat ("Never before have party lines been more completely ignored"). In 1863, when Democrats controlled both the council and the legislature, they finally annexed the "two or three hundred Irish Democrats" of Bridgeport and drew a sixteen-ward map that, like the proposed Republican twenty-three, abandoned the segmented design.[89] (See map 4.) The parties had been trying since 1857 to replace the real estate ward map. By 1863, the Democrats were powerful enough to draw the first partisan gerrymander.

By 1863, as the next chapter will show, Chicagoans also had begun to dismantle the segmented system, using the public works process to redistribute wealth by granting favors to powerful industrial interests. The Bridgeport annexation would be important less for its partisan intent than for the jurisdiction that it gave the city over the packinghouses that polluted the river.[90] As for the BPW, its members ran for office on party slates but tended to be engineers educated in public works technology. They prepared special assessment ordinances for aldermen to pass, advised them on timing, and coordinated the city's response to court actions. The council and BPW fought when property owners pressured one to speed up projects delayed by the other and when partisanship encouraged squabbling. Yet property owners insisted that both apply the segmented logic to special assessment issues. As late as 1866, when the city assessed 1 percent penalties for late payment of special assessment charges, the BPW and council undercut complaints by resolving to spend the penalties only on the particular improvement projects for which they had been collected. Chicagoans created the BPW not to centralize decision making or to redistribute wealth, but to coordinate administration in order to preserve property owners' local control.[91]

The Panic of 1857 paralyzed a special assessment system that was none too healthy anyway. The new party politics blocked an effective response to its problems until after the depression had magnified them. The four-year delay in creating the BPW probably would have mattered little had they been years of prosperity. Property owners

89. Ibid., 139–43; *Tribune*, March 16, 20, 1861; Illinois, *Private Laws, 1863*, 41–42. The *Times* is not available for late 1860 and early 1861.

90. Louise Carroll Wade, *Chicago's Pride: The Stockyards, Packingtown, and Environs in the Nineteenth Century* (Urbana: University of Illinois Press, 1987), 37, argues that the pollution issue motivated the annexation but, as the *Tribune* asked, December 14, 1862, "Who does not see a brilliant Democratic idea in this?"

91. CP, 1861/62:338, 1863/64:327, 473, 1864/65:18, 1865/66:867, 1866/67:662.

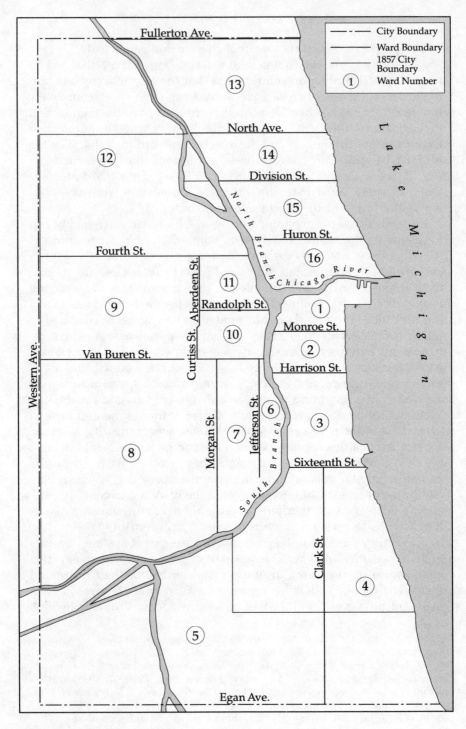

MAP 4 CHICAGO WARDS IN 1863

would have complained of inefficiency, but they would have paid assessments with less resistance. The litigation of the late 1850s developed precedents that would be important in the postwar conservative legal environment. Although, as the last chapter noted, the BPW privatized the extension of water service and lobbied for special assessments for sewers, it also provided a central pressure point for the powerful groups who soon would champion new public interests for the city. Thus, after the war, the BPW tried to favor downtown property in scheduling public works construction. They informed aldermen in 1866 that their schedules "have not been made without some general plan or system." They did "not mean to be understood as expressing the opinion that no other improvements should be made," but thought street work should proceed "from the centre outwards."[92] Aldermen rejected this attempt to sever special assessment financing from local control of decision making, but others would destroy the segmented system. The BPW was created to save the system, despite the fact that the agency would be among the architects of its destruction.

THROUGHOUT the 1850s, Chicago's property owners, organized on a segmented basis, were the constituents of the city's government. Aldermen, mayors, and, after 1857, the comptroller tried to minimize general fund spending for public services that all Chicagoans—or all Chicago property owners—enjoyed in common. Nonpartisanship was not a necessary condition for this attitude; during the liquor fight, it was a hindrance. While Republicans professed their loyalty to property owners in a partisan rhetoric inherited from the Whigs, however, Democrats claimed to champion the working class. The 1863 charter is interesting in this context. This Democratic production annexed Bridgeport, drew the sixteen-ward map, and segregated the schools. It also abolished the regressive street tax and extended segmented taxation to new forms of "interested" property. The city took the fire insurance tax from the Benevolent Society and levied new taxes on marine and life insurance, all dedicated: fire to the fire department, marine to the harbor, and life to public health. That council Democrats settled part of John McBean's claim from the general fund suggests that their "public" may have been a bit wider than that of the Republicans, though this would be tested during the war.[93]

Although the segmented system did not survive the political and

92. Ibid., 1866/67:766–67.
93. Illinois, *Private Laws, 1863*, 98–99, 129; CP, 1862/63:123. The segregation clause was repealed in 1865; Illinois, *Private Laws, 1865*, 286.

economic shocks of the late 1850s unchallenged, it survived them intact nonetheless. The failure of public works retrenchment during the panic was distressing to city officials and costly to street contractors, but it was an unqualified victory for the localized sovereignty of Chicago's property owners. Even as strong-willed a comptroller as Samuel D. Ward failed to impose his own policies from the center—even though they were popular policies—and the BPW was created with a sharply restricted role in decision making. Chicagoans had adopted the segmented system to facilitate the construction of public works during a land boom, but declining values after 1857 only enhanced their commitment to it. Local control worked both ways: it allowed property owners not only to build infrastructure, but also to prevent its construction. Whatever their choices were at any particular time, local groups of property owners made these choices locally.

Yet the defeat of temperance reform was the more remarkable triumph for segmentation because unlike public works debates, the debate about liquor was ethnocultural, class-based, morally charged, thoroughly partisan, and wide open in terms of participation. Everyone could claim to be "interested" in the temperance fight. The temperance battle pitted Chicago's predominantly Yankee elite against its predominantly immigrant working class on the issue of segmentation or, alternatively, on the issue of the existence of a citywide public interest. Some of the temperance men had been among the loudest proponents of segmented government as Whigs in the 1840s, including Scammon, Throop, and, to a lesser extent, even Levi Boone. Yet it was the orthodox Jacksonian Elihu Granger who remained consistently true to the segmented logic, if not to the party of Jackson. Granger always knew where he stood on municipal issues. He could join with men of much greater wealth and status to write the 1847 charter and, as an alderman, harangue these same men on the defense of segmented policy. Once city politics was charged with nationally significant partisan issues, however, Elihu Granger was lost. There was no obvious way to campaign either in defense of segmentation or in opposition to "monopoly."

This may be the most significant aspect of the Kansas-Nebraska Act as a political issue in Chicago and perhaps across much of the North. In the 1856 city election, Douglas wrapped slavery and liquor into one segmented package: the Democratic party stood for popular sovereignty on slavery and personal liberty on liquor. It opposed a politics in which some coerced others to promote one view of public morality or the public interest. Kansans should decide for themselves whether it was right to hold slaves, and Chicagoans should decide for themselves whether it was right to drink liquor. Yet Lincoln and other

Republicans attacked the Kansas-Nebraska Act in the very same terms in which Douglas defended it. This is why they called it "the repeal of the Missouri Compromise." The Republicans' stress on the threat of a "slave power conspiracy" was a defense of segmented policy making. They argued that the Kansas-Nebraska Act, especially when combined in 1857 with the Dred Scott decision, was part of a conspiracy to end the national practice of segmenting debate about slavery and freedom, and to end it by making slavery the uniform policy of the United States. "We shall lie down," as Lincoln put it in his House Divided speech, "pleasantly dreaming that the people of Missouri are on the verge of making their State free, and we shall awake to the reality instead, that the Supreme Court has made Illinois a slave state."[94] The "people" of Missouri and Illinois, Lincoln insisted, should make these decisions themselves.

In Chicago, the anti-Nebraska coalition could not build a winning Republican party until they embraced Douglas's position on liquor, until they sloughed off the ethnocultural baggage of the Know Nothings and Whigs. In places with stronger Whig traditions, Republicans might continue to use the ethnocultural appeals and even attack slavery on the abolitionist ground of public morality, but these strategies could never have worked in Chicago. The antislavery argument in Chicago—and in Illinois as a whole—had to be a segmented argument. It had to be a Jacksonian attack on monopolistic slave-power conspirators. Concretely, the Republican party in Chicago needed John Wentworth to win elections. It needed a Republican mayor in 1860 who had Jacksonian credentials on the individual's right to drink liquor. Part of the genius of Abraham Lincoln, and the moral ambiguity of his legacy, lies in his grasp of these Republican imperatives. Despite serious challenges in the late 1850s, segmentation survived as both the language of politics and the organizational principle of city government in Chicago.

94. The interpretation of Lincoln and Republican ideology contained in this and the next paragraph has been influenced by Don E. Fehrenbacher, *Prelude to Greatness: Lincoln in the 1850s* (Stanford: Stanford University Press, 1962), chap. 4; Fehrenbacher, *Slavery, Law, and Politics*; and Foner, *Free Soil, Free Labor, Free Men*, chaps. 3–5.

6

The New Public Interest

ON JUNE 2, 1863, delegates from all but three of the loyal states met in Chicago for the National Ship Canal Convention. Since Congress had defeated a bill to deepen the Illinois and Michigan Canal in February, Chicagoans had been busy planning this reprise to their 1847 booster triumph. Modelled on the River and Harbor Convention, this meeting also voiced Chicagoans' bipartisan demand for federally financed internal improvements. With Vice-President Hannibal Hamlin wielding the gavel and over a third of Congress in attendance, delegates debated the military necessity—and thus the national interest—of a canal that could shuttle gunboats between the Mississippi River and the Great Lakes.[1] Chicago won national attention on June 2, but not for its patriotism. General Ambrose Burnside chose this moment to suppress the Copperhead Chicago *Times*, provoking an embarrassing display of disunity. Like its predecessor, this convention also suggests important changes in Chicago. While another decade of rapid growth had convinced Chicagoans that they could exert national political power, their municipal politics now were enmeshed in a vigorous national party system. Chicagoans also were adopting a new idea of their local public interest. Like their interest in the Union war effort, this local interest submerged party in the urgency of government action. It also destroyed the segmented system.

1. Chicago *Tribune*, June 3, 1863; Committee on Statistics for the City of Chicago, *The Necessity of a Ship-Canal between the East and the West* (Chicago: Tribune Co., 1863), 32–45. No delegates came from California, Oregon, or, more significantly, Pennsylvania.

WELCOMING CANAL delegates to Chicago, the *Tribune* proclaimed "the dawning of a new era" in American politics. Never again would the states of the Mississippi Valley beg for the federal government's fostering care. Rather, they would demand their rights "as coequal sovereignties of the Great Republic" and insist that "their vast commerce" receive "a share of the concern which the common legislature bestows upon the commerce of the sea-board States." Even if Chicago lost its bid for the ship canal, the West would demonstrate its power "and hereafter the equality which she asserts among the other sections of the Union—equality that does not stop at mere words—will never be the subject of dispute or of dissent. The West will henceforth be a partner in the Union, entitled to all the immunities and privileges of her place."[2] The West, in other words, was ready to play power politics on the national level. In the 1840s westerners had debated whether to advance their sectional interests by allying with the Northeast or South. By 1847, after southern politicians had stopped courting them with promises of internal improvement, they had chosen the northern alliance.[3] Now, with the southern states in rebellion and their representatives absent from Congress, the West expected dividends on its political investment.

When the expectation was frustrated, especially by the 1861 Morrill Tariff, western Peace Democrats had a potent propaganda issue. Copperhead leader Clement Valladingham of Ohio declared himself "a western sectionalist" and the Chicago *Times* condemned the federal government for levying tariff and excise taxes on the West while it "requires nothing from Puritan patriots who are fattening upon the spoils of war."[4] This was the backdrop for the Republican *Tribune*'s celebration of western power. In their brief for the ship canal, Chicago's bipartisan "committee on statistics" argued that western congressmen had voted for military spending to protect eastern ocean commerce "and now they have a right to demand, as a matter of justice and reciprocal good feeling, that appropriations shall be made for *Lake* commerce." The ship canal "would establish, between the East and the West, closer commercial and political affiliations, and forge a chain which no convulsion could sever."[5] If historians have ques-

---

2. *Tribune*, June 2, 1863.

3. See Mentor L. Williams, "The Background of the Chicago River and Harbor Convention, 1847," *Mid-America* 30 (1948): 219–32.

4. Frank L. Klement, *The Copperheads of the Middle West* (Chicago: University of Chicago Press, 1960), 3–11; Helen Elizabeth Breckenridge, "The *Chicago Times* During the Civil War" (M.A. thesis, University of Chicago, 1931), 28.

5. *Necessity of a Ship-Canal*, 41, 45 (emphasis in original).

tioned the sectional basis of Copperheadism in the Midwest, contemporaries used western sectional rhetoric as an important tool in the high-stakes politics of 1863.[6]

It is significant that what Chicagoans called the "National Ship Canal," Congress called the "Illinois Ship Canal." While a Philadelphia newspaper thought the project a scheme to enhance New York's commerce at the expense of its own—and New York support for the bill had been bought with provisions to enlarge the Erie and Oswego canals—a Boston paper complained that "these plans *leave out the New England States.*" Congressmen from border states whose trade depended on the Ohio River rather than the Great Lakes also opposed the bill. Even the intense logrolling of the first Civil War Congress could not save it. Democrats voted against the canal overwhelmingly, while Republicans registered only a bare majority in support. Thus Leonard Curry has concluded that commercial rather than political rivalries killed it.[7] In 1846, Illinois congressmen had managed to link a Chicago harbor improvement to thirty-nine other western projects in a single river and harbor package. By this strategy they had forced President Polk to veto "western" interests. But Isaac Arnold, who represented Chicago in Congress in 1863, was no match for the Stephen Douglas who had constructed the 1846 omnibus (Douglas died in 1861).

This time, Chicagoans could not even count on their Great Lakes neighbors. No sooner had they mailed their convention invitations, than the Milwaukee Chamber of Commerce announced that it would oppose them on the convention floor. "Because it would build up local interests exclusively, to the injury of . . . all the northwestern States save one," Illinois should pay for its own ship canal. Not only were there better ways to move gunboats, but the canal could not be finished in time to be useful in the Civil War.[8] Chicagoans answered with the timeless threat of a British invasion from Canada and, under the rubric "How to Conduct a Long War," cited the Netherlands' ability "to carry on a war for eighty years" with the aid of internal improvements, though they presumably did not expect the Civil War

6. See Richard O. Curry's articles, "Copperheadism and Continuity: the Anatomy of a Stereotype," *Journal of Negro History* 57 (1972): 29–36, and "The Union As It Was: A Critique of Recent Interpretations of the 'Copperheads,'" *Civil War History* 13 (1967): 25–39.

7. Leonard P. Curry, *Blueprint for Modern America: Non-military Legislation of the First Civil War Congress* (Nashville: Vanderbilt University Press, 1968), 136–48 (Boston *Post* quoted on 143, emphasis in original).

8. Chicago *Times*, May 20, 1863.

to last quite that long.[9] In their convention planning sessions, Chicagoans admitted their cynical use of national defense: if they called the canal a commercial project, they would encounter not only the old Jacksonian constitutional objection—that Congress could not finance an improvement that lay within a single state—but also localized commercial rivalries.[10] It didn't work. The National Ship Canal Convention refused to endorse the ship canal.

As they had done in 1847, Chicagoans painted the ship canal as an issue above party politics. Democrats and Republicans both helped to plan the convention. This time, however, rather than a single mass citizens committee, Chicagoans created four committees that remained autonomous while planning the convention in joint meetings. The need for four committees—from the council, Board of Trade, Mercantile Association, and "citizens generally"—is unclear.[11] It may have reflected the existence of the commercial bodies, both founded after 1847, but it probably reflected party. While the citizens committee—a committee of prominent politicians—was scrupulously bipartisan and no evidence suggests partisanship in the Mercantile Association, the council and Board of Trade were in conflict. The board was Republican; two months before convention planning began, it had banned the *Times* from its reading room for disloyalty, prompting the Democratic state legislature to charter a rival Chamber of Commerce, though nothing came of this.[12] The council had a weak Democratic majority when planning began, but Chicago then held its first election using the 1863 ward map. The Democrats had gerrymandered the city well; after the election they outnumbered Republicans two to one.[13]

9. *Necessity of a Ship-Canal*, 35–36, 39–40.
10. *Times*, April 29, 1863.
11. Ibid., March 20, 27, 1863.
12. Ibid., January 5, 27, 1863. In 1861 Douglas's editor James Sheahan left the *Times* to found the *Post*, organ of the city's War Democrats. Cyrus McCormick operated the *Times* briefly and then sold it to Wilbur Storey, whose earlier editorial policies had reflected a racism exceptional even by antebellum standards. See Justin E. Walsh, "Radically and Thoroughly Democratic: Wilbur F. Storey and the Detroit *Free Press*, 1853 to 1861," *Michigan History* 47 (1963): 193–225.
13. This follows the *Times*, April 25, 1863, in classifying two War Democrats with the Republicans, but the *Tribune*, April 23, 1863, counted them separately. On the War Democrats generally, see Joel Silbey, *A Respectable Minority: The Democratic Party in the Civil War Era, 1860–1868* (New York: W. W. Norton, 1977), 55–59. The 1863 charter also saved seats for two incumbent Democrats in the remapped and now Republican First Ward; Illinois, *Laws, 1863*, 154; *Tribune*, May 6, 1863. While the convention committees were organizing, Republican aldermen were boycotting council meetings to block the

Like the convention planners of 1847, those of 1863 assumed that the city's government would pay for the convention. At the first joint planning meeting on March 24, the "general expression seemed to be in favor of requesting the Common Council to vote an amount necessary." On April 2 the committees debated the form in which they should petition the council and whether each committee member would have to sign the petition in person. The Republican alderman who planned to present it demanded individual signatures so that "there would be no dodging it in the future. There would be no loopholes left." Another planner, noting that the petition "would be a subject of criticism in the future," seconded the call for careful drafting.[14] This was silly. Public works petitions required careful drafting; from 1861 to 1863 they were, at least in theory, subject to litigation in special assessment cases. No city charter ever linked general fund spending to petitions. The debate actually had nothing to do with the legitimacy of the committees' petition. Republicans wanted an impressive document so they could use the convention funding issue to embarrass council Democrats. Unlike the 1847 funding debate, this one was thoroughly partisan.

Indeed, the 1863 planners had a much weaker case for funding. While they argued that all Chicagoans were "directly interested" in the ship canal, the River and Harbor Convention had itself been a public good for the booster city. By 1863, Chicago needed no advertising. Not only had it hosted the 1860 Republican national convention that nominated Lincoln, but the Ship Canal Convention was only one of five national conventions that met in the city on the same day.[15] Chicago was the ninth largest city in the United States in 1860 and the third largest city in the West, trailing only Cincinnati and St. Louis. The war, moreover, paralyzed St. Louis's Mississippi River trade but brought an economic boom to Chicago, whose population rose 63 percent from 109,200 in 1860 to 178,500 in 1865. At the hub of a massive railroad network when the war began, Chicago was the nation's primary market for corn, wheat, and lumber and one of its

---

assembly of a quorum. They finally appeared and engineered the midnight passage of "Loyal League Resolutions" to suspend partisanship for the duration of the war. Mayor Sherman vetoed these April 1, kicking off the city election campaign. After the election the council's Democratic majority reconsidered and rejected them. See *Times*, March 25, 1863; *Tribune*, May 19, 1863; Chicago City Council Proceedings Files [hereafter CP], 1863/64:14, 62.

14. *Times*, March 27, April 3, 1863.

15. CP, 1863/64:55; *Times*, May 16, June 2, 1863. Also meeting on June 2 were the National Medical Association, National Christian Association, National Manufacturers Association, and major city Young Men's Christian Associations.

leading producers of agricultural implements. With the help of Union army contracts, Chicago also replaced Cincinnati in the 1861/62 packing season as "hog butcher to the world."[16] The reception of a few thousand convention delegates—only a few hundred actually came— could hardly be described as a public good worthy of municipal funding. Nobody even tried.

Rather, the convention was a tool in partisan conflict. Republicans tried to make it a military spectacle. In a discussion of "the class of persons" to invite, Congressman Arnold suggested the president, the cabinet, and the generals and admirals of the Union. Democrats responded that the generals were irrelevant, their views were always available, generals on active wartime service should not be attending conventions, and "anything that would be apt to give a political complexion to the assembly was to be deprecated." The planners compromised by inviting military officers who had specific knowledge about the project.[17] Funding was harder to compromise. At the first joint convention planning session, Thomas B. Bryan—a War Democrat about to challenge the incumbent, regular Democratic mayor Francis C. Sherman on a Republican-dominated Union slate— was deliberately ambiguous, stating that "the interests of the people and property holders of Chicago, in this enterprise, would warrant the levying of a tax upon them for this money, unless they should subscribe liberally without such compulsory process." Republicans, however, delayed circulating a subscription list to test the possibilities of voluntarism.[18] They preferred to force a council vote that would tar Democrats as enemies of the ship canal.

The joint committee suspended meetings during the city campaign, but submitted a petition for $10,000 one week before the April 21 election. Republican aldermen tried to avoid committee reference in order to force a quick preelection vote, but Democrats, though they favored the ship canal "as much as any man in Chicago," refused to be rushed into a hasty appropriation of "the people's money."[19] The *Times* suggested that the council had no power to

16. Howard P. Chudacoff and Judith E. Smith, *The Evolution of American Urban Society*, 3d ed. (Englewood Cliffs: Prentice-Hall, 1988), 71; Homer Hoyt, *One Hundred Years of Land Values in Chicago* (Chicago: University of Chicago Press, 1933), 483; Bessie Louise Pierce, *A History of Chicago* (3 vols.; Chicago: University of Chicago Press, 1937–57), 2:77–117; Margaret Walsh, *The Rise of the Midwestern Meat Packing Industry* (Lexington: University Press of Kentucky, 1982), 50–51, 57–60.

17. *Times*, April 24, 27, 29, 1863.

18. Ibid., March 27, 1863.

19. The Board of Trade also submitted its own petition; CP, 1863/64:55; *Times*, April 14, 1863.

pay for the convention and announced its election platform the next day, condemning the Lincoln administration for military conscription, suspensions of habeas corpus, and the Emancipation Proclamation. The Republicans, meanwhile, nominated Bryan to head their Union ticket, campaigned by charging the Democrats with disloyalty, and labeled Mayor Sherman, whose son was the colonel of a Board of Trade regiment, a blundering "tool" of the Copperheads. Admitting afterwards that the conscription law had cost votes, the *Tribune* blamed the Republicans' rout on the annexation of Bridgeport's "debased and ignorant" Irish voters. The Democrats, it complained, might as well have annexed the state penitentiary.[20] The election had three consequences for convention funding: the council's committee was automatically dissolved, the appropriation process had to begin again from scratch, and funding now clearly was a partisan issue.

It also became a test of wills. Democrats insisted that the charter's rules governing appropriations precluded a vote before June 1, the night before the convention, and then only if consent were unanimous. An objection by any alderman would cost another two weeks. Democrats urged the joint committee to circulate a subscription list but Republicans refused to take action before the council voted. Meanwhile, the committee mailed 7,000 invitations and one Republican threatened that if aldermen denied funding he would stand up at the convention, "let the infamy rest where it belonged," and take up a collection among the city's visitors (this was Grant Goodrich, the old anti-theater crusader). By May 21, some planners were worried. The committee had raised no money—Arnold used his congressional privileges to frank the invitations—and the city's Democratic comptroller hinted that the charter contained legal obstacles to funding (this was Samuel S. Hayes, who had exhibited less legal scruple over his sale of Union Park). Corporation counsel B. F. Ayer, also a Democratic member of the joint committee (though a relative newcomer to politics), suggested the circulation of a subscription list just in case aldermen voted funding down, without revealing that he had prepared an adverse legal opinion for their use. Chicago, Democrat Thomas Hoyne now feared, faced a "loss of rank among the sisterhood of cities in the scale of civilization." (Hoyne was the brawling Douglasite district attorney in 1856.)[21]

On May 25 the council voted—not on an appropriation, but on a resolution endorsing the corporation counsel's opinion that they could not pay for the convention. Funding was dead. The 18–9 vote

20. *Times*, April 15, 16, 1863; *Tribune*, April 18, 19, 22, 23, 1863.
21. *Times*, April 3, May 1, 15, 20, 22, 1863.

was almost entirely partisan. Both War Democrats but only one regular Democrat voted with the Republicans for funding and only two Republicans joined the Democrats in opposition. The joint committee raised $7,740 in subscriptions in a single day and by June 1 they had $8,400.[22] Chicago's guests arrived on June 2 and rejected the ship canal on June 3, the same day Burnside's soldiers stormed the *Times* office and destroyed several thousand copies in the street. Any guests still in the city that evening watched indignation meetings against the suppression. Arnold joined in wiring President Lincoln on June 2 to reverse Burnside's order and then denied that he had done so when local Republicans decided they wanted the *Times* suppressed after all. Historians of this incident, puzzled by the behavior of Arnold and other Illinois Republicans, have neglected the fact that Chicago had hundreds of dignitaries in town for a show of patriotism designed to convince Congress of the military necessity of an internal improvement.[23] The National Ship Canal Convention was a fiasco.

It was, however, a revealing fiasco. Chicagoans had seen that the Civil War promised opportunities of government subsidy to those who were powerful enough to snatch them. The public interest of a nation at war could justify the political redistribution of its wealth. One of the first war measures that aldermen considered was Arnold's request that they lobby for an armory. "Chicago," the congressman warned in booster fashion, "must not expect that her superior natural advantages will secure the prize without zealous and energetic efforts of her citizens."[24] Chicagoans had overestimated their clout in both the West and the nation: the West may have been ready to play power politics, but Chicago could not muscle its ship canal through Congress. As in 1847, Chicagoans endorsed a redistributive federal improvement policy and a politics of interest-group competition to implement it. This time, however, they did not have to squirm on the issue of strict construction. Democrats and Republicans both exploited the overriding public good of the Union war effort. Yet, Chicagoans again were cautious about applying this notion of public interest within the city. And this time, the municipal government did not fund the convention.

"ALL THE OPPOSITION came from 'non tax-payers,'" Republican alderman A. D. Titsworth said of the convention funding vote,

22. CP, 1863/64:24; *Tribune*, May 26, 1863; *Times*, May 26, 27, June 1, 1863.
23. See Craig D. Tenney, "To Suppress or Not To Suppress: Abraham Lincoln and the Chicago *Times*," *Civil War History* 27 (1981): 248–59.
24. CP, 1861/62:145, 218.

and he "did not think that class ought to have anything to do with the matter." If the opposition actually came from Democrats, Chicago politicians tended to confuse class and party. When the *Tribune* compared Bridgeport to the penitentiary and the *Times* found it "beyond question that the producing classes . . . are bearing the [tax] burden of the war," the parties claimed that they represented class interests. Sherman boasted that he was "personally familiar with the habits and interests of the laboring classes," which he doubtless was, employing many laborers in his brickyard, but Titsworth, as a clothing manufacturer, probably had a similar familiarity.[25] It is easy to dispute these claims of class representation. While Republicans clearly coveted workers' votes, Illinois Democrats enacted the antilabor LaSalle Black Laws in 1863. Yet there was a class component in party rhetoric. John Wentworth, explaining his own political isolation, expressed it in Jacksonian vernacular: "men who were sound on the banking question were rotten on the negro question, and men who were sound on the negro question were rotten on the banking question."[26]

Convention funding was a partisan but not a class issue. Democrats used strict construction to show partisan independence by evoking the image of Jacksonian populism. Jacksonian strict construction never was an ideology of "non tax-payers." It banned all political redistribution of wealth—upward, downward, and horizontal—in order to protect opportunity for "producers," prevent exploitation by "monopolists," and create an economy that allowed individuals to compete in a race that was fair. At the urban level, Chicagoans banned redistribution in the segmented system by refusing to recognize the existence of a public interest that would be defined through political conflict. During the Civil War, the segmented system met two challenges far more serious than convention funding. One, linked directly to the war, defined a public interest that justified downward redistribution while the other, linked to public health, defined an interest in upward redistribution. Chicagoans rejected the downwardly and embraced the upwardly redistributive interest, but party was irrelevant to these decisions. As they had created the segmented system by nonpartisan consensus in the 1840s, they now also destroyed it in a nonpartisan manner.

The potential for downward redistribution reflected Chicago's public interest in the Union war effort. The federal recruiting system,

25. *Times*, May 26, 1863; Breckenridge, "Chicago Times," 28; CP, 1862/63:1.

26. Don E. Fehrenbacher, *Chicago Giant: A Biography of "Long John" Wentworth* (Madison, Wis.: American History Research Center, 1957), 193; David Montgomery, *Beyond Equality: Labor and the Radical Republicans, 1862–1872* (Urbana: University of Illinois Press, 1967), 90–127.

by delegating responsibility to local communities, ensured that local and national interests converged during the war. Both the 1862 Militia Act and the 1863 Enrollment Act reserved drafting as a threat that the federal government held over communities that failed to meet enlistment quotas with volunteers. Counties, cities, and towns throughout the Union soon entered into bidding wars for recruits; those that offered the highest bounties could attract the most volunteers and thereby improve their chances of avoiding conscription. The local bounty market was organized. While bounty brokers and jumpers made a business out of abusing it, communities advertised to spread price information. Potential recruits became sophisticated consumers who could shop for high local bounties to supplement those offered by the federal government, states, and counties.[27]

Local communities recruited men in two ways. First, they paid bounties that attracted both local men and outsiders. Bounty payments were the most direct method by which a community could meet its recruitment quotas. Second, communities paid relief stipends that encouraged local men to volunteer by promising that their families would be supported in their absence. Because soldiers earned only about two-thirds of the wages of home front laborers, received their wages sporadically, and had no regular system for sending their earnings home, family stipends addressed an important obstacle to enlistments. When these methods failed and the federal government imposed a draft, communities engaged in two other practices. Some, particularly after the New York City draft riot of July 1863, paid the $300 commutation fees to exempt local draftees from service, though this supplied no men and thus hampered rather than aided recruiting. Communities also purchased substitutes for draftees, a practice that both appeased potential rioters and supplied men for the army. All of these recruiting methods were expensive. While bounty and substitute prices rose with each call for troops, relief stipends had to keep pace with rapid inflation during the war.[28]

None of these practices were necessarily functions of municipal

27. Eugene Converse Murdock, *Patriotism Limited, 1862–1865: The Civil War Draft and the Bounty System* (Kent, Ohio: Kent State University Press, 1967), 16–41. See also Murdock, *One Million Men: The Civil War Draft in the North* (Madison: State Historical Society of Wisconsin, 1971); Murdock, *Ohio's Bounty System in the Civil War* (Columbus: Ohio State University Press, 1963); James W. Geary, "Civil War Conscription in the North: A Historiographical Review," *Civil War History* 32 (1986): 208–28. For the theme of local public interest, Michael H. Frisch, *Town into City: Springfield, Massachusetts, and the Meaning of Community, 1840–1880* (Cambridge: Harvard University Press, 1972), 60–71.

28. Murdock, *Patriotism Limited*, 19–27; Geary, "Civil War Conscription," 213–14.

government. While the federal, state, and county governments paid bounties, local recruiting also was conducted by voluntary patriotic associations, business organizations that mobilized commercial resources into the war effort, and insurance societies that purchased substitutes for their drafted members. As Eugene C. Murdock has pointed out, local governments rarely had the authority to raise money for recruiting. In New York State, cities and counties ignored restrictions on their borrowing powers and contracted large illegal recruitment debts in the hope that the legislature would approve them retroactively, which it did in 1863. Massachusetts, by contrast, authorized local recruitment borrowing in advance. Because it also promised to reimburse towns after the war, the construction of local power and the definition of local public interest were less urgent issues in that state.[29] Illinois pursued a more ambiguous policy. In 1861 the legislature empowered counties and cities to levy annual five mill taxes (fifty cents per $100 of assessed property) for bounties and stipends, and in 1863 it retroactively legalized debts and taxes higher than five mills for eight counties including Cook.[30]

Chicago's recruiting efforts were successful enough to avoid a draft until September 1864 and even then only fifty-nine Chicagoans entered the army as conscripts. Cook County and its Chicago subdistricts—each ward was a subdistrict—continually met their quotas. The city's government played a minor role in the activities that accomplished this feat. It spent a total of $120,000 on bounties and $91,000 on stipends, for an aggregate of $211,000. While the comparison has a limited application because of legal distinctions between Massachusetts and Illinois in regard to county government, Chicago's municipal bounty spending may be placed in some perspective by comparing it with the $175,000 spent by Springfield, Massachusetts, a city one-eighth of Chicago's size. It was not that Chicagoans paid fewer government bounties. Cook County spent $2.6 million on them, much of it in Chicago. For stipends, the county and city divided responsibility; the county paid in towns outside Chicago and the city handled relief within its boundaries. Even for sti-

29. Murdock, *Patriotism Limited*, 29–30; Frisch, *Town into City*, 61. Ohio did not allow local taxes or debts until March 1864, and its communities waited for authorization; Murdock, *Ohio's Bounty System*, 17–18.

30. Illinois, *Laws, Extraordinary Session, 1861*, 24–25 and *Public Laws, 1863*, 25, 39–41, 51, 56, 85–86. The legislature might have included more counties or passed a general ratification like New York's, but Republican Governor Richard Yates prorogued it to block a Democratic legislative program and even before that, Republicans had been boycotting sessions. It thus is difficult to assign legislative intent. See Arthur Charles Cole, *The Era of the Civil War, 1848–1870* (Chicago: A. C. McClurg, 1919), 298–99.

pends, however, the Board of Trade and Mercantile Association together spent three times as much as the city's government.[31]

What is remarkable, is that Chicagoans spent municipal funds on these items at all. They did it with reluctance. The war tax never approached the authorized five mills. The council levied two mills in 1861, 1.25 in 1862, three in 1863, and no war tax in 1864. For other general objects, meanwhile, aldermen taxed at the maximum rate that the charter allowed for each category of expenditure.[32] When they levied the first war tax in 1861, they had not yet decided how to spend it. The legislative authorization was broad. Counties and cities could raise war taxes "for the purpose of aiding in the formation and equipment of volunteer companies mustered into the service of the United States or of this state, for the purpose of enforcing the laws, suppressing insurrection or repelling invasion, and to aid in the support of the families of members of such companies, while engaged in such military service."[33] Thus, the city could appropriate its war tax proceeds for bounties and stipends to aid in recruiting or for the purchase of weapons, the organization of local defense forces, and almost any other war-related purpose.

When the Republicans controlled the council early in 1862, two voluntary associations asked for war fund appropriations—the tax had not yet been collected. The Union Defense Committee (UDC), which handled much of Chicago's recruiting by organizing patriotic demonstrations to collect subscriptions, wanted aldermen to give them the fund to buy weapons for local defense. The UDC also was a Republican party adjunct, having declared the previous August that only "traitors and their abettors" still remained Democrats. The council refused to arm the UDC, but it did authorize them to administer loyalty oaths.[34] The Chicago Sanitary Commission (CSC), meanwhile,

---

31. Frisch, *Town into City*, 65. Cook county recruiting is detailed in Weston A. Goodspeed and Daniel D. Healy, eds., *History of Cook County* (2 vols.; Chicago: Goodspeed Historical Association, 1909), 1:448–96. For the totals, A. T. Andreas, *History of Chicago* (3 vols.; Chicago: Andreas, 1884–86), 2:168. The city comptroller reckoned total bounty spending at $125,000; CP, 1865/66:724. See also Robin L. Einhorn, "The Civil War and Municipal Government in Chicago" in *Toward a Social History of the American Civil War: Exploratory Essays*, Maris Vinovskis, ed. (Cambridge: Cambridge University Press, 1990), 127–32.

32. *Tribune*, August 28, 1861; *Times*, September 3, 1862, October 6, 1863, October 4, 1864; Edmund J. James, ed., *The Charters of the City of Chicago* (2 pts.; Chicago: University of Chicago Press, 1898–99), 156–57 (1851 charter); Illinois, *Private Laws, 1863*, 96–97.

33. Illinois, *Laws, Extraordinary Session, 1861*, 24.

34. CP, 1861/62:104, 189, 1862/63:96; *Times*, August 28, 1861; Pierce, *History*, 2:261–62.

a branch of the U.S. Sanitary Commission, wanted the fund for its work with sick and wounded soldiers at the front. Aldermen appropriated $10,000, of which the CSC got $5,000 immediately and a promise of $5,000 more if necessary. It demanded the second $5,000 within a month, but a city election had intervened in May 1862, resulting in a bare Democratic majority, and most aldermen now wanted to spend the fund in the city rather than transfer it to the front. Although the *Times* later would call the CSC a "rank partisan concern" of "abolition fanatics," the newly elected Mayor Sherman and a bipartisan majority of the council now stressed the city's own needs.[35]

In July 1862, when aldermen considered how to spend the $70,000 war fund collected in the 1861 tax levy, recruiting was still relatively easy in Chicago. The Board of Trade raised a battery of troops so quickly that its members decided to raise a regiment. Express companies offered their employees half-pay for enlisting, the railroads raised a regiment, and by August 15, the deadline for avoiding a draft under that month's 600,000 troop call, the Board of Trade was organizing its third regiment, which it filled in September. The county paid bounties of only $60 per volunteer; two years later it paid $300.[36] In this situation, aldermen who wanted to reject the CSC's second $5,000 needed alternative, local spending objects. The UDC, in one of its weekly mass rallies, resolved to organize a Home Guard of men too old to join the army, and renewed its demand for weapons. The council, then meeting only monthly, reclaimed the CSC's second $5,000 and appropriated the rest of the war fund for $30,000 of arms and $35,000 of stipends. They rejected bounties, endorsing Cook County's bounty taxation, but Republican aldermen could not prevent Democrats from linking the council's "unqualified approval" to the effort to "restore the Union as it was."[37]

The *Times* approved the arms appropriation, printing a speech by Sherman about the threat posed by Confederate prisoners-of-war held in the city, but the *Tribune* was cool toward stipends. Not only was the war fund intended for the local prevention of "riotous proceedings," but the Republican county board rather than the Democratic city council should pay stipends in Chicago.[38] The CSC still

35. CP, 1861/62:319, 399; *Times*, February 2, 1863.

36. Goodspeed and Healy, *Cook County*, 1:457–59, 488–89.

37. CP, 1862/63:99, 101, 121, 139; *Tribune*, July 29, 1862; *Times*, July 29, 1862.

38. *Times*, July 29, 1862; *Tribune*, August 28, 1861, July 29, 1862. Some 17,000 prisoners were held at Camp Douglas on Chicago's south side during the war. It was the focus of a farcical conspiracy to use Confederate prisoners to lead an insurrection

wanted its $5,000 and the UDC complained that Sherman was block-
ing the Home Guard project by keeping their weapons boxed in a
warehouse. In September 1862, Sherman rejected a second call for
city bounties, claiming there was no legal way to appropriate money
for them once the war fund was exhausted, and council Democrats
again rebuffed the CSC, this time with a strict construction of the war
fund law. The fund was intended for "the thousands of families
whose natural protectors are away from them . . . and when we have
these calls at home of those for whom the fund was specially raised
we feel we cannot report in favor of an appropriation of any part of
said fund to any other purpose & especially to one to which we think
it cannot be legally diverted or appropriated."[39] Thus, while Chicagoans still disputed the purpose of the war tax, they agreed that its
revenue should be spent in the city. The Sanitary Commission did
not try again.

By the spring of 1863, a new $40,000 war fund from the 1862 tax
levy gave the now predominantly Democratic council another opportunity to define Chicago's public interest in the war. Recruiting
had become more difficult, military officials completed a statewide
enrollment in May, and a draft in July appeared likely. On June 15
aldermen appropriated the whole fund to stipends. Within a month,
however, New York City exploded and the Democrats called for a
bounty ordinance.[40] They abandoned the strict construction with
which they had rejected bounties before; the present emergency
overrode the charter's appropriation rules. Aldermen placed an extra
mill on the 1863 war tax, raising it from two to three, and appropriated $120,000—the whole sum—to procure substitutes or pay com-
mutations for drafted Chicagoans. The ordinance classified enrolled
men by income, limiting eligibility to those who earned less than $800
per year and granting priority to those who earned under $600,
though a version excluding draftees who owned over $1,000 of prop-
erty failed to pass. The city paid bounties under this ordinance, but
because Chicago met its quota, it bought no substitutes and paid no
commutations.[41]

By late 1863, the threat of a draft had increased. Council Democrats

in the North in 1864. Andreas, *History*, 2:301–3, 307–9; Wood Gray, *The Hidden Civil
War: The Story of the Copperheads* (New York: Viking Press, 1942), 206–7.

39. CP, 1862/63:152, 265; *Tribune*, December 13, 1862.

40. Goodspeed and Healy, *Cook County*, 1:471–75; CP, 1863/64:239. See also
Robert E. Sterling, "Civil War Draft Resistance in Illinois," *Journal of the Illinois State
Historical Society* 64 (1971): 254–55.

41. CP, 1863/64:236.

wanted to correct the city's enrollment but military officials would not let them see the list. Aldermen authorized $75 city bounties in December but by February 1864 the war fund was exhausted. On the motion of a Republican, aldermen resolved that the city had no power to borrow money for bounties, sending responsibility back to the county and private agencies. The city continued to pay stipends, but by September 1864 aldermen had limited their recruiting activity to regulating substitute brokers who credited Chicago enlistees to other states, "frustrating the efforts and sacrifices of our best citizens to enable our City to escape the disgrace of a Draft by voluntarily filling our quota."[42] In October, when they saw that "the utmost good humor prevailed" among crowds at Chicago draft lotteries, the council passed a tax ordinance that omitted war spending entirely. Some aldermen revived the call for city bounties in March 1865, but most no longer dreaded conscription. Reinterpreting the 1861 war tax legislation yet again, the council decided that it had no power to pay bounties after all. Chicago avoided drafting for its March quota only because the war ended in April.[43]

Municipal bounty and stipend payments redistributed wealth in a downward direction for the public purposes of raising troops and avoiding the draft. Although historians dispute the economic impact of conscription, particularly whether workers could afford the $300 commutation fee, the economic impact of municipal recruiting is less complex.[44] The war tax was a general property tax, but the city paid bounties to anyone who took them and stipends to families who required relief. Presumably, few wealthy men took bounties. While social pressures must have curbed temptation (bounties were paid at public rallies), volunteering by the wealthy could rest solely on personal motives such as patriotism. But to fill local quotas, communities had to attract men who would worry about their families' provision in their absence and to whom army wages represented a pay cut that bounties could compensate. Chicagoans met the challenges of recruiting with enthusiasm and success. The Union Defense Committee, Board of Trade, Mercantile Association, other business groups, ward committees, trade unions, and especially Cook County raised enough money and men to fill most local quotas. Only at the

42. Ibid., 1864/65:219. See also 1863/64:31, 60, 554, 576–77, 582, 1864/65:167, 238, 377. The war fund committee raised part of its fund from subscriptions. Appealing for donations of old clothes in 1863, the chairman said the needy families were not beggars but he was: "I glory in it"; *Tribune*, February 4, 1863.

43. *Times*, October 4, 1864; CP, 1864/65:451; Goodspeed and Healy, *Cook County*, 1:495.

44. See Geary, "Civil War Conscription," 216–26.

municipal level did Chicagoans exhibit caution. There, Republicans and Democrats both endorsed strict construction arguments that limited the city's role.

The city's highest war tax, the three mills of 1863, was a small commitment. It was Chicago's response to the most extreme threat that the war posed for cities, a local version of the New York draft riot. Republicans and Democrats agreed that the county was the proper jurisdiction for pursuing a public interest that redistributed wealth downward. The county always had handled poor relief in Chicago, though without notable generosity. The city had made only one relief appropriation in its antebellum history—$1,500 in 1857. If the stipends were a departure from earlier policy, however, that departure was temporary. After the war, aldermen did pursue something they considered a relief policy, waiving peddlers license fees for disabled veterans, soldiers' widows, and others unable to support themselves because of age or illness, but even this meager charity effort violated assumptions about the purpose of municipal government.[45] In 1872 aldermen stopped granting free licenses after the corporation counsel delivered a legal verdict resonant of Jacksonian strict construction:

> I am aware that the practice of granting free licenses, to individuals . . . has prevailed for many years, and that some hardships may result from the discontinuance of the practice, but it must be also considered that special exemptions from the operation of general ordinances, or special privileges granted for individual (not the public) benefit, lessens the respect of the people for the City ordinances in general, and creates a discontent which renders their enforcement both difficult and uncertain.[46]

Many historians have shown the temporary nature of the national public interest created by the Civil War. The wartime expansion of federal authority was curtailed quickly enough to doom a meaningful Reconstruction of the South. The retreat also had major implications for redistributive government in the North. A recent study of county-level relief policy finds "little doubt that Appomattox rendered relief less legitimate, if no less necessary." Harold Hyman has argued that Republicans shaped the federal-level policies of both the war and Reconstruction with the same Jacksonian constitutionalism that Demo-

45. See the hundreds of free peddlers license petitions, their dispositions marked, in the Chicago City Council Proceedings Files for the years 1859–72. In 1867 aldermen formalized the practice to the extent of detailing a policeman to investigate applicants' claims of poverty.

46. CP, 1872/73:275.

crats claimed as their party's exclusive inheritance.[47] At the urban level, the Republicans and Democrats of Chicago shared an inheritance of segmentation. In the segmented system, municipal government existed to serve property in a manner that minimized the public interests even of the property owners themselves. The property owners comprised the "public," but Chicagoans combined a strict construction of the city's general spending powers with segmented financial instruments to serve these owners without redistributing their wealth. Chicago did adopt a new public interest during the Civil War but not, in any direct sense, because of it.

IN THE SAME COUNCIL meetings and newspaper columns in which Chicagoans debated their municipal interest in the Civil War, they also discussed another urgent public interest. The Chicago River had become a sewer whose "perfume is so intense that it permeates our dwellings and mingles its nastiness with the air we breathe, with the water we drink and the food we eat." Not only did the river serve as a harbor for Great Lakes commercial traffic and flow through Chicago's most populous neighborhoods, but it also emptied into Lake Michigan near the point at which the city drew its water supply. The river's pollution was a serious public health problem that the *Tribune* considered "the duty of the authorities and of every citizen to meet." The *Times* also demanded municipal action. "No tax-payer," it insisted, "will object to furnish his share of the expense for remedying an evil which is so palpable to his senses that he cannot escape it wherever he goes."[48] Chicago's public interest in cleaning the river was probably the only issue on which the *Tribune* and *Times* agreed during the war. Yet despite this partisan consensus, other Chicagoans thought that the responsibility for cleaning the river should rest with those who were polluting it. They demanded a segmented solution.

The Chicago River was really three rivers: the main river and its North and South branches.[49] The short main river emptied into Lake

47. Glenn C. Altschuler and Jan M. Saltzgaber, "The Limits of Responsibility: Social Welfare and Local Government in Seneca County, New York, 1860–1875," *Journal of Social History* 22 (1988): 517; Harold M. Hyman, *A More Perfect Union: The impact of the Civil War and Reconstruction on the Constitution* (New York: Knopf, 1973). See also Morton Keller, *Affairs of State: Public Life in Late Nineteenth Century America* (Cambridge: Harvard University Press, 1977).

48. *Tribune*, July 26, 1863; *Times*, December 30, 1862.

49. For general studies of the pollution problem, Louis P. Cain, *Sanitation Strategy for a Lakefront Metropolis: The Case of Chicago* (DeKalb: Northern Illinois University Press, 1978); James C. O'Connell, "Technology and Pollution: Chicago's Water Policy,

Michigan at the entrance to Chicago's harbor. Lined with wharves and grain elevators, it split just west of today's Loop into the two branches. The stagnant North Branch was lined with distilleries and hog pens. Distillers fed their industrial wastes to hogs and then washed the hogs' wastes into the river through drains mounted on its banks. The South Branch contained much of the city's wharfage and most of its meat-packing industry. Like the North Branch distillers, the South Branch packers mounted drains on the riverbank to run blood, offal, and other filth into the river. While the South Branch did not flow quickly, it did flow. Thus Chicago's packing wastes travelled north down the South Branch, east through the main branch, and into the lake near the water intake. Unless it restrained the distillers, the city could do nothing about the North Branch short of building a canal to create an artificial current. The South Branch, however, already had a canal connection: it met the Illinois and Michigan Canal at Bridgeport. If the Illinois and Michigan Canal could be deepened, therefore, the Chicago River could be reversed so that the packing wastes flowed away from rather than into Lake Michigan.

Chicagoans called this project the National Ship Canal. When the convention planners argued that the government should build it "primarily as a war measure, and incidently to afford an enlarged outlet to the constantly-increasing products of the North-west," their lie was double.[50] If Congress rejected the ship canal on commercial grounds, few seem to have realized that what Chicagoans really wanted the federal government to build was a sewer. This was common knowledge within the city, where the project had been under consideration for years. Ellis Chesbrough, now chief engineer of the Board of Public Works, had recommended it in 1856 when he designed the city's sewerage system. Among the four plans he presented at that time, deepening the canal to reverse the river was the most expensive option but the only one that he regarded as a permanent solution. He recommended it again in 1860 and 1862. In January 1863, while the ship canal was pending in Congress, the *Tribune* listed it along with four other ways to clean the river.[51] If the U.S. government would not

1833–1930" (Ph.D. diss., University of Chicago, 1980). The official history of the Chicago Sanitary District not only is useful but has a descriptive subtitle: G. P. Brown, *Drainage Channel and Waterway: A History of the Effort to Secure an Effective and Harmless Method for the Disposal of the Sewage of the City of Chicago, and to Create a Navigable Channel between Lake Michigan and the Mississippi River* (Chicago: R. R. Donnelly & Sons, 1894).

50. CP, 1863/64:55.
51. O'Connell, "Technology and Pollution," 37–39; *Tribune*, January 16, 1863.

solve Chicago's pollution problem, Illinois seemingly could not. The 1848 constitution banned internal improvements because the ambitious plans of 1837 had bankrupted the state.[52]

Chicago was going to have to clean up its own pollution. But whose pollution was it? The industrial polluters and the press claimed the sewer system caused the pollution, making river cleansing a public responsibility. The river, the *Times* argued, was "a great ditch, into which the filth of a whole city flows. Added to this, the offal of packinghouses and distilleries is but a small item." Chesbrough answered that his sewers could not be blamed for "the large quantities of blood and other waste and foul substances" in the river.[53] In July 1862, the council hired a chemist, one Dr. Mahla, to settle the question through scientific analysis. Explaining that the location of ammonia concentrations in the river "must lead to the discovery of the parties by whom the nuisances are produced," Mahla blamed the industries. While no sewers emptied into the North Branch, it had high ammonia concentrations and was "almost as impure as one of our most important sewers." The council hired Mahla in the summer, when the packinghouses were closed, but he urged further testing during the packing season. He exonerated all but one of the south side sewers and found an industrial culprit even there, since the gas company dumped into the only large sewer on the South Branch.[54]

In addition to hiring Mahla, the council sent a series of delegations, dubbed the "aldermanic smelling committees," to the industrial districts. The 1862 committee was "convinced beyond a doubt" of the distillers' role in North Branch pollution, having seen them pour a "constant stream of Liquid Poison" through their riverbank drains. The distillers "cheerfully" agreed to close the drains. After a South Branch tour, the committee ordered the packers to stop dumping and again the businessmen promised to comply. Conditions on the South Branch were uneven; some packers carted their wastes away and others dumped them into the river.[55] Yet the major packers' claim that although small firms polluted, the larger ones were clean, is questionable. Of thirty-four South Branch firms visited by the smelling committee, twelve were deemed clean (three of them not in operation),

52. Theodore Calvin Pease, *The Frontier State, 1818–1848* (Springfield: Illinois Centennial Commission, 1918), 408–9.

53. *Times*, December 30, 1862; CP, 1861/62:337.

54. CP, 1862/63:120, 144.

55. Ibid., 1862/63:237; Louise Carroll Wade, *Chicago's Pride: The Stockyards, Packingtown, and Environs in the Nineteenth Century* (Urbana: University of Illinois Press, 1987), 41.

five unclean, and seventeen both dirty and dumping into the river. If most of the small firms were filthy and most of the clean firms were large, such major businesses as Culbertson and Jones, Harbeck and Kreigh, and A. E. Kent numbered among the offensive. These were not fly-by-night operations.[56]

The council responded with a nuisance ordinance in December 1862. Packers, distillers, slaughterers, and renderers had to take licenses and give bonds to ensure that they (1) did not dump blood, offal, and the like into the river, (2) did not allow these substances to remain on their premises for more than one day in the summer or two days in the winter, (3) buried their wastes twelve feet under ground at least forty rods away from the river, the lake, and any dwelling or public street in the city, and (4) kept their premises clean.[57] The press greeted the ordinance with outrage. Both the *Times* and the *Tribune* found it "oppressive to manufacturers," and the *Tribune* actually applauded the river's use as a meat packer's sewer. Its disposal facilities were the reason the packers were in Chicago; to deny them its use "and thereby narrow the margin for profit" would drive them away, "and the men who are now clamoring for the removal of 'nuisances' would find when they have gone, that they had removed a large percentage of the population of the city along with them." The *Times* was more subtle. It stressed the sewers and appealed to civic pride. "If Chicago is so poor, and so inconsiderable, that she cannot [clean the river], she deserves to endure the evil. But she is not."[58]

The packers met the ordinance by organizing the Chicago Pork Packers Association, dedicated to fighting it through a license boycott. While most of its officers operated packinghouses that the smelling committee had deemed clean, one director who claimed to be carting his wastes away had been spotted by a bridge tender running his blood into the river.[59] He was unlucky, though his detection il-

56. Wade, *Chicago's Pride*, 35; CP, 1862/63:237. In 1868, the reorganized Culbertson, Blair and Co. was Chicago's largest meat-packing firm, A. E. Kent came in fourth, and Culbertson's former partner Jones—now a partner in Jones, Hough and Co.—was fifth. Kreigh, no longer in partnership with Harbeck, was seventh, and Reid and Sherwin, another unclean 1862 firm, was sixth. Only two "clean" firms made the top ten in 1868. See John S. Wright, *Chicago: Past, Present, Future* (Chicago: Horton & Leonard, 1868), 210.

57. CP, 1862/63:245.

58. *Tribune*, January 1, 1863; *Times*, December 30, 1862.

59. *Times*, February 4, 1863; CP, 1862/63:237. Wade describes the association's goals as production standards in an industry where small firms produced inferior products (*Chicago's Pride*, 34–35). While this may have been the case later, it defined its objectives at its first meeting as "mutual benefit and protection, and uniting upon some course of action in regard to the recent ordinance of the City Council upon the subject of slaugh-

lustrated a fundamental problem with smelling committees. A committee that inspected the South Branch in 1864 visited not only in the off-season, but with an escort from the packers association, "who generously furnished carriages" for the tour. Needless to say, the packinghouses closed for the summer were "in a neat and tidy condition." While the committee reported that the packers had stopped dumping, they obviously did not observe this. By 1864, the distillers also had radicalized. The smelling committee had watched them run swill, dung, and other filth into the North Branch and asked them to stop, "but they were unanimous in saying it was out of the question to do so and carry on the business."[60] The industrialists demanded a publicly financed solution to the pollution problem that would allow them to continue to dump waste into the river.

Chicago's pollution problem was not new. During the cholera epidemic of 1849, when many Chicagoans had blamed slaughterhouse pollution for the spread of the disease, aldermen had considered proposals to ban meat packing in the city. The packers wanted a compromise that would guarantee them "security from molestation." Relocation would entail "great pecuniary sacrifice" and nobody had "a deeper interest in the health, or prosperity of our city" than the packers.[61] They asked for a nuisance ordinance to prevent blood and offal from being dumped into the river, allowed to saturate the ground, or kept on hand for more than one day. Some aldermen were skeptical: "whether such vast numbers of cattle sheep & hogs can be *Yearly & even daily* slaughtered within the limits of the present Corporation without creating a nuisance is the *question*, with all due *defference* [sic] to the opinions of others. Your Comm[ittee] consider it *verry* [sic] doubtful to say the least of it."[62] The council enacted a license ordinance in 1850 like that which the packers requested—but would boycott a decade later—and ordered out of the city all lard renderers, soap makers, and others who "steam or render any animal substance in such a manner as to occasion any offensive smell." Most of the packers also left, moving south along the South Branch to Bridgeport.[63]

The more significant response to the 1849 cholera epidemic, of

---

tering establishments." Its first action was the boycott. See *Times*, December 31, 1862, for aldermen's recognition of this pressure.

60. CP, 1864/65:148.
61. Ibid., 1850/50:6673.
62. Ibid. (emphasis in original).
63. Wade, *Chicago's Pride*, 29–30; George Manierre, ed., *The Revised Charter and Ordinances of the City of Chicago* (Chicago: Daily Democrat, 1851), 216.

course, was the construction of the waterworks in 1852. The citywide provision of Lake Michigan water replaced hundreds of private wells easily contaminated by privy vaults; apparently everyone who drank from one north side well died of cholera. In 1856, the city also began to replace the privy vaults with the sewerage system.[64] Yet these public responses were tied to the nuisance rules. No outcry met the exodus of the packers. Although they had asked for concessions because their industry was "already a very important branch of the commerce of this city," their sanitary costs still outweighed their economic benefits.[65] This changed during the Civil War. Chicago's packing industry grew throughout the 1850s but tripled in size from 1861 to 1863. Union army contracts stimulated demand everywhere but favored suppliers in large cities, while the war disrupted the southern commercial ties and river transportation of St. Louis and Cincinnati. Chicago, whose trade was oriented eastward by lake and railroad, reaped the benefits. As Margaret Walsh has shown, the war accelerated the concentration of the industry in large cities generally and in Chicago particularly.[66]

The rapid rise of the packing industry transformed Chicago's economy. The packers handled 272,000 hogs in 1860/61, 506,000 in 1861/62, and 970,000 in their peak 1862/63 season. Production then dropped, but never below 500,000 hogs per year. As the industry concentrated in Chicago, it remained concentrated within Chicago. In 1858/59, nine Chicago area firms packed at least 5,000 hogs and none packed more than 50,000. The three largest firms packed half of the city's total pork production. In 1871/72, the first year that total production surpassed the 1862/63 peak, twenty-six firms packed at least 5,000 hogs, seven packed over 50,000, and three packed more than 100,000. Now the three largest firms accounted for one-third and the five largest for half of the city's pork production. These were huge businesses. The packing industry produced 12 percent of the city's total manufacturing output in 1860 and one-fourth in 1868—and the total expanded between five and six times over.[67] By the end of the

64. O'Connell, "Technology and Pollution," 12. Also chap. 4 above.

65. CP, 1850/50:6673.

66. Wade, *Chicago's Pride*, 32–33; Walsh, *Midwestern Meat Packing Industry*, 55–60. In the Illinois Central Railroad, Chicago also had a route other than the blockaded Mississippi River to the Union armies fighting in the West, making it easy to provision these armies from Chicago.

67. Andreas, *History*, 2:382; Elias Colbert, *Chicago: Historical and Statistical Sketch of the Garden City, from the Beginning until Now* (Chicago: P. T. Sherlock, 1868), 79. In 1867/68 four firms packed over 50,000 and one over 100,000. The concentration was the same as in 1871/72. See Wright, *Chicago*, 210.

war, Chicago was indeed "porkopolis." Because the city's residents could taste their prosperity in their water, the Civil War had an important indirect effect on the development of the new public interest.

One additional characteristic of the packing industry shaped the politics of pollution in the city. In Chicago as elsewhere, most packers had begun packing as a sideline to general mercantile operations. Leading packers also were livestock traders, grain shippers, commission merchants, and lumber dealers.[68] As a result of the industry's commercial base, the packers were members of the Board of Trade. The implications of this link for the ship canal were obvious. In 1863, when the board insisted on the national interest in building the canal and the municipal interest in financing the convention, the city's leading packer, John L. Hancock, simultaneously was the president of the board and the vice-president of the Pork Packers Association.[69] If all Board of Trade members clearly would have favored an "enlarged outlet to the constantly-increasing products of the North-west," Hancock and the other packers saw the ship canal as an alternative to the nuisance ordinance they were boycotting. When the board demanded that the council provide "immediate relief from the sickening & putrifying waters of [the Chicago] river," therefore, the appeal to public health did not emanate from disinterested representatives of the public interest.[70]

None of this seems particularly scandalous today, when cities and states define their public interests broadly enough to include all sorts of subsidies for "economic development." Indeed, looking back on this debate, most modern critics would side with the Board of Trade and the newspapers rather than Dr. Mahla and the smelling committees. From a public health perspective, it does not matter who was polluting the river. That only Chicago's poorest residents lived near it—the wealthy lived as far away as possible—increases the sense in which the opponents of a public solution obstructed a progressive pursuit of Chicago's real public interest. The city's health was at stake, the Tribune thundered, and this "is no time to argue who is to blame."[71] But to other Chicagoans, blame was the crucial issue. In the segmented system, the "privatism" that modern critics deplore was elevated to an ideology of government purpose. The articulation of a public interest in public health, therefore, was a departure many

68. Walsh, Midwestern Meat Packing Industry, 60–63 for Chicago and passim for the industry.

69. Times, February 4, 1863; Charles H. Taylor, ed., History of the Board of Trade of the City of Chicago (3 vols.; Chicago: Robert O. Law, 1917), 1:297, 303, 310.

70. CP, 1862/63:63.

71. Tribune, July 26, 1862.

property owners contested. The fight was less over the definition of the public interest—nobody said that public health was a bad thing—than over whether the city's property owners should redistribute their wealth to promote that interest. At an extreme level, it was about whether a homeowner who could not afford to drain his own yard should have to subsidize the drainage costs of meat-packing firms.

From the property owners' point of view, a publicly financed river project would redistribute their wealth toward the packers. An alternative and segmented solution existed in the rules for nuisance assessment. By this procedure, when the city abated a nuisance, it levied a special assessment against those who had created it.[72] In theory, the city could have cleaned the river by appointing assessors to determine the relative responsibility of the sewers and industries for its pollution, apportioning the cost between the public and the industries through mechanisms that in the segmented system most Chicagoans had deemed equitable. It was not considered. Chesbrough, who by 1864 had given up defending his South Branch sewers, made the obvious argument about the North Branch distillers: "Inasmuch as the City, in its corporate capacity, is doing nothing to pollute the North Branch, but has thus far kept the sewers from emptying into it, there is no sufficient reason why private individuals should be allowed to pollute it. It is believed that no other large city in the civilized world permits such nuisances, and why should Chicago?"[73] Why indeed? The answer was that in addition to its interest in public health, Chicago was adopting a public interest in its economy. A profitable packing industry, as the *Tribune* explained in its defense of the packers' dumping, was a public good. While the distillers had far less power, the packers could and did threaten that if the city did not grant them public subsidies, they would leave and take a large chunk of Chicago's economy with them.

In the 1840s and 1850s, the city had promoted its public interest in commerce by dredging the river through special assessment. But the packers had power in the 1860s on an entirely new scale. They could not prevent the Bridgeport annexation because that was a partisan issue: the Democrats who controlled both the council and the legislature wanted Bridgeport's Democratic voters to vote in Chicago. But once annexed, they shaped city policy. The 1862 nuisance ordinance was Chicago's last attempt to clean the South Branch solely by re-

72. Illinois, *Laws, 1863,* 92.
73. CP, 1864/65:148. The packers produced 25 percent of the city's manufacturing output in 1868 but the distillers produced only 3 percent; Colbert, *Chicago,* 78–79.

straining its polluters. Beginning in 1863, the council took limited public steps. The Illinois and Michigan Canal board had built pumps at Bridgeport that fed the canal with river water in dry seasons. From 1863 to 1866 the city paid the canal board periodically to reverse its pumps, flushing the South Branch with clean water from the canal.[74] This took care of the river's smell, but was not a solution; it pumped the pollution directly toward the water intake in the lake. Solutions were expensive. Had the federal government stepped in with the National Ship Canal, Chicagoans would not have had to face their pollution problem during the war. They might have postponed the new public interest a bit longer.

Instead, the city inaugurated two huge public works projects in 1865. First, it built a tunnel under Lake Michigan that moved the water intake two miles away from the shore. Completed in 1867 at a cost of $2.5 million, the tunnel was a spectacular engineering achievement that won international acclaim. The Board of Public Works celebrated its triumph by capping the project with the castellated gothic water tower that would be one of the only buildings on Chicago's north side to survive the Great Fire of 1871. The pumping works across the street succumbed, ending all hope of fighting the Fire, but the tower remains as Chicago's monument to its pre-Fire history.[75] Second, the city deepened part of the Illinois and Michigan Canal. Completed in 1871, with $2.5 of its $3.3 million cost assumed ultimately by the state, this second engineering feat solved Chicago's pollution problem for a decade.[76] In 1881 the city reinstalled the Bridgeport pumps and in 1900, under the jurisdiction of the Chicago Sanitary District, built the "Chicago Sanitary and Ship Canal," finally naming the project correctly. Ship canal politics from 1880 to 1900 was complex, but Chi-

74. O'Connell, "Technology and Pollution," 37; CP, 1850/50:6602, 1861/62:14, 1862/63:238. Note that the canal board reversed its pumps, flushing canal water into the river rather than river water into the canal. Cain, *Sanitation Strategy*, 62–63, describes the "discovery" that the board's regular pumping "removed considerable quantities of sewage from the river. . . . That the suspended sewage would flow into the canal along with the water seems self-evident today." It also was self-evident then; hence the pumps' reversal. That Chicago ultimately sent its sewage downstate through the canal owed more to political power than technological "accident."

75. O'Connell, "Technology and Pollution," 42–47; Cain, *Sanitation Strategy*, 46–57. See also *The Tunnels and Water System of Chicago: Under the Lake and under the River* (Chicago: J. M. Wing & Co., 1874).

76. Cain, *Sanitation Strategy*, 59–82; O'Connell, "Technology and Pollution," 39–41. Even before these projects were completed, the largest packing firms left anyway, for the new Union Stock Yards in the adjacent town of Lake. The stockyards were built in 1865 by a syndicate of railroads to simplify livestock marketing and transshipment, and thus offered packers convenience in addition to a local government that would not interfere with their dumping. See Wade, *Chicago's Pride*, 47–60.

cagoans had established the general pattern in their demands for outside funding in 1863 and 1865.

Chicago financed the 1865–71 canal project by issuing bonds under the authority of the state's 1865 "Act to provide for the completion of the Illinois and Michigan Canal, upon the plan adopted by the state in 1836."[77] This law gave the city a lien on $2.5 million of future canal revenue to begin in 1871, when the state liquidated its original canal debt. Chicago based its claim to this revenue on the canal's early history. When Illinois first authorized it in 1836, the state adopted a "deep cut" plan. The canal board ran out of money during the Panic of 1837, but when it resumed construction in 1845 it substituted a cheaper "shallow cut." Thus, Chicagoans now argued, the state owed the city its original plan, which incidentally would enhance shipping facilities for farmers across northern Illinois. The legislature passed the canal act with no debate of any kind.[78] Soon, however, communities along the canal line realized that a deepened canal would divert Chicago's sewage to them. Thus, at the 1870 constitutional convention, some delegates tried to authorize the state to sell the canal, jeopardizing Chicago's lien on its future revenue.[79]

Chicago delegate Elliott Anthony explained to the convention that the 1865 act had been unrelated to Chicago's pollution. The canal board itself had wanted to deepen the canal to save the cost of pumping in dry seasons, had met with city authorities, "and it was finally decided, as the canal had not the money sufficient to go forward with the work, the city of Chicago should do it—should deepen the canal; and they called it a sanitary measure."[80] By 1870, with an eighth of Illinois's population and economic clout that the state had begun to address with antimonopoly Granger laws, Chicagoans tried to exert in Illinois the power they had failed to exert nationally. As they had

77. Illinois, *Public Laws*, 1865, 83–84.

78. Illinois, House, *Journal* (1865), 861, 992, 1247; Illinois, Senate, *Journal* (1865), 576. For the "shallow cut," James William Putnam, *The Illinois and Michigan Canal: A Study in Economic History* (Chicago: University of Chicago Press, 1918), 55–56.

79. Delegates from southern Illinois also supported the sale of a canal that now seemed to benefit only northern Illinois; Ernest Ludlow Bogart and Charles Manfred Thompson, *The Industrial State, 1870–1893* (Chicago: A. C. McClurg, 1922), 10–11. Within Chicago, meanwhile, north siders felt "wronged" in having to pay taxes for a project that abated only south side pollution; CP, 1869/70:777.

80. Elliott Anthony, *Sanitation and Navigation* (Chicago: Chicago Legal News, 1891), 117. By 1891 Anthony had improved the scenario: the 1836 deep cut had been planned with the intention of carrying "the prospective sewage of Chicago" into the canal. The town was laid out as part of the canal plan "and those who were invited to settle on the banks of what was then a stagnant bayou [the Chicago River], were promised a perfect means of sewage disposal" (p. 67).

defined their municipal interest as that of the packers, they tried to define Illinois's interest as that of Chicago. Anthony scolded the downstaters: "A state is sometimes denominated a body politic. We are all members of that body politic, and are all interested in its welfare. It is a great partnership, in which each one composing the partnership is supposed to act for the good of the whole; and we do not understand that type of statesmanship which limits its grasp to the door-sills of one's own country village."[81] The convention did not approve the sale of the canal and when much of Chicago burned to the ground in 1871, the governor paid the $2.5 million canal lien in a lump sum as the state's contribution to the city's rebuilding. Downstate communities not only had taken Chicago's sewage, but also had paid for it. If this was their "partnership" with Chicago, they refused to remain partners. Chicago eventually built its own Sanitary and Ship Canal. As Jon C. Teaford has shown, the "door-sill" model was precisely the way most state legislatures worked in the late nineteenth century.[82] Anthony's political theory was, to say the least, ahead of its time.

The debate about Chicago's pollution involved similar issues at each level of government. Naming was everything. After the Jacksonians developed their formal rules for defining national public interests, subsidies could be justified only by redefining "local" interests. Emergencies could justify new public interests, whether they were defined as the need to win the Civil War or the threat, as the Board of Trade put it, that "sickness and death [will] surround us on every hand throughout the city."[83] But the powerful had clear advantages in defining emergencies. While Chicagoans subsidized the packers, the city also tried to force local butchers to use a monopolistic central slaughterhouse operated by one of the largest meat-packing firms. This too was a sanitary measure.[84] A politics that banned calls for redistribution banned downward redistribution effectively. Even free peddlers licenses became unfair "special privileges" (as sewer extensions were becoming "local interests"). Only the powerful could re-

81. Ibid., 113.

82. Jon C. Teaford, "Special Legislation and the Cities, 1865–1900," *American Journal of Legal History* 23 (1979): 189–212. Also Bogart and Thompson, *Industrial State*, 13; O'Connell, "Technology and Pollution," 39.

83. CP, 1862/63:63.

84. On the central slaughterhouse, ibid., 1865/66:710, 798, 836, 860, 1867/68: 422–23. After debate in the council and courts much like that concerning New Orleans's slaughterhouse law, the Illinois supreme court voided Chicago's action in *Chicago v. Rumpff*, 45 Ill. 90 (1867). See Chicago v. Rumpff, case file 15325, Supreme Court of Illinois papers, Illinois State Archives.

define the public interest as their own. It was better, the Jacksonians
had argued, to have no public interest to define.

IN 1864 THE ILLINOIS supreme court announced that Chicago's
new public interest extended to the street-building arrangements at
the heart of the segmented system. The technical issue in *Chicago v.
Larned* was narrow: whether Chicago could limit special assessments
for paving to abutting lots, assessing each lot by its frontage on the
street being paved. The 1861 and 1863 charters had substituted this
administrative short-cut, which the city's special assessors had used
in practice for years and the council had adopted by ordinance in
1859, for the traditional direction to levy assessments "on the real
estate of the persons benefited, in proportion, as nearly as may be, to
the benefits resulting to each."[85] Rejecting the short-cut in order to
harmonize special assessment with the taxation clauses of the state
constitution, the court also questioned the logic of the segmented system. In practical terms, it directed the city to mix special assessment
with general property taxation when the cost of any improvement
exceeded the "special benefits" it conferred. While this in itself was a
blow to the system's privatization, the judges also went further:

> We cannot understand how it is, that a law which places the burden
> upon the property adjacent to the improvement is a more equitable
> apportionment than if imposed upon the entire property of the city,
> ward or district. Nor is it true that the grading, paving, etc., of a
> street in Chicago, or other large and growing city, is a mere local
> improvement, the expense of which adjacent property should wholly
> bear. It is a matter of public benefit, extending throughout the char-
> tered limits of the city. Are not the owners of property on . . . the
> most remote street in Chicago . . . benefited by [the improvement of
> downtown] streets?[86]

The *Larned* decision reversed the legal doctrine that had governed
special assessments in Illinois since the state court had defined them
in the 1851 *Canal Trustees* case, holding that they were "imposed for a
special purpose, and not for a general or public object." The court
now all but rejected the idea that benefit could be localized: "In these
improvements, the whole public is interested."[87]

85. *Chicago v. Larned*, 34 Ill. 267 (1864). For the quoted language in the 1837 and
1851 charters, James, *Charters*, 52, 161, 167. For the 1859 ordinance, CP, 1858/59:966-A.
For the short-cut, Illinois, *Laws, 1861*, 123, and *Private Laws, 1863*, 89.
86. *Chicago v. Larned*, 281.
87. Ibid., 282; *Canal Trustees v. Chicago*, 12 Ill. 403 (1851). The court cited *Canal Trustees* in defining special assessment as an exercise of the eminent domain power. In

The court did not reject special assessment completely, admitting that street projects conferred special as well as public benefits, but its stress on the public side was a crucial shift in emphasis. Legal historians have charted the nineteenth-century development of public interest doctrines in several branches of American law. What Harry N. Scheiber has called "the road to *Munn*," the idea that a private business could be "affected by a public interest" and thus subject to regulation, was also a road to *Larned*. Scheiber traces the road through the law of eminent domain and the devolution by states of the power to take property.[88] States delegated taking powers to private companies in order to promote such public interests as turnpikes, canals, railroads, gristmills, and, by the 1830s in Massachusetts, textile factories. By the 1870s, according to Scheiber, the redistribution of wealth through eminent domain law had expanded to the point where judges "merely paused to assert prescriptively that one private interest or another—mining, irrigation, lumbering or manufacturing—was so vitally necessary to the common weal as to be a public use by inference." By the 1880s, individuals with "public" interests also won immunity in nuisance cases.[89]

Like the longer road to *Munn*, the road to *Larned* involved transportation. The first case to assert a public interest in Chicago's streets was not a special assessment case, but a railroad case. In 1859, the Illinois supreme court rejected an argument that a railroad in the center of a street unjustly damaged the property of abutters, who defended their property right by citing a special assessment they had paid to improve the street for their own use. The judges mocked the abutters' claim, assuming without argument that the railroad served a greater public interest. "To say that a new mode of passage shall be banished from the streets, no matter how much the general good may

---

Larned, however, while assessments less than or equal to benefit were eminent domain and could be levied proportionally, those greater than benefit were taxes and had to be assessed uniformly on all property. For a critique of this reasoning, unique to the Illinois court, see John F. Dillon, *Treatise on the Law of Municipal Corporations* (Chicago: James Cockcroft & Co., 1872), 574–75.

88. Harry N. Scheiber, "The Road to *Munn:* Eminent Domain and the Concept of Public Purpose in the State Courts," *Perspectives in American History* 5 (1971): 329–402. Also Morton J. Horwitz, *The Transformation of American Law, 1780–1860* (Cambridge: Harvard University Press, 1977); Clyde E. Jacobs, *Law Writers and the Courts: The Influence of Thomas M. Cooley, Christopher G. Tiedeman, and John F. Dillon upon American Constitutional Law* (Berkeley: University of California Press, 1954), esp. 98–159.

89. Harry N. Scheiber, "Property Law, Expropriation, and Resource Allocation by the Government: The United States, 1789–1910," *Journal of Economic History* 33 (1973): 243.

require it, simply because streets were not so used in the days of Blackstone, would hardly comport with the advancement and enlightenment of the present age." Although irrelevant to the case at hand, the court extended its ruling to the new transit technology of horse railways, then being introduced in Chicago. On this issue, the judges contrasted the "convenience of those who live a greater distance from the center of the city" against the rights of abutters, who "must submit to the burthen when the Common Council determine that the public good requires it."[90]

Of course, as urban historians have shown, street railways generally were built less to serve the transit needs of people who lived far from downtown than to convince them to buy outlying and suburban lots in the first place. Transit facilities led rather than followed subdivision. Like the streets, horse railways were tools in a competitive real estate market. Thus, the actual contrast of rights in early street railway cases was not between commuters and property owners, but among the property owners who had invested in different parts of the city.[91] If the owners of outlying tracts could identify their interests with the "public good" of urban transit, they gained an advantage that the segmented system had been designed to prevent. This was the very issue that had structured the 1856 debate about the extension of Clybourn Avenue, in which the developers of far north side property had failed to extend the street through a neighborhood whose owners would not sacrifice their own interests for interests in other properties.[92] By the time of the *Larned* decision, however, the rules of the Clybourn debate no longer applied. The streets belonged to the "public."

When the council first authorized street railways in Chicago, aldermen tried to follow a segmented procedure. In 1855 and 1856 they allowed a company to operate horse cars on specified streets for twenty-five years on the condition that the company obtain permission from abutting property owners before laying track. The effort to cajole or purchase this permission proved too difficult, however, and the company forfeited its grant. In 1858, the council made a new

90. *Moses et al. v. Pittsburgh, Fort Wayne and Chicago Railroad Company*, 21 Ill. 515 (1859).

91. Sam Bass Warner, Jr., *Streetcar Suburbs: The Process of Growth in Boston, 1870–1900*, 2d ed. (Cambridge: Harvard University Press, 1978); Kenneth T. Jackson, *Crabgrass Frontier: The Suburbanization of the United States* (New York: Oxford University Press, 1985), 39–42; Jerome D. Fellman, "Pre-Building Growth Patterns of Chicago," *Annals of the Association of American Geographers* 47 (1957): 59–82; Ann Durkin Keating, *Building Chicago: Suburban Developers and the Creation of a Divided Metropolis* (Columbus: Ohio State University Press, 1988), 69.

92. See chap. 4 above.

grant. This time, it did not give abutters a veto power and as soon as the company began laying track, the abutters won an injunction that questioned the council's authority to let the company use the streets.[93] The company lost little time. In 1859, the legislature incorporated it as the Chicago City Railway Company, affirmed the council's grant, and allowed the company to lay track and operate horse cars on any streets on the city's south and west sides that the council permitted it to use. The law also chartered the North Chicago City Railway Company with the same powers for the north side, and a separate law of 1861 created the Chicago West Division Railway Company, which bought the west side franchise from the City Railway Company.[94]

Thus, a segmented approach was rejected from the start. It was impossible to build street railways if each abutting owner could determine for himself whether a railway on his street benefited him because the railways did not benefit most abutters by definition. They linked outlying property to downtown in order to benefit the outlying and downtown properties. When the North Chicago City Railway Company built a line to Clybourn in 1859, the far north side developers won part of what they lost in 1856. William B. Ogden, whose real estate firm had been assessed for 10 percent of the benefits on the Clybourn assessment, was one of the five incorporators of the North Chicago company; presumably, his property interests influenced his company's routing policies.[95] Chicago's street railway ordinances, however, like those of other cities, offered abutters a compensation. Because the companies held obvious interests in the condition of streets that they used, the ordinances required them to pay one-third of all paving costs on those streets, thus slashing the costs chargeable to abutters. Had the city been able to hold the companies to this, it might have preserved a measure of segmentation even given the nature of street railways.[96]

93. CP, 1855/56:362, 1859/60:222; Pierce, History, 2:324–25; Andreas, History, 2:119; Samuel Wilber Norton, Chicago Traction: A History Legislative and Political (Chicago: By author, 1907), 19.

94. These charters, the basis of litigation into the twentieth century, are explained in a large polemical and social science literature, e.g., Norton, Chicago Traction, 20–24; John A. Fairlie, "The Street Railway Question in Chicago," Quarterly Journal of Economics 21 (1907): 372–74; Harry P. Weber, comp., An Outline History of Chicago Traction (Chicago: Chicago Railways Company et al., 1936), 5–8. Note that the three companies did not compete; each held a territorial monopoly.

95. CP, 1855/56:2099; Weber, Outline History, 379.

96. The one-third share represented the physical proportion of street that the railways occupied. This issue deserves more research. For the standard view, Ernest S. Griffith and Charles R. Adrian, A History of American City Government: The Formation of

Abutters, meanwhile, tried to block construction altogether. One group, protesting the use of Clark Street by the City Railway Company, listed their abutting frontage, complained that "there were no petitions for the passage of said Ordinance," and demanded that aldermen revoke the ordinance until the company "secured the consent of the owners of two thirds of the property upon said street." A group fighting the North Chicago company used another tactic. The company had laid tracks 18.5 feet apart and nine feet off-center in one street but their ordinance required a 13.5 foot gap in the center. They had built the track this way after consultation with city officials and in order to preserve the recently planked street. Claiming to "represent 9/10 of the whole of the property owners" involved, the abutters opposed an ordinance to legalize the track as laid; the illegal track "gives us a remedy for consequential damages against said North Chicago railway company." Aldermen tried to balance the claims of the abutters and companies, but their interests were diametrically opposed. The issue on every street was railway or no railway, or, as yet another group of abutters put it, "who should legitimately have the benefit of the [streets]."[97]

Aldermen were caught in the middle. On one side, the city's property owners, organized on a segmented basis, had comprised the municipal "public" for more than a decade. The council could not ignore them when they described themselves as "the people" and the railways as "monopolists." On the other side, however, street railway companies provided a service to part of a group that aldermen dubbed "the travelling public" in 1860—those who used the streets.[98] This was the group the court noticed in *Larned* when it required the city to supplement special assessments with "equal and uniform taxation" of all property. The "public" still consisted of property owners; the court dropped only the location of property from its definition. The next step was inevitable. Once the railways were in operation, with franchises stipulating the council's right to regulate them, the council began to represent a new group of "interested par-

---

Traditions, 1775–1870 (New York: Praeger, 1976), 100: "Typically a franchise made some minor provisions for the obligations of the utility . . . but these were often vague, and frequently no attempt was made to enforce [them] in court." This was attempted in Chicago. The abutters lost. For an intermediate view, Eugene P. Moehring, *Public Works and the Patterns of Urban Real Estate Growth in Manhattan, 1835–1894* (New York: Arno Press, 1981), 113.

97. For the quotations, CP, 1859/60:796, 839, 1861/62:160. See also 1859/60:495, 1863/64:498, 512.

98. Ibid., 1859/60:839, 1861/62:160.

ties." When aldermen tried to influence fares and schedules, they represented streetcar riders—whether the riders owned real estate or not. Now even "non tax-payers" (or, more precisely, non–property tax-payers) had an "interest" in city policy because they paid fares for public transportation. The payment of streetcar fares, as one alderman explained, gave riders a "direct personal and pecuniary interest" in street railway policy.[99]

In this ambiguous situation, the companies held a strategic position. They played one public against the other, representing themselves as the servants of both. When they wanted to build a new line, the public consisted of riders who would benefit from expanded service. When they did not want to build a line, which happened often in the early 1860s, they championed the abutters, angering abutters who knew they were being manipulated in a game to which their interests were irrelevant. Each street railway ordinance vested one of the companies with the exclusive right to lay track and operate cars for twenty-five years in specified streets. If the company did not begin service on any street in a certain amount of time, usually five years, it would forfeit its right-of-way for that street. Encouraged by the prospect of twenty-five-year monopolies, the companies asked for and received grants much larger than they could use, especially in the chaotic financial environment of the Civil War years. They began to petition the council for time extensions almost immediately, citing abutters' resistance to railways as a reason to postpone their construction. Now the abutters demanded construction, hoping to force the companies to forfeit their grants.[100]

The volume of street railway ordinances mushroomed as the council repealed and modified the originals; the city attorney counted fifty pages of confusing and contradictory street railway ordinances in 1868.[101] Had aldermen been able to continue to amend them, this would have been unimportant. But in 1865, the companies engineered a coup that would continue to structure "the Chicago traction question" into the twentieth century: the legislature passed "An Act concerning Horse Railways in the City of Chicago," otherwise known as the Ninety-nine Year Act. This law froze the railway ordinances in their condition as of the date of its passage, February 6, 1865, and extended all contracts based on the ordinances from twenty-five to ninety-nine years, or to 1958. Not only was the council barred from

99. Ibid., 1867/68:425. See 1865/66:926, 1866/67:725, 753, 1868/69:1186, 1189, 1285, 1360.

100. Ibid., 1859/60:798, 1860/61:238, 1861/62:160. The abutters also won ordinances excluding streets from railway use; 1863/64:499–500, 667–68.

101. Ibid., 1867/68:1356.

amending the ordinances without the companies' consent, but any amendments it made would remain in force for the full ninety-nine years. The conditions under which legislators enacted this law—it was rushed through both houses before protest leaders could travel from Chicago to Springfield—suggested corruption on a major scale. Nevertheless, after the governor vetoed it (he later claimed to have been offered a $100,000 bribe for his signature), and despite huge protest meetings in Chicago, the legislature overrode the veto with equal speed, binding the city to a series of contracts whose particular language suddenly assumed immense importance.[102]

The Ninety-nine Year Act was an outrage. The legislature previously had passed three laws affecting Chicago without the council's consent: it forbade 999-year wharfing privileges in 1836, banned liquor licenses in 1852, and took the police away from Wentworth in 1861. It would top even the Ninety-nine Year Act in 1869, handing Chicago's lakefront and harbor to three railroad companies in the Lake Front Act, though it repealed this in 1873. The Ninety-nine Year Act remained in force until 1906, when the U.S. Supreme Court finally voided part of it. In the 1880s and 1890s, it made the spectacular financial and political frauds of traction baron Charles T. Yerkes possible.[103] Its impact in the 1860s, if more modest, was important. First, the rhetoric of segmentation, the demonstration of "interest" in policy, became obsolete in the face of the companies' new power. The definition of the "public" was clarified—everyone except the companies—but this too was irrelevant. Second, the abutters lost any chance to contest the use of the streets. Their leverage evaporated when the ordinances became unamendable contracts. Finally, armed with the contracts, the companies launched a final offensive against the segmented system.

Having vanquished the abutters on routing, the companies set out to evade the one-third share of paving assessments that was the abut-

102. Illinois, *Private Laws, 1865,* 597–98; Norton, *Chicago Traction,* 28–45; Fairlie, "Street Railway Question," 375–77; Henry Demarest Lloyd, *The Chicago Traction Question* (Chicago: George Waite Pickett, 1903), 10–20; R. E. Heilman, *Chicago Traction,* Publications of the American Economic Association, 3d ser., vol. 9, no. 2 (Princeton, N.J., 1908), 3–6.

103. The city considered the Lake Front Act invalid from the start. Despite its repeal, litigation continued to 1910. See CP, 1868/69:2138, 2163, 1869/70:144-I, 744; Lois Wille, *Forever Open, Clear and Free: The Historic Struggle for Chicago's Lakefront* (Chicago: Henry Regnery, 1972), 36–37. For Yerkes's accomplishments, see Ray Ginger, *Altgeld's America: The Lincoln Ideal Versus Changing Realities* (New York: Funk & Wagnalls, 1958), 106–10; Willard E. Hotchkiss, "Chicago Traction: A Study in Political Evolution," *Annals of the American Academy of Political and Social Science* 28 (1906): 385–404; Fairlie, "Street Railway Question," 393–95.

ters' single compensation in the railway ordinances. The *Larned* decision now assumed a significance opposite to that which its text suggested. The Illinois court, which had emphasized the public use of the streets in 1864, retreated from this position in 1866, when it would have required a subsidy for the monopolists responsible for the Ninety-nine Year Act. In *Chicago v. Baer*, the court cited the *Larned* ruling that assessments had to include all benefited property, but it now did not hesitate to name the beneficiaries:

> Can any thing be clearer than that, if one-third or one-quarter of all the benefits to be reaped by property holders from this improvement accrues to the railway company, and yet they are wholly exempted from the assessment, the other property holders are unequally and unjustly taxed to the extent of that portion which, in the ratio of benefits, should have been assessed against the railway? In other words, their property is taken for the benefit of the railway.[104]

An alternative view might have held that the railways' benefits were public benefits, and that the abutters therefore should pay only for their "special benefits" while general taxation financed the railways' share. This would have been a more logical application of the *Larned* decision. After the Ninety-nine Year Act, however, such claims by the companies were superfluous. They no longer bothered to identify themselves with the public interest.

The company, in the *Baer* case the North Chicago City Railway Company, rested its claim to exemption from paving assessments on its contract with the city, the content of which the litigants disputed. Evidence before the court revealed that over the crucial section of the company's franchise ordinance, which also was a contract between the city and the company, "is pasted a strip of paper, on which is written what purports to be a portion of the provisions of this section. The writing underneath this pasted paper is not obliterated, and, by being held against a strong light, can be read." While the original version required the company to pay one-third of paving assessments, the "writing on the pasted paper is so worded as to make the company liable for only ordinary repairs." The court refused to rule on whether the pasted paper was a forgery as the abutters contended. Because the council routinely amended ordinances by cutting and pasting—and had amended the railway ordinances many times—forgery was tough to prove, but also improbable. The court ignored

---

104. *Chicago v. Baer*, 41 Ill. 310 (1866). This was a special assessment case; the city was on the company's side because it was defending an assessment that exempted the company. The city's interest throughout the litigation was in valid assessments. For the city's brief on the abutters' side in an 1867 case, see CP, 1867/68:971.

this argument, decided the case on grounds of equality in taxation, and urged the city to adopt a system "that shall not leave in doubt what the ordinances really are under which their people live." The council adopted an engrossment procedure several months later.[105]

Loopholes in the railway ordinances multiplied as litigation continued and the pasted section was subjected to reinterpretation. Perhaps the most extreme claim, made by the companies in 1868, was that because their 1859 ordinances were passed before the Board of Public Works was created in 1861, and thus did not mention that agency, it had no authority to charge them even for the "ordinary repairs" specified in their version of the meaning of the pasted section.[106] In 1867, meanwhile, the companies offered a compromise. Aldermen had been trying to persuade them to increase the number of cars on crowded lines. They would run more cars, they suggested, if the council either allowed them to raise fares or "exempted [them] from taxation and assessment of every kind for the improvement or repair of [the] streets," in return for which they would pay 2 percent of their revenues into a fund for the maintenance of streets that they occupied. Thus aldermen could choose which public's interest to sacrifice for the railways—the riders' or the abutters'—and the choice would be binding for the full ninety-nine years. The city refused this offer.[107] The companies, however, had another plan.

After the Illinois court voided the assessment involved in the *Baer* case, the Board of Public Works made a new assessment for the same street, this time assessing the North Chicago company. Now a nonresident stockholder in that company sued in the federal courts and won an injunction blocking the assessment. The city appealed, reaching the U.S. Supreme Court in 1869. In *Chicago v. Sheldon*, this court found for the company, citing the sanctity of contract and defining the contract as the exemption interpretation of the pasted section. The Court determined the latter point by what the justices called the "practical construction" of the contract by its parties: in the first assessment (the one voided in *Baer*), the city had exempted the company and the company had agreed to its exemption. The abutters were irrelevant because they were not parties to a contract between the city and the North Chicago company, and *Baer* was irrelevant because these abutters were the litigants. Even if, as the city argued, the *Larned* decision declared the contract to be unconstitutional—the *Baer*

---

105. *Chicago v. Baer*, 308–9; CP, 1866/67:1045, 1867/68:971.
106. CP, 1867/68:1356. See also 1867/68:971, where the city argued that the pasted section actually permitted railway assessment.
107. Ibid., 1867/68:425.

ruling, which the Supreme Court rejected—the Illinois state court could not impair a contract that had been valid at the time it was made (supposedly this contract, including both the pasted section and its "practical construction," was dated 1859). As a final proof of the contract's validity, the justices made an oblique reference to the Ninety-nine Year Act: "We need only say that . . . the contract itself has been since ratified by [the state legislature]." [108]

The subject was closed and the street railways exempted from paving assessments. Unlike the packers, who had beaten segmented nuisance rules by exerting their power in a public debate in Chicago, the street railways evaded special assessment by applying outside pressure on Chicago. Where the packers had redefined the city's public interest, the railways flouted it. They might have followed the packers' route; the *Larned* case certainly laid a foundation for this strategy. In fact, Edwin C. Larned, the property owner who won public contributions to assessments, was part of the legal team defending railway exemption in *Baer*. But the Ninety-nine Year Act was such an outrageous grab that the companies no longer could win this way in Chicago politics or Illinois law. Whoever the public might have become at that ambiguous juncture, it would not be them. *Sheldon* was an amazing show of force. The city argued that the case concerned Chicago and an Illinois corporation, but the U.S. Supreme Court accepted jurisdiction. The city argued that *Baer* was binding in special assessment cases, but the Court ruled that this was a contract case. The elaborate arrangements through which the segmented system had arbitrated competing interests were not dismantled. They were ignored.

THE RECORD OF Chicago's government during the Civil War might be read as a series of stunning achievements, a vigorous mobilization of public power for public objectives. After more than a decade of segmented localism, Chicagoans used city government to help meet their recruiting quotas, clean a desperately polluted river, and build a transit system. Each of these accomplishments had progressive effects. The bounty and stipend programs provided for the welfare of impoverished families, the river project abated a nuisance from which the poor suffered the most because they lived next to it, and the transit system helped to relieve a housing shortage not

---

108. *Chicago v. Sheldon*, 9 Wall. 50 (1869). But see *Parmalee et al. v. Chicago*, 60 Ill. 267 (1871), in which the Illinois court charged a railway company in a "widening" assessment because the pasted section, now conceded to exempt the companies from paving, omitted that word.

FIG. 7 CHICAGO FROM THE LAKE, 1871

through the construction of tenement apartments, as some proposed, but by increasing the supply of accessible land on which workingmen could build, buy, or rent their own houses.[109] Chicagoans met some of the most pressing urban problems generated by rapid growth in a public manner and they did it by a nonpartisan consensus that overcame even the visceral party conflict of the war years. If the city retreated quickly from its involvement in relief, the locally based interests that opposed the river project and street railway construction were beaten irrevocably.

Chicagoans reshaped their government to strike a new balance between public and private, keeping privatism for the many along with new public interests for a few. Underlying this new balance, was a change in the city's social structure. Chicago historians generally agree that during the Civil War the city's booster elite began to be replaced by a new elite of Gilded Age millionaires who took less active roles in the community. Where the boosters had participated personally in charitable causes, the millionaires hired others to administer private welfare bureaucracies. Where the boosters had served in routine government posts, the millionaires influenced government

109. *Times*, April 10, 1863; Hoyt, *One Hundred Years*, 96–97.

indirectly.[110] Chicago's wartime economic boom lured many ambitious men, some of whom parlayed its opportunities into extraordinary fortunes. Frederick Cople Jaher has found not only that one-third of all Chicagoans whose incomes exceeded $10,000 in 1863 would be represented either personally or by family on an 1892 list of Chicago millionaires, but also that one-third of the 1892 millionaires had made the 1863 high-income list.[111] Two distinctions with political importance separated the millionaires (or future millionaires) from the boosters: the millionaires rarely competed with one another and municipal government was much less important to them than it had been to the boosters.

Most of the boosters had engaged in a similar combination of economic ventures. They shipped commodities, operated banks, invested in railroads, sold insurance, pursued legal careers, and sometimes even built factories, but they made their fortunes by speculating in real estate. Attracted to Chicago initially by the land boom of the 1830s, they continued to invest in its property. Throughout the 1850s, real estate development remained a major source of wealth in Chicago. This was why the boosters simultaneously joined in so many activities that promoted the city's growth. They depended on that growth to raise the value of their properties. It also was the reason they created the segmented system. Successful real estate development required the physical improvements city government provided: streets, bridges, sidewalks, and sewers. Because no single booster or small group of boosters dominated the real estate market, all needed access to infrastructure to compete. The booster system, which had distributed public works politically, had led to paralysis as each competitor resisted subsidizing the speculations of his rivals. In the segmented system, all could receive the projects they wanted because each paid for his own projects.

The millionaires were different. First, they were not competitors. Engaged in specialized industries or commercial pursuits, they became millionaires either by creating new fields or by eliminating the competition to dominate older ones. Thus George Pullman dominated in sleeping cars, Cyrus McCormick in agricultural machinery, Marshall Field in retailing, Philip Armour and Gustavus Swift in

---

110. Rima Lunin Schultz, "The Businessman's Role in Western Settlement: The Entrepreneurial Frontier, Chicago, 1833–1872" (Ph.D. diss., Boston University, 1984); Kathleen D. McCarthy, *Noblesse Oblige: Charity and Cultural Philanthropy in Chicago, 1849–1929* (Chicago: University of Chicago Press, 1982); Frederick Cople Jaher, *The Urban Establishment: Upper Strata in Boston, New York, Charleston, Chicago, and Los Angeles* (Urbana: University of Illinois Press, 1982), 453–575.

111. Jaher, *Urban Establishment*, 494–97.

meat, and the railroad-warehouse oligopoly in grain. Second, except for men like Potter Palmer, who specialized in real estate, the million-aires bought property more as a manifestation than a source of wealth. They acquired real estate for the same reason they deposited their money in banks or bought stocks and bonds. They may have wanted public works on occasion, but their businesses did not de-pend on the regular provision of physical infrastructure. The day-to-day operation of municipal government mattered only inasmuch as the millionaires shared an interest in keeping their tax assessments low, which they achieved on a scandalous scale.[112] In fact, these busi-nessmen did not depend on Chicago at all. As the packers reversed the booster logic in the pollution debate, so could the new elite as a group. Chicago's economy depended on them.

The members of this new elite could think about government as an annoyance, something that taxed and in some instances even threat-ened to regulate them. In the segmented system, the older elite had devised a set of rules that fostered active government policy. They had tied decision-making power to financial responsibility in order to ensure that they could get what they were willing to pay for. Aggres-sive real estate promoters did not have to worry about tax resistance from those who owned only single houselots. Unless they lived next door, such owners would raise no opposition to public works because they would not be asked to pay for them. If they did live next door, they either had to pay or to move to a place where their neighbors agreed on improvement priorities. The new elite, however, were them-selves the tax resisters. As the owners of large tracts of property throughout the city, they were liable both to heavy property tax bills and large special assessment charges. They wanted these charges reduced and exploited the legal weakness of special assessment to reduce them. This was the significance of the *Larned* case: a public interest in the streets spread the costs of their improvement.

Charter amendments in the 1860s also undermined local control in the assessment process. Where the 1861 charter had barred the Board of Public Works from levying assessments without petitions from the owners of three-fourths of the affected property, the 1863 law dropped this rule, letting the board determine whether a project was "necessary and proper." In 1865, it gained even greater autonomy; it could finance street projects from revenue on hand and assess

112. C. K. Yearley, *The Money Machines: The Breakdown and Reform of Governmental and Party Finance in the North, 1860–1920* (Albany: State University of New York Press, 1970); Robert Murray Haig, *A History of the General Property Tax in Illinois* (Urbana: University of Illinois, 1914).

for them later, when property owners no longer could argue about whether they wanted them.[113] The Board of Public Works made some of its decisions based on the public interest in street improvements. Since the powerful had advantages in defining this interest, they still could get projects they wanted as long as their opponents were weak. Since these now publicly determined improvements were financed by special assessment, however, the result was a forced subsidy not by the whole city—as in the packers' case—but by those who were assessed for each individual project. This was the street railway scenario on a citywide scale. Like the railways, moreover, wealthy property owners also extended their victory from decision making to finance. They too evaded special assessment in the courts.

A burst of litigation after *Sheldon* convinced some Chicagoans that the city should scrap the special assessment system altogether. Where the city attorney had reported some $100,000 in assessments pending before the courts in 1860, only a small fraction of it before the state supreme court, Mayor Joseph Medill found in 1871 that almost $1 million was pending, over half of it "either by injunction or on appeal to the supreme court, principally to the latter."[114] In a series of 1870 decisions, the Illinois supreme court subjected all assessments to litigation, opened all aspects of the assessment process to judicial inquiry, granted remonstrants jury trials on disputed points, held that a defect in the assessment of any particular lot would invalidate an entire assessment roll, and barred reassessment when courts voided original assessments. After making the process this uncertain, it then suggested that contractors could sue the city for their claims under voided assessments even though both the charter and their contracts included explicit statements to the contrary. "The court," Medill explained, "has so construed the law that there seems to be no possible way of making a special assessment . . . that may not be disputed by any interested party who resists payment."[115]

While Medill saw general taxes as the only alternative, some aldermen demanded the restoration of segmented decision making by the petition rule. They based this demand on a class argument the boost-

---

113. Illinois, *Private Laws, 1863*, 83 and *Private Laws, 1865*, 276. The 1867 charter added a provision that after a street had been paved once, the general fund would finance repavings; Illinois, *Private Laws, 1867*, 762.

114. CP, 1860/61:200, 1872/73:128.

115. Ibid., 1872/73:128; *Creote v. Chicago*, 56 Ill. 422 (1870); *Rue v. Chicago*, 57 Ill. 435 (1870); *Rich v. Chicago*, 59 Ill. 286 (1871). *Beygeh v. Chicago*, 65 Ill. 189 (1872), the contractor case, was reversed before publication. See Beygeh v. Chicago, case file 17490, Supreme Court papers.

ers would have recognized. "Improvements to be paid for by special assessments," they argued,

> frequently greatly embarrass poor people. It is not a sufficient reply to urge that such improvements are a good investment. Are the people prepared to make the investment? Will they be compelled to mortgage at great sacrifice and perhaps lose their premises? Marble fronts are good investments, but we cannot all afford to build them. Who is to judge of the ability of persons, living on the line of a contemplated improvement to pay? We reply the people themselves.[116]

These aldermen did not suggest that the city subsidize public works for those who could not afford to build them (and their "poor people" consisted only of property owners). They did not even hint at a downwardly redistributive alternative to special assessment. Rather, their class-based argument was a Jacksonian antimonopoly call for the localism that historians generally have considered a weakness of late nineteenth-century American city government. It is an illustration of Teaford's "unheralded triumph" view that in 1870 the council rejected this version of localism out of hand.[117]

The segmented system was gone. In its place, was a system that used government to redistribute wealth in accordance with public policy decisions made through power politics and interest–group competition. In demanding this nationally in 1863, Chicagoans preached what they were beginning to practice at home. Despite the legal crisis of 1870, Chicagoans salvaged the special assessment process and used it until the 1930s. They used it, however, as a revenue expedient rather than a policy instrument. The scrupulous concern that city government had shown for the interests of individual property owners disappeared. So too did the materialistic rhetoric of personal interest. Now Chicagoans debated policy in a more lofty vocabulary of the public interest. Although the ability to define this interest was limited to a narrow portion of Chicago's elite in the 1860s—and, to some extent, for the rest of the nineteenth century—this elite, the Gilded Age millionaires, had established the existence of a public interest that could be redefined as the distribution of political power changed in the twentieth century.[118] Some redefinitions would retain

116. CP, 1870/71:479–80.

117. Jon C. Teaford, *The Unheralded Triumph: City Government in America, 1870–1900* (Baltimore: Johns Hopkins University Press, 1984).

118. See Maureen A. Flanagan, *Charter Reform in Chicago* (Carbondale: Southern Illinois University Press, 1987), for the role of the Chicago Federation of Labor in articulating a popular vision of the purposes of municipal government in the Progressive Era.

the upwardly redistributive character of the new public interests of the 1860s. Others, however, would abandon the Jacksonians' pessimism and marshall the resources of government to serve a more democratically defined public. These redefinitions would attempt to scrap "privatism" for everyone.

Special assessment had been one of two characteristic policy-making tools of the segmented system. The other, the fire limit, now also assumed a new meaning that dropped local control as an objective. With much of the city in ashes after the Great Fire, Chicagoans debated new fire limit boundaries in an open and angry rhetoric of class conflict. They defined at that point what would remain the municipal "public" of the late nineteenth century.

Epilogue
The Great Fire and the New Public

AFTER MRS. O'LEARY'S cow kicked over the lantern on Sunday night, October 8, 1871, the Great Chicago Fire burned out of control for twenty-seven hours. By the time a rainstorm finally put it out, it had killed 300 people, left 100,000 of the city's 300,000 residents homeless, and levelled 18,000 buildings on four square miles. It spared most of the city's west side, but burned almost every building in the south side business district and on the north side, including commercial, industrial, and residential areas.[1] Such devastation presented an emergency more pressing than any that had inspired Chicago's new public interests in the 1860s, and in coping with it, Chicagoans revealed how much they had altered their uses of municipal government and politics. No longer a mechanism for serving "interested parties," government was an arena for class conflict. No longer a choice of agents for public works investment, politics was an ongoing battle between "bummers"—machine politicians—and "reformers." Both of these new groups defended aspects of the lost segmentation, the bummers its decentralization and the reformers its dedication to property interests. Yet both actually were products of the new public interest. While the bummers exploited the political incentives of redistributive policy making, the reformers demanded a vigorous pursuit of public interests that they claimed the right to define. Unlike the architects of the segmented system, the reformers of the 1870s refused to see that a government that was public, was inevitably political.

1. For a complete narrative, Robert Cromie, *The Great Chicago Fire* (New York: McGraw-Hill, 1958).

ROSWELL B. MASON, formerly the chief engineer of the Illinois Central Railroad, a street railway promoter, and a Board of Public Works member appointed for the canal-deepening project, was mayor of Chicago when the city burned. The city's first "reform" mayor, Mason had been elected in 1869 on a Citizens Reform ticket pledged to check the depredations of a corrupt council "ring." Although it is difficult to know how corrupt Chicago aldermen were, the particular charges made against them are instructive. They were accused of accepting bribes from the Chicago Gas Light and Coke Company, soliciting them from those attempting to sell park land to the city, auctioning jobs and the municipal printing contract, and selling their votes for local improvement projects.[2] Except for the printing, whose importance to a partisan press always had subjected it to chicanery, none of these frauds had been possible in the 1850s. Special taxes had restrained the gas company, special assessments had encouraged "interested" owners to monitor park costs, and the privatization of other services had minimized official power over jobs. Most important, the special assessment decision rules, with their myriad of legal checks, had prevented any hint of fraud in the public works process.

Citizens Reform, moreover, was a new kind of nonpartisanship. Where the reformers of 1848 had banished the Locofocos by banishing party altogether, Citizens Reformers created a temporary reform party to oppose the now dominant Republicans. Nonpartisan elections in the 1850s had been unorganized—no endorsements, no tickets, candidates "on their own hooks," and a formal agreement by party leaders, including a reluctant John Wentworth, to stay out of city elections. Citizens Reformers, however, nominated a bipartisan slate endorsed by most of Chicago's newspapers. Even the *Workingman's Advocate*, organ of the Trade and Labor Assembly, endorsed Mason, only to recoil from his brand of reform after the Fire. Indeed, the five-year-old assembly had grievances against aldermen and the Republican party that were unrelated to their corruption. In 1866, when the assembly demanded the eight-hour day for city workers, ostensibly supportive Republican aldermen passed a resolution asking the Board of Public Works to employ on an eight-hour basis "so far as practicable." The board found this impracticable and ignored it. In 1867, when the Republican legislature passed a statewide eight-hour-day law, the result was similarly futile. After Chicago manufac-

2. A. T. Andreas, *History of Chicago* (3 vols.; Chicago: Andreas, 1884–86), 2:51; Bessie Louise Pierce, *A History of Chicago* (3 vols.; Chicago: University of Chicago Press, 1937–57), 2:297–99.

turers refused to obey the law, the assembly called a general strike that failed, in part, because the city police supported the employers.[3]

Neither Mason nor the aldermen elected with him succeeded in purifying the council. Only the disaster of the Fire allowed them to act on their views of reform. While the city's north side was still burning—the south side downtown, including the city hall, already had been destroyed—several aldermen met in a west side church to re-establish municipal authority and begin the work of relief. They declared the church a temporary city hall, summoned Mason to issue a proclamation pledging the city's credit to relief, opened churches and schools to the homeless, deputized special policemen to guard against looting and arson, and met the relief delegations of other cities as they arrived at surviving rail depots with money, food, clothing, and other supplies. The aldermen constructed temporary houses, distributed water—the waterworks had burned—by commandeering "every vehicle which would not volunteer to aid in the noble work," arranged free rail passes so that Fire victims could leave Chicago, and tried to safeguard the relief fund by placing it in the care of the city treasurer so as to "meet the approval of the Country at large whose moneys were then enroute here for our succor."[4]

This municipal activity lasted for three days. On Thursday, October 12, Mayor Mason delegated the entire relief effort—and turned over the $5 million relief fund—to the Chicago Relief and Aid Society (CRAS). A voluntary association, the CRAS had been established on a permanent and professionalized basis in 1867, modelled on the New York Association for the Improvement of the Condition of the Poor. By the time of the Fire, the CRAS had a salaried director, paid visitors who distinguished worthy from unworthy paupers, and a board of directors composed of Gilded Age millionaires including Marshall Field and George Pullman. Unlike the "benevolent" boosters who had staffed the society's earlier, temporary incarnations, the reorganized CRAS eschewed personal charity in favor of professional humanitarianism. It distributed food, coal, and clothing and coordinated temporary lodging arrangements but, as Kathleen McCarthy has shown, it soon subordinated individual relief measures to a program of endowment grants to charitable institutions. Over the next decade, the CRAS used the huge fund that it accumulated from outside con-

3. Pierce, *History*, 2:297; Chicago City Council Proceedings Files [hereafter CP], 1865/66:968, 993, 1018, 1315, 1866/67:254, 840; Richard Schneirov and John B. Jentz, "The 1867 Strike and the Origins of the Chicago Labor Movement," Working Paper, Origins of Chicago's Industrial Working Class Project, Newberry Library.

4. CP, 1870/71:1239; Andreas, *History*, 2:761–73.

tributions to Chicago's relief as a lever with which to mold and discipline the city's benevolent establishment.[5]

Mason's decision to place the relief fund in private rather than public hands reflected his view—the view of Chicago's elite as a whole—that a corrupt council could not be trusted with the money. His efforts to maintain public order revealed a similar mistrust, in this case of the Board of Police Commissioners. He declared martial law and vested full police authority in General Philip Sheridan, who was headquartered at Chicago. Sheridan sent to Washington for regulars, mustered 1,100 volunteers—most of them college students—into a regiment, and relieved the militia units sent by Governor John M. Palmer. The governor criticized Mason's illegal appeal to federal authority and asked him to relieve Sheridan. Only after one of the general's volunteers accidentally killed an attorney, however, did the mayor recommend that Sheridan disband his force. Nevertheless, four days after the regulars left, business leaders including the CRAS president, Board of Trade secretary, *Tribune* editor Joseph Medill, and three bank presidents asked Sheridan to recall them—and the general complied over the governor's protest. Palmer then appealed to President Grant in an exchange that foreshadowed the later Pullman Strike correspondence between Governor Altgeld and President Cleveland.[6]

The police board also protested against the use of federal troops. Commissioner T. B. Brown later testified that he and Commissioner Mark Sheridan had tried both to prevent Mason from calling the troops and, once they arrived, to limit their use to the burnt district, an interference that General Philip Sheridan rejected. With a municipal force of 450 policemen, 200 specials, 500 deputized private watchmen, 220 firemen (also deputized), and 1,000 specials hired since the Fire, Brown thought the police board—especially when bolstered by state militia—possessed adequate resources to maintain order. The problem, of course, was not the size of the force but its control. After the 1867 strike, Chicago's labor movement had concentrated its political efforts on a sympathetic police board and won its first victory in the 1870 election of Mark Sheridan, a Democratic alderman from Bridgeport who had been an Irish revolutionary before he fled to

5. Kathleen D. McCarthy, *Noblesse Oblige: Charity and Cultural Philanthropy in Chicago, 1849–1929* (Chicago: University of Chicago Press, 1982), 64–72. Also Karen Sawislak, "Smoldering City: Class, Ethnicity, and Politics in Chicago at the Time of the Great Fire" (Ph.D. diss., Yale University, 1990), chap. 3.

6. Andreas, *History*, 2:773–80; Illinois, House, Select Committee on Governor J. M. Palmer's Messages of Nov. 15 and Dec. 9, 1871, *Report* (Springfield: Illinois State Journal, 1872).

America in 1848.[7] The CRAS's role in redeploying the troops was not lost on either its supporters or its critics. Neither was Mason's coupling of the martial law order with an order mandating early saloon closing not just in the burnt district, but throughout the city. Rather than direct responses to the Fire's destruction, these actions represented—and were intended to represent—a show of force by Chicago's elite.

Opponents of the relief privatization had no political voice at all. Even C. C. P. Holden, a "bummer" Republican alderman who ran for mayor in November 1871 and wrote a narrative of his relief activities as a campaign document—with testimonials from the visiting committees to the safety of their donations in his hands—failed to criticize this move.[8] Opponents of the army deployment included state officials at the highest level, but they were thwarted by President Grant himself. On another measure dear to the city's elite, however, opposition was not only loud, but for a time even successful. This measure was a citywide extension of the fire limit in order to guarantee that Chicagoans rebuilt a "fireproof" city. For the November 7 election, one month after the Fire, "reputable" Republicans and Democrats nominated a Fireproof Reform ticket led by Medill for mayor. Their opponents, according to Medill's *Tribune*, comprised only "irresponsible soreheads." The Fireproof ticket swept the election. Although turnout in burned wards fell to about half that of the off-year election of 1870, Medill would have beaten Holden even if all of the "missing" voters had voted against him.[9] With much of the city still in ashes, Chicagoans voted overwhelmingly for "reform."

In his inaugural, Medill deplored "the alarming deterioration of integrity of municipal administration," urging a 20 percent pay cut for city workers, the immediate discharge of "hundreds of persons" (unspecified), and a "searching investigation . . . for the purpose of ascertaining where it is possible to retrench expenses." His only examples of municipal "vice and dishonesty," however, were from New York, whose Tweed Ring had just been toppled. Medill also, as the last chapter noted, analyzed the 1870 special assessment crisis, con-

7. Committee on Palmer's Message, *Report*, 19–22; M. L. Ahern, *The Great Revolution: A History of the Rise and Progress of the People's Party in the City of Chicago and County of Cook* (Chicago: Lakeside Publishing & Printing, 1874), 139–41.

8. CP, 1870/71:1239.

9. Medill won 16,125 votes to Holden's 5,988. Turnout fell in eight burnt wards—all five north side and three of the six south side wards—by 7,738. Had Holden captured all of these votes, his total would have been 13,726, still well below Medill's. For election returns, see appendix 1.

cluding that the city could build no public works except "by *general* taxation." His most important reform, however, was the fire limit. He was "unalterably opposed from this time forward to the erection of a single wooden building within the limits of Chicago." The Fire had shown the interdependence of the city's neighborhoods. After starting in a working-class district far from downtown, where the O'Learys and their neighbors owned frame cottages crowded two and three to a lot, the fire was "propelled by an autumn gale in time of drought" into the business district, where one of its many victims was the recently completed *Tribune* building, itself a model of fire-proof design. A citywide fire limit, Medill insisted, was the only democratic policy; the construction of "incendiary" buildings was a "special privilege" that was "odious in a Republican country." [10]

To others, however, this "special privilege" meant access to home-ownership by workingmen. The fire limit, as Chicagoans had argued since the 1840s, determined the market in frame buildings. The cheapness of wood put houses within reach of those who could not afford to build or buy the brick or stone buildings required in limited areas. Chicagoans disputed the actual cost difference between wood and brick construction. Estimates varied from a 10 to 20 percent figure—offset by lower heating costs—calculated by Medill's allies, to an insistence that the citywide limit would "compel [workingmen] to sell our land, to greedy land speculators, at ruinous prices." [11] In analyzing this debate, Christine Rosen has concluded not only that brick cost more than twice as much as wood, but that the Fireproof reformers "had no understanding of how costly their improvement would be in human terms." The lack of understanding increased when a march on city hall led by the north side German Republican Anton Hesing—a "bummer" later jailed in the Whiskey Ring scandal— elevated the citywide fire limit, for its advocates, into "the only way of vindicating the authority and dignity of the city government against the assaults of mob violence." [12] Thus, the fire limit became a class issue.

The marchers combined several aspects of workers' discontent with post-Fire reform. Their banners not only asked aldermen to "Leave a Home for the Laborer," but also deplored "The Relief, Temperance, and Fire Limits Swindle." It is not obvious that the fire limit would have become a class issue in 1871 and 1872. Several of Chica-

10. CP, 1872/73:128 (emphasis in original).

11. Ibid., 1872/73:151-B (files 2–3).

12. Christine Meisner Rosen, *The Limits of Power: Great Fires and the Process of City Growth in America* (Cambridge: Cambridge University Press, 1986), 100; CP, 1872/73:181-B (file 3).

go's leading real estate men—boosters who now qualified as old residents—endorsed Hesing's call for a small extension with a traditional argument: the citywide limit "would be equivalent in many cases to a total prohibition against building." Medill's allies found it "eminently unjust, to draw an imaginary line . . . and permit the inhabitants on one side of a street, to build of wood, & compel those on the other side to build of brick."[13] Since the creation of Chicago's fire limit in 1845, however, this "imaginary line" had been its essential feature. Manufacturers, lumber dealers, and other businessmen unable to comply with it, always had opposed its extension to their properties. Speculators who leased out their unimproved landholdings also had opposed it consistently. Its only sure supporters had been the owners of commercial buildings. Now, however, the fire limit had a broader constituency. Now, in Rosen's words, "most middle and upper class people saw [it] as an essential environmental reform."[14]

There are several plausible explanations for this, none of which can be tested with currently available evidence. First, middle-class homeowners probably had shifted to brick and stone construction methods before the Fire. Second, lumber dealers and manufacturers may have thought they could evade a citywide limit by gaining personal exemptions from the Board of Public Works, the police board, or whatever agency ultimately assumed what had been an administratively mobile task in the 1860s. Third, and least likely, Chicago's physical development to 1871 may have reduced the economic importance of speculation in unimproved property. Fourth, and supported by later events, the preference for brick among middle-class homeowners may have reflected the pressure of insurers whose huge losses made them keenly interested in the outcome of this debate. Finally, the debate's class basis may have been something of a sham. "Bummers" could have organized constituencies of workers on the real issue of homeownership, but for the purpose of bolstering one side in a struggle between factions of Chicago's elite. All of these explanations, however, share an assumption: that it is the conversion of the elite, or part of it, to the citywide limit that needs to be explained.

In light of the ease with which reformers privatized relief and maintained martial law, and of the elitist nature of the new public

13. For the quotations, CP, 1872/73:181-B (file 1). For the march, Rosen, *Limits of Power*, 100–103; Richard Schneirov, "Class Conflict, Municipal Politics, and Governmental Reform in Gilded Age Chicago, 1871–1875" in *German Workers in Industrial Chicago, 1850–1910: A Comparative Perspective*, Hartmut Keil and John B. Jentz, eds. (DeKalb: Northern Illinois University Press, 1983), 188.

14. Rosen, *Limits of Power*, 97–98.

interests adopted in the 1860s, this assumption seems reasonable. It is difficult to conclude that Chicago's workers exerted very much power by 1871. Richard Schneirov, who has examined this issue closely, finds that only by the late 1870s had workers built institutions through which they could even "exert a presence in the rest of society."[15] The fire limit fight was an important moment in the creation of this presence; some elite Chicagoans thought (or, more accurately, feared) that the fire limit march was a "communist" uprising. Statistical evidence does suggest that workers had a stake not only in the fire limit but in segmented policy making in general. Federal census data show a rising rate of property holding by workers in the 1850s, but a slight drop in the 1860s as segmentation was dismantled.[16] By extending the fire limit over the whole city, reformers wanted to change it from a segmented zoning device into a citywide building code. The opponents of this code defended a decentralized system of land-use regulation that allowed workingmen to own cheap houses—as the special assessment system, which Medill was quite willing to scrap, allowed them to avoid public works costs.

Although the ownership rate had dropped over the past decade, Chicago's population of property owners still embraced one-fifth of the city's adult men in 1870, including 20 percent of the skilled and 17 percent of the unskilled workers in the city. The wealthiest 10 percent of the property owners owned an estimated 66 percent of the real estate value, a figure substantially lower than the 74 percent of 1860 or the 82 percent of 1850. Some outlying wards had extremely high rates of working-class ownership in 1870. At the northern and southern corners of the west side, about three-fourths of the property owners were workingmen (compared with 61 percent of the owners citywide), and these working-class owners lived in wards with median values far below the citywide median of $2,500. Untouched by the Fire, these owners could have been hurt seriously by a fire limit that banned wood construction.

The working-class property owners with the most to lose from a citywide limit, however, were the north siders who already had lost their houses and workshops to the Fire. The destruction of the heavily German north side meant that the Fire hit German-born prop-

15. Richard Schneirov, "Haymarket and the New Political History Reconsidered: Workers' Class Presence in Chicago's Municipal Politics, 1873–1894," *Journal of American History* (forthcoming). This essay is more skeptical about working-class power in the 1870s than Schneirov's earlier "Class Conflict, Municipal Politics, and Governmental Reform."

16. For more detail on this data and that reported in the next two paragraphs, see appendix 2 below.

erty owners especially hard: 44 percent of Chicago's German property owners lived in wards destroyed by the Fire, compared with only 25 percent of the native-born and 21 percent of the Irish and other immigrant owners. In Chicago's most heavily German wards, the far north side Sixteenth and Seventeenth, 75 percent of the property owners were German (64 percent of the adult men in these wards were German). The Sixteenth Ward also had one of the highest property ownership rates (42 percent) and lowest median property values ($1,500) in the city. For these property owners, as the city hall marchers made clear, a citywide fire limit would have been devastating. It would have prevented them from rebuilding their houses.

Segmentation itself had become a class issue in Chicago, and the one post-Fire issue on which the city's workers seem to have won. The city hall marchers achieved their objective, a small extension of the fire limit to cover only the downtown commercial district and the residential neighborhoods of the very rich. For two weeks of what one alderman described as "a long, laborious and exciting struggle," Chicago's property owners did what they had been doing for twenty-five years: they petitioned and remonstrated about their particular blocks until the council drew a line that seemed to place most prolimit proprietors inside and most antilimit proprietors outside the fire limit.[17] Citywide reform had failed. The danger that outlying "tinderboxes" could ignite downtown "fireproof" buildings remained, enhanced by the fact that the fire limit ordinance did not pass until February 1872, by which time even blocks within its boundaries had been rebuilt with wood. No fire limit ever had mandated the demolition of existing structures. The 1872 limit, however, was the first that should have. It was the first fire limit in Chicago's history that was enacted for the purpose of preventing fires.

IN JULY 1874, a second runaway fire reversed this working-class victory (if that is what it was) and prompted the city's elite reformers to organize as the Citizens Association of Chicago, the oldest permanent municipal reform organization in the United States and a model for "structural reformers" across the country.[18] Through a police reorganization and a hopeless revival of the temperance issue, Medill's administration had alienated enough Chicagoans by 1873 to enable the "bummers" to sweep back into office as the People's party. This victory, following loud and direct appeals to workers' economic

17. For the quotation, CP, 1872/73:364.
18. Schneirov, "Class Conflict," 192–95; Sidney I. Roberts, "Ousting the Bummers, 1874–1876," typescript, Chicago Historical Society, 1956, 2–5.

grievances, convinced Chicago's elite that radical reform had become necessary. Unless they could empower "the best part of the community" over "the baser elements of the people," a fireproof city was impossible. "How," they asked, "can you be sure of finding a set of men severely anxious about the protection of property who themselves have no property to protect?" When they dismissed universal suffrage in municipal government as an "immoderate fancy," the Citizens Association assumed that its enemies, the bummers, represented only the propertyless.[19] The reformers refused to accept the fact that many of Chicago's workers both owned property and wanted their city government to protect it—not from fire, but from the new public interest in "structural" municipal reform.

It is not clear that Chicago's workers would have questioned the Citizens Association's view that municipal government was "largely a mere management of property."[20] Still clinging to the defensive Jacksonian mistrust of "monopolists"—a mistrust easily justified in the age of George Pullman, Cyrus McCormick, and Marshall Field— most workers seem to have championed limited government and what remained of segmentation.[21] But the structural reformers did not explore this possibility. They had begun to forge a new ideal of municipal government that differed from the older ideal of segmentation, a new strategy for achieving the objective of a municipal "corporation" responsive to the demands of its "stockholders." They now demanded a government that was centralized and apolitical at the same time. They wanted to elevate the bias with which Chicago had adopted new public interests in the 1860s into a system of government for the future. Thus, they demanded active public policies but declared their own interests to be above politics and exempt from debate. They considered themselves to be the only legitimate municipal "public." Although they won the citywide fire limit in 1874— aided by a national insurance embargo—the reformers could not continue indefinitely to have it both ways. If municipal government was to be a public institution that redistributed wealth, the majority

19. "Address by President Franklin MacVeagh, September 11, 1874," *Address and Reports of the Citizens Association of Chicago, 1874–1876* (Chicago: Hazlitt & Reed, 1876), 4–5. For People's party appeals, see Ahern, *Great Revolution*, 83–99.

20. "Address by President Franklin MacVeagh," 4.

21. It is difficult to know the political ideas of "most workers," of course, but see esp. David Montgomery, *Beyond Equality: Labor and the Radical Republicans, 1862–1872* (Urbana: University of Illinois Press, 1967), 334, 432, and passim. On the analytical problem, Richard Oestreicher, "Urban Working-Class Political Behavior and Theories of American Electoral Politics, 1870–1940," *Journal of American History* 74 (1988): 1257–86.

eventually would demand a voice in determining the direction of redistribution. Eventually, a "social reform" critique of privatism itself would transform public works and other city services into public goods. Eventually, paved streets would become rights that city governments owed all urban residents.

These developments would not occur for several decades, of course, decades that in Chicago would witness extraordinarily violent class conflict: Haymarket, the Pullman Strike, and numerous other bloody clashes. The "bummers" would expand their activities into the machinery of exploitation and fraud associated with "Bathhouse John" Coughlin, Michael "Hinky Dink" Kenna, and the other "Gray Wolves" of the late nineteenth-century council. As long as Chicago's elite was the only group capable of organizing to assert its political interests, this elite would remain the only dynamic force in the continual shaping and reshaping of municipal government. Some workers would adapt and find advantages in any system that the elite designed. Thus, in the segmented system, they "opted out" of public works costs in order to own their own houses, though only at a price that in hindsight looks painfully high: the basic physical infrastructure that made urban life safe and healthy. Some workers also would derive benefits from machine politics—the turkeys at Christmas, help in the police court for children in trouble, and, of course, lax enforcement of the liquor laws. But these too fetched a price: land-use regulations that favored the wealthy, systematic exploitation by utility companies, and a debasement of electoral politics that blocked democratic redefinitions of both the public and the policies that would serve its interests.

The transition from segmented government to the new public interest in Chicago was the transition from Jacksonian to Gilded Age politics in the United States. The Jacksonian "personal interest" rhetoric was replaced by a pluralist rhetoric more familiar to modern ears. Where the Jacksonians avoided the conflict of competing interest groups, Gilded Age politics was (and our politics is) defined by such conflict. Where the Jacksonians "solved" problems of banking, internal improvements, and especially slavery by refusing to debate them except in geographically segmented forums limited to "interested parties," Gilded Age politics consisted in broad, national debates about the public interest. As the interests of businessmen with foreign investments became public, the United States protected "American interests" with imperialism. As the interests of railroads and major shippers became public, the government helped to "rationalize" transportation. It took much longer for the interests of child laborers and tenement workers to become public interests in "social justice," and the adoption of a public interest in racial justice has been excruciatingly slow and incomplete, but these developments also would take the form of pluralist redefinitions of the public interest. Pluralism—the competition of interest groups to define public interests—had few democratic outcomes in Gilded Age America. It was, and often still is, the means by which elites gained upward redistributions of wealth from government. But the idea that something called the public interest did in fact exist, was a precondition for democratic policies that would have been inconceivable to the Jacksonians.

The Jacksonian rejection of pluralism was double-edged. The refusal to recognize the existence of broad, national public interests built a barrier against the appropriation of government power by commercial and industrial elites—a barrier that collapsed dramatically after the Civil War—but it also, and probably more fundamentally, erected a barrier protecting slavery. To decide which barrier was fundamental and which incidental is to analyze the power structure within which the national rules were adopted. In one northern city, the rules were adopted to serve elite land speculators by making government a neutral force in a competitive real estate market. The Jacksonians believed that "a house divided against itself" could stand. Actually, they believed that *only* such a house could stand given the economic, social, and moral conflicts of their society. And that house did stand for three decades. Some Jacksonians, radical antibank Locofocos like the New York writer William Leggett, thought that the divided, or segmented, house guaranteed a system of equal economic opportunity for its residents and, on their own (white male) terms for residency, they were right. But this populism was not the source of segmentation even in a relatively undeveloped, overwhelmingly Democratic, and rapidly growing antebellum city on the northwestern frontier. The Republicans believed, of course, that a house divided against itself could not stand. It remained for them to define, in the Gilded Age, the power relations of the residents of their more integrated public household.[22]

22. For a description of this definition process at the federal level, Margaret Susan Thompson, The "Spider Web": Congress and Lobbying in the Age of Grant (Ithaca: Cornell University Press, 1985). At the urban level, esp. David C. Hammack, Power and Society: Greater New York at the Turn of the Century (New York: Russell Sage, 1982). Most discussions of laissez-faire link Jacksonian and Gilded Age rhetoric in arguments for ideological continuity, e.g., Sidney Fine, Laissez-faire and the General-Welfare State: A Study of Conflict in American Thought, 1865–1901 (Ann Arbor: University of Michigan Press, 1956), chap. 1, and Philip S. Paludan, "Law and the Failure of Reconstruction: The Case of Thomas Cooley," Journal of the History of Ideas 33 (1972): 597–614. Yet this begs

At the urban level, this integration resulted in machine politics. Historians generally have defined the politics of the late nineteenth-century American city by its decentralization, comparing it with what replaced it in the twentieth century. When it is compared with what preceded it, however, it is its integration that stands out. For all the noisy ward politics of late nineteenth-century urban elections, the men who were elected made political decisions to redistribute wealth in the pursuit of objectives that they defined as public interests. That this was the origin of machine politics, and that the public it served was, at least in Chicago, defined in elitist terms, makes it impossible to describe this politics as populistic or to ascribe its origin to the rising power of a socially decentralized urban working class. It was Chicago's first government transition, from boosterism to segmentation, that was decentralizing. It was the second transition, however, that brought bummers and machine politics. Neither of these transitions can be described as democratizing.

In nineteenth-century Chicago, city government was reshaped again and again, but power barely changed hands at all. Democratization would await a new kind of reform in the twentieth century—not the downtown "structural" call for centralized elitism, but the "social reform" call for a government whose policies were economically progressive. This government, built only after the Great Depression, began, however tentatively, to redistribute some urban wealth in a downward direction. Although elites and many middle-class property owners resisted through new strategies, especially by flight to the suburbs, this new city government marshalled some of its resources for democratic objectives. This city government sometimes attempted to offset rather than enhance the inequities of the private economy. In this government, paved streets—and even housing— became rights that cities owed all of their residents. Even though today's cities often fail to deliver these services, particularly since the gutting in the 1980s of the downwardly redistributive federal policies that helped to finance them, nobody justifies the failure to provide the services by calling them the private "investments" of those who hold "stock" in the city. Nobody champions inequality in the distribution of services, even in the name of low taxes. Nobody mistakes these failures of city government for successes. Public works now are conceived as public goods. Equity now consists of something more

---

rather than answers the key question: how and why did an antebellum anticorporation ideology become a postwar justification for unrestrained corporate power? How, in other words, did the laissez-faire ideology change hands?

democratic than the nineteenth-century ideal of getting only what you can pay for. This ideological change is very important. It would be more important still, if cities had the resources to act on it.

By 1871, Chicago had become a big industrial city not very different from those of the East. Its rapid development had enabled it not only to catch up with the East but to provide leadership in the Gilded Age movement for "structural" municipal reform. No longer copying their laws from New Yorkers, Chicagoans had begun to set national precedents themselves. Perhaps it is no accident that few historians of nineteenth-century Chicago have embraced the populistic, "poor man's friend" view of machine politics. This city's Gilded Age elite displayed their power in too autocratic and sanguinary a fashion for romantic denial. They were not subtle people. Even today, Chicago politics is characterized by a peculiar honesty, a rhetoric that rarely attempts to hide the real sources of local conflict no matter how bad they may sound to outsiders. But it is the honesty, rather than the conflict, that makes Chicago unique.

$$\boxed{1}$$

Citations for Poll Books and Election Returns in the Chicago City Council Proceedings Files

ELECTION YEAR	FILE YEAR	DOCUMENT NUMBERS
1837	37/37	319–24
1838	38/38	587–92
1839	39/39	785–90
1840	40/40	920–25
1841	41/41	1098–1103
1842	42/42	1295–99
1843	43/43	1565–69
1844	44/44	1882–86, 1913–18
1845	45/45	2418–24
1846	46/46	3030–35, 3049
1847	47/47	3709–16
1848	48/48	4393–4401
1849	49/49	5163–71, 5184
1850	50/50	5968–76
1851	51/52	179–94
1852	51/52	1626–34
1853	52/53	1264–72
1854	53/54	1657–66
1855	54/55	1798–1806
1856	55/56	2148–56
1857	56/57	1826–38
1858	57/58	1351–61
1859	58/59	977–87
1860	59/60	977–86

ELECTION YEAR	FILE YEAR	DOCUMENT NUMBERS
1861	60/61	329–48, 376
1862	61/62	378–98
1863	62/63	340–56
1864	63/64	698–729
1865	64/65	529–60
1866	65/66	1244–76
1867	66/67	1139–70
1868	67/68	1415–49
1869	68/69	3019
1870	69/70	2113-B
1871	70/71	1241–42, 1254
1872	72/73	1323

APPENDIX

Analysis of Census Data

A. OVERVIEW OF THE SAMPLES

1. The Database

This database was constructed by the Origins of Chicago's Industrial Working Class Project under the direction of John B. Jentz and Richard Schneirov.[1] It consists of samples of "occupied" people from the federal manuscript census schedules of 1850, 1860, and 1870, or samples of the population for which census takers listed occupational titles. The samples were drawn systematically in 1850 and by a random number process in 1860 and 1870. The restriction to "occupied" people limited the number of women and children sampled. The 1850 sample is 96 percent male, the 1860 sample 84 percent, and the 1870 sample 82 percent. The rise in the number of women who had what census takers recognized as "occupations" may be historically significant, but for the purpose of this analysis—which focusses on property ownership—all women as well as men under the age of 21 have been excluded from the database since neither group tended to own real estate. Only 5 percent of the "occupied" women in 1850 owned any, and this dropped to 2 percent in 1860, and 1 percent in 1870.[2] A sample of men aged 21 and over

1. This project was funded by NEH grant RS-20393-83 and based at the Newberry Library from 1983 to 1985. Its full results will be reported in John B. Jentz and Richard Schneirov, *Workers, Immigrants, and Urban Politics during the Civil War Era: Chicago, 1848–1877* (University of Illinois Press, forthcoming).

2. Males under 21 comprised a larger proportion of "occupied" people than women did in 1850 and roughly the same proportion in 1860 and 1870 (12, 15, and 18 percent, respectively), but the census found only 1 percent of them owning property in any of the years. It is probable, of course, that "unoccupied" women owned property more often than their "occupied" sisters, who tended overwhelmingly to be servants or to hold similarly unskilled service jobs. Nevertheless, the inclusion of "occupied" women and young men would have biased the ownership analysis without adding any infor-

also provides a reasonable proxy for the population of eligible voters; from 1848 to 1865, unnaturalized immigrants could vote after one year in the state only if they had been in Illinois in 1848, but in 1865 even this restriction was dropped.[3] The samples are fairly large: 1,474 men 21 and over in 1850; 1,908 in 1860; and 2,118 in 1870. Occupational titles were aggregated into four levels (high white-collar, low white-collar, skilled, and unskilled) using the coding system of the Philadelphia Social History Project with one exception: land and real estate dealers, among the wealthiest individuals in the Chicago data, were moved from the low to the high white-collar category.[4]

2. General Social Characteristics

Although Chicago's total population grew dramatically from one census year to the next—from 30,000 in 1850 to 109,000 in 1860 to 300,000 in 1870—the basic structure of the population of adult males remained stable. A large majority were immigrants in every year: 66 percent in 1850 and 72 percent in 1860 and 1870. Among immigrants, the German-born proportion rose from 21 percent of the men in 1850 to 29 in 1860, dropping back to 26 in 1870, while the Irish-born comprised 26 percent in 1850, 27 in 1860, and 20 in 1870. The occupational categories also were stable; the proportions of high white-collar and skilled workers dropped and those of low white-collar and unskilled rose, but these changes all were of less than five percentage points.[5] Overall, the samples are about one-fifth low white-collar, two-fifths skilled, and one-third unskilled, with the rest in the high white-collar group. More interesting, is the huge overlap between ethnicity (measured by birthplace) and class (measured by the occupational categories). In all three years, native-born men comprised 70 percent of the high white-collar and half of the low white-collar categories, but only 15 percent of the unskilled workers. The native-born pro-

---

mation beyond the statement that, among the population listing occupations, the property owners were, first and foremost, adult males.

3. Edmund J. James, ed., *The Charters of the City of Chicago* (2 pts.; Chicago: University of Chicago Press, 1898–99), 138–39; Bessie Louise Pierce, *A History of Chicago* (3 vols.; Chicago: University of Chicago Press, 1937–57), 2:315.

4. Theodore Hershberg and Robert Dockhorn, "Occupational Classification," *Historical Methods Newsletter* 9 (1976): 59–98.

5. These changes over time are all statistically significant (chi square at .0001) because of the large sample size (for all three years together, $N = 5500$), but they are unimportant. Using the "proportional reduction in error" measure Lambda, in no case did knowledge of the year reduce the error in predicting the categories of the other variables by as much as 0.5 percent. Lambda will be used as a measure of association for nominal variables in this analysis. It is better than measures based on chi square because it is independent of sample size (and thus comparable across samples), varies between 0 and 1, and can be interpreted as the reduction of errors in predicting the category of a dependent variable when the category of an independent variable is known. See Hubert M. Blalock, Jr., *Social Statistics*, 2d ed. (New York: McGraw-Hill, 1979), 307–11.

portion of skilled workers varied more, dropping from 31 percent in 1850 to 22 in 1860 and 23 in 1870, but the important point is that Chicago's working class was composed overwhelmingly of immigrants. Taking skilled and unskilled workers together, 80 percent of Chicago's working-class men were foreign-born in 1850, and 82 percent in 1860 and 1870.[6]

One important population shift was in the geographical distribution of the city's population, particularly the development of the west side after 1850. While west siders accounted for only 25 percent of the population (of adult males) in 1850, they comprised 41 percent in 1860 and 48 percent in 1870. The south side proportions dropped from 44 percent in 1850 to 35 in 1860 and 30 in 1870, while the north side dropped from 30 percent in 1850 to 24 in 1860 and 22 in 1870.[7] The relatively large growth of the west side population was a change of great social significance.

B. PROPERTY OWNERSHIP

1. Who Owned Property?

Property owners comprised a minority of the adult males in Chicago, though hardly a negligible one: 19 percent of the men owned at least some real estate in 1850, 25 in 1860, and 22 in 1870. The 1850 figures are low across the board (only 28 percent even of those with high white-collar occupations in 1850 reported owning real estate, compared with 52 in 1860 and 38 in 1870), but they are consistent with Craig Buettinger's analysis of the 1849 and 1850 tax lists, which found that one-fourth of the adult men owned all of the real property in the city.[8] The left panel of table 1 presents ownership rates by categories of age, class, and birthplace. Considered separately, none of these variables explains much of the variation in the likelihood of property ownership, though they all had statistically significant effects (F at .001) except for birthplace in 1860, when the nativity groups had very similar ownership

6. Controlling for age revealed a suggestive difference between native-born and immigrant unskilled workers, though there are too few cases for statistical significance. The proportion of native-born men who were unskilled dropped with rising age: fewer of the men over 40 than of those in their twenties were unskilled. In the immigrant categories (German, Irish, and a grab-bag "other") this pattern was reversed: a greater proportion of the men over 40 than of those in their twenties were unskilled in all three years (except among "other" immigrants in 1870).

7. This geographical distribution over time is significant (chi square at .0001) and has a Lambda association of 8 percent.

8. Craig Buettinger, "Economic Inequality in Early Chicago, 1849–1850," *Journal of Social History* 11 (1978): 414. The ownership figures rise when they are calculated for the population of household heads only, to 28 percent in 1850, 31 in 1860, and 30 in 1870. Even so, the Chicago figures for 1850 and 1860 are much lower than those for Milwaukee, where 36 percent of household heads owned some real property in 1850 and 39 percent in 1860. See Kathleen Neils Conzen, *Immigrant Milwaukee, 1836–1860: Accommodation and Community in a Frontier City* (Cambridge: Harvard University Press, 1976), 77.

TABLE 1 PROPERTY OWNERSHIP

	Ownership Rate (percent)			Median Value (dollars)		
	1850	1860	1870	1850	1860	1870
Total	19	25	22	1000	1000	2500
Age						
21–29	10	12	7	500	1000	2000
30–39	22	30	22	1000	1000	2000
40 plus	26	37	39	1000	2000	3000
E^2	.03	.05	.10	.06	.07	—
Occupation						
High white-collar	28	52	38	3500	6500	13000
Low white-collar	16	26	27	2000	4000	4000
Skilled	22	27	20	800	1000	2500
Unskilled	14	18	17	500	600	1500
E^2	.01	.04	.01	.23	.32	.24
Birthplace						
U.S.	21	24	22	1450	5000	7000
German	26	29	27	500	1000	2000
Irish	12	23	19	800	800	2000
Other	16	23	18	1000	1000	2250
E^2	.02	—	.01	.13	.22	.15

rates. In general, property owners were older than nonowners and more likely to have occupations in the higher class categories, but also quite likely to be immigrants. German-born men had the highest ownership rates, followed (when occupational class is not controlled) by the native-born. The Irish had a very low rate in 1850, but it doubled in 1860 before dropping back

9. The low Irish figures for Chicago are consistent with those of Milwaukee in 1850 and 1860 and of Buffalo, New York, in 1855, but the Irish were more likely than others to own property in Hamilton, Ontario, in 1871 (there were few Germans). The rates for the native-born, however, are much lower in Chicago (and Buffalo) than Milwaukee: only 31 percent of native-born household heads in Chicago owned property in 1850, compared with 48 percent in Milwaukee; for 1860, the figures are 31 percent in Chicago and 51 in Milwaukee. In Buffalo in 1855, as in Chicago in 1850, German household heads were significantly more likely than the native-born (or others) to own property. This was not the case in Milwaukee, where the native-born owned property more often than Germans. See Conzen, *Immigrant Milwaukee*, 77; Michael B. Katz, Michael J. Doucet, and Mark J. Stern, *The Social Organization of Early Industrial Capitalism* (Cambridge: Harvard University Press, 1982), 138–43, 147.

TABLE 2 PROPERTY OWNERSHIP:
MULTIVARIATE ANALYSIS (MCA)

	Ownership			Value (log)		
	1850	1860	1870	1850	1860	1870
Age						
21–29	−.08	−.12	−.15	−.21	−.20	−.24
30–39	.02	.05	.00	.03	−.01	−.06
40 plus	.08	.09	.17	.08	.12	.08
Beta	.17	.21	.31	.19	.18	.20
Occupation						
High white-collar	.07	.25	.12	.46	.37	.46
Low white-collar	−.03	.04	.06	.18	.30	.13
Skilled	.03	.02	−.01	−.10	−.10	−.02
Unskilled	−.04	−.09	−.05	−.24	−.28	−.27
Beta	.10	.20	.13	.40	.41	.40
Birthplace						
U.S.	.00	−.05	−.01	.12	.24	.17
German	.00	.05	.05	−.13	−.09	−.12
Irish	−.04	.02	.00	−.05	−.13	−.08
Other	−.02	−.03	−.04	.01	.01	.02
Beta	.10	.09	.08	.19	.25	.23
Multiple R^2	.05	.09	.12	.31	.40	.31

with the overall rate in 1870.[9] The influence of birthplace within the occupational classes is smaller, remaining significant (F at .001) only among the unskilled in 1850 and 1870; the German unskilled rate was double that for unskilled workers overall in 1850 and 50 percent higher in 1870. Native-born unskilled workers (of which there were few) were particularly unlikely to own property.

Age, however, was the variable most closely related to ownership, as other scholars have found for the era before the long-term home mortgage.[10] In all three years, age explained more of the variation in ownership than either occupational class or birthplace. The left panel of table 2 disentangles the effects of these variables through multiple classification analysis. The coefficients show the increased (or decreased) probability that an individual in any given category would own property, holding the other variables constant.

10. See Eric H. Monkkonen, *America Becomes Urban: The Development of U.S. Cities and Towns, 1780–1980* (Berkeley: University of California Press, 1988), 198–202, for a review of this literature.

Thus, men aged 40 and over had a 17 percent higher ownership rate in 1870 than the population as a whole, controlling for occupational class and birth-place.[11] As the table's last row shows, these variables explain quite little of the variation in ownership: 5 percent in 1850, 9 in 1860, and 12 in 1870. Age is stronger than the others, though occupational class also is powerful for 1860, with the high white-collar men 25 percent more likely to own property than the population as a whole. The disproportionate German ownership remains evident, though less pronounced, but the most obvious result of the analysis is its lack of overall explanatory power. Although notably older, the popula-tion of property owners was not very different from the total population of men in birthplace or occupational class. While this analysis has done little to explain the social bases of property ownership, it has illustrated a point with political significance. A city government that was designed to serve property owners ruled in the interests of a minority, but membership in that minority crossed lines of ethnicity and class (though not of gender).

2. How Much Did They Own?

The right-hand panels of tables 1 and 2 consider the value of the property owned among those who did own property (i.e., the nonowners were ex-cluded). Birthplace and occupational class are far more closely related to property value than to the rate of property ownership. While owners with white-collar occupations, as one would expect, owned much larger amounts of property than working-class owners, native-born owners also owned more than immigrant owners, and this relationship held within the occupational classes. Thus, the median property value for native-born owners in every occupational class exceeded the overall median for that class in all three years, with the exception of the high white-collar group in 1870 (when a handful of "other" immigrants ($N = 5$) had a higher median than the high white-collar owners as a whole). Among workers, this means that although native-born workers were less likely than immigrant workers to own any property, those working-class natives who owned some owned more than did working-class immigrant owners. This relationship is clear in table 2: occupational class is the most powerful determinant of property value, but birthplace remains im-portant when class (as well as age) is controlled. Thus, the value of property owned by native-born owners was 12 percent higher than the overall average value in 1850, 24 percent higher in 1860, and 17 percent higher in 1870. The negative figures for German owners are striking when compared with the high German ownership rates: German men owned property more often than others, but they owned a good deal less of it. Finally, age clearly is related to property value; older property owners owned more than younger property owners.

11. I ran the test with more precise measurements of age, first using its exact value as a covariate and then using a quintile breakdown as a factor category, but in both cases—for property value as well as for the ownership rate—the more exact measure-ments reduced rather than enhanced the total R^2 for the tables. Clearly, age is not related to property holding in a linear fashion.

While age, occupational class, and birthplace explained very little of the variation in property ownership, they explain about one-third of the variation in property value. This still is not a particularly powerful figure. Obviously, most of the variation in both ownership and value is attributable to variables not considered in this analysis. Thus, in their sophisticated analysis of property ownership in Buffalo, New York, in 1855, Katz, Doucet, and Stern found that length of residence in the city was an important determinant of ownership; while those who had lived in Buffalo less than two years had a 13 percent chance of owning property, the probability jumped to 25 percent at 2–5 years, and 42 percent at 6–9 years, continuing to rise the longer someone lived in Buffalo.[12] Those with high-ranking commercial occupations (comparable to the high white-collar group here) tended to own property more often than others, though among workers a job in the construction trades also increased the likelihood of ownership. Yet in Chicago, there was at least one other important variable, especially for the probability of ownership: whether a man lived on the south, west, or north side of the city. The inclusion of this variable in the multiple classification analyses raised their overall explanatory power for 1850 and 1860, though not for 1870.[13] It did not change the other coefficients by very much, but it reveals an important geographical pattern: the development by 1860 of a separate neighborhood of immigrant, working-class property owners.

3. The West Side in the 1850s: The Tenth Ward

Men who lived on the west side were more likely to own property than those on the north or south sides in both 1850 and 1860, and these more numerous owners tended to own smaller amounts of property (table 3, top panel). While 25 percent of the west siders in 1850 and 32 percent in 1860 were owners, however, these figures mean different things because the population of the west side changed substantially (table 3, bottom panel). In 1850, the west side was 32 percent native-born and 22 percent white-collar, but in 1860 it was only 20 percent native-born and 16 percent white-collar. Yet while the Irish proportion on the west side rose only slightly (and the "other" immigrant share dropped a bit), the German proportion almost doubled, from 15 percent in 1850 to 27 percent in 1860. The 1857 charter amendment split the west side Fifth Ward, placing the southern two-thirds of its area into the new Tenth Ward. In 1860 the Tenth had both the highest ownership rate

12. Katz, Doucet, and Stern, *Social Organization*, 146. Conzen, *Immigrant Milwaukee*, 77, makes a similar point, attributing the low German rates in 1850 and 1860 to "the continuing arrival of new immigrants." The most influential statement linking persistence with ownership has been Stephan Thernstrom, *Poverty and Progress: Social Mobility in a Nineteenth Century City* (Cambridge: Harvard University Press, 1964), 117–18.

13. The multiple R^2 for the analysis of ownership with division included is .07 in 1850 and .11 in 1860. For property value, it is .33 in 1850 and .41 in 1860. The inclusion of division had very little effect in 1870, yielding R^2s of .12 for ownership and .32 for value.

TABLE 3 WEST SIDE OWNERSHIP

A. Property Ownership in the Divisions

	Ownership Rate (percent)			Median Value (dollars)		
	1850	1860	1870	1850	1860	1870
South	16	18	20	1100	3500	3750
West	25	32	23	800	1000	2000
North	17	26	22	1000	1000	2600
E^2	.01	.02	.00	.05	.11	.02

B. The West Side Wards in 1850 and 1860

	1850			1860			
	Fifth	Sixth	Total	Fifth	Sixth	Tenth	Total
Birthplace (percent)							
U.S.	32	33	32	42	20	11	20
German	12	18	15	13	22	37	27
Irish	34	24	29	26	24	43	33
Other	22	26	24	18	34	9	20
Occupational Class (percent)							
High white-collar	7	6	7	10	4	6	6
Low white-collar	15	15	15	25	10	4	10
Skilled	45	47	46	40	51	28	38
Unskilled	33	32	32	25	35	62	45
Ownership Rate (percent)	28	22	25	15	27	42	32
Median Value (dollars)	800	800	800	3000	1000	750	1000

(42 percent) and the highest proportion of unskilled workers (62 percent) of any ward in the city. No other ward even approached these figures. (See map 7.) The north side Ninth was second in both ownership (33 percent) and proportion unskilled (41 percent), but the ownership figure of the Ninth also reflected the fact that it had the second highest proportion of men with high white-collar occupations, as the home of some of the wealthiest businessmen in Chicago (e.g., William B. Ogden, Walter Newberry, and Richard J. Hamilton). The native-born comprised 34 percent of the Ninth but only 11 percent of the Tenth; the high white-collar group accounted for 13 percent of the Ninth but only 6 percent of the Tenth. Most telling, Ninth Ward owners had a median property value of $9,000; the median among Tenth Ward owners was $750.

The development of the west side, in other words, and especially of that part of it that became the Tenth Ward, created opportunities for working-class ownership that are reflected in the high overall ownership rate for 1860. Not only did two-fifths of all Tenth Ward men own property in 1860, but for skilled and unskilled workers the figures are 56 percent (double the citywide rate for skilled workers) and 28 percent, respectively. Even the Irish had a high rate in the Tenth, 41 percent compared with a citywide Irish owner-ship rate of 23 percent—and the Tenth was by far the most heavily Irish ward in 1860 (43 percent, compared with 28 percent in the Seventh, the second most heavily Irish ward). The similarly high west side ownership figures for 1850 and 1860 mask major changes over the decade. The west side in 1850 was a vast tract of undeveloped land. Its population was disproportionately working-class but its ethnic breakdown was similar to that of the city as a whole. In 1850, low median values on the west side probably reflected gen-erally low west side land values and the fact that Chicago's wealthiest men (who owned property everywhere) lived in the elite enclaves of the north and south sides. In 1860, the west side had a far larger population, still heavily working-class (now more unskilled than skilled), but also disproportionately immigrant (80 percent versus 72 for the city). By 1860, moreover, the creation of the Tenth made a finer geographical distinction visible. While the Sixth still had a fairly low median value, the even lower value of the Tenth can be interpreted with confidence as the ownership of a home and no other property. Chicago's Tenth Ward in the 1850s clearly enjoyed a level of working-class ownership comparable to those of late nineteenth- and early twentieth-century cities.[14]

The similarity between Chicago's Tenth in the 1850s and Milwaukee's Fourteenth half a century later is striking. As Roger Simon has shown, some of Milwaukee's outlying neighborhoods had extremely high rates of immi-grant and working-class home-ownership in the decades around 1900. In the Fourteenth Ward in 1905, 55 percent of the household heads owned their homes or at least part of the equity in them. Half of the skilled, 40 percent of the semiskilled, and 55 percent of the unskilled household heads were home-owners. Simon has explained some of the strategies by which Milwaukee's working-class owners obtained their properties: they "doubled up," dividing their houses into apartments while they paid off their mortgages (sometimes living in the worst part of the house to collect higher rents on the best), and they delayed the installation of physical infrastructure that would have re-quired them to pay special assessments.[15] Simon's sources, particularly the building permits that allow him to measure the time lag between house con-struction and public works extension, are unavailable for Chicago in the

14. See esp. Jules Tygiel, "Housing in Late Nineteenth-Century American Cities: Suggestions for Research," *Historical Methods* 12 (1979): 91.

15. Roger D. Simon, *The City-Building Process: Housing and Services in New Milwaukee Neighborhoods, 1880–1910*, Transactions of the American Philosophical Society, vol. 68, pt. 5 (Philadelphia, 1978), esp. 35–45.

1850s (one did not need permits to build houses), but the logic of Simon's analysis can be extended backwards in light of the organization of segmented government.

Working-class owners on Chicago's north and south sides had wealthy neighbors whose larger holdings gave them greater power in the property-based decision-making process. If it was important that working-class owners avoid special assessment costs, it made sense for them to buy in a place like the Tenth. Not only was the land cheaper (because relatively undeveloped), but a homogeneous population of property owners could protect a struggling working-class owner against assessment costs that he would have found harder to avoid in other parts of the city. Christine Rosen has argued that Chicago's high working-class ownership rates resulted, in part, from the absence of fire limit restrictions in working-class neighborhoods; it seems reasonable to guess that there was a connection between the west side fire limit fight of the mid 1850s and the creation of an independent Tenth Ward in 1857.[16] In the Tenth Ward in 1860, 78 percent of the property owners were workers and 42 percent of them were unskilled workers. Although there obviously were noneconomic reasons for ethnic and class-based residential clustering—i.e., a simple preference for neighbors similar to oneself—segmented city-building policies may well have influenced the settlement pattern.[17] There were few men in the Tenth who would have been likely to initiate an expensive improvement proposal, much less able to force it on their neighbors through the power of their greater property holdings.

C. THE SIGNIFICANCE OF WARD POLITICS

1. Introduction

This section presents statistical evidence about the generalizations in chapter 3 concerning the 1847 ward map. I argued that the real estate map was designed to facilitate the special assessment process *rather than* to create a council in which aldermen represented the class and ethnic interests of neighborhood-based wards. There was no direct evidence of this intention; none of the charter-drafters said "I want a map that will ignore class and ethnicity." The map's functional utility was clear: aldermen in the 1850s played vital roles as ward-based consensus builders in the assessment process. Their solicitude for the interests of property owners also was clear; when class and ethnic hostilities were politicized in 1855, it took a riot to

16. Christine Meisner Rosen, *The Limits of Power: Great Fires and the Process of City Growth in America* (Cambridge: Cambridge University Press, 1986), 99. The west side fire limit never extended into what became the Tenth, but the political salience of the issue may well have encouraged working-class owners to take steps to protect themselves.

17. This influence need not be considered purely voluntary: wealthy owners could have manipulated special assessment, like the fire limit, to force poorer neighbors to sell out. The most important discussion especially of ethnic clustering in a nineteenth-century city is Conzen, *Immigrant Milwaukee*, esp. chap. 5.

TABLE 4 EXPLANATORY POWER OF WARD MAPS

		Birthplace Lambda	Occupation Lambda	Ownership E^2	Value (log) E^2
1850					
Divisions		.046	.001	.009	.051
Wards		.079	.032	.020	.091
	South	.040	.010	—	—
Wards	West	—	—	—	—
	North	—	—	—	—
1860					
Divisions		.142	.044	.018	.110
Wards		.183 [.166]	.110 [.094]	.044 [.026]	.350 [.330]
	South	.000	.005	—	.348
Wards	West	.101 [.056]	.154 [.109]	.047 [—]	.140 [.063]
	North	.074	.042	—	.302
1870					
Divisions		.084	.000	—	—
Wards		.244	.136	.062	.316
	South	.083	.156	.090	.349
Wards	West	.234	.175	.042	.247
	North	.139	—	.066	.310

Note: the bracketed figures for 1860 represent hypothetical west side values on the measures if the Tenth Ward had not been separated from the Fifth in 1857.

persuade some aldermen to pay attention to the ethnocultural and class-based preferences of the voters in their wards. While the analysis of census data cannot substitute for direct evidence of intentionality, it can determine whether the ward boundaries actually were significantly less important as social boundaries in the 1850s than they were later, when the ward maps at least look like they might have reflected neighborhoods. The creation of the Tenth Ward in 1857 did not alter any other boundaries; on the north and south sides, therefore, the 1847 map remained in force throughout the 1850s. Ideally, the 1847 map should be compared with the one that the Democrats introduced in 1863, but this is impossible because no census canvassed the wards of that map, and the north and west side boundaries were substantially redrawn when the city annexed new territory in 1869. The 1870 data are based on 20 rather than 16 wards (which appear to reflect a Republican as opposed to the earlier Democratic gerrymander).

Maps 5 through 10 present basic data for the wards in 1850, 1860, and 1870: percent owning property, median property value, percent immigrant, and percent unskilled. Table 4 presents the results of the full ward map analysis, using all of the categories on the birthplace and occupational class variables rather than only those on the maps. For each year, table 4 shows the statistical association between (1) the divisions, wards, and wards within the divisions, and (2) birthplace, occupational class, property ownership, and property value. The first two columns can be interpreted as the proportional reduction in the error of predicting an individual's birthplace or occupational class category when his division (or ward, or ward within a division) of residence is known. The third and fourth columns measure the proportion of the variation in ownership and property value that is explained by the divisions and wards. All of the measures included in the table represent statistically significant relationships (chi square at .001 for birthplace and occupational class, F at .001 for property ownership and property value). The bracketed figures for 1860 are hypothetical values for these measures if the Tenth Ward had not been separated from the Fifth in 1857.

2. The 1847 Map in 1850 and 1860

In 1850, none of these geographical boundaries was a very important predictor of the social variables, though when taken together the wards performed better than the divisions. The four south side wards differed from one another in 1850 even though they were drawn in long rectangles only two blocks wide (additional north-south streets were added later). The distinction between the lakefront First Ward and the riverside Fourth is especially clear: the First was 60 percent native-born and 22 percent high white-collar, while the Fourth was only 27 percent native-born and 6 percent high white-collar. The proportions also drop in order moving westward from the lakefront, with those of the Second lower than those of the First and those of the Third lower than those of the Second but higher than those of the Fourth. In terms of birthplace and occupational class, in other words, it did make some social sense to draw north-south lines on the south side in 1850. The lines were drawn in 1847, however, and there is reason to suspect that developments in these three years (Chicago's population nearly doubled) had particularly important effects on the First and Fourth wards: in the First, the establishment of the elite neighborhood on the lakefront, which was connected with negotiations for the Illinois Central Railroad and lake shore protection barrier (these were concluded in 1852);[18] and in the Fourth, the southward expansion of wharfage and warehousing along the river's South Branch. It also can be argued, on the other hand, that the charter drafters anticipated these developments; we know that they anticipated the city's growth, and most of them were key players in causing the more specific changes.

In any case, the 1847 ward boundaries reduced the error in predicting birthplace and occupational class on the south side in 1850 by only 4 percent and 1 percent, respectively. Ten years later, these same boundaries in a city three times as large did not reduce the error for birthplace at all, and reduced

18. See Robin L. Einhorn, "A Taxing Dilemma: Early Lake Shore Protection," *Chicago History* 18 (1989): 34–51.

it for occupational class by only .5 percent. The 1847 ward boundaries were not statistically significant for either property ownership or property value on the south side in 1850 (though the Fourth had a markedly lower ownership rate than the others), but in 1860 they were important determinants of property value. The median value of property in the First Ward was $10,000 in 1860 (it was only $2,000 in 1850); the lakefront clearly was home to many quite wealthy men in 1860. The median value in the Fourth, by contrast, was only $1,250 ($1,200 in 1850); the valuable riverfront properties of the Fourth may well have belonged to men who lived in the First. It is possible that the ward boundaries influenced this outcome directly, that the 1860 value differentials actually resulted from ward-based public works decision making in the 1850s.

Moving to the north side, the 1847 ward boundaries explained nothing in 1850. By 1860, however, the north side wards reduced the error for birthplace by 7 percent and occupational class by 4 percent. While the Eighth and Ninth had similar ethnic distributions in 1860, the Seventh had a far lower percentage of native-born residents. The Seventh was 50 percent German and 28 percent Irish in 1860, which no doubt contributed to its strikingly low percentage of high white-collar men (1 percent, compared with 8 percent in the Eighth and 13 percent in the Ninth). The Eighth and Ninth differed in their occupational class distributions: the Eighth had a much larger low white-collar and much smaller unskilled proportion than either the Seventh or Ninth; the Eighth's proportion of skilled workers was much higher than the Ninth's but close to the Seventh's.[19] Thus, although the 1847 ward boundaries do not reduce much of the error in predicting birthplace and occupational class on the north side in 1860, the wards did differ from one another. It probably is fair to call the Eighth a middle-class ward, the Seventh a working-class ward, and the Ninth a ward containing both social extremes (much like the near north side in the twentieth century, with its "gold coast and slum"). For the property variables, the wards still had no effect on ownership in 1860, but a relatively strong effect on value. Like the south side First, the north side Ninth had an elite residential area. The median values are consistent with the occupational class figures, $9,000 in the Ninth, $5,000 in the Eighth, and $800 in the Seventh; the ward boundaries explain 30 percent of the variation in north side values in 1860.

For birthplace and occupational class, however, the real change from 1850 to 1860 occurred on the west side, particularly because of the 1857 creation of the Tenth Ward. Almost half of the reduction in error for birthplace on the west side in 1860 is attributable to the Tenth, though only one-third of that for occupational class can be explained this way. The Fifth was much more heavily native-born than either the Sixth or Tenth, but its native-born percentage drops to 20, about equal to the Sixth's, when it is figured using the 1847 ward boundaries. The Fifth Ward in 1860 also had an unusually high

19. The 1860 north side percentages are: for low white-collar, 17 in the Seventh, 28 in the Eighth, and 20 in the Ninth; for skilled workers, 42 in the Seventh, 41 in the Eighth, and 27 in the Ninth.

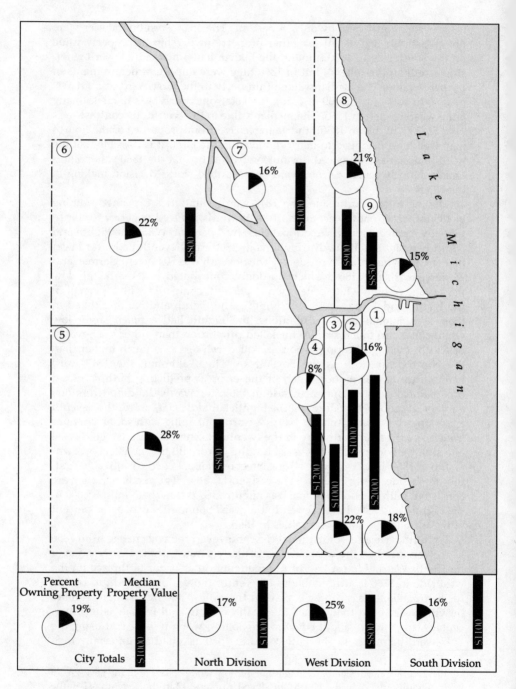

Percent Owning Property   Median Property Value

City Totals
19% $1000

North Division
17% $1000

West Division
25% $550

South Division
16% $1100

MAP 5 PROPERTY OWNERSHIP, 1850

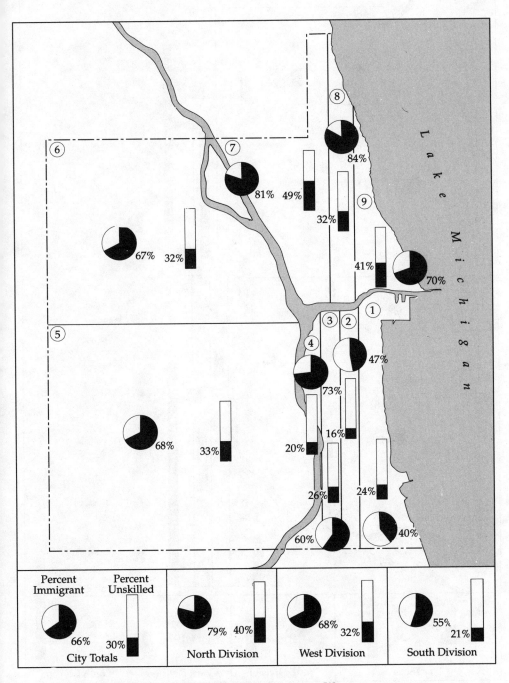

Percent Immigrant
Percent Unskilled

66%
30%
City Totals

79% 40%
North Division

68% 32%
West Division

55% 21%
South Division

MAP 6 IMMIGRANTS AND UNSKILLED WORKERS, 1850

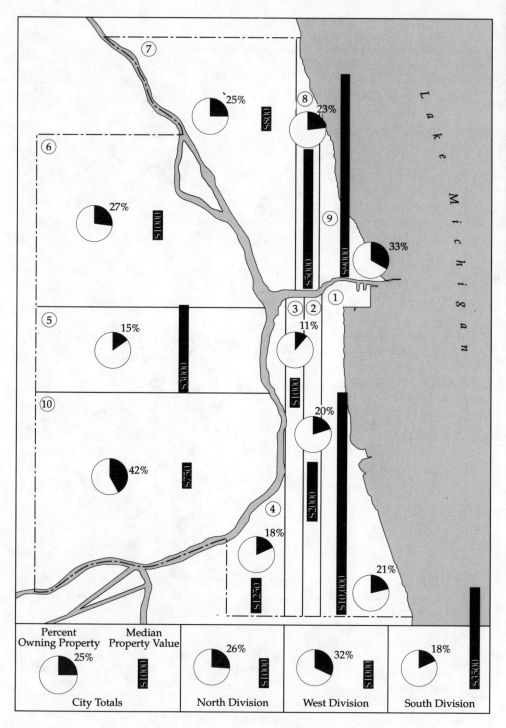

Lake Michigan

7

25% $800

8   23%

6

27% $1000 $3000   9   33% $9000

5   15% $3000   3 2 1   11% $1000

10   20% $2000

42% $750   4 $10,000

18% $250   21% $350

Percent Owning Property	Median Property Value				
25%	$1000	26%	$1000	32%	$1000	18%	$350
City Totals		North Division		West Division		South Division	

MAP 7 PROPERTY OWNERSHIP, 1860

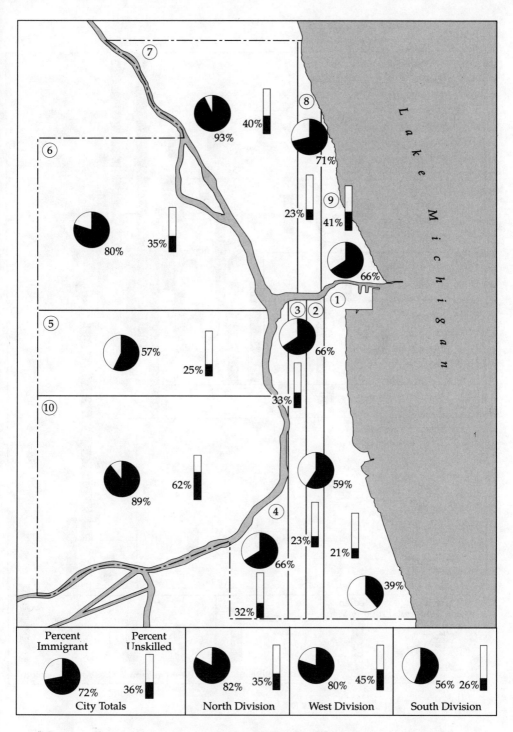

Percent
Immigrant

Percent
Unskilled

72% 36%

City Totals

82% 35%

North Division

80% 45%

West Division

56% 26%

South Division

MAP 8 IMMIGRANTS AND UNSKILLED WORKERS, 1860

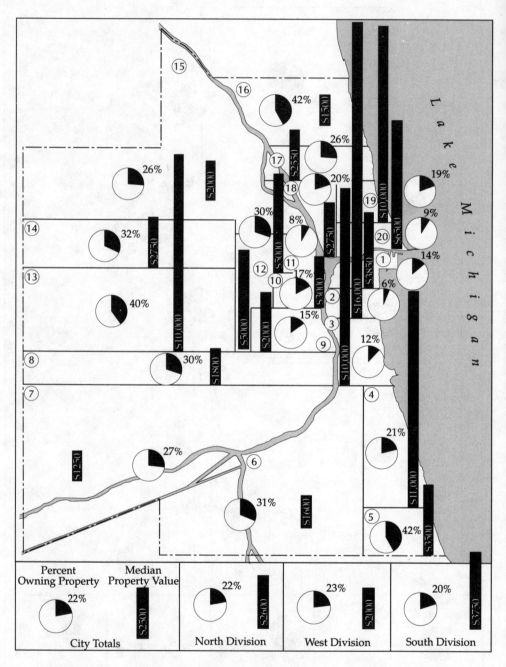

42%
$1500

26%
$2350

20%

19%

26%
$3000

32%
$2750

30%

8%

9%

14%

40%
$10,000

17%

15%

6%

12%

30%
$1800

21%

27%
$1250

31%
$1600

42%
$350

$2000

$3000

$2000

$5000

$2750

$3000

$16,000

$10,000

$11,000

$500

$4000

MAP 9 PROPERTY OWNERSHIP, 1870

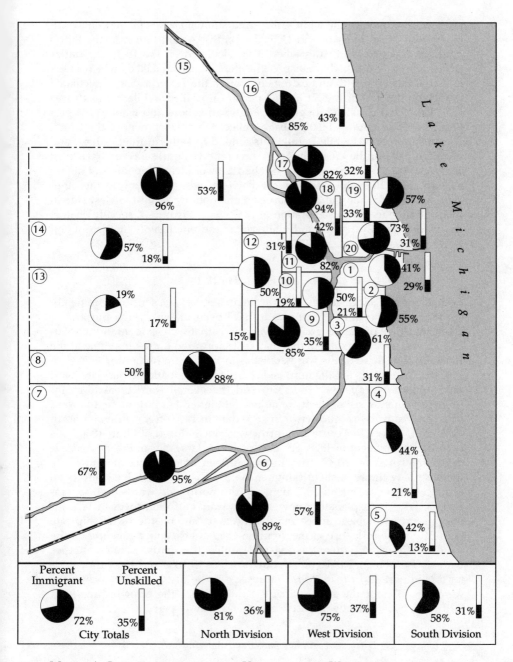

Percent Immigrant 72% Percent Unskilled 35% City Totals

81% 36% North Division

75% 37% West Division

58% 31% South Division

MAP 10 IMMIGRANTS AND UNSKILLED WORKERS, 1870

proportion of men in the white-collar occupational classes (35 percent, compared with 14 in the Sixth and 11 in the Tenth). Again, however, the Fifth's figure is closer to the Sixth's when it is calculated on the 1847 boundaries (18 percent). The key difference is the percentage unskilled, which is extremely low in the Fifth and extremely high in the Tenth. When recalculated to include the Tenth, the Fifth is 52 percent unskilled, while the Sixth was only 35 percent unskilled. In general, high native-born and white-collar proportions of the Fifth in 1860 probably reflect the development of the Union Park neighborhood, while immigrants tended to settle in the northern and southern parts of the West Division. The property figures already have been analyzed, but to summarize, the Fifth had a lower ownership rate and higher median value than the west side as a whole, with the Tenth at the other extreme. Thus, while the 1847 map explains nothing about the west side in 1850 and little in 1860, its alteration in 1857 created two new, socially distinct wards: one heavily Yankee and white-collar and one heavily immigrant and working-class.

3. The 1869 Map in 1870

Even a cursory glance at the 1869 ward map suggests its sensitivity to neighborhood characteristics. It appears to have been drawn for the purpose of capturing some of the geographical variations that were evident in the 1850s and, on the west side, others that may have appeared for the first time in the 1860s. All but three of the ward statistics in table 4 are higher for 1870 than 1860 (the exceptions are the north side wards for occupational class, the west side wards for property ownership, and the overall ward breakdown for property value). Most of them are quite a bit higher. For birthplace, the ward map reduces twice as much error in 1870 than in 1860 on the west and north sides and, where the south side error was not reduced at all in 1860, it is reduced by 8 percent in 1870. For occupational class, the south side figure is thirty times higher in 1870 than in 1860 (fifteen times higher than in 1850); the west side figure is slightly higher in 1870 than in 1860, but there is no significant relationship in 1870 between the north side wards and occupational class. The explanatory power of the wards also improves in 1870 for the property variables, appearing for the first time on the ownership rate (aside from the influence of the Tenth in 1860), and almost doubling on the west side for value. Where the divisions, unlike the wards, were boundaries with statistical significance on all four variables in 1850 and 1860, they were far less important in 1870. Most impressive is the overall importance of the wards in 1870 for the social variables: they reduce the error in predicting birthplace by 24 percent and occupational class by 14 percent.

4. A Note on Gerrymandering

The 1870 wards varied in size: the largest ward contained four times as many of the adult males as the smallest. Only 2 percent of the men lived in each of the smallest wards, the Thirteenth and Nineteenth, and it cannot be a coincidence that the Thirteenth had by far the highest native-born proportion in the city. The largest ward, meanwhile, the Ninth, contained 8 percent of the men—and a large immigrant population. In fact, the correlation between percent native-born and percent of the adult males in a ward in 1870 was −.58; wards with high native-born populations were smaller than others. Conversely, the correlation between percent Irish and percent of the men was .73; the more heavily Irish wards contained more potential voters.[20] There are more sophisticated ways to measure gerrymandering, but these figures certainly suggest that Republicans benefited from the 1869 map. The 1863 map drawn by the Democrats (map 4) is even more suggestive. That map divided the heavily immigrant Tenth of 1860 (plus the newly annexed Bridgeport packing district to the south) into three wards and moved the northern boundary of the Fifth (1857) substantially farther north before splitting it. In 1869, the Republicans created a new Yankee ward on the south side by separating the Fifth from the Fourth (1863), while on the north side they carved the tiny (and wealthy) Nineteenth from the lakefront part of the Fifteenth (1863). The point of all this is its contrast with the 1847 map and 1850 data. While the smallest ward in 1850, the north side Ninth, contained 7 percent of the men, every other ward contained between 10 and 13 percent. The 1863 and 1869 maps seem clearly to have promised partisan benefits but, assuming no major reshuffling between 1847 and 1850, the 1847 map did not.

5. Conclusion

The 1847 ward map proved more important as a map of social boundaries on the south side—where almost half the city's adult males lived—in 1850 than expected, but the east-west lines of the 1869 map performed twice as well for birthplace and fifteen times as well for occupational class. On the north side, while north-south lines explained nothing in 1850 and little in 1860, the east-west lines captured a fair amount of the ethnic difference, but none of that in occupational class. Nor did they do much better on the property variables. The 1857 creation of the Tenth certainly drew a boundary with social significance on the west side, but the 1869 map improved the prediction of birthplace almost twice as well. In sum, the analysis of the census data did not provide a perfect demonstration that the 1847 map was drawn in order to ignore social boundaries, but that map clearly was much less sensitive to them than the maps drawn in 1857 (for the west side) and 1869.[21]

20. These correlations are not significant for 1850 or 1860.

21. It might be objected that a map with twenty wards would tend to explain more variation than a map with only nine or ten, but a larger number of boundaries would be as likely to achieve more perfect randomness as more pronounced clustering. It depends, as most politicians know, on where you draw the lines. See Bruce E. Cain, *The Reapportionment Puzzle* (Berkeley: University of California Press, 1984).

Bibliography

Primary Sources

Unpublished Government Documents

Chicago City Council Proceedings Files, 1833–1872, Illinois State Archives.
Illinois Supreme Court papers, Illinois State Archives.
U.S. Census, Population and Manufactures, manuscript schedules, 1850–1870, courtesy of the Origins of Chicago's Industrial Working Class Project, NEH grant RS-20393-83, based at the Newberry Library from 1983–85.

Published Government Documents

The Charters of the City of Chicago. Edited by Edmund J. James. 2 pts. Chicago: University of Chicago Press, 1898–99.
Chicago. Department of Finance. *Annual Statement, 1877.* Chicago: Hazlitt & Reed, 1878.
Chicago. *Revised Charter and Ordinances.* Edited by George Manierre. Chicago: Daily Democrat, 1851.
A Compilation of the Messages and Papers of the Presidents, 1789–1897. Compiled by James D. Richardson. 10 vols. Washington, D.C.: Government Printing Office, 1896–99.
Illinois. Constitutional Convention. *The Constitutional Debates of 1847.* Edited by Arthur Charles Cole. Springfield: Illinois State Historical Society, 1919.
Illinois. House of Representatives. *Journals.*
Illinois. House of Representatives. Select Committee on Governor J. M. Palmer's Messages of Nov. 15 and Dec. 9, 1871, *Report.* Springfield: Illinois State Journal, 1872.
Illinois. *Laws* (titles vary).
Illinois. Senate. *Journals.*
Illinois. Supreme Court. *Reports.*

Private Manuscript Collections

Ante-Fire Subdivision Plats, Chicago Title and Trust Company.
Thomas Barbour Bryan papers, Chicago Historical Society.
David Davis papers, Chicago Historical Society.
Stephen A. Douglas papers, University of Chicago Library.
Henry Greenebaum papers, Chicago Historical Society.
Richard J. Hamilton Letterbook, Chicago Historical Society.
Illinois Central Archives, Newberry Library.
Edmund Stoughton Kimberly papers, Chicago Historical Society.

Newspapers

Chicago *American*, 1835–42.
Chicago *Democrat*, 1833–52.
Chicago *Journal*, 1845–56.
Chicago *Times*, 1855–68.
Chicago *Tribune*, 1853–68.

Other Publications

Anthony, Elliott. *Sanitation and Navigation*. Chicago: Chicago Legal News, 1891.
Chicago River-and-Harbor Convention. Compiled by Robert Fergus. Fergus Historical Series, no. 18. Chicago: Fergus Printing Co., 1882.
Committee on Statistics for the City of Chicago. *The Necessity of a Ship-Canal between the East and the West*. Chicago: Tribune Co., 1863.
MacVeagh, Franklin. "Address by President Franklin MacVeagh, September 11, 1874." In *Addresses and Reports of the Citizens Association of Chicago 1874–1876*. Chicago: Hazlitt & Reed, 1876.
Reception to the Settlers of Chicago Prior to 1840. Chicago: Calumet Club, 1879.
The Tunnels and Water System of Chicago: Under the Lake and Under the River. Chicago: J. M. Wing & Co., 1874.

SECONDARY SOURCES

Abbott, Carl. *Boosters and Businessmen: Popular Economic Thought and Urban Growth in the Antebellum Middle West*. Westport: Greenwood Press, 1981.
Adrian, Charles R., and Griffith, Ernest S. *A History of American City Government: The Formation of Traditions, 1775–1870*. New York: Praeger, 1976.
Ahern, M. L. *The Great Revolution: A History of the Rise and Progress of the People's Party in the City of Chicago and County of Cook*. Chicago: Lakeside Publishing and Printing, 1874.

Allswang, John M. *Bosses, Machines, and Urban Voters: An American Symbiosis.* Port Washington: Kennikat, 1977.

Altschuler, Glenn C., and Saltzgaber, Jan M. "The Limits of Responsibility: Social Welfare and Local Government in Seneca County, New York 1860–1875." *Journal of Social History* 22 (1988): 515–37.

Anderson, Alan D. *The Origin and Resolution of an Urban Crisis: Baltimore, 1890–1930.* Baltimore: Johns Hopkins University Press, 1977.

Andreas, A. T. *History of Chicago.* 3 vols. Chicago: Andreas, 1884–86.

Bailey, Robert E., et al., eds. *Chicago City Council Proceedings Files, 1833–1871: An Inventory.* Springfield: Illinois State Archives, 1987.

Baker, Jean H. *Affairs of Party: The Political Culture of Northern Democrats in the Mid-Nineteenth Century.* Ithaca: Cornell University Press, 1983.

Balestier, Joseph N. *The Annals of Chicago.* 2d ed. Fergus Historical Series, no. 1. Chicago: Fergus Printing Co., 1876.

Benson, Sumner. "A History of the General Property Tax." In *The American Property Tax: Its History, Administration, and Economic Impact.* By George C. S. Benson, et al. Claremont, Calif.: College Press, 1965.

Bergquist, James Manning. "The Political Attitudes of the German Immigrant in Illinois, 1848–1860." Ph.D. diss., Northwestern University, 1966.

Biographical Sketches of Some of the Early Settlers of the City of Chicago. Part 2. Fergus Historical Series, no. 6. Chicago: Fergus Printing Co., 1876.

Blackmar, Elizabeth. *Manhattan for Rent, 1785–1850.* Ithaca: Cornell University Press, 1989.

Blake, Nelson Manfred. *Water for the Cities: A History of the Urban Water Supply Problem in the United States.* Syracuse: Syracuse University Press, 1956.

Bogart, Ernest Ludlow, and Thompson, Charles Manfred. *The Industrial State, 1870–1893.* Chicago: A. C. McClurg, 1922.

Boorstin, Daniel J. *The Americans: The National Experience.* New York: Random House, 1965.

Booth, Douglas E. "Transportation, City Building, and Financial Crisis: Milwaukee, 1852–1868." *Journal of Urban History* 9 (1983): 335–63.

Boyer, Paul. *Urban Masses and Moral Order in America, 1820–1920.* Cambridge: Harvard University Press, 1978.

Breckenridge, Helen Elizabeth. "The Chicago *Times* during the Civil War." Ph.D. diss., University of Chicago, 1931.

Bridges, Amy. "Becoming American: The Working Classes in the United States Before the Civil War." In *Working Class Formation: Nineteenth Century Patterns in Western Europe and the United States.* Edited by Ira Katznelson and Aristide Zolberg. Princeton: Princeton University Press, 1986.

———. *A City in the Republic: Antebellum New York and the Origins of Machine Politics.* Cambridge: Cambridge University Press, 1984.

Brown, G. P. *Drainage Channel and Waterway.* Chicago: R. R. Donnelly, 1894.

Brown, M. Craig, and Halaby, Charles N. "Machine Politics in America, 1870–1945." *Journal of Interdisciplinary History* 17 (1987): 587–612.

Bryce, James. *The American Commonwealth.* Rev. ed.; 2 vols. New York: Macmillan, 1914.

Buder, Stanley. *Pullman: An Experiment in Industrial Order and Community Planning, 1880–1930.* Chicago: University of Chicago Press, 1977.

Buettinger, Craig. "The Concept of Jacksonian Aristocracy: Chicago as a Test Case." Ph.D. diss., Northwestern University, 1982.

————. "Economic Inequality in Early Chicago, 1849–50." *Journal of Social History* 11 (1978): 413–18.

Bushnell, George D. "Chicago's Rowdy Firefighters." *Chicago History* 2 (1973): 232–41.

Cain, Louis P. "Raising and Watering a City: Ellis Sylvester Chesbrough and Chicago's First Sanitation System." *Technology and Culture* 13 (1972): 353–72.

————. *Sanitation Strategy for a Lakefront Metropolis: The Case of Chicago.* DeKalb: Northern Illinois University Press, 1978.

Callow, Alexander B., Jr. *The Tweed Ring.* New York: Oxford University Press, 1966.

Chudacoff, Howard P., and Smith, Judith E. *The Evolution of American Urban Society.* 3d ed. Englewood Cliffs: Prentice-Hall, 1988.

Cleaver, Charles. *Early-Chicago Reminiscences.* Fergus Historical Series, no. 19. Chicago: Fergus Printing Co., 1882.

Colbert, Elias. *Chicago: Historical and Statistical Sketch of the Garden City, from the Beginning until Now.* Chicago: P. T. Sherlock, 1868.

Cole, Arthur Charles. *The Era of the Civil War, 1848–1870.* Chicago: A. C. McClurg, 1922.

Cole, Bruce McKitterick. "The Chicago Press and the Know-Nothings, 1850–1856." M.A. thesis, University of Chicago, 1948.

Conzen, Kathleen Neils. "Community Studies, Urban History, and American Local History." In *The Past Before Us: Contemporary Historical Writing in the United States.* Edited by Michael Kammen. Ithaca: Cornell University Press, 1980.

————. *Immigrant Milwaukee, 1836–1860: Accommodation and Community in a Frontier City.* Cambridge: Harvard University Press, 1976.

————. "The New Urban History: Defining the Field." In *Ordinary People and Everyday Life: Perspectives on the New Social History.* Edited by James B. Gardner and George Rollie Adams. Nashville: American Association for State and Local History, 1983.

————. "Quantification and the New Urban History." *Journal of Interdisciplinary History* 13 (1983): 653–77.

Cooley, Thomas M. *A Treatise on the Law of Taxation.* Chicago: Callaghan & Co., 1876.

Cromie, Robert. *The Great Chicago Fire.* New York: McGraw-Hill, 1958.

Curry, Leonard P. *Blueprint for Modern America: Non-military Legislation of the First Civil War Congress.* Nashville: Vanderbilt University Press, 1968.

Curry, Richard O. "Copperheadism and Continuity: The Anatomy of a Stereotype." *Journal of Negro History* 57 (1972): 29–36.

————. "The Union As It Was: A Critique of Recent Interpretations of the 'Copperheads.'" *Civil War History* 13 (1967): 25–39.

Dahl, Robert A. *Who Governs? Democracy and Power in an American City.* New Haven: Yale University Press, 1961.

Dana, David D. *The Fireman: The Fire Departments of the United States.* 2d ed. Boston: James French, 1858.

Dawley, Alan. *Class and Community: The Industrial Revolution in Lynn.* Cambridge: Harvard University Press, 1976.

Dawley, Alan, and Faler, Paul. "Working-Class Culture and Politics in the Industrial Revolution: Sources of Loyalism and Rebellion." *Journal of Social History* 9 (1976): 466–80.

Diamond, Stephen. "The Death and Transfiguration of Benefit Taxation: Special Assessments in Nineteenth-Century America." *Journal of Legal Studies* 12 (1983): 201–40.

Dickerson, O. M. *The Illinois Constitutional Convention of 1862.* Urbana: University [of Illinois] Press, 1905.

Dillon, John F. *Treatise on the Law of Municipal Corporations.* Chicago: James Cockcroft & Co., 1872.

Doebele, William A.; Grimes, Orville, Jr.; and Linn, Johannes F. "Participation of Beneficiaries in Financing Urban Services: Valorization Charges in Bogotá, Colombia." *Land Economics* 55 (1979): 73–92.

Doyle, Don Harrison. *The Social Order of a Frontier Community: Jacksonville, Illinois, 1825–70.* Urbana: University of Illinois Press, 1978.

Durand, Edward Dana. *The Finances of New York City.* New York: Macmillan, 1898.

Einhorn, Robin L. "The Civil War and Municipal Government in Chicago." In *Toward a Social History of the American Civil War.* Edited by Maris Vinovskis. New York: Cambridge University Press, 1990.

———. "A Taxing Dilemma: Early Lake Shore Protection." *Chicago History* 18 (1989): 34–51.

Elkins, Stanley, and McKitrick, Eric. "A Meaning for Turner's Frontier." *Political Science Quarterly* 69 (1954): 321–53.

Ely, Richard T. *Taxation in American States and Cities.* New York: Thomas Y. Crowell, 1888.

Erie, Steven P. *Rainbow's End: Irish Americans and the Dilemma of Machine Politics.* Berkeley: University of California Press, 1988.

Ethington, Philip J. "The Structures of Urban Political Life: Political Culture in San Francisco, 1849–1880." Ph.D. diss., Stanford University, 1989.

———. "Vigilantes and the Police: The Creation of a Professional Police Bureaucracy in San Francisco, 1847–1900." *Journal of Social History* 21 (1987): 197–227.

Fairlie, John A. "The Street Railway Question in Chicago." *Quarterly Journal of Economics* 21 (1907): 371–404.

Farnham, Wallace D. "'The Weakened Spring of Government': A Study in Nineteenth-Century American History." *American Historical Review* 68 (1963): 662–80.

Fehrenbacher, Don E. *Chicago Giant: A Biography of "Long John" Wentworth.* Madison: American History Research Center, 1957.

————. "The Judd-Wentworth Feud." *Journal of the Illinois State Historical Society* 45 (1952): 197–211.

————. *Prelude to Greatness: Lincoln in the 1850s*. Stanford: Stanford University Press, 1962.

————. *Slavery, Law, and Politics: The Dred Scott Case in Historical Perspective*. New York: Oxford University Press, 1981.

Fellman, Jerome D. "Pre-Building Growth Patterns of Chicago." *Annals of the Association of American Geographers* 47 (1957): 59–82.

Fine, Sidney. *Laissez-Faire and the General-Welfare State: A Study of Conflict in American Thought*. Ann Arbor: University of Michigan Press, 1956.

Fischel, William A. *The Economics of Zoning Laws: A Property Rights Approach to American Land Use Controls*. Baltimore: Johns Hopkins University Press, 1985.

Fisher, Glenn W., and Fairbanks, Robert P. *Illinois Municipal Finance: A Political and Economic Analysis*. Urbana: University of Illinois Press, 1968.

Fitzgerald, Faith. "Growth of Municipal Activities in Chicago, 1833 to 1875." M.A. thesis, University of Chicago, 1933.

Flanagan, Maureen A. *Charter Reform in Chicago*. Carbondale: Southern Illinois University Press, 1987.

Fleming, George Joseph, Jr. "Canal at Chicago: A Study in Political and Social History." Ph.D. diss., Catholic University, 1951.

Flinn, John J. *History of the Chicago Police from the Settlement of the Community to the Present Time*. Reprint ed. New York: AMS Press, 1973.

Foner, Eric. *Free Soil, Free Labor, Free Men: The Ideology of the Republican Party before the Civil War*. New York: Oxford University Press, 1970.

————. *Reconstruction: America's Unfinished Revolution, 1863–1877*. New York: Harper & Row, 1988.

Formisano, Ronald P. *The Birth of Mass Political Parties: Michigan, 1827–1861*. Princeton: Princeton University Press, 1971.

Fox, Kenneth. *Better City Government: Innovation in American Urban Politics, 1850–1937*. Philadelphia: Temple University Press, 1977.

Frisch, Michael H. *Town into City: Springfield, Massachusetts, and the Meaning of Community, 1840–1880*. Cambridge: Harvard University Press, 1972.

Gale, Edwin O. *Reminiscences of Early Chicago and Vicinity*. Chicago: Fleming H. Revell, 1902.

Geary, James W. "Civil War Conscription in the North: A Historiographical Review." *Civil War History* 32 (1986): 208–28.

Gere, Edwin A., Jr. "Dillon's Rule and the Cooley Doctrine: Reflections of the Political Culture." *Journal of Urban History* 8 (1982): 271–98.

Gienapp, William E. "The Crime against Sumner: The Caning of Charles Sumner and the Rise of the Republican Party." *Civil War History* 25 (1979): 218–45.

————. *The Origins of the Republican Party, 1852–1856*. New York: Oxford University Press, 1987.

————. "'Politics Seems to Enter into Everything': Political Culture in the North, 1840–1860." In *Essays on American Antebellum Politics, 1840–1860*.

Edited by Stephen E. Maizlish and John J. Kushma. College Station: Texas A&M University Press, 1982.

Ginger, Ray. *Altgeld's America: The Lincoln Ideal Versus Changing Realities*. New York: Funk & Wagnalls, 1958.

Glaab, Charles N., and Brown, A. Theodore. *A History of Urban America*. 2d ed. New York: Macmillan, 1976.

Goldfield, David R. *Urban Growth in the Age of Sectionalism: Virginia, 1847–1861*. Baton Rouge: Louisiana State University Press, 1977.

Goldfield, David R., and Brownell, Blaine A. *Urban America: A History*. 2d ed. Boston: Houghton Mifflin, 1990.

Goldscheid, Rudolf. "A Sociological Approach to Problems of Public Finance." In *Classics in the Theory of Public Finance*. Edited by Richard A. Musgrave and Alan T. Peacock. London: Macmillan, 1964.

Goodrich, Carter. *Government Promotion of American Canals and Railroads, 1800–1890*. New York: Columbia University Press, 1960.

———. "The Revulsion against Internal Improvements." *Journal of Economic History* 10 (1950): 145–69.

Goodspeed, Weston A., and Healy, Daniel D., eds. *History of Cook County, Illinois*. 2 vols. Chicago: Goodspeed Historical Association, 1909.

Gray, Wood. *The Hidden Civil War: The Story of the Copperheads*. New York: Viking Press, 1942.

Groves, Harold M. *Tax Philosophers: Two Hundred Years of Thought in Great Britain and the United States*. Madison: University of Wisconsin Press, 1974.

Gunn, L. Ray. *The Decline of Authority: Public Economic Policy and Political Development in New York State, 1800–1860*. Ithaca: Cornell University Press, 1988.

Haeger, John Denis. *The Investment Frontier: New York Businessmen and the Development of the Old Northwest*. Albany: State University of New York Press, 1981.

Haig, Robert Murray. *A History of the General Property Tax in Illinois*. Urbana: University of Illinois, 1914.

Haines, Deborah L. "City Doctor, City Lawyer: The Learned Professions in Frontier Chicago, 1833–1860." Ph.D. diss., University of Chicago, 1986.

Hammack, David C. *Power and Society: Greater New York at the Turn of the Century*. New York: Russell Sage, 1982.

———. "Problems in the Historical Study of Power in the Cities and Towns of the United States." *American Historical Review* 83 (1978): 323–49.

Hammond, Henry L. *Memorial Sketch of Philo Carpenter*. Chicago: Fergus Printing Co., 1888.

Handlin, Oscar. *The Uprooted*. 2d ed. Boston: Little, Brown, 1973.

Handlin, Oscar, and Handlin, Mary Flug. *Commonwealth: A Study of the Role of Government in the American Economy, Massachusetts, 1774–1861*. Rev. ed. Cambridge: Harvard University Press, 1969.

Hansen, Stephen L. *The Making of the Third Party System: Voters and Parties in Illinois*. Ann Arbor: University Microfilms International, 1980.

Harris, Carl V. *Political Power in Birmingham, 1871–1921*. Knoxville: University of Tennessee Press, 1977.

Hartog, Hendrik. *Public Property and Private Power: The Corporation of the City of New York in American Law, 1730–1870.* Chapel Hill: University of North Carolina Press, 1983.

Hartz, Louis. *Economic Policy and Democratic Thought: Pennsylvania, 1776–1860.* Cambridge: Harvard University Press, 1948.

Haydon, James Ryan. *Chicago's True Founder: Thomas J. V. Owen.* Lombard, Ill.: Owen Memorial Fund, 1934.

Hays, Samuel P. "The Changing Political Structure of the City in Industrial America." *Journal of Urban History* 1 (1974): 6–38.

———. "The Politics of Reform in Municipal Government in the Progressive Era." *Pacific Northwest Quarterly* 55 (1964): 157–69.

Heale, M. J. "From City Fathers to Social Critics: Humanitarianism and Government in New York, 1790–1860." *Journal of American History* 63 (1976): 21–41.

Heilman, R. E. *Chicago Traction.* Publications of the American Economic Association. 3d. ser., vol. 9, no. 2. Princeton, N.J., 1908.

Herrman, Donald D. *The Special Assessment in Oak Lawn.* Carbondale: Public Affairs Research Bureau, Southern Illinois University, 1962.

Hirsch, Susan E. *Roots of the American Working Class: The Industrialization of Crafts in Newark, 1800–1860.* Philadelphia: University of Pennsylvania Press, 1978.

Holli, Melvin G. *Reform in Detroit: Hazen S. Pingree and Urban Politics.* New York: Oxford University Press, 1969.

Hollingsworth, J. Rogers, and Hollingworth, Ellen Jane. *Dimensions in Urban History: Historical and Social Science Perspectives on Middle-Size Cities.* Madison: University of Wisconsin Press, 1979.

Holt, Glen E. "The Birth of Chicago: An Examination of Economic Parentage." *Journal of the Illinois State Historical Society* 76 (1983): 82–94.

Holt, Thomas. *Black over White: Negro Political Leadership in South Carolina during Reconstruction.* Urbana: University of Illinois Press, 1977.

Horwitz, Morton J. *The Transformation of American Law, 1780–1860.* Cambridge: Harvard University Press, 1977.

Hotchkiss, Willard E. "Chicago Traction: A Study in Political Evolution." *Annals of the American Academy of Political and Social Science* 28 (1906): 385–404.

Hoyne, Thomas. "The Lawyer as a Pioneer." In *Chicago Bar Association Lectures.* Part 1. Fergus Historical Series, no. 22. Chicago: Fergus Printing Co., 1882.

Hoyt, Homer. *One Hundred Years of Land Values in Chicago.* Chicago: University of Chicago Press, 1933.

Hurst, James Willard. *Law and the Conditions of Freedom in the Nineteenth-Century in the United States.* Madison: University of Wisconsin Press, 1956.

Huse, Charles Phillips. *The Financial History of Boston.* Cambridge: Harvard University Press, 1916.

Huston, James L. *The Panic of 1857 and the Coming of the Civil War.* Baton Rouge: Louisiana State University Press, 1987.

Hyman, Harold M. *A More Perfect Union: The Impact of the Civil War and Reconstruction on the Constitution.* New York: Knopf, 1973.

Jackson, Kenneth T. *Crabgrass Frontier: The Suburbanization of the United States.* New York: Oxford University Press, 1985.

Jacobs, Clyde E. *Law Writers and the Courts: The Influence of Thomas M. Cooley, Christopher G. Tiedeman, and John F. Dillon upon American Constitutional Law.* Berkeley: University of California Press, 1954.

Jaher, Frederic Cople. *The Urban Establishment: Upper Strata in Boston, New York, Charleston, Chicago, and Los Angeles.* Urbana: University of Illinois Press, 1982.

James, F. Cyril. *The Growth of Chicago Banks.* 2 vols. New York: Harper & Bros., 1938.

Jentz, John B., and Schneirov, Richard. "Class and Politics in an Antebellum Commercial Boom Town, Chicago, 1848 to 1861." Working Paper, Origins of Chicago's Industrial Working Class Project, Newberry Library.

Johannsen, Robert W. *Stephen A. Douglas.* New York: Oxford University Press, 1973.

Jones, Stanley L. "Agrarian Radicalism in Illinois' Constitutional Convention of 1862." *Journal of the Illinois State Historical Society* 48 (1955): 271–82.

Katz, Michael B.; Doucet, Michael J.; and Stern, Mark J. *The Social Organization of Early Industrial Capitalism.* Cambridge: Harvard University Press, 1982.

Katznelson, Ira. *City Trenches: Urban Politics and the Patterning of Class in the United States.* Chicago: University of Chicago Press, 1981.

Keating, Ann Durkin. *Building Chicago: Suburban Developers and the Creation of a Divided Metropolis.* Columbus: Ohio State University Press, 1988.

———. "From City to Metropolis: Infrastructure and Residential Growth in Urban Chicago." In *Infrastructure and Urban Growth in the Nineteenth Century.* Chicago: Public Works Historical Society, 1985.

———. "Governing the New Metropolis: The Development of Urban and Suburban Governments in Cook County, Illinois, 1831–1902." Ph.D. diss., University of Chicago, 1984.

Keefe, Thomas M. "The Catholic Issue in the Chicago Tribune before the Civil War." *Mid-America* 57 (1975): 227–45.

———. "Chicago's Flirtation with Political Nativism, 1854–1856." *Records of the American Catholic Historical Society of Philadelphia* 82 (1971): 131–58.

Keller, Morton. *Affairs of State: Public Life in Late Nineteenth Century America.* Cambridge: Harvard University Press, 1977.

Klement, Frank L. *The Copperheads of the Middle West.* Chicago: University of Chicago Press, 1960.

———. "Middle Western Copperheadism and the Genesis of the Granger Movement." *Mississippi Valley Historical Review* 38 (1951–52): 679–94.

Lane, Roger. *Policing the City: Boston, 1822–1885.* Cambridge: Harvard University Press, 1967.

Laurie, Bruce. "Fire Companies and Gangs in Southwark: The 1840s." In *The Peoples of Philadelphia: A History of Ethnic Groups and Lower-Class Life, 1790–1940.* Edited by Allen F. Davis and Mark H. Haller. Philadelphia: Temple University Press, 1973.

———. *Working People of Philadelphia, 1800–1850.* Philadelphia: Temple University Press, 1978.

Levine, Bruce Carlan. "Free Soil, Free Labor, and *Freimänner*: German Chicago in the Civil War Era." In *German Workers in Industrial Chicago, 1850–1910: A Comparative Perspective*. Edited by Hartmut Keil and John B. Jentz. DeKalb: Northern Illinois University Press, 1983.

Lewis, Lloyd. *John S. Wright: Prophet of the Prairies*. Chicago: Prairie Farmer Publishing Co., 1941.

Lewis, Nelson P. *The Planning of the Modern City: A Review of the Principles Governing City Planning*. New York: Wiley, 1916.

Lloyd, Henry Demarest. *The Chicago Traction Question*. Chicago: George Waite Pickett, 1903.

Lowi, Theodore. "American Business, Public Policy, Case-Studies, and Political Theory." *World Politics* 16 (1964): 677–715.

Lurie, Jonathan. *The Chicago Board of Trade, 1859–1905: The Dynamics of Self-Regulation*. Urbana: University of Illinois Press, 1979.

McCarthy, Kathleen D. *Noblesse Oblige: Charity and Cultural Philanthropy in Chicago, 1849–1929*. Chicago: University of Chicago Press, 1982.

McCormick, Richard L. *The Party Period and Public Policy: American Politics from the Age of Jackson to the Progressive Era*. New York: Oxford University Press, 1986.

McDonald, Terrence J. "The Burdens of Urban History: The Theory of the State in Recent American Social History." *Studies in American Political Development* 3 (1989): 3–29.

———. *The Parameters of Urban Fiscal Policy: Socioeconomic Change and Political Culture in San Francisco, 1860–1906*. Berkeley: University of California Press, 1986.

———. "The Problem of the Political in Recent American Urban History: Liberal Pluralism and the Rise of Functionalism." *Social History* 10 (1985): 323–45.

———. "Putting Politics Back into the History of the American City." *American Quarterly* 34 (1982): 200–209.

McDonald, Terrence J., and Ward, Sally K., eds. *The Politics of Urban Fiscal Policy*. Beverly Hills: Sage, 1984.

McKivigan, John R. *The War against Proslavery Religion: Abolitionism and the Northern Churches, 1830–1865*. Ithaca: Cornell University Press, 1984.

McLear, Patrick E. "The Galena and Chicago Union Railroad: A Symbol of Economic Maturity." *Journal of the Illinois State Historical Society* 73 (1980): 17–26.

———. "John Stephen Wright and Urban and Regional Promotion in the Nineteenth Century." *Journal of the Illinois State Historical Society* 68 (1975): 407–20.

———. "William Butler Ogden: A Chicago Promoter in the Speculative Era and the Panic of 1837." *Journal of the Illinois State Historical Society* 70 (1977): 283–91.

McShane, Clay. "Transforming the Use of Urban Space: A Look at the Revolution in Street Pavements, 1880–1924." *Journal of Urban History* 5 (1979): 279–307.

Macon, Jorge, and Mañon, Jose Merino. *Financing Urban and Rural Develop-*

ment through Betterment Levies: The Latin American Experience. New York: Praeger, 1977.

Mandelbaum, Seymour J. *Boss Tweed's New York*. New York: Wiley, 1965.

Marcus, Alan I. "The Strange Career of Municipal Health Incentives." *Journal of Urban History* 7 (1980): 3–29.

Martineau, Harriet. "Chicago in 1836." In *The Present and Future Prospects of Chicago*. Fergus Historical Series, no. 9. Chicago: Fergus Printing Co., 1876.

Mayer, Harold M., and Wade, Richard C. *Chicago: Growth of a Metropolis*. Chicago: University of Chicago Press, 1969.

Merriam, Charles Edward. *Report of an Investigation of the Municipal Revenues of Chicago*. Chicago: City Club of Chicago, 1906.

Merton, Robert K. *Social Theory and Social Structure: Toward the Codification of Theory and Research*. Glencoe: Free Press, 1949.

Miller, Zane L. *Boss Cox's Cincinnati: Urban Politics in the Progressive Era*. Chicago: University of Chicago Press, 1968.

Moehring, Eugene P. *Public Works and the Patterns of Urban Real Estate Growth in Manhattan, 1835–1894*. New York: Arno Press, 1981.

———. *Public Works and Urban History: Recent Trends and New Directions*. Chicago: Public Works Historical Society, 1982.

Monaghan, Jay. *The Man Who Elected Lincoln*. Indianapolis: Bobbs-Merrill, 1956.

Monkkonen, Eric H. *America Becomes Urban: The Development of U.S. Cities and Towns, 1780–1980*. Berkeley: University of California Press, 1988.

Montgomery, David. *Beyond Equality: Labor and the Radical Republicans, 1862–1872*. Urbana: University of Illinois Press, 1967.

Murdock, Eugene Converse. *Ohio's Bounty System in the Civil War*. Columbus: Ohio State University Press, 1963.

———. *One Million Men: The Civil War Draft in the North*. Madison: State Historical Society of Wisconsin, 1971.

———. *Patriotism Limited, 1862–1865: The Civil War Draft and the Bounty System*. Kent: Kent State University Press, 1967.

Musgrave, Richard A. *The Theory of Public Finance: A Study in Public Economy*. New York: McGraw-Hill, 1959.

Musgrave, Richard A., and Peacock, Alan T., eds. *Classics in the Theory of Public Finance*. London: Macmillan, 1958.

Nelson, Robert H. *Zoning and Property Rights: An Analysis of the American System of Land Use Regulation*. Cambridge: MIT Press, 1977.

Netzer, Dick. *Economics of the Property Tax*. Washington, D.C.: Brookings Institution, 1966.

Nichols, Roy F. "The Kansas-Nebraska Act: A Century of Historiography." *Mississippi Valley Historical Review* 43 (1956–57): 187–212.

Norton, Samuel Wilber. *Chicago Traction: A History Legislative and Political*. Chicago: By the Author, 1907.

O'Connell, James C. "Technology and Pollution: Chicago's Water Policy, 1833–1930." Ph.D. diss., University of Chicago, 1980.

O'Connor, Edwin. *The Last Hurrah*. Boston: Little, Brown, 1956.

O'Connor, James. *The Fiscal Crisis of the State*. New York: St. Martin's Press, 1973.

Oestreicher, Richard. "Urban Working-Class Political Behavior and Theories of American Electoral Politics, 1870–1940." *Journal of American History* 74 (1988): 1257–86.

Paludan, Philip S. "Law and the Failure of Reconstruction: The Case of Thomas Cooley." *Journal of the History of Ideas* 33 (1972): 597–614.

Pease, Theodore Calvin. *The Frontier State, 1818–1848*. Springfield: Illinois Centennial Commission, 1918.

Pessen, Edward. *Riches, Class, and Power before the Civil War*. Lexington: D. C. Heath, 1973.

Peterson, Jacqueline. "The Founding Fathers: The Absorption of French-Indian Chicago, 1816–1837." In *Ethnic Chicago*. Rev. and exp. Edited by Melvin G. Holli and Peter d'A. Jones. Grand Rapids: William B. Eerdmans, 1984.

Peterson, John A. "The Impact of Sanitary Reform upon American Urban Planning, 1840–90." *Journal of Social History* 13 (1979): 83–103.

Pierce, Bessie Louise, comp. *As Others See Chicago: Impressions of Visitors, 1673–1933*. Chicago: University of Chicago Press, 1933.

———. *A History of Chicago*. 3 vols. Chicago: University of Chicago Press, 1937–57.

Polsby, Nelson W. *Community Power and Political Theory: A Further Look at Problems of Evidence and Inference*. 2d ed. New Haven: Yale University Press, 1980.

Potter, David M. *The Impending Crisis, 1848–1861*. New York: Harper & Row, 1976.

Pratt, Harry E., ed. "John Dean Caton's Reminiscences of Chicago in 1833 and 1834." *Journal of the Illinois State Historical Society* 28 (1935): 5–25.

Putnam, James William. *The Illinois and Michigan Canal: A Study in Economic History*. Chicago: University of Chicago Press, 1918.

Rawley, James A. *Race and Politics: "Bleeding Kansas" and the Coming of the Civil War*. Philadelphia: Lippincott, 1969.

Renner, Richard Wilson. "In a Perfect Ferment: Chicago, the Know-Nothings, and the Riot for Lager Beer." *Chicago History* 5 (1976): 161–70.

Richardson, James F. *The New York Police: Colonial Times to 1901*. New York: Oxford University Press, 1970.

Roberts, Sidney I. "Ousting the Bummers, 1874–1876." Typescript, 1956, Chicago Historical Society.

Rodgers, Daniel T. "In Search of Progressivism." *Reviews in American History* 10 (1982): 113–32.

Rosen, Christine Meisner. *The Limits of Power: Great Fires and the Process of City Growth in America*. Cambridge: Cambridge University Press, 1986.

Rosenberg, Charles E. *The Cholera Years: The United States in 1832, 1849, and 1866*. Chicago: University of Chicago Press, 1962.

Rosewater, Victor. *Special Assessments: A Study in Municipal Finance*. New York: Columbia University, 1898.

Rybeck, Walter. "The Property Tax as a Super User Charge." In *The Property*

Tax and Local Finance. Proceedings of the Academy of Political Science. Vol. 35. Edited by C. Lowell Harriss. New York, 1983.

Scheiber, Harry N. "Government and the Economy: Studies of the 'Commonwealth' Policy in Nineteenth-Century America." *Journal of Interdisciplinary History* 3 (1972): 135–51.

———. "Property Law, Expropriation, and Resource Allocation by the Government: The United States, 1789–1910." *Journal of Economic History* 33 (1973): 232–51.

———. "The Road to *Munn*: Eminent Domain and the Concept of Public Purpose in the State Courts." *Perspectives in American History* 5 (1971): 329–402.

Schiesl, Martin J. *The Politics of Efficiency: Municipal Administration and Reform in America, 1880–1920.* Berkeley: University of California Press, 1977.

Schlesinger, Arthur M. "The City in American History." *Mississippi Valley Historical Review* 27 (1940–41): 43–66.

Schneider, John C. *Detroit and the Problem of Order, 1830–1880: A Geography of Crime, Riot, and Policing.* Lincoln: University of Nebraska Press, 1980.

———. "Riot and Reaction in St. Louis 1854–1856." *Missouri Historical Review* 68 (1974): 171–85.

Schneirov, Richard. "Class Conflict, Municipal Politics, and Governmental Reform in Gilded Age Chicago, 1871–1875." In *German Workers in Industrial Chicago, 1850–1910: A Comparative Perspective.* Edited by Hartmut Keil and John B. Jentz. DeKalb: Northern Illinois University Press, 1983.

———. "Haymarket and the New Political History Reconsidered: Workers' Class Presence in Chicago's Municipal Politics, 1873–1894." *Journal of American History* (forthcoming).

Schneirov, Richard, and Jentz, John B. "Social Republicanism and Socialism: A Multi-Ethnic History of Labor Reform in Chicago, 1848–1877." Paper presented to the Social Science History Association, November, 1985.

———."The 1867 Strike and the Origins of the Chicago Labor Movement." Working Paper, Origins of Chicago's Industrial Working Class Project, Newberry Library.

Schultz, Rima Lunin. "The Businessman's Role in Western Settlement: The Entrepreneurial Frontier, Chicago, 1833–1872." Ph.D. diss., Boston University, 1985.

———. *The Church and the City: A Social History of 150 Years at Saint James, Chicago.* Chicago: Cathedral of Saint James, 1986.

Schultz, Stanley K., and McShane, Clay. "To Engineer the Metropolis: Sewers, Sanitation, and City Planning in Late-Nineteenth Century America." *Journal of American History* 65 (1978): 389–411.

Schumpeter, Joseph A. "The Crisis of the Tax State." Translated by W. F. Stolper and R. A. Musgrave. *International Economic Papers* 4 (1954): 5–38.

Scott, Mel. *American City Planning since 1890.* Berkeley: University of California Press, 1969.

Seligman, Edwin R. A. *Essays in Taxation.* New York: Macmillan, 1895.

Sennett, Richard. *Families against the City: Middle Class Homes of Industrial Chicago, 1872–1890.* New York: Vintage, 1970.

Shefter, Martin. "The Emergence of the Political Machine: An Alternative View." In Willis D. Hawley, et al. *Theoretical Perspectives on Urban Politics*. Englewood Cliffs: Prentice-Hall, 1976.

―――. "Trade Unions and Political Machines: The Organization and Disorganization of the American Working Class in the Late Nineteenth Century." In *Working Class Formation: Nineteenth Century Patterns in Western Europe and the United States*. Edited by Ira Katznelson and Aristide Zolberg. Princeton: Princeton University Press, 1986.

Shoup, Donald C. "Financing Public Investment by Deferred Special Assessment." *National Tax Journal* 33 (1980): 413–29.

Silbey, Joel. *A Respectable Minority: The Democratic Party in the Civil War Era, 1860–1868*. New York: W. W. Norton, 1977.

Simon, Roger D. *The City-Building Process: Housing and Services in New Milwaukee Neighborhoods, 1880–1920*. Transactions of the American Philosophical Society. Vol. 68, pt. 5. Philadelphia, 1978.

―――. "Housing and Services in an Immigrant Neighborhood: Milwaukee's Ward 14." *Journal of Urban History* 2 (1976): 435–58.

Skowronek, Stephen. *Building a New American State: The Expansion of National Administrative Capacities, 1877–1920*. Cambridge: Cambridge University Press, 1982.

Sterling, Robert E. "Civil War Draft Resistance in Illinois." *Journal of the Illinois State Historical Society* 64 (1971): 245–66.

Sterne, Simon. "The Administration of American Cities." *International Review* 4 (1877): 631–46.

Still, Bayrd. *Milwaukee: The History of a City*. Madison: State Historical Society of Wisconsin, 1948.

―――. "Patterns of Mid-Nineteenth Century Urbanization in the Middle West." *Mississippi Valley Historical Review* 28 (1941–42): 187–206.

Strevey, Tracy Elmer. "Joseph Medill and the Chicago *Tribune* during the Civil War Period." Ph.D. diss., University of Chicago, 1930.

Tarr, Joel A. "The Evolution of the Urban Infrastructure in the Nineteenth and Twentieth Centuries." In *Perspectives on Urban Infrastructure*. Edited by Royce Hanson. Washington, D.C.: National Academy Press, 1984.

―――. "The Separate vs. Combined Sewer Problem: A Case Study in Urban Technological Design Choice." *Journal of Urban History* 5 (1979): 308–39.

Taylor, Charles H., ed. *History of the Board of Trade of the City of Chicago*. 3 vols. Chicago: Robert O. Law, 1917.

Taylor, George Rogers. *The Transportation Revolution, 1815–1860*. New York: Harper & Row, 1951.

Teaford, Jon C. "Finis for Tweed and Steffens: Rewriting the History of Urban Rule." *Reviews in American History* 10 (1982): 133–49.

―――. *The Municipal Revolution in America: Origins of Modern Urban Government, 1650–1825*. Chicago: University of Chicago Press, 1975.

―――. "Special Legislation and the Cities, 1865–1900." *American Journal of Legal History* 23 (1979): 189–212.

―――. *The Unheralded Triumph: City Government in America, 1870–1900*. Baltimore: Johns Hopkins University Press, 1984.

Tenney, Craig D. "To Suppress or Not To Suppress: Abraham Lincoln and the Chicago *Times*." *Civil War History* 27 (1981): 248–59.

Thelen, David P. "Urban Politics: Beyond Bosses and Reformers." *Reviews in American History* 7 (1979): 406–12.

Thernstrom, Stephan. *Poverty and Progress: Social Mobility in a Nineteenth Century City*. Cambridge: Harvard University Press, 1964.

Thompson, Margaret Susan. *The "Spider Web": Congress and Lobbying in the Age of Grant*. Ithaca: Cornell University Press, 1985.

Thompson, Wilbur R. *A Preface to Urban Economics*. Baltimore: Johns Hopkins Press, 1965.

Thornton, J. Mills, III. "Fiscal Policy and the Failure of Radical Reconstruction in the Lower South." In *Region, Race, and Reconstruction: Essays in Honor of C. Vann Woodward*. Edited by J. Morgan Kousser and James M. McPherson. New York: Oxford University Press, 1982.

Tiebout, Charles M. "A Pure Theory of Local Expenditures." *Journal of Political Economy* 64 (1956): 416–24.

Townsend, Andrew Jacke. "The Germans of Chicago." Ph.D. diss., University of Chicago, 1927.

Tygiel, Jules. "Housing in Late Nineteenth-Century American Cities: Suggestions for Research." *Historical Methods* 12 (1979): 84–97.

Tyrrell, Ian R. *Sobering Up: From Temperance to Prohibition in Antebellum America, 1800–1860*. Westport: Greenwood Press, 1979.

Vickrey, William W. "General and Specific Financing of Urban Services." In *Public Expenditure Decisions in the Urban Community*. Washington, D.C.: Resources for the Future, 1963.

Wade, Louise Carroll. *Chicago's Pride: The Stockyards, Packingtown, and Environs in the Nineteenth Century*. Urbana: University of Illinois Press, 1987.

Wade, Richard C. *The Urban Frontier: Pioneer Life in Early Pittsburgh, Cincinnati, Lexington, Louisville, and St. Louis*. Chicago: University of Chicago Press, 1959.

Wallenstein, Peter. *From Slave South to New South: Public Policy in Nineteenth-Century Georgia*. Chapel Hill: University of North Carolina Press, 1987.

Walsh, Justin E. "Radically and Thoroughly Democratic: Wilbur F. Storey and the Detroit *Free Press*, 1853 to 1861." *Michigan History* 47 (1963): 193–225.

Walsh, Margaret. *The Rise of the Midwestern Meat Packing Industry*. Lexington: University Press of Kentucky, 1982.

Warner, Sam Bass, Jr. *The Private City: Philadelphia in Three Periods of Its Growth*. Philadelphia: University of Pennsylvania Press, 1968.

———. *Streetcar Suburbs: The Process of Growth in Boston, 1870–1900*. 2d ed. Cambridge: Harvard University Press, 1978.

Watts, Eugene J. *The Social Bases of City Politics: Atlanta, 1865–1903*. Westport: Greenwood Press, 1978.

Weber, Harry P., comp. *An Outline History of Chicago Traction*. Chicago: Chicago Railways Company, et al., 1936.

Weinstein, James. *The Corporate Ideal in the Liberal State, 1900–1918*. Boston: Beacon Press, 1968.

Weisberger, Bernard A. "The Newspaper Reporter and the Kansas Imbroglio." *Mississippi Valley Historical Review* 36 (1949–50): 633–56.

Wiebe, Robert H. *The Opening of American Society: From the Adoption of the Constitution to the Eve of Disunion.* New York: Knopf, 1984.

———. *The Segmented Society: An Introduction to the Meaning of America.* New York: Oxford University Press, 1975.

Wilentz, Sean. *Chants Democratic: New York City and the Rise of the American Working Class, 1788–1850.* New York: Oxford University Press, 1984.

Wille, Lois. *Forever Open, Clear, and Free: The Historic Struggle for Chicago's Lakefront.* Chicago: Henry Regnery, 1972.

Williams, Mentor L. "The Background of the Chicago River and Harbor Convention, 1847." *Mid-America* 30 (1948): 219–32.

———. "The Chicago River and Harbor Convention, 1847." *Mississippi Valley Historical Review* 35 (1948–49): 607–26.

Winter, William O. *The Special Assessment Today, with Emphasis on the Michigan Experience.* Ann Arbor: University of Michigan Press, 1952.

Wolfinger, Raymond E. "Why Political Machines Have Not Withered Away and Other Revisionist Thoughts." *Journal of Politics* 34 (1972): 365–98.

Wolper, Gregg. "Winning the Battle but Losing the War; Building-Raising and Sanitation in Mid-Nineteenth-Century Chicago." Seminar paper, University of Chicago, 1983.

Wright, John S. *Chicago: Past, Present, Future.* Chicago: Horton & Leonard, 1868.

Yearley, C. K. *The Money Machines: The Breakdown and Reform of Governmental and Party Finance in the North, 1860–1920.* Albany: State University of New York Press, 1970.

Zunz, Olivier. *The Changing Face of Inequality: Urbanization, Industrial Development, and Immigrants in Detroit, 1880–1920.* Chicago: University of Chicago Press, 1982.

Unpublished

Bergquist, James Manning. "The Political Attitudes of the German Immigrant in Illinois, 1848–1860." Ph.D. diss., Northwestern University, 1966.

Breckenridge, Helen Elizabeth. "The Chicago *Times* during the Civil War." Ph.D. diss., University of Chicago, 1931.

Buettinger, Craig. "The Concept of Jacksonian Aristocracy: Chicago as a Test Case." Ph.D. diss., Northwestern University, 1982.

Cole, Bruce McKitterick. "The Chicago Press and the Know-Nothings, 1850–1856." M.A. thesis, University of Chicago, 1948.

Ethington, Philip J. "The Structures of Urban Political Life: Political Culture in San Francisco, 1849–1880." Ph.D. diss., Stanford University, 1989.

Fitzgerald, Faith. "Growth of Municipal Activities in Chicago, 1833 to 1875." M.A. thesis, University of Chicago, 1933.

Fleming, George Joseph. "Canal at Chicago: A Study in Political and Social History." Ph.D. diss., Catholic University, 1951.

Haines, Deborah L. "City Doctor, City Lawyer: The Learned Professions in

Frontier Chicago, 1833–1860." Ph.D. diss., University of Chicago, 1986.

Jentz, John B., and Schneirov, Richard. "Class and Politics in an Antebellum Commercial Boom Town, Chicago, 1848 to 1861." Working Paper, Origins of Chicago's Industrial Working Class Project, Newberry Library.

Keating, Ann Durkin. "Governing the New Metropolis: The Development of Urban and Suburban Governments in Cook County, Illinois, 1831–1902." Ph.D. diss., University of Chicago, 1984.

O'Connell, James C. "Technology and Pollution: Chicago's Water Policy, 1833–1930." Ph.D. diss., University of Chicago, 1980.

Roberts, Sidney I. "Ousting the Bummers, 1874–1876." Typescript, 1956, Chicago Historical Society.

Schneirov, Richard, and Jentz, John B. "Social Republicanism and Socialism: A Multi-Ethnic History of Labor Reform in Chicago, 1848–1877." Paper presented to the Social Science History Association, November, 1985.

———. "The 1867 Strike and the Origins of the Chicago Labor Movement." Working Paper, Origins of Chicago's Industrial Working Class Project, Newberry Library.

Schultz, Rima Lunin. "The Businessman's Role in Western Settlement: The Entrepreneurial Frontier, Chicago, 1833–1872." Ph.D. diss., Boston University, 1985.

Strevey, Tracy Elmer. "Joseph Medill and the Chicago *Tribune* during the Civil War Period." Ph.D. diss., University of Chicago, 1930.

Townsend, Andrew Jacke. "The Germans of Chicago." Ph.D. diss., University of Chicago, 1927.

Wolper, Gregg. "Winning the Battle but Losing the War; Building-Raising and Sanitation in Mid-Nineteenth-Century Chicago." Seminar paper, University of Chicago, 1983.

Index